S. Spencer

FANNY FERN

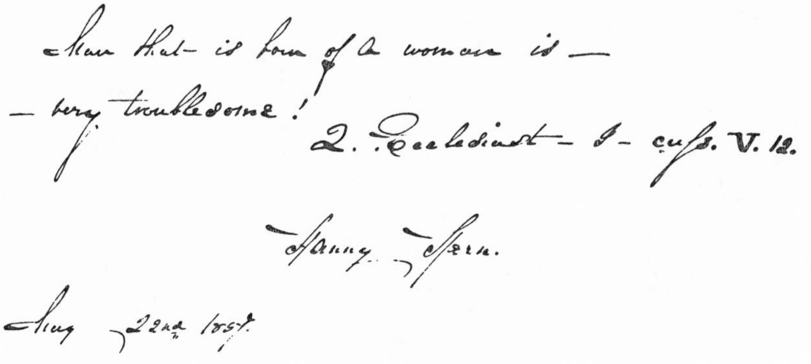

[handwritten note]

Man that is born of a woman is —
— very troublesome!
2. Ecclesiast — I — cap. V. 12.

Fanny Fern.

Aug 22nd 1857.

"Man that is born of a woman is—very troublesome."
Fern's statement is a satirical variation on a passage from the Bible, Job 14:1.

JOYCE W. WARREN

꒒꒛꒜꒛꒜꒛

Fanny Fern

AN INDEPENDENT WOMAN

Rutgers University Press
NEW BRUNSWICK, NEW JERSEY

Library of Congress Cataloging-in-Publication Data

Warren, Joyce W.
    Fanny Fern : an independent woman / Joyce W. Warren.
        p.   cm.
    Includes bibliographical references and index.
    ISBN 0-8135-1763-X (cloth)
        1. Fern, Fanny, 1811–1872—Biography.   2. Feminism and literature—
    United States—History—19th century.   3. Novelists, American—19th
    century—Biography.   4. Journalists—United States—Biography.
    I. Title.
    PS2523.P9Z97   1992
    813'3—dc20
    [B]   91-20382
                                                                      CIP
            British Cataloging-in-Publication information available

FRONTISPIECE:

Fanny Fern Collection (#8378),
Clifton Waller Barrett Library,
Manuscript Division, Special Collections Department,
University of Virginia Library.

For my children—
VICTORIA,
CATHERINE,
CHARLOTTE,
and FRANK
*—who so graciously welcomed
Fanny Fern into the family.*

ACKNOWLEDGMENTS

I WANT TO THANK THE MANY PEOPLE who have helped to make this book possible. My research was greatly assisted by a year's grant from the National Endowment for the Humanities in 1987. I also want to express my appreciation to the University Seminars of Columbia University for assistance in preparing the manuscript for publication. Material drawn from this work was presented to the University Seminar on Women and Society. The work for this book has been conducted with the cooperation of libraries all over the country, as well as the British Museum Library in London and the Bibliothèque Nationale and the Bibliothèque de L'Institut de France in Paris. I wish to thank the many librarians and archivists with whom I have worked, particularly Jeffrey Kaimowitz at the Watkinson Library in Hartford, Connecticut, Susan Boone in the Sophia Smith Collection at Smith College, Keith Arbour, former Head of Readers' Services, at the American Antiquarian Society in Worcester, Massachusetts, and Mary MacKenzie and Harold P. Worthley, archivists at the Park Street Church and Congregational Library in Boston.

I also want to thank the many scholars with whom I have exchanged ideas about nineteenth-century American women writers, particularly Mary Kelley and Joanne Dobson, who read early versions of the manuscript and made many helpful suggestions, and my colleagues at Queens College and at the Women and Society Seminar at Columbia University, who provided numerous opportunities to discuss and evaluate literature and culture. I am also grateful to the students in my classes at Queens College, whose enthusiasm about Fern's writings over the years has encouraged me to continue my work. I particularly want to thank Leslie Mitchner, executive editor at Rutgers University Press, whose sensitivity to persons as well as to manuscripts and literature, has made her a valued friend and literary confidante. I am also grateful to Willa Speiser, whose careful editing helped to make this a better book. I owe a special debt of gratitude to James Parton II, the great-grandson of Fanny Fern, who from the first was enthusiastic and willing to help in any way—with family information and artifacts as well as friendship and advice. Finally, I want to give posthumous thanks to the early Fern scholar, Florence Bannard Adams, who at a time when few people had heard of Fern (or seemed to want to hear of her) had the foresight and perseverance to read all of the articles Fern wrote during her sixteen years at the *New York Ledger*, and wrote of Fern's work with insight and understanding. Adams's pioneering pamphlet, *Fanny Fern, or a Pair of Flaming Shoes*, was privately printed in 1966.

I also want to thank the editors and publishers who provided a forum for my ideas on Fern during the years that I was working on this book. Selected material was published previously in the following sources: *Legacy* (Fall 1985 and Fall 1991); Introduction to *Ruth Hall and Other Writings by Fanny Fern* (Rutgers University Press, 1986); *Patrons and Protégées: Gender, Friendship, and Writing in Nineteenth-Century America*, ed. Shirley Marchalonis (Rutgers University Press, 1988); *Politics, Gender, and the Arts*, ed. Ronald Dotterer and Susan Bowers (Susquehanna University Press, 1991); and *Joinings and Disjoinings: The Significance of Marital Status in Literature*, ed. JoAnna S. Mink and Janet D. Ward (The Popular Press, Bowling Green University, 1991).

Permission has been granted by the following sources to quote from unpublished manuscript material: from the Fanny Fern Collection (#8378), Clifton Waller Barrett Library, Manuscripts Division, Special Collections Department, University of Virginia Library; from the Harriet Beecher Stowe material in the Yale Collection of American Literature, Beinecke Rare Book and Manuscript Library, Yale University; from the letters of James Parton and Ellen Chandler Moulton, courtesy of the Trustees of the Boston Public Library; from the Drowne Papers in the Brown University Library; from the letters of James Parton, the Department of Special Collections, University Research Library, UCLA; from letters of Fanny Fern, courtesy of the Chicago Historical Society; from the letter of Fanny Fern and James Parton in the William L. Clements Library, University of Michigan; from the letters of Nathaniel Parker Willis in the Typographic Collection, Rare Book & Manuscript Library, Columbia University; from the manuscript of Richard S. Willis, courtesy of the Burton Historical Collection, Detroit Public Library; from the Special Collections Department, the William R. Perkins Library, Duke University; from the private collection of Richard F. Eckert; from the William Dean Howells Collection, Rutherford Hayes Presidential Center; from manuscript material in the James Parton Papers, by permission of the Houghton Library, Harvard University; from letters of James Parton in the Huntington Library; from the letters of Horace Mann, courtesy Massachusetts Historical Society; from the diary of Thomas Butler Gunn, Missouri Historical Society; from the letters of Fanny Fern, Lloyd W. Smith Collection, Morristown National Historic Park; from a letter of Clifford Thomson, courtesy of The New-York Historical Society; from the Robert Bonner Papers and the Horace Greeley Papers, Rare Books and Manuscripts Division, the New York Public Library, Astor, Lenox and Tilden Foundations; from letters of Nathaniel Parker Willis and James Parton, the Historical Society of Pennsylvania; from a letter by Nathaniel Parker Willis, Pennsylvania State University Libraries; from the letters of Nathaniel Parker Willis in the Scribner's Archives, published with permission of Princeton University Library and Charles Scribner's Sons, an imprint of Macmillan Publishing Company and the Owners of the letters, all rights reserved; from the papers of William Sloane Kennedy, Mss. Ac. 541, Special Collections and Archives, Rutgers University Libraries; from the papers of Sara Willis Parton (Fanny Fern) in the Sophia Smith Collection, Smith College, Northampton, Massachusetts; from the papers at the Stowe-Day Foundation, Hartford, Connecticut. I want to thank Hannah Locke Carter and James Parton II for permission to publish manuscript material by Nathaniel Parker Willis and by Fanny Fern, James Parton, Ethel Parton, Grace Eldredge Thomson, and Ellen Eldredge Parton.

Finally, but most importantly, I want to thank my husband, Frank, for the understanding and sympathy he has shown over the years, as well as for the practical help he has provided. I also want to thank my children for generously sharing their life with Fanny Fern. Just how much Fanny Fern had become a part of my family life became clear to me several years ago when I sat reading the Sunday paper and my six-year-old son asked of the article I was reading, "Is it by Fanny Fern?" His question made me laugh, but it also made me realize that Fanny Fern had indeed become a part of my family life if my six-year-old was aware of her name (at that time he was probably the only six-year-old in the country who had even heard of Fanny Fern). I thought about how different it was in Fern's own day when her name was on the tongue of every adult and child in the country. And, I thought that perhaps my son's generation would be different from my own if my work—and the work of other scholars working on forgotten women writers—bore fruit. Perhaps once again the name Fanny Fern would be, if not on everyone's tongue, at least in many people's consciousness.

My biggest thanks, then, go to my family for sharing my interest in Fanny Fern. I think of conversations at the dinner table or in the car, on the beach at midday or in the house at midnight, random comments or earnest talks— with my husband, daughters, or son, singly or as a group, they listening to Fern anecdotes, commenting on the wisdom of her practical philosophy, laughing at her satire, and—most valuable of all—offering interpretation and analysis from their own reading and from their own experience. I have derived important insights from other sources, but it is this unselfconscious involvement of Fern in my everyday life that has made Fanny Fern come alive for me.

CONTENTS

LIST OF ABBREVIATIONS

The following frequently cited works are referred to in the text by the designated initials.

EP   Ethel Parton, "Fanny Fern, An Informal Biography." Unpublished manuscript in the Sophia Smith Collection at Smith College.

FF   Fanny Fern, "Fanny Ford," in *Fresh Leaves* (New York: Mason Brothers, 1857). Originally published serially in the *New York Ledger*, 1855.

FL   Fanny Fern, *Fern Leaves from Fanny's Portfolio*. Auburn, N.Y.: Derby and Miller, 1853.

FOLLY   Fanny Fern, *Folly As It Flies; Hit at by Fanny Fern*. New York: G. W. Carleton, 1868.

JP   James Parton, *Fanny Fern, A Memorial Volume*. New York: G. W. Carleton, 1873.

LF   Fanny Fern, *Little Ferns for Fanny's Little Friends*. Auburn, N.Y.: Derby and Miller, 1853.

MWT   New York *Musical World and Times*, 1853–1855. New York Public Library.

NSB   Fanny Fern, *A New Story Book for Children*. New York: Mason Brothers, 1864.

NYL   *New York Ledger*, 1855–1872. The Watkinson Library, Trinity College, Hartford, Conn.

OB   Boston *Olive Branch*, 1851–1855. American Antiquarian Society, Worcester, Mass.

RC   Fanny Fern, *Rose Clark*. New York: Mason Brothers, 1856.

RH   Fanny Fern, *Ruth Hall and Other Writings*. Edited by Joyce W.
          Warren. New Brunswick, N.J.: Rutgers University Press, 1986.

SEP   Philadelphia *Saturday Evening Post*, 1853–1854. Philadelphia
          Public Library.

TF   Boston *True Flag*, 1851–1855. American Antiquarian Society,
          Worcester, Mass.

FANNY FERN

What it is to write a biography. . . . It is to hunt through a dozen libraries for a bit of information in the shape of a date which occupies
one single line. . . . This it is to write a biography.

Fanny Fern, *New York Ledger,* May 19,1860

Let a biographical notice be a *true* transcript. . . . The world is nauseated
with this fulsome biographical whitewash.

Fanny Fern, *New York Ledger,* December 20, 1856

PROLOGUE

Who Is Fanny Fern?

I am sick, in an age which produced a Brontë and a [Barrett] Browning, of the prate of men who assert that every *woman should be a perfect housekeeper, and* fail *to add,* that every man should be a perfect carpenter.

(Fanny Fern, NYL, November 17, 1860)

A NUMBER OF YEARS AGO, when I was doing research for my book *The American Narcissus: Individualism and Women in Nineteenth-Century American Fiction* (1984), I came upon an 1855 letter from Nathaniel Hawthorne to his publishers; in it he modified the comments he had made in a previous—now famous—letter criticizing the "damned mob of scribbling women":

> In my last, I recollect, I bestowed some vituperation on female authors. I have since been reading "Ruth Hall"; and I must say I enjoyed it a good deal. The woman writes as if the devil was in her; and that is the only condition under which a woman ever writes anything worth reading. Generally women write like emasculated men, and are only distinguished from male authors by greater feebleness and folly; but when they throw off the restraints of decency, and come before the public stark naked, as it were—then their books are sure to possess character and value. Can you tell me anything about this Fanny Fern? If you meet her, I wish you would let her know how much I admire her.[1]

At the time that I had read this I had never heard of *Ruth Hall* or of Fanny Fern. But, Hawthorne's praise having piqued my curiosity, I took some time out from my research to read *Ruth Hall* (1855). I found that I shared Hawthorne's high opinion of the novel, and I went on to read some of the collected newspaper articles by its author, Sara Willis Parton, pseudonym Fanny Fern. The more I read, the more I concluded that the author of these works did not deserve the oblivion to which she had been consigned.

The question asked by the title of this chapter, "Who is Fanny Fern?" had a different meaning in the nineteenth century than it has today. For the first several years of Fern's career, her identity was a well-kept secret, and readers all over the United States and across the Atlantic were eagerly asking, "Who is Fanny Fern?"; today, however, the question might be asked because the questioner has not heard of Fanny Fern at all. Fanny Fern (1811–1872) was a successful novelist, as well as the first American woman newspaper columnist and most highly paid newspaper writer of her time. This book will trace the rise to worldwide fame of Fanny Fern during her lifetime and her subsequent descent into oblivion in the twentieth century; it will examine the major reasons for the decline in her literary reputation, primarily the tendency of twentieth-century critics to equate "popular nineteenth-century woman writer" with "sentimental nonentity," and, without reading her works, to dismiss the popular Fanny Fern as a "tear-drenched" sentimentalist.[2]

Anyone who has read Fern's works knows the absurdity of this label; Fern's satirical, down-to-earth prose far outweighed the tender writings that helped her gain respectability at the beginning of her career. Although her work grew out of the same tradition as that of the domestic women writers, and reflects some of the same concerns (the importance of day-to-day domestic life; the importance of the central female figure in literature), in other respects it is very different from that of other popular writers of the time, both men and women. A pioneer in the use of the vernacular and understatement, Fern was acclaimed by *Harper's* in 1854 as the welcome harbinger of a new writing style, which, the editors hoped, marked the end of the "stilted rhetoric" and "parade and pomp" of literature.[3] Fern was also praised by the British press for her ability to write without the "affectation of extreme propriety" which, the editors felt, inhibited other American women writers.[4]

Thematically also, Fanny Fern was a pioneer. Her best-selling novel *Ruth Hall,* for example, is nearly unique in its portrayal of a woman as the self-reliant American individualist, a role that nineteenth-century Americans regarded as designed exclusively for men; like the male heroes of countless "rags-to-riches" novels of the period, Ruth Hall realizes the American Dream—gaining wealth and success solely by her own talents and industry. And, unlike the other women's novels of the era, the novel ends not with Ruth Hall's acquisition of a husband but with her acquisition of ten thousand dollars in bank stock.

In her twenty-one-year career as a journalist, Fern was noted for her courageous and independent stance. She was the first woman to praise Whitman's *Leaves of Grass* in print; she wrote fearlessly on such taboo subjects as venereal disease, prostitution, birth control, and divorce; she expounded ideas on education and child rearing that have become accepted practice today; she questioned male authority and conventional marriage patterns; she condemned narrowness in religion; she urged prison reform; she criticized platitudinous religious reformers and sought real solutions for poverty and crime.

The underlying theme in all her work, however, was her concern for women's rights. She was not an active member of the women's rights movement; she never gave a speech or participated in a meeting. Her practical feminism derived from the exigencies of her own life experience. Most important was her advocacy of economic independence for women, a revolutionary concept at the time. Impatient with her society's double standard with respect to financial success, she wrote in 1861:

There are few people who speak approbatively of a woman who has a smart business talent or capability. No matter how isolated or destitute her condition, the majority would consider it more "feminine" would she unobtrusively gather up her thimble, and, retiring into some out-of-the-way place, gradually scoop out her coffin with it, than to develop that smart turn for business which would lift her at once out of her troubles; and which, in a man so situated, would be applauded as exceedingly praiseworthy. (NYL, June 8, 1861)

Most of the ideas in Fanny Fern's columns were contrary to the prevailing attitudes of her culture. And, although she was not unique in expressing them, what was unique was that she was so popular even though many of her ideas were not. For years readers mobbed the offices of the *New York Ledger* on the day the paper came out, eager to be the first to see what Fanny Fern had to say. And throughout her career she was deluged with fan mail, far beyond the expectations for any writer of the period. Nor was she forgotten by the literati. In 1855, at the opening of the Crystal Palace in New York to which the most distinguished literary people of the time were invited, Fanny Fern was included in the "gathering of immortals" presided over by the president of the Publishers' Association.

This immense popularity can be attributed to her original style and the vivid rendering of her ideas. Almost as important as the ideas themselves is her presentation of them in plain language and her ability to give dramatic life to the flaws she saw in society. The popularity of her columns also derived from her pungent satire. She stripped people—particularly men—of their grandiose airs and pompous self-complacency, and she satirized folly and pretension in all facets of life. Antiromantic and often cynical, Fanny Fern was the originator of the now-famous phrase, "The way to a man's heart is through his stomach" (TF, April 23, 1853).

Fern's humor is not in the tradition of the sprightly playfulness of a Grace Greenwood. It is sharp and cutting. Her closest rival was Gail Hamilton, who began contributing to the newspapers some years after Fern and whose barbs Fern praised in her 1868 biographical sketch of Hamilton. The seriousness behind Fern's wit is apparent in her reply to a reader who wanted to meet her because of the humor in her articles: "You labor under the hallucination that I felt *merry* when I wrote all that nonsense! *Not a bit of it*; it's a way I have when I can't find a razor handy to cut my throat!" (OB, January 31, 1852).

It is Fern's ability to transcend convention that makes her writing so valuable today. She challenges the restrictions of convention, while at the same time portraying the more rational mores of her era. In addition, she writes in a pungent, unforgettable idiom that renders her work powerful and unique. Writing from within her culture and from the perspective of a woman, yet uninhibited by the restrictions that impeded conventional femininity, she gives us an accurate and realistic portrayal of people and events, bringing to her assessment a critical eye, a sense of humor, and a fearlessness and frankness that provide us with unusual insights into the thought and customs of her time.

Fanny Fern was a remarkable woman and a pioneering writer whose work is as interesting today as when it was written. There are weaknesses in her work that one cannot ignore; for example, her overuse of death and dying in her early sentimental works, when she herself, having experienced the deaths of five loved ones in two years, seemed to be obsessed with loss. But my principal objective in this biography, in addition to chronicling Fern's life and analyzing her works, is to reveal the extent of her contribution to American literature and American culture, both as a creative artist and as a social critic, and to attempt to remedy the serious error in literary scholarship that has hitherto ignored so important a figure.

I

Deacon's Daughter

I was a "deacon's daughter," and that means in plain English that what good qualities I possessed nobody would see, and those that were bad, were ten times magnified—because I was expected to be as good as my father.

Fanny Fern, OB, August 9, 1851

FANNY FERN WAS BORN SARAH PAYSON WILLIS in Portland, Maine, on July 9, 1811.[1] Her father, Nathaniel Willis, had undergone a religious conversion four years before she was born and had decided that if his fifth child was a boy he would name the baby after the Reverend Edward Payson, the minister of the Second Congregational Church in Portland whose eloquent preaching had brought about Willis's conversion. When the baby was born a girl, Willis, not to be deterred from paying homage to his minister, determined to name the child after Payson's mother, Grata Payson. Payson urged the Willises not to burden the child with the name Grata, however; his mother, he said, had never even liked the name. The baby was named Sarah Payson Willis. In adult life, she usually signed her name Sara, without the final *h*, and that is how most sources today spell her first name.[2]

When Sarah Willis was born, she seemed an unhealthy infant, suffering from spasms and unable to catch her breath. She was hurriedly baptized, but, her parents reported, when the Reverend Payson touched her forehead, she suffered her last spasm, gave a loud howl, and afterward was healthy and robust throughout her infancy and childhood (EP, 14). There were nine Willis children. The eldest was Lucy Douglas, named after their father's mother and born in 1804. In 1806 Nathaniel Parker was born. In 1807 and 1809 Louisa Harris and Julia Dean, respectively, were born. Sarah came next, in 1811. After the family moved back to Boston, four more children were born to the Willises: Mary Perry in 1813, Edward Payson in 1816 (named for the Reverend Edward Payson), Richard Storrs in 1819, and Ellen Homes in 1821.

The father of these nine children, Nathaniel Willis, before his religious conversion in 1807, had loved dancing and pretty girls. After his conversion, however, he frowned on dancing and other "frivolous" pursuits, not only for himself but for his family. Although he retained a dry sense of humor, he was a strict Calvinist whose primary concern was the immortal soul. In Boston he was a deacon of the Park Street (Congregational) Church. The Park Street Church gained the nickname Brimstone Corner partly because it had been a repository for gunpowder during the War of 1812 and partly because of the fiery sermons that issued from its pulpit. Fanny Fern's memory of her father was of a sober man whose somber religiosity placed a pall on the household. Ethel Parton, Fern's granddaughter, described him in her biography of her grandmother as a man with "no poetry in his nature, little imagination, less tolerance; little will and little capacity to understand any disposition different from his own" (EP, 23). Fern portrayed him as an inhibiting and gloomy figure in the family in her novel *Ruth Hall* (1855), where the father is clearly based on Fern's own father, and she suggests the same qualities in this passage from an 1853 newspaper article:

"Father is coming!" and little, round faces grow long, and merry voices are hushed, and toys are hustled into the closet; and mamma glances nervously at the door; and baby is bribed with a lump of sugar to keep the peace; and father's business face relaxes not a muscle; and the little group huddle like timid sheep in a corner, and tea is despatched as silently as if speaking were prohibited by the statute book; and the children creep like culprits to bed, marvelling that baby dare crow so loud, now that "Father has come." (OB, April 1, 1853)

Fortunately for the children, the warmth and cheerfulness of their mother, Hannah Parker Willis, provided the anchor that they needed against their father's stern disposition. Ethel Parton calls her "a tenderly playful, deeply sympathetic, imaginatively understanding mother, with whom her children could share their joys and sorrows" (EP, 22). Throughout her life Fern referred to her mother with warm affection. She wrote in 1871, the year before she died and twenty-seven years after her mother's death, that she had never ceased to miss her (NYL, April 29, 1871). Her 1864 description of her mother suggests the debt that she felt she owed to her:

If there is any poetry in my nature, from my mother I inherited it. . . . Had my mother's time not been so constantly engrossed by a fast-increasing family, had she found time for literary pursuits, I am confident she would have distinguished herself. Her hurried letters, written with one foot upon the cradle, give ample evidence of this. She *talked poetry unconsciously!* (NSB, 10–13)

James Parton, Fern's third husband, confirmed this view of her parents in his biographical sketch of Fern. Her father, he said, was "an honest, plodding gentleman, . . . not remarkable either for breadth of view or vivacity of mind." It was "unquestionably" from their mother, Parton felt, that Fanny Fern and her brothers and sisters "derived the talent which all of them, in some measure, inherited" (JP, 16).

Also of importance to Fanny Fern was her mother's ability to maintain her cheerfulness within the family in spite of her husband's lack of cheer. In 1864 Fern described an incident that she had witnessed in her childhood, which she later realized was a profound example of her mother's strength and forbearance in the face of insult and harsh treatment.

One scene I well remember. It occurred in our little sitting room at home. My mother had entered, with her usual soft step and pleasant tones, and addressed some question to me concerning the lesson I was learning, when a person entered, upon whom she had every claim for love, the deepest and strongest. To some pleasant remark of hers, this individual returned an answer so rude, so brutal, so stinging, that every drop of blood in my body seemed to congeal as the murderous syllables fell. I looked at my mother; the warm blood rushed to her temples, the smile faded from her face; then her eyes filled with tears. . . . With a meek, touching grace I shall never forget, she glided voiceless from the room. . . . When I next saw her, save that her voice had an added sweetness, no trace of the poisoned arrow, so ruthlessly aimed at her peace, remained. (NSB, 15–16)

Fern respected her mother for having the patience she felt that she herself never could have had under such treatment. She recognized the cost to her mother of this effort and recognized also that it was only because of this effort that her mother was able to make their childhood home the warm and cheerful place that it was. In later years she commented on the hard lot that she had come to realize had been her mother's:

Well I remember when too young to know what life *meant for a woman*, hearing one who I have since learned had suffered and forgiven much, murmur to herself as she wearily laid her head upon her pillow, "God be thanked for sleep and forgetfulness!" (NYL, June 23, 1866)

Although Fanny Fern herself had no interest in her ancestry, maintaining that she had no desire to "climb her family tree" (EP, 3–4), her ancestors were among the first European settlers in Massachusetts. The earliest Willis in the New World was George Willis, a brickmaker and builder who was born in England around 1602 and settled in the Massachusetts Bay Colony in 1630. The great-great-grandson of this "distinguished Puritan" was Charles Willis, who married Abigail Belknap, a descendant of the brother of the Reverend John Bailey, the Puritan divine who was memorialized in Cotton Mather's *Magnalia*. Abigail Belknap was an aristocratic woman who was remembered for her insistence that one "should never eat brown bread when he can eat white" and for her refusal to drink the herb tea brewed in resistance to the British tariff on tea. Her son, Nathaniel, however, Fanny Fern's grandfather, was among the "Indians" who dumped tea into Boston Harbor in 1773, and in 1774 he began publishing the ardently patriotic *Independent Chronicle* in the Boston printing offices where Benjamin Franklin had worked as a printer.[3]

After the Revolutionary War, Nathaniel Willis married Lucy Douglas, and in 1780, Nathaniel, Fern's father, was born. In 1784, after his wife's death, the elder Nathaniel moved west, where he remarried and established two other newspapers, one in Virginia and one in Ohio.[4] His son remained in Boston until he was seven, when his father sent for him to help him in his printing office. When he was almost sixteen, Nathaniel Willis, Fern's father, who did not get along with his stepmother, returned to Boston, where he worked as a printer on the *Independent Chronicle*.

In 1803 Nathaniel Willis, Jr., married Hannah Parker of Holliston and Boston and was called to Portland, Maine, by a group of Republicans who wanted to establish a newspaper to counter the Federalist organ in Portland. Willis began as printer and became sole editor of the journal, the *Eastern Argus*. He published his first issue on September 8, 1803, announcing that he would support the current "happy Administration" and inculcate "Republican sentiments in the common country."[5] However, a series of articles in his newspaper by an overzealous politician resulted in a libel suit, and Willis, unable to pay the fine, was put in jail for ninety days. His Republican friends did not support him, and after his release, although he succeeded in paying his debts, he edited the paper in his own way. Becoming more and more religious since his conversion in 1807, Willis began to publish more religious articles and fewer political articles. The Republicans complained that the *Argus* was becoming a "milk-and-water paper," and in 1809, about six years after its inception, Willis sold the *Eastern Argus* to his partner, Francis Douglas, and opened a grocery store. The store failed—partly because of the poor economic situation and partly because Willis's religious fervor would not allow him to sell any alcoholic beverages. It was during these times of economic hardship that Sarah Willis was born in a two-story wooden frame house at 72 Franklin Street (then Essex Street), one block south of Federal Street.

The house was destroyed in the Portland fire of 1866.[6] Ethel Parton describes the house thus: "It was unpretentious outside, and its furnishings within were no more than sufficient for reasonable comfort, with no margin for extra expense in quality or decoration" (EP, 13). The only item of luxury in the house was a fine mahogany cradle, in which all of the Willis babies were rocked. Hannah Willis was determined to have a good cradle for her babies, but her husband could not afford one, and she would not ask him for the money. Instead she agreed to do the washing for Francis Douglas, at that time an apprentice printer who boarded with the family. After a year of doing Douglas's washing, she was able to buy the cradle (EP, 14).

Sarah, the fifth of the Willis's nine children, was the last to be born in Portland. When she was still an infant, the family moved back to Boston. By September 1812, her father was advertising his printing business in the Exchange Building on Devonshire Street, where he printed primarily religious books and tracts. Later he moved his office to 76 State Street, and in January 1816 Willis began printing the *Boston Recorder,* which was the first religious newspaper in America. In 1827 he founded the *Youth's Companion,* the first children's periodical in the country.

The family lived at first in rented quarters on Sweetsers Court and then on School Street, but on May 1, 1819, Willis bought a three-story brick house and some additional land at 31 Atkinson Street (later Congress Street), near Fort Hill, and this was the home in which Sarah Willis grew up.[7] She was a pretty child, with silky straw-colored curls covering her head, a rosy complexion, and dimples (EP, 7). She was merry and high-spirited, popular among the other children, exuberant and quick to learn.

Ethel Parton writes that although her grandmother never told her stories about her illustrious ancestors, she told her story after story about her own childhood and life in the Willis family:

As a child, I coaxed from her many stories of family incidents, accidents and achievements; but few of them had been handed down from a period beyond her own recollection, and those few have not remained clearly in my memory. She was a delightful story-teller, though, rather curiously, she never told me any "made-up" stories or stories of fantasy. The stories she told were always true ones. (EP, 4–5)

This was the principal characteristic of Fern's writing throughout her career. The stories she told were true ones, that is, they were based on her own observation and experience. Although she showed the "human comedy" in her portrayal of life, heightening the comedy of what sometimes were tragic situations, she did not soften or romanticize her subject matter. In fact, it was her tendency to write candidly, particularly in her autobiographical novel *Ruth Hall,* that brought so much criticism down upon her from her contemporaries. But it is also her ability to tell what she felt to be the truth about her society, without covering up the unpleasantnesses, that gives her work such value for today's reader.

According to her granddaughter, Sara loved the old house on Atkinson Street and remembered every inch of it. In the back of the house there was a garden. It was not large, but it held a quince bush, rhubarb plants, a few pole bean plants, and squash vines. One summer when Sara was a very little girl, she broke her doll and was given a crookneck squash to play with. She later described as "the first tragedy of her life" the time her squash doll was accidentally cooked for dinner and her brother Nat told her that she was a cannibal because she had eaten it (EP, 9; NYL, October 25, 1862, January 20, 1872).

Ethel Parton describes how vividly her grandmother remembered the house on Atkinson Street, particularly winter afternoons in the comfortable parlor with the icy branches of the apple tree outside and the biblical scenes on the wallpaper and fireplace tiles within (EP, 18). The family held religious services in the parlor every Sunday evening, and Deacon Willis told stories deriving from these biblical scenes. The children were eager to listen to the stories, which came at the end of a day on which toys, games, and books were forbidden except for religious books, including the Bible and Fox's *Book of Martyrs*, with its gory illustrations of tortures. Deacon Willis said that he sometimes used these stories in the *Recorder,* and that it was from telling these biblical stories to his children that he derived the idea of starting a magazine solely written for children (EP, 46).[8]

The family also held morning prayer in the parlor every morning. In 1866 Fern described the family gathered for prayers and for breakfast afterward:

I hear, now, the soft rustle of my mother's dress, as she rose after the "amen." I see the roguish face of my baby brother, whose perfected beauty was long since hid under the coffin lid. I see black curly heads, and flaxen curly heads, of all sizes, but *all* "curly," ranged round the breakfast table. (NYL, November 10, 1866)

She also remembered playing on the Boston Common on Saturday afternoons when she was a girl, picking buttercups and giving the cows a wide berth, her mother's only stipulation being that she be home before sundown. Sometimes she and her playmates would go up to the top of the State House. Children were not rushed through their childhood in those days, she said. She and her sisters played with dolls until they were fifteen, and she climbed fences "like a cat" (NYL, April 5, 1862).

Other memories were not so pleasant. The old sexton at the Park Street Church was her nemesis: "I know he hated me for my rollicking laugh, and the merry twinkle in my eye." He was the only person or thing, she said, that could take "all the color" out of her face and make her "look as sober as the Deacon himself." She was so afraid of this man, who she said looked like a distorted tombstone carving of old Father Time, that she exacted a promise from her father that he would never let the old sexton touch her (NYL, November 22, 1856; OB, August 9, 1851). Another unpleasant memory of childhood was the memory of being forced to kiss adults who were repulsive to her. Particularly offensive were the old men who took snuff, flourishing their handkerchiefs full of brown spittle. Those "snuffy kisses," she said, were "followed in many cases by actual nausea, and in all by a vigorous facial ablution on my part, after the repulsive ceremony" (NYL, April 5, 1862).

The home at 31 Atkinson Street was always open to visiting clergymen. In 1852 Fern wrote an article describing "The Prophet's Chamber," the room that was kept for visiting men of the cloth. The article refers to her grandfather and grandmother, but she is describing her parents' home:

> My grandfather's house was, to all intents and purposes, a ministerial tavern;—lacking the sign. . . . [A]lmost every steamboat, stage, and railroad car brought them a visitor. . . . You should have seen the "Prophet's Chamber,"—that never, within my recollection, was unoccupied more than time enough to clear it up. . . . There was a very orthodox atmosphere in that room, you may be sure; and when my grandmother used to send me up,—then a little girl,—with some dainty morsel, prepared by her own skillful hands for the "good minister," I used to stop at the door, till I imagined my little round face was drawn down to the proper length, before I dare show it on the other side. How glad I was when that dyspeptic Mr. Ney's visit was at an end, with his protracted walkings up and down, and across the floor, and his sighs and groans. . . . And how I used to wonder if my heart was as "awful hard and dreadful wicked," as he used to tell me! (OB, March 13, 1852)

Although young Sara was told over and over again by her father and by visiting clergymen that she was wicked and that if she did not make a religious commitment she would go to hell when she died, and although hell was often described to her in graphic scenes of horror, she refused to be frightened. Other members of the Willis family experienced tremors and fears, and her brother Nathaniel Parker worked himself up to the exaltation of conversion at the age of fifteen when he was a student at Andover. Young Sara, however, never reached conversion. The records at the Park Street Church indicate that although Fern's brother Nathaniel Parker, and her sisters Lucy, Louisa, Julia, and Mary all became church members in the 1820s when they were in their early teens, Sara was not recorded as a member until 1840, two years after her first child was born.[9] Even then her decision to become a member did not come as the result of a conversion experience; as she said in *Ruth Hall* and in a later newspaper article, it came with her acceptance of the responsibility of motherhood (RH, 29; NYL, August 23, 1862).

Nathaniel Willis was worried about his daughter Sara's lack of religious devotion. She was quick to learn the Assembly's Catechism and the biblical passages she was assigned, but she did not seem to her father to reflect the proper seriousness with respect to religion. She was not fearful of hell, nor did she worry about her wickedness (NSB, 18–19). The child Sara would run and hide when she felt that one of the visiting clergymen was going to lecture her about the state of her soul: "I was a wild slip in those days, that's why they always wanted 'a little conversation with Sarah.' . . . I ran out the nearest door after meals rather than hear it again." Fern says that she did not hate the ministers for trying to "darken" her childhood; nor did she hate church, although she was "driven there to hear so many 'seventeenthlies' at the point of a bayonet; and when skewered up on the seat between rows of big folks, felt as if little ants were creeping out from under my fingernails, so fidgety did I get for the blessed outdoors" (NYL, June 19, 1869).

James Parton felt that both his wife's father, Nathaniel Willis, and her brother Nathaniel Parker Willis had been psychologically warped by the oppressiveness of their religion. A respected biographer, Parton was asked to write a biography of N. P. Willis in 1867, and also of Nathaniel Willis in 1868 by Nathaniel Willis himself.[10] He refused in both instances because of his family connections, commenting privately that he could not write a positive biography. In both cases, he felt, their religion was the reason for their defects in character. On February 13, 1867, he wrote to James T. Fields, who had asked him to write the biography of N. P. Willis:

With regard to N. P. Willis, I am the only person living who could truly expound him. I alone have the requisite knowledge of him, from before his birth to his death. But it would be improper for me to use that knowledge unless I could use it to the credit of his family. This I could not do. He was one of the millions of victims of the baneful thing, called evangelical religion. His old dad was one kind of victim; the son, another kind.[11]

Fanny Fern, Parton said, had "escaped this evil, if it was an evil, by being something of a rebel against the leading doctrine of the orthodox church." From childhood to the end of her life, as Parton said he had often heard her say, she was "unable to believe either that she was a very depraved sinner, or that she was in any danger of everlasting perdition" (JP, 28).

It was not that Fern rejected religion entirely; what she rejected was the fear and horror of Calvinism. In this respect, she was similar to some of the other women writers of the period (for example, Catharine Beecher and Harriet Beecher Stowe) who struggled against and ultimately rejected the oppressive Calvinistic creed of their fathers but retained a strong religious belief. The difference was that whereas Beecher and Stowe believed in but later rejected Calvinism, Fern *never* accepted her father's creed; even as a child she refused to capitulate to his grim teachings. Throughout her career as a journalist, she wrote on the cruelty of bringing up children in an oppressive and fearful religious atmosphere. Sunday, she wrote in 1853, should not "be a day for puzzling the half-developed brain of childhood with gloomy creeds" (MWT, August 27, 1853). Children, she said, should not be "fettered" with "chains of *fear*" (NYL, September 13, 1862).

In her adult life Fern associated Christianity with the nurturing warmth of motherhood rather than with the fearful punishment of a patriarchal God. "Who but God can comfort like a mother," she wrote; "there is no word save God which is so . . . heart-satisfying" (NSB, 26; NYL, April 29, 1871). In 1864 Fern described a childhood incident that apparently had an important effect on her in terms of her association of Christianity with maternal love rather than with her father's stern creed:

One summer, while I was yet a child, we were located in a very lovely spot near Boston. Connected with the church where my mother worshiped, was a female prayer meeting, held alternately at the houses of its different members. One warm summer afternoon, my mother passed through the garden where I was playing, and asked me if I would like to go too. I said yes, because I liked to walk with my mother anywhere; so we sauntered along the grassy path under the trees, till we came to a small, wooden house, half hidden by a tall hedge of lilacs. Then my mother led me through the low doorway, and up a pair of clean wooden stairs, into an old-fashioned raftered chamber, through whose open window the bees were humming in and out, and the scent of flowers, and song of birds, came pleasantly enough to my childish senses. Taking off my sunbonnet, and brushing back my curls, she seated me on a low stool at her feet, while one of the old ladies commenced reading the Bible aloud. All this time I was looking around curiously, as a child will, at the old-fashioned paper on the walls, with its pink shepherdesses and green dogs; at the old-fashioned fireplace, with its pitcher of asparagus branches, dotted with little red berries; at the high-post bedstead, with its rainbow-colored patchwork quilt, of all conceivable shapes and sizes. . . .

After the tremulous old lady had done reading, they asked my mother to pray. I knelt with the rest; gradually my thoughts wandered from the china parrot, and patchwork quilt and sampler, to the words my mother was speaking. Her voice was low, and sweet, and pleading, as if God was very near, instead of on the "great, white throne," far away from human reach, where so many good people are fond of placing Him. . . . Of course, these thoughts did not then, even to myself, find voice as now, but that was my vague, unexpressed feeling. . . . It was with a new, delicious feeling I slid my hand within hers, as we passed through the low doorway, and back by the pleasant, grassy paths, to our home. (NSB, 13–15)

It is significant that it was in a community of women in a domestic setting that Fanny Fern was able to find meaning in religion. As a journalist, she was to rebel against the way in which a patriarchal society oppressed women. Portraying real-life situations in the lives of women, she used her

biting satire to attack the cruelties and injustices to which women were
subjected in their daily lives—as wives, mothers, sisters, daughters, and as
exploited workers. She urged women to rebel, to refuse to bow their heads
to the authority of men—husbands, brothers, fathers, employers, politi-
cians, even ministers—if those men acted unjustly, selfishly, and without
regard to the individual rights of women. The training ground for the public
rebellion of Fanny Fern was in her youthful struggle to resist the pressures to
submit to the image of a patriarchal God of fear and punishment. That she
was able to maintain her independence despite the constant pressure she
was under within her family and among her peers indicates a strong will and
an unusual ability to believe in herself. This experience—resisting the pressure of her father and other authority figures and the example of her brother
and sisters and peers—trained her well in the ability to resist public disfavor
and go against the tide. This ability stood her in good stead when, after the
publication of her critical articles and especially after the publication of
Ruth Hall, she did not capitulate to public opinion, but was able to maintain her unpopular opinions despite overwhelming criticism.

The only clergyman who visited her family from whom the child Sara did
not run away was the Reverend Edward Payson, after whom she had been
named. She was reluctant to meet him the first time he came, but she found
that he did not lecture her about her wickedness as the other ministers did;
he was gentle and kind. Although from the pulpit he preached on the fearful
subject of "man's depravity," in person he apparently was a "tender human
being" (JP, 19–20). It was he, she said, a different kind of minister, who
came between her and the "grim creed" that was driving her to disbelieve
(NYL, October 2, 1858). Preachers like Jonathan Edwards, she wrote in
1868, were wrong to preach of hell and damnation; she could not accept
their "Avenger" God (NYL, August 1, 1868). As she said in 1864, "The
God *my eyes* see, is not a tyrant, driving his creatures to heaven through fear
of hell" (NSB, 20).

In an early newspaper article called "Deacons' Daughters and Ministers'
Sons," Fern described what it was like growing up as the daughter of the
good Deacon Willis. A deacon's daughter, she said, was supposed to be
exemplary, so that people always noticed and commented on what she did.
Behavior that was acceptable in other children was frowned upon in a deacon's daughter:

I'm sure I could tell you of a hundred girls wilder than ever *I* was. Besides
I'd like to know if my papa's mantle of gravity was expected to be capa-
cious enough to cover us . . . when he accepted the office of deacon. Does
goodness come by *inheritance?* tell me *that*! . . . Not a bit of it; the consequence is, I was born an untameable romp—and a romp I remained, and
nobody would have thought of noticing it, either, if *Deacon* hadn't been
prefixed to my papa's name. (OB, August 9, 1851)

The first school that Sara Willis attended was a local girls' school in Boston. Her granddaughter tells the story of how on the first day of school, when the teacher asked little Sara to recite a piece from the Bible, her older sister Julia raised her hand and said: "Please, teacher, my little sister hasn't learned any Bible text for today, because it is her first day, and she is so little, and Mother thought that by tomorrow she would be used to the class and not be too shy, if you would be kind enough to wait. Mother asked me to explain." But before the next child in line could begin to recite, little Sara stood up. "Breathlessly, at top speed, without a stumble or a stop, she galloped through a passage from the Bible as long as Julia's." When the sisters came home from school, Julia told her mother what had happened and said that she had been made to appear foolish. "Don't ever ask me to explain Sarah again," she said. "Sarah can't be explained" (EP, 1).

The school day for Sara Willis as a very young child began with a morning of schoolwork. At twelve, the children "went home hungry to a good, sensible dinner." After dinner they "romped" till three, when they went back to school, and to the "benevolent face" of their teacher. In the afternoon they sewed while one of the girls read aloud from some "nice book." During her career as a journalist, Fern opposed the long school day of the 1850s and 1860s, the lack of time for outdoor play, and the excessive homework given to very young children. In her day, she said, when children were dismissed from school, they "*didn't* walk in a sepulchral procession"; they "jumped and skipped" and arrived home with bright eyes and bright cheeks, rather than the pale faces and dull eyes of the overworked children of the later period who, after spending all day in school with no time for outdoor play, carry home piles of books at night, thus destroying their health and their spirit (NYL, April 17, 1858, November 29, 1862).

Later Sara apparently attended a coeducational school in Boston, where she had what she called her "first lesson in the perfidy of man." A little boy named Georgie was fond of her. He brought her gingerbread, wrote notes to her on his slate, and played with her at recess. One day the teacher saw the two whispering in school, and for punishment made them come to the front of the room and stand on the platform back to back with their arms tied together with twine. Georgie, his arms protected by the thick sleeves of his jacket, tugged at his bonds, spitefully cutting and bruising Sara's bare arms, to show the other little boys that he did not care about her. Sara did not cry out or protest. But the next day when Georgie came running up to her as if nothing had happened and held out a stick of red-and-white striped candy as a peace offering, Sara tipped her chin in the air and walked by without looking at him or his candy. Nor would she listen as he ran by her side urging her to "make up" (NYL, May 7, 1870; EP, 20–21). In a similar incident when Sara was twelve, there was a "little blue-eyed boy" who used to walk to school with her. One day she gave him one of her long yellow curls. Another boy saw him take it, and, fearing the "world's jeer," the blue-eyed boy said he "hated girl's hair" and threw the curl into the gutter. The next day, when no one else was around, he ran up to her with a handful of "three-cornered nuts," but the nuts "followed" the curl into the gutter (NYL, September 11, 1869). She could not forgive Georgie or the blue-eyed boy for their betrayal—just as the adult Fanny Fern could not forgive her brother and father for their betrayal of her when she was slandered by her second husband and left in poverty. Moreover, in later years, when she was criticized and shunned by her family, her friends, and the public, she proved that, unlike the boys whose cowardly fear of the opinions of others had disgusted her, she herself did not capitulate before the "world's jeer."

As a little schoolgirl, Sara was dressed neatly and tidily, usually in made-over dresses carefully sewn. Seeing overdressed schoolgirls many years later, Fern compared them with the girls of her day. "Gingham and calico were good enough then," she said (NYL, July 13, 1861). The Willises thriftiness did not permit the purchase of novelty items of fashion. One item of fashion that Sara coveted, however, was pantalettes. Her mother thought they were unnecessary and did not like them; she said she did not want her girls to look like "hens with feathered legs." Sara was determined to have pantalettes like other girls in her school, and one day she found in a chest in the attic two lace-trimmed pillowcases. She cut and basted them and folded them among her schoolbooks. The next morning she left the house without pantalettes, but on the way to school she stepped into a doorway and pinned the pillow cases around her legs, enabling herself on that day at least to walk proudly into school wearing an elegant pair of pantalettes. Never able to maintain a deception, however, that evening Sara told her mother what she had done, and that was the end of the pantalettes (EP, 22).

In 1822 young Sara and her sisters Louisa and Julia were sent to boarding school at the Reverend Joseph Emerson's Ladies' Seminary in Saugus, Massachusetts, a little village eight miles northeast of Boston. Emerson was a second cousin of Ralph Waldo Emerson.[12] A circular dated October 26, 1824, states of Saugus, "It is expected that the place will soon be accommodated with a stage and a mail," and outlines the course of study at the school: the younger students studied "Orthography and Definitions of English Primitives, Reading, Arithmetick, English Grammar, Modern Geography, and the use of the Globes."[13] The school year consisted of two terms of twelve weeks each, with a vacation in between. The students paid six dollars per term in addition to board of between a dollar and a dollar seventy-five (excluding fuel, lights, and washing).[14]

The school opened in May 1822. When they started at the school, Sara was almost eleven, Julia thirteen, and Louisa fifteen. The girls boarded with local residents. The school was so popular for two years that boarding accommodations were difficult to find.[15] The Reverend Emerson was a popular preacher and supplied the church's pulpit most of the time. At one time there was a preparatory school attached to the seminary; it was taught by Mrs. Emerson and Miss Z. B. Cheever.[16]

Nathaniel Willis's motivation in sending his daughters to Saugus apparently derived from his knowledge of Emerson's orthodox Calvinism and emphasis upon religion. Emerson was famous as the author of the *Evangelical Primer,* a conservative religious tract that sold over two hundred thousand copies. Emerson exhorted the students "to evangelize the world," to "read and study the Bible much."[17] Mary Lyon, who was a student of Emerson's at Byfield, wrote to her mother that a strong "spirit of piety" was "mingled with all of Mr. Emerson's instructions." There was a constant "anxiety for [religious] revival" in the school, she said.[18] When Emerson moved from Byfield to Saugus, he invited one of his former students, whose religious fervor matched his own, to assist him. This was Zilpah Polly Grant, who, Emerson said, was necessary to help him combat the "atheistic teaching" of the age.[19] The "best book for instruction," according to Emerson, was Jonathan Edwards's *A History of the Work of Redemption;* Timothy Dwight's *Theology* was "one of the greatest works in the world."[20] At his school in Byfield, Zilpah Grant reported, much emphasis was placed on bringing the young ladies to "divine grace," and much concern was expressed when there seemed to be insufficient numbers of students affected.[21] Under the guidance of Emerson and Grant, the school at Saugus clearly continued the pressures upon young Sara to profess religion.

Despite his orthodoxy in religion, Emerson's educational ideas were progressive, and his school provided the beginnings of a useful education for the future Fanny Fern. A circular advertising the school in 1824 stated: "Unwearied pains will be taken to inspire a thirst for knowledge, to cultivate the understanding, and fix ideas rather than mere words in the minds of the pupils."[22] "Logic, the art of using reason well, is the parent of all other arts," Emerson told his female students, thus indicating that he did not share the common opinion that women were unreasoning creatures.[23] His comments on composition, which he also considered important, are interesting with respect to Fern's later career, particularly her lifelong penchant for writing candidly: "Young people should be trained in much composing. . . . You will be happily successful if you write the truth and nothing but the truth."[24]

Emerson's opinions on the position of women were also advanced. In 1820 he told his students at Byfield:

Females are the foundation of society; they need sound judgment, energy, and vigor. Has the woman nothing to do but obey? . . . Woman has far more of commanding than of obeying to do. The sexes are mutually dependent. It is worse than foolish for one to speak against the other.[25]

While the Willis girls were at Saugus, their brother, Nathaniel Parker, who was a student at Andover, wrote several letters to Louisa, who, only one year younger than he, was the closest to his age of the three at Saugus.[26] In a letter written in late September 1822 he says that he plans to visit

Saugus and hopes to meet their parents there. The letter provides an interesting picture of the girls' teacher, probably Mrs. Emerson, whom Willis calls an "old hag" in another letter:

Dear Louisa:

Julia says, I owe you two letters. If so I did not know it—for I always make it my rule, never to let a communication go unanswered. But, you know Memory's fallacious.—& perhaps I had forgotten them. So *excusez moi.*

Mary Woods was married the night of the exhibition. Louis Dwight, brideman, & Elizabeth Adams bridemaid. . . .

How do you come on at Saugus.—& how is your old beldame,—I wish I had her nose between my thumb & finger. I would tweak it nicely for her—But after all perhaps she is better than I, (though I doubt it,)—so Heaven bless her oddities, and give her old crazy carcass one grace at least before she dies.—

Probably, I shall be at Saugus soon to meet Pa & Ma.—He mentioned it to me in his letter, so you may expect me. Dorrance will come with me. Give my respects to his sister, & tell her that her brother's health is very poor indeed. . . .

Give my love to Sarah. My *respects* to Miss Lord.—By the way I expected to see her at exhibition.—I told E. Adams she was coming, and was disappointed at her non-appearance. Love to Francis & all my friends.

Your Aff'te Brother
N. P. Willis[27]

In another letter to Louisa at Saugus, Willis indicates that he was a frequent visitor to Saugus. That Willis mentions so many other young ladies in this and other letters suggests that the reason for his frequent visits to Saugus was not only to see his sisters:

We are coming to Saugus next Lotus day—if weather and other circumstance permit—Don't you mention it in your letters to Pa, for he thinks I go there too often, and that Mrs. Emerson don't like it, and perhaps would write to me not to go—I don't care for the old hag myself, but he might—. . . . How is S.—Write me soon—my best love to her—and all my friends at S's—Respects to Miss Dorrance—I called on her when in Andover. Remember me to Augusta, Miss Boardman, Miss Bigelow, &c And I am

Your affectionate Brother
N. P. Willis

In another undated letter to Louisa, Willis gives us an idea of the requirements of the school. Louisa had apparently asked him to write an essay on fiction that she could use for her school's exhibition exercises. Willis was ultimately to develop a taste for dancing, the theater, and fiction—all of which in his Calvinist home were considered implements of the devil. His opinions on fiction would consequently not be acceptable at the Reverend Emerson's orthodox school:

It is a shame, Louiza [sic], to defraud you of my promise, though it was a foolish one. My remarks on Fiction I find are such as would not be esteemed orthodox at your College, and might subject the author to the charge of heresy. I shall therefore withhold them. Many thoughts on many subjects have occupied my mind since I saw you. I have thought of the advantages of cultivating a taste for poetry and the fine arts—of harmony of character, and the danger of extremes—of ambition—and a thousand other little things—But none of them are fit for you. I have therefore concluded to rid me of my engagement by sending a few lines of what the world calls "the sentimental." I am strongly of Mr. Emerson's opinion that the young ladies would as well to indulge themselves in occasional flights into the regions of fancy and to cherish the talent for poetry—whenever it is possessed in the smallest degree.

It is interesting that Fanny Fern, who was also a student at Emerson's school, never wrote poetry in her life, so that Emerson's belief that "young ladies" should poetize apparently did not convince her. Within a few years, however, Willis himself was famous as a poet while he was an undergraduate at Yale.

In the fall of 1823, after two years of great popularity for the Emerson Ladies' Seminary, there was a typhoid fever epidemic at the school. A number of students became ill, and some died. As a result of this scare, many of the students were withdrawn—including the Willis girls. The following year the Reverend Emerson retired for reasons of health, and although the school continued for two more years, religious conflicts within the parish resulted in 1826 in a split within the church and the dissolution of the seminary.[28]

In December 1823, after Sara and her sisters had come home, their sister Mary wrote a letter from home to their brother Nathaniel, who had entered Yale University that fall:

Dear Brother:

As Mother has gone to Mrs. Peters' to pass the evening, I will improve this opportunity of writing to you. In the first place I must tell you that God has been very good to us since you have been gone[.] [W]e have all been in good health and very comfortable[.] [W]e should have been happy had we been holy but sometimes when I think I shall have a very pleasant day I indulge in some angry feeling and do some wicked thing which spoils it all[.] [I]s it so with you my brother? [D]o you find occasion to mourn over sin that dwelleth in you or have you gained the victory[?]

[D]o you write to me and tell me if you have any feelings of this sort and what you do in such a case[.] Now I will tell you something about the family[.] Lucy comes over every evening to drink tea[.] [L]ittle Ellen grows finely and begins to talk very fast and says brother Atta (Nat) gone[.] [T]he boys have grown very noisy and pa has the headache very often. Julia's eyes have grown so weak poring over her books that she cannot see how to hem a ruffled shirt[.] Mother is very busy as usual. Pa is going over to South Boston tomorrow with Mr. Dwight as delegate from our church to form a church which Mr. Hawes has gathered there and over which he is to be pastor. Richard and Edward send their love[.] I shall expect a letter very soon.

Your affectionate Sister
Mary[29]

Mary's letter is interesting as a chronicle of events in the Willis household at the time. Her comments about her father—that "pa has the headache often" because her little brothers are noisy—confirms Fanny Fern's portrayal of Nathaniel Willis in "Father is Coming," where the father's arrival home casts a pall on the household. The boys, Edward and Richard, were seven and four at the time. Mary's comments about Julia's reading interfering with her sewing suggests the priorities of society and of her family with respect to women's activities. Her letter is also interesting as an example of the piety and seriousness that Nathaniel Willis sought in his children. Mary, who was two years younger than Sara, had just turned ten when she wrote the letter. Unlike Sara, who rebelled against her father's grim Calvinistic creed, Mary describes how she is tortured by guilt because of her wickedness and sin.

Sara's eldest sister, Lucy, married Josiah F. Bumstead, Jr., on July 21, 1823, and set up housekeeping in Boston. On May 31, 1824, Louisa, who was four years older than Sara, married Louis Dwight, a friend of her brother's (the "brideman" in the September 27 letter from N. P. Willis to Louisa at Saugus), and Louisa and Julia, who was never to marry, remained in Boston, their education apparently complete.

In November of 1823 Emerson's principal assistant at Saugus, Zilpah Polly Grant, had become principal of the newly organized Adams Female Academy in Derry, New Hampshire. With her she brought another former student of Emerson's, Mary Lyon, who in 1837 founded Mount Holyoke Seminary. The names of Sarah P. Willis and her younger sister, Mary P. Willis, are listed in the catalog of the Adams Female Academy for 1826, along with the name of Ellen Tucker, Ralph Waldo Emerson's first wife. It is not clear whether Sara, who had returned home after the typhoid scare at Saugus in the fall of 1823, began attending Adams Female Academy at its inception in the spring of 1824, or if she began in 1826, when her name appears in the catalog.

Jacob Adams had died in 1822, bequeathing four thousand dollars to endow a female academy, and the Adams Female Academy became the first institution for women in the country to be founded with funds from a legacy left specifically for the academic education of women.[30] The school was incorporated in June of 1823, and "a large, commodious building" was erected that summer.[31] It was the first incorporated institution for women in the state.[32] A statement written by Zilpah Grant and issued by the secretary of the corporation on December 3, 1823, outlined the course of study and terms for the new school, which was to open with sixty young ladies in April of 1824:

> As the exclusive object of this institution is the improvement of female education, and as its permanency is secured by funds, the trustees are disposed to avail themselves of the advantages which they possess to adopt a more systematic and thorough course than has been usually pursued in the education of females. . . .
>
> There shall be three regular classes, denominated junior, middle, and senior classes. . . . For admission into the junior class it is expected that the young ladies will be familiarly acquainted with the fundamental rules of arithmetic, particularly with the arithmetical tables; that they be able to write legibly; that they have a good general acquaintance with modern geography, and a sufficient knowledge of English grammar to parse easy sentences. The junior class will attend to reading, spelling, defining, chirography, pen-making, arithmetic, modern and ancient geography, English grammar, and composition. . . . Except in special cases, no one will be admitted into the junior class under the age of thirteen years.[33]

The school year at the Adams Female Academy consisted of two terms of fourteen weeks each. The first term began in mid-April. After a two-week vacation in August, the second term ran until mid-November. The school was not in session during the winter. As Mary Lyon said in a letter to Hannah White in 1824, the location in New Hampshire was not "favorable" to a winter term because of the severe climate.[34]

Since Fanny Fern would have been thirteen in July 1824, she was either a member of the junior class or of the preparatory class; if she entered in 1826, she would have been fifteen in July. So stringent were the requirements of the school that as Mary Lyon wrote in 1824, "We have but very few under fifteen years of age who can enter the regular classes."[35]

If Fern was at the Adams Female Academy in June 1825, she would have been present at the historic visit of General Lafayette to the academy. Hannah Chickering, one of the teachers, described the event in a letter to her mother:

> At nine o'clock in the morning the young ladies all assembled, dressed in white, and wearing bunches of natural flowers fastened in their pink belts.

Their heads were ornamented only by the combs that confined their glossy locks. We arranged them in five rows, the tallest at the back.

After waiting all day, the students finally got to greet Lafayette at five o'clock. Dr. Dana told him that "this was one of the public institutions in our country for the education of females, and taught exclusively by them, designed principally to give them a solid training." Lafayette shook hands with each of the pupils, whose faces were "solemn with an expression of intense feeling."[36]

Mary Lyon admired Zilpah Grant's teaching methods and the "systematic arrangement" that she proposed to follow.[37] Her teaching was thorough and intense. The words on the official seal of the academy were "Drink deep or taste not."[38] Both Grant and Lyon regarded their calling as a God-given trust. As Linda Guilford says in her biography of Grant, *The Use of a Life*, "they received the young and tender minds committed to their guidance as deposits of infinite preciousness for which they were to give account at the day of judgment."[39] Lyon wrote to a friend in 1824 that Grant's method was superior to Emerson's because it was more thorough and did not make the mistake of presupposing knowledge that did not exist.[40] The academy's reputation rose rapidly, and after the first term the number of students had more than doubled.[41]

Fanny Fern would receive a good education at this new academy. Unfortunately for the young rebel against Calvinism, however, Grant was not only dedicated to the improvement of the minds of the young ladies in her charge; she was passionately concerned with her pupils' immortal souls. According to Fanny Fern's daughter, Zilpah Grant was a friend of the Willises and was often a visitor in their home.[42] Again Nathaniel Willis had chosen a school where he felt his daughters would be immersed in his brand of religion. Grant told the trustees before the school opened that "her aim would be not only the development of the intellect, but the training of the character according to the Word of God," and she stipulated that she would use one-seventh of the time in Bible instruction. As her plan was put into effect, however, it became apparent that the religious instruction was the center around which everything else revolved, and in 1826 there was a constant increase in religious seriousness.[43] Instead of a treatise on ethics, all students every week had to study the Scriptures, and there were daily Bible lessons, individually and in groups.[44] More time was spent in Bible study at Adams Academy than at any other educational institution, except a theological seminary.[45] For years Grant had prayed that she might have an institution where women could be trained to serve God as men were trained.[46] Guilford describes Grant's emphasis on religion at Adams:

It was Miss Grant's habit to make, during the first few days of the term, a division of the pupils on the question, "Are you a professing Christian?"

She made it a point to ascertain as nearly as possible the religious state of every one. No school ever brought afterwards under either herself or Miss Lyon had so small a number of church members. But one after another heard and obeyed the call to a more devoted life, and the careless awoke to eternal things.[47]

Young Sara, apparently, was one of the few who did not "hear the call." In this respect she was like Emily Dickinson, who, at Mount Holyoke twenty years later, resisted the call to make a commitment to Christianity and was classed among the "no hopers."[48] After having withstood the pressures of her father, her siblings, the visiting clergymen, and the religious teachings at the Reverend Emerson's seminary in Saugus, Sara also was able to resist Zilpah Grant's passionate urgings in spite of the daily example of the girls around her who were brought to profess their religion.

In 1874, after Fern was dead, her daughter and granddaughter coincidentally found themselves in a boardinghouse in Newburyport, Massachusetts, with Zilpah Polly Grant Banister, who remembered the youthful Sara Willis. Ethel Parton, Fern's granddaughter, who was eleven at the time of the meeting, recalled that her grandmother had often spoken of "Zilpah Polly," and she was sure that "as preceptress of the old school" Mrs. Banister would disapprove of her (Ethel). When Ellen, Fern's daughter, recounted an amusing incident to Mrs. Banister, however, the former preceptress was delighted: "My dear! my dear! you certainly have your mother's capacity for dramatic narration." Mrs. Banister told them a great deal about Sara Willis as a schoolgirl, and Ethel Parton describes the retired principal's impression of her grandmother:

As a pupil, she had been bright, but not studious, and dangerously inclined to levity. To a teacher [like Grant] so serious, so given to bringing the slightest actions of youth to the bar of moral and religious judgment, Sarah's behavior must certainly have been a trial. She could never have been harsh or unkind in either action or opinion, I feel assured; but Sarah's airy recklessness troubled and bewildered her. . . . She was even faintly troubled in conscience because of her own leniency toward . . . [Sarah] over other girls more attentive to their studies, more correct in their deportment, and more inclined to meditation and piety. Even though she committed no outward injustice, and cherished her preference secretly, in her own heart it did not seem to her quite fair. "Such good girls, my dear; such good girls! But Sarah—" (EP, 38–41)

Although Sara Willis was not a "good girl" by Zilpah Polly Grant's standards of deportment and piety, her experience in New Hampshire ironically did have an influence on her attitude toward religion—although not the influence that her father and Grant hoped that it would have. Although she never accepted Calvinism, her Sundays spent in the simple country church in Derry, New Hampshire, gave her a standard against which to measure religious devotion. Many years afterward, when she was living in New York, she wrote of the hypocrisy of people who went to church only to show off their new clothes or because it was fashionable to do so, and she contrasted their false piety with the genuineness and sincerity of the country people in the old church she attended in New Hampshire (NYL, May 12, 1860, September 16, 1865, June 15, 1867).

During the years 1826 and 1827 the religious teaching at the Adams Female Academy was its most intense. Sara Willis's father was in agreement with Zilpah Grant's theology, but there were other parents who were not. The executive committee became increasingly alarmed at the intense religious instruction taking place at the school. In July 1826 the committee issued a formal request that Grant and all of her teachers keep a record of the time spent each day in religious instruction. Grant and the teachers complied with the request but continued the instruction, and Grant later wrote that "during the next term, the religious interest was deep and extensive."[49] Then, on November 13, 1827, the trustees proposed adding courses in music and dancing to the curriculum. Grant, who had not been consulted regarding the new department, opposed the new courses. In December 1827 the trustees advertised for a new principal:

It was the original design of the trustees to establish this seminary on liberal principles. They regret that the institution has acquired the character of being strictly Calvinistic in religious instruction. This character has grown up in opposition to the sentiments and wishes of a majority of the trustees.[50]

Zilpah Polly Grant left the Adams Female Academy early in 1828 and moved to Ipswich, where she founded the Ipswich Female Seminary. Forty of her pupils followed her from Derry to Ipswich, but Sara and Mary Willis were not among them. Nor did they remain in Derry after the trustees made their break with Calvinism. They both returned to the house at 31 Atkinson Street. Sara was glad to be home. She had had enough of boarding school. But Nathaniel Willis was even more concerned about Sara's lack of piety than he had been before. Her brother, Nathaniel Parker, while at Yale, had begun the backsliding from his commitment to Calvinism that was to result in his being excommunicated from the Park Street Church in 1829.[51] Nathaniel Willis began to look for a way to ensure that Sara would become more seriously religious. The new minister at Park Street Church was Edward Beecher, the son of Lyman Beecher. His sister Catharine Beecher had in 1823 begun the Hartford Female Seminary, which was so successful that in 1827, having raised sufficient funds by subscription to erect a new building on Pratt Street with a lecture hall, a library, six recitation rooms, and a study hall for a hundred and fifty persons, she obtained a charter and established a board of trustees. The school opened in November with seven teachers.[52] Beecher was known to have successfully conducted a religious awakening among her pupils. In her *Educational Reminiscences* she said that for several years every term at the Hartford Female Seminary "witnessed what would be called a 'revival of religion.'"[53] If anyone could bring Sara to religion, said Edward Beecher, it was his sister.

Thus it was decided. Sara was to go to Catharine Beecher's school. Mary, who did not present a problem in terms of seriousness and religiosity, would remain home. Insisting that she wanted to stay home also, Sara declared that she did not like boarding school. As an adult, Fanny Fern remembered the young Sara Willis's objections to boarding school and refused to send her own daughters or her granddaughter away to school. Her newspaper articles on the subject give us an idea of her opinion of boarding schools. She objected to the "license allowed, or if not allowed, stealthily taken"; to the unventilated sleeping quarters; to the "insufficient food; and stolen confectionary to make up the deficiency"; and to the "over-dressed, vain, vapid, brainless" girls who have been put there because their parents think it is the fashionable thing to do (NYL, March 27, 1858, April 18, 1858).

Life at home had become more interesting as Sara entered her teens and beaux became numerous. With her yellow curls, clear rosy complexion, dimples, and rounded figure, she was never lacking in admirers. In the afternoons, they went for walks, or a row on the river, or coasting. In the evenings, the young people went to meeting, or to a neighborhood party with no dancing, or stayed at home, talking, playing games, or popping corn over the open fire. Sometimes her younger sister Mary would win away a beau by bringing in cookies and cider. Sara laughed and called Mary "little slyboots." It was hard for Sara to leave these activities to go to boarding school. Ethel Parton describes her grandmother's reluctant departure for the Hartford Female Seminary as it was told to her:

She wept when she said goodbye. She wept when her bandboxes were stowed aboard the stage-coach. She wept when the driver cracked his whip to start, and when he whoaed the horses to a stop before the Seminary door. She wept when she was shown to her room. Her room-mate had not yet arrived. Left to herself, she dropped down upon her hair-trunk studded with brass nails, screwed around to lean her hot forehead against a cool window-seat, and wept still harder. Presently, she caught the sound of sobs echoing her own and paused to listen. Perhaps there was somebody in the next room—as homesick as she? There was. On the two sides of the thin partition, two tearful girls were presently taking turns in sobbing and listening for each other's sobs. . . . Tears turned to laughter, and they were soon cheering and comforting each other. (EP, 55)

fannfern

2

❧

Hartford Female Seminary

*Something must be speedily done, to curb her imagination, demolish
her airy castles; in short, to convert her into a plain, sober, matter-of-
fact damsel, without a thought beyond her Murray's Grammar or
Daboll's Arithmetic. All this was wound up with the suggestion, that it
would be wise to send me to school without further delay.*[1]

DESPITE HER OBJECTIONS, Sara, now sixteen, was sent to the Hartford Female Seminary for three years. The school year consisted of two terms of
twenty-two weeks each. The summer term began in May and ended in October; the winter term began in November and ran through April of the
following year. The evidence indicates that Sara Willis was a student at the
seminary from May 1828 through April 1831.[2]

The trip from Boston to Hartford in 1828 took seventeen hours by stage
coach. Some young ladies traveled to Worcester the first day, stayed overnight at the Temperance Hotel, and then proceeded to Hartford.[3] The Hartford of 1828 was very different from the Hartford of today. Major John
Parsons, a resident of Hartford who was a young college student at the time
that Sara Willis was in Hartford, described the 1828 town at a reunion of
the Hartford Female Seminary in 1892:

> The town of Hartford at that time included West Hartford, and the whole
> population was about 9,500. . . . There were only a few scattered dwell-
> ings west of Trumbull Street. Of the fifty-two original subscribers to the
> stock of the Seminary, all but four or five resided on Main Street, and
> streets to the east of Main. . . . There was no bridge over Little River
> except on Main Street. In summer, the stages from New York and Boston
> arrived about dusk, and left again at daybreak.[4]

A classmate of Sara Willis's, a young woman named Mary Kingsbury
Talcott, described the Hartford Female Seminary in a composition written
at the school in 1830. The composition is interesting not only for its physical description of the seminary and of the composition class, but also for its
tone, which seems to be slightly tongue in cheek. Despite the rules that the

author describes, her tone suggests that the school which would permit such a tone in a composition did not suffer from an oppressive atmosphere:

The Hartford Female Seminary is a brick building, situated in Pratt St. nearly in the centre of the city. . . . It is surrounded by a grassy yard, enclosed by a white fence, and has its entrance by means of two gates in front. The front door, to which ascent is afforded by a flight of wooden steps, is surmounted by a large window, from which when open, many bright faces may be seen peeping forth, at certain times of liberty. Upon the east side, is another door, designed for the ingress and egress of the pupils, which, doubtless, for wise reasons best known to the rulers of the institution, are not allowed entrance, by the door in front. . . . Should any one enter this [composition] room, . . . at the *present* time, he would see in the midst of the class, a young lady, with more than an ordinary share of dignity, yet with an arch smile in the corners of her mouth, endeavouring to perform the duties of Teacher in Composition, during the absence of the rightful lady of the room.—Two rows of young ladies, ranged around the room, would afford him ample subject of meditation. . . . On the whole, he would *probably* think it a very fine class, and a pattern for all school girls to imitate. . . . At another time he would behold the pupils, grouped in little circles, or meandering in pairs, or trios, around the various rooms, and yard, of the institution, enjoying the delights of a few moments of *partial* liberty, during recess. The spectator would, doubtless, be unable to leave this establishment, without a feeling of admiration and pleasure, at the sight of so many young ladies, walking in the path of wisdom and knowledge.[5]

Catharine Beecher's school provided the religious emphasis that Nathaniel Willis wanted for his daughter. In her *Educational Reminiscences* published in 1874, Beecher described her religious methods at Hartford. Through the use of prayers and conversation with both teachers and students, she said, "a silent religious influence pervaded the school." Teachers and students who had "commenced a religious life" were requested to select at least one member of the school who was not thus committed, and suggestions were made as to the best way to "exert an influence."[6]

In spite of this religious emphasis, Sara Willis continued to maintain her independence, and in May 1829, after Sara had been at the school for a year, Catharine Beecher had to confess to the Willises that, although she had no criticism of Sara's moral character, she had been unable to bring her to a commitment to a religious life: "I do not feel much confidence in Sarah's *piety* but I *do* think that religious influence has greatly improved her character. She is very lovely & tho' her faults are not all eradicated, & tho' I still fear the world has the *first* place, yet I think religion occupies much of her thoughts. She now rooms alone, & has much time for reading & reflection.

As soon as I can get my school organized I can do more for her spiritual improvement."[7]

Although Beecher's religious influence permeated the school, the emphasis was not on the fear of damnation, nor was the atmosphere oppressive. Beecher herself preached to her students, and, as she said later, she "endeavored to present God as a loving Father, and to make it plain that his 'glory' . . . consisted in the virtue and true happiness of all his children."[8] Moreover, although Beecher had conducted a religious revival earlier, at about the time that Sara Willis came to the school she had decided to focus on "character, not conversion"—which is ironic considering Nathaniel Willis's principal motivation in sending his daughter to Hartford. Beecher's biographer, Kathryn Kish Sklar, explains this shift by the fact that the new school attracted many students from outside New England, many of whom were not Congregationalist. She also suggests that Beecher's emphasis on the development of character may have been an attempt to find a universal religious principle.[9]

Beecher's father, the Reverend Lyman Beecher, was considered "the big gun of Calvinism," and in 1824 he had characterized Calvinism as the "Faith once delivered to the Saints." He was called to Boston in 1826 to save the city for Calvinism in the struggle against Unitarianism, which Lyman Beecher regarded as a "soul-destroying heresy."[10] Catharine Beecher did not preach orthodox Calvinism, however. In 1829 she had difficulty raising money because most of the well-to-do were orthodox Calvinists and they objected to her lack of orthodoxy. They felt that it was a waste of money to support a school that educated souls without conversion; such souls, they reasoned, would only be on earth a short time and then would spend an eternity in hell. Catharine Beecher also refused contributions that would force her to bind her school to any one sect, maintaining that "while Christianity was essential to proper education, sectarianism was both irrelevant and injurious."[11] Beecher's school was apparently also not orthodox enough for Zilpah Polly Grant, who had been young Sara's principal in Derry, New Hampshire. In 1829, Beecher wrote to Grant offering her a position in the school. Grant declined, saying that the Hartford Female Seminary was too "worldly" for her; she objected to Beecher's emphasis on "taste and refinement" rather than religion.[12]

If Fern did not escape religious pressures in Hartford, at least the religious teaching at the Hartford Female Seminary was more palatable to her than the fire and brimstone preached by her father and the visiting clergymen. Beecher's emphasis on character rather than conversion also included an interest in benevolent activities. Angelina Grimké, who was in Hartford from 1829 to 1833, remembered much emphasis on such activities.[13] From 1828 to 1830, for example, Beecher was very involved in the protest against the removal of the Cherokees from their land.[14] To a certain extent, Beecher's religious perspective confirmed the feelings that had been evolving in the young Sara Willis. The adult Fanny Fern never subscribed to the grim creed of Calvinism; she also severely criticized doctrinaire sectarianism in religion, and throughout her journalistic career she took a strong stand against all forms of injustice.

In the history of education in the United States, however, it is not Catharine Beecher's religious teachings that make the Hartford Female Seminary important; it is the educational value of her methods and ideas. At a time when colleges were not open to women, Fern received at the Hartford Female Seminary as close to a college education as was available to any woman of the period. The editor of the *American Journal of Education* pointed out that the seminary offered "to young women a pretty fair opportunity of keeping pace, in some measure, with those of the other sex, who enjoy the advantages of a classical education."[15] In 1828 when Sara Willis entered the Hartford Female Seminary, Emma Willard's school in Troy, New York, was probably the only other school in the country that offered a comparably high level of education for women.

In 1829 Catharine Beecher outlined her educational philosophy and the methods she used at her school in a paper entitled *Suggestions on Education*, which she presented to the trustees of the school. First of all, she said, she wanted to "secure a division of labor and responsibility peculiar to our college system." Women and small children were often taught by one teacher, who was expected to teach all subjects. This resulted in a superficiality of knowledge. Beecher's method was to hire a teacher to teach only one or two branches of learning so that the teacher would have sufficient knowledge of the subject to enable the students to learn it in depth. Second, Beecher formed her classes into small groups of students equal in abilities and acquirements so that "none were hurried forward and none retarded for the sake of others." Third, Beecher's concept of education emphasized ideas rather than rote memorization; she sought to teach students "to think and reason, to invent, discover." Finally, she included in her school a regular program of physical education, emphasizing the importance of physical exercise at a time when women were often regarded as semi-invalids. Beecher regularized education for women, establishing regular terms and a regular course of study. In order to counteract the tendency of young girls of the period to flit from school to school, a tendency that derived from the failure to take the education of women seriously, she specified in her advertisements that students would only be admitted at the beginning of the term and that all students would be expected to complete the required three-year course of study. She also required that each student take four regular classes, with a certain degree of proficiency required for each.[16]

As in other educational institutions of the day, particularly those designed specifically for young women, life at the Hartford Female Seminary was regimented and carefully supervised. In the seminary's 1831 catalog Catharine Beecher described a typical school day:

The daily routine of school duty is as follows. The young ladies are required to study *two hours in silence* out of school, and thus to prepare
their lessons for the morning recitations. The scholars first assemble in the
entrance room. . . . At ten minutes before nine, the bell is rung to summon
them to the Hall, where they are expected to seat themselves quietly and
in silence. The first three quarters of an hour is devoted to instructions
from the Principal, on various duties, enforced by the authority of the
Bible, and concluded by prayer to God. After this the school journal is
read aloud, in which is recorded an account of the behaviour and recitation of the several classes during the preceding day. The *cases* are stated of
those who are faulty in each class, but the *names* are omitted. . . .

After the school journal is read, the scholars are requested to forward
to the Governess, on slips of paper, an account of all the rules they have
violated since the preceding morning, which are to be recorded by the
Governess. . . . After the scholars have passed their accounts to the Governess, they are all requested to rise. Then those who can recollect that they
have violated no rule, are requested to sit. This gives an opportunity for
the teachers and scholars to notice those who remain standing, and thus
learn whether all have recollected the rules they have been observed by
others to neglect. . . . After this, the Governess calls out the classes in
succession, when they form themselves in regular file of two and two, in
the centre of the Hall, and pass to meet their teachers in the several recitation rooms. A monitor is placed at the head and at the foot of the stairs, to
record any who are disorderly in going or returning. Those who do not
recite the first hour, remain in the Hall either to write or to study. At the
end of an hour, the bell is rung, and the classes all return and are again
seated in the Hall. The Governess then calls out the classes to exercise in
Calisthenics, and they all pass to the various rooms, where, under the
direction of the teachers, they perform the regular course of exercise. After this a recess of ten minutes is given, in which the free use of the tongue
and the limbs is allowed. The scholars are then again assembled in the
Hall, and at each successive hour, are sent to recitations or remain to
study in the Hall. In the afternoon also, the general exercise in Calisthenics succeeds the first recitation hour.[17]

What becomes clear from this description is the seriousness of Beecher's
commitment to her undertaking and the organized nature of her system;
even the calisthenics are integrated into the regular course of study. It is also
apparent that much emphasis was placed on proper behavior. Although
Beecher did not believe in what she called "espionage," and discouraged the
girls from reporting on each other (she preferred if possible to rely on the
girls' honesty), the catalog contains a long list of rules: no young lady "during school hours, *in any part of the building* may communicate ideas to
another, by mouth, by the fingers, or by writing"; no young lady may leave

the building; no pupil may sit up later than 11 in the evening; each young lady must attend church; young ladies may not visit other rooms after 10 in the evening; "no pupil may spend more than 12 ½ cents in any kind of confectionary without leave"; no young lady "may visit or receive company except Friday evenings and Saturdays"; young ladies may "never remain abroad till dark; and young ladies are forbidden to walk or ride with a gentleman without permission.[18] In both of these areas so important to the founder of the school—proper behavior and seriousness of purpose—the young Sara Willis was found wanting.

Sara Willis had two nicknames while she was in Hartford. One was "Yellowbird" because of her yellow hair. The other was "Sal Volatile" because of her scintillating personality. Harriet Beecher Stowe, who was the same age as Sara, was a pupil-teacher in her sister's school at the time that Sara Willis was there. Harriet was studious and quiet, and although they liked each other, Harriet was somewhat in awe of the popular, high-spirited Sara. In a letter to her friend Mary Dutton on May 25, 1830, Harriet mentioned some of the girls who were at the school that term. "S. Willis," she said, "is as well & lively as ever—She is a lovely girl but a proud one. I want to be acquainted with her but have not. She is sometimes a sort of 'Noli me tangere.'"[19]

Many years later, Stowe wrote to James Parton, Fern's husband, thanking him for his defense of her in his article urging an international copyright law. In the course of the letter she referred to Fanny Fern, reminding her of their school days in Hartford:

I believe you have claim on a certain naughty girl once called Sarah Willis in whom I still retain an interest who, I grieve to say one night stole a pie at Mrs. Dr. Strong's and did feloniously excite unto sedition and rebellion some five or six other girls,—eating said pie between eleven & twelve o'clock in defiance of the laws of the school & in breach of the peace—ask her if it isn't so—& if she remembers curling her hair with leaves from her geometry?—Perhaps she has long been penitent—*perhaps*—but ah me—when I read Fanny Fern's articles I detect sparks of the old witch-craft—& say as poor Mrs. Strong used to when any new mischief turned up—That's Sarah Willis, I know![20]

The pie raid that Stowe describes was one of several raids on the pantry. Catharine Beecher was fond of experimentation, and one of the fields she experimented in was diet. She believed that hearty eating deadened the mental faculties as well as causing obesity. At one time the food was carefully weighed and second helpings were discouraged. Sara, who always had a good appetite, rebelled at the skimpy servings and, along with several other girls, stole a pie from the pantry and ate it in her room at night. The problem was that after they had consumed the pie they wanted to get rid of the evidence—the pie plate. Throwing the metal plate out of Sara's window, they heard someone cry out. Looking down they found that the plate had narrowly missed hitting Dr. Strong, the matron's husband, on his bald head. He of course reported the incident, and they were found out (EP, 60–62).

Two other raids on the pantry in which Sara Willis was the ringleader give us an idea of her position at the seminary. One night Sara and several other girls stole a rice pudding. They were interrupted on the stairs and dropped the pudding, all of the girls running through it in their hurried retreat to their rooms. The grains of rice adhered to their bare feet, and in the morning the culprits were discovered by the rice in their beds. Another raid proved equally disappointing. Having gone to a great deal of trouble to steal a jar of pickles, the girls gathered in Sara's room only to find that the pickles had been only recently put in brine and consequently were inedible. This time Sara was more careful in disposing of the evidence. She wrapped the jar in a newspaper and, stuffing it in her reticule, carried it downtown the next day and left it in a gutter (EP, 62).

Another incident concerning food involved justice, something that was always important to Fanny Fern. The teachers and students sat together at a long table for their meals. The housekeeper, apparently to save money, was in the habit of putting better-quality food at Catharine Beecher's end of the table. One day Sara came into the dining room just before dinner and switched the butter dishes. At dinner Beecher helped herself to butter and called the housekeeper over. "This butter is not the same as usual," she said. "There is something the matter with it. It is very nearly rancid." Before the housekeeper could reply, Sara Willis stood up and, picking up the butter dish at the students' end of the table, carried it to Beecher.

"Oh, no, Miss Beecher; it's just the same, only we have your dish, and you have ours." Beecher, who had not been aware of the discrimination, spoke to the housekeeper, and after that the butters were equal (EP, 63).

Despite their differences in personality, Harriet Beecher Stowe remembered Sara Willis very fondly. On February 6, 1868, she wrote to James Parton regarding his wife: "Please say to her that my heart is just as warm to her as when she was a bright laughing witch of a half saint half sinner in our school here in Hartford."[21] She recalled in a letter to Fanny Fern later in 1868 how she, as a more serious young girl, "used to hector and lecture" her "in the old times."[22] The young Sara Willis called her "Miss Harriet," although they were the same age, because of Stowe's role as pupil-teacher and because of her seriousness. In another letter Stowe referred to Sara Willis as "Sister Katy's best-loved pupil, her torment and her joy" (EP, 62).

Henry Ward Beecher, the brother of Harriet and Catharine who was to become the famous and charismatic preacher of the Plymouth Church in Brooklyn, was also a friend of Sara Willis. Less intimidated than Harriet, he sometimes went on clandestine horseback rides with Sara when he visited his sisters at the seminary. Fanny Fern referred to their friendship in an exchange in the *New York Ledger* in 1870: "I mind me of a young man, of your name, who once came to a boarding-school, where I, at sixteen, was placed for algebra and safe-keeping, both of which I hated, and who invited me to take several surreptitious rides with him, which I did" (NYL, February 26, 1870). Beecher later described the young Sara Willis to J. C. Derby, her publisher:

When I was a boy in college, she attended Catharine Beecher's school in that city [Hartford]. The latter kept a stable full of horses for the girls to ride horseback, my sister Harriet among them. I used to go with Fanny on horseback. She was a blonde, had a very fair face and flowing flaxen hair. She was quite a bewitching little creature. One of the prettiest girls in Hartford.[23]

Coupled with this description of Sara Willis by Henry Ward Beecher we have another description by an admirer in Hartford. Signing himself an "old fogy," he wrote to the then famous Fanny Fern telling her of how he had admired her in silence thirty years before:

Many years ago I was *electrified* by a jaunty straw flat [Leghorn hat], a green veil, long flaxen curls. Oh! how witchingly beautiful! One blue eye—the other was under the veil, which was perseveringly held down and set the jaunty hat slightly awry—a lithe, supple form, perfect in its proportion and movement! Talk of the poetry of motion! *that* is nothing; poetry, painting, music and dancing *all* in action! T'won't do! Well, school was out. The vision vanished, but it has come and gone a thousand times during the many years that have passed, and always the same fresh, enchanting thing of memory. (EP, 74)

Another anonymous admirer focused on the way Sara Willis walked: "Other girls, when we were young, tripped or teetered or minced when they walked, or if they tried to step out freely, they strode. Not Sarah Willis! Sara walked like a nymph" (EP, 74).

The only surviving memento of Fern's days at the Hartford seminary is an autograph album, which was a gift from her brother Nathaniel Parker, whom she called Nat. It is a brown leather-bound volume with gold leaf around the border of the front cover where the name "Sarah P. Willis" is engraved in gold in the center. Her friends, including Harriet Beecher Stowe, wrote in it, inscribing romanticized names under often melancholy poems. Harriet wrote a translation from the German and signed her initial H————. Fanny Fern later wrote in her full name. Some of the poems are written in by Fern herself from such poets as Byron, Moore, and Southey.[24]

As Harriet Beecher Stowe's comments suggest, Catharine Beecher liked and respected her wayward pupil. Even while scolding her, Beecher would find herself laughing at Sara's exploits. Sara Willis's high spirits and amusing ways won over Catharine Beecher, who even as principal of her own school retained a vast store of the Beecher sense of humor. In a letter to Fanny Fern in 1868, Harriet Beecher Stowe describes the young Sara Willis and indicates her sister's attitude toward her:

> You also I remember with your head of light crepe curls with your bonnet always tipped on one side and you, with a most insidious leaning towards that broad sound of laughing & conjuration which is the horror of well regulated school ma'ams, & the many scrapes which occasioned for you secret confabulations with Sister Katy up in her room. She had always a warm side toward you.[25]

Many years after Sara left the Hartford Female Seminary she was shopping in a Boston store with her young children when she saw Catharine Beecher. She went up to her and said, "Why, Miss Beecher!" Then she paused and added, "But you had so many girls, you could not remember them all; I suppose you don't know me."

"Know *you*, Sarah Willis," Catharine Beecher exclaimed. "You were the worst behaved girl in my school—and I loved you the best!"[26]

Although Sara Willis was called in to see the principal on many occasions, Catharine Beecher did not feel that her infractions were serious. She wrote to Mr. and Mrs. Willis that Sara's conduct, "though frequently gay and unthinking," is never such as to invite "serious reprehension." "Her manners," she said, "are indeed as engaging as her person, and her apprehension is as ready as her smile." In Beecher's opinion, however, this did provide some cause for concern:

> This agreeable conjunction, generally deemed so fortunate, offers to my mind the chief cause for anxiety on her behalf. When mind, manners and countenance unite to charm, it becomes difficult in face of the world's delightful flattery for a young woman to retain the docility and retiring grace which should characterize her age and sex. (EP, 65–66).

Catharine Beecher's concern that Sara Willis was not retiring enough was particularly apparent in the principal's comments to a man who admired her pupil at one of Beecher's receptions at the school. Beecher believed that her young ladies should not only be well trained morally and intellectually, but should have some training in the social graces as well. Throughout the school term she held regular social gatherings for the students, teachers, and for other ladies and gentlemen whom she chose to invite. The girls looked forward to these levees, as Beecher called them, and when it was known that certain favorites were to attend, much time was spent in preparing for the event. At one of the levees, a stranger told Catharine Beecher that Sara

Willis was "a remarkably brilliant girl." Many years later the man wrote to Fanny Fern to tell her Catharine Beecher's response. "Brilliant!" Beecher had exclaimed, regretfully. "That is what I feared." She explained to him that although Sara possessed "unusual abilities, which it had been her duty to develop," she knew that it was also her duty to mold character. When a stranger's first comment was "What a brilliant girl," she said, it made her doubt her success. If he had said, "What a sweet girl," she would have been pleased. In her opinion, "A perfectly bred young lady pleases, but rarely scintillates. Brilliance is too conspicuous for youth, of which a prime virtue should be modesty" (EP, 66).

Catharine Beecher had another concern about Sara Willis: she spent money unwisely, Beecher felt. The principal wrote to Sara's parents in 1829:

I have *tried* to make her as economical as possible but have not succeeded as I could wish. She never would do anything she *knew certainly* I would disapprove, but is withal very *thoughtless* as you well know—So she sometimes has borrowed money of the girls which I of course could not refuse to return, & in vacation brought in some bills to me which I knew nothing about.[27]

Enclosed with this letter is a list of Sara Willis's expenses, including $61 for board, fuel, and lights; $22.87 for tuition and French lessons; $10 for washing: books, stationery, pins, and needles $10; 50¢ for a physician's bill; and $3.89 for postage and a seat in church. The other expenses include $4.25 for gloves and a spring bonnet; $2 for presents for companions; $7.75 for other articles; $7.25 for "corsettes"; and $2.77 for shoes. Sara was $44.56 over budget, which balance Catharine Beecher directed the Willises to pay to her brother Edward in Boston.

The physician's fee of fifty cents listed on the bill Catharine Beecher sent to Mr. and Mrs. Willis in 1829 may have been the fee charged by the doctor who was called in to see their daughter on the Friday before one of Catharine Beecher's levees. At breakfast that morning Sara had complained that she did not feel well. The matron had advised her to go back to bed and, against Sara's protest, had sent for the doctor. The doctor came and examined her. When they were alone, the doctor, who was a friendly old man with many years of experience, reproached her: "Now, now, Sarah Willis, what's the meaning of this nonsense? There's nothing the matter with you!"

"Oh, yes, there is, doctor," Sara responded very seriously. "I have the snipping fever. I have it badly."

"The *what* fever?" asked the doctor.

"The snipping fever." Sara reached under the bedclothes and pulled out a dress, partially ripped, and yards of narrow ruffles which she was scalloping, then pinking, and which when sewed onto her dress would create a dress of the very latest fashion. She would never finish it in time for the levee if she could not remain in her room all day, she said. The amused doctor agreed to go along with the plot. He prescribed a bread pill and told the matron he was sure she would be recovered soon—which she was, and appeared at the levee wearing a dress that was the envy of all her friends. Characteristically, however, after the levee was over, she went to see Catharine Beecher and confessed. In the process of telling what she had done, she made the story so hilarious that Beecher, although she tried to reprove her, ultimately broke down into helpless laughter and Sara escaped with "the lightest possible punishment" (EP, 61–62).

At another levee, Beecher decided to reward Sara Willis, who had been behaving herself unusually well for the past two weeks, by asking her to entertain a distinguished clergyman who, with his nephew, a very good-looking young man, had been invited to the levee. During the evening, Beecher was pleased to see that the gentleman seemed to be enjoying himself immensely, that he was even laughing, although he was ordinarily very sober. The next day, however, Beecher was dismayed to hear Sara say to a group of her friends that she "thought she should have died amusing that terrible old Humpty Dumpty."

"Sarah! Sarah!" exclaimed Beecher, coming up to the group. "How *can* you! Dr.——— is a man of remarkable intellect and lofty character. You should think of that and not of his person."

"But, Miss Beecher," protested Sara, innocently. "I didn't mention Dr.———. I only spoke of Humpty Dumpty."

Beecher laughed. The resemblance to Humpty Dumpty was so pronounced that she could not help knowing whom Sara meant. But she nevertheless reproved Sara, pointing out that making fun of the man was a poor way to repay the opportunity to entertain a distinguished clergyman, particularly when such an opportunity had been given to her as a reward. "You don't deserve it, Sarah," she protested. "Indeed you don't."

"I know it, Miss Beecher," Sara admitted. "Next time don't you think you'd better reduce me to entertaining his nephew as a punishment?"

"Oh, Sarah! Sarah!" Beecher sighed. "You don't deserve that either! But you will probably get it just the same"—and, according to Ethel Parton, who got the story from her grandmother, Sara did (EP, 66–67).

Also included in the bill that Catharine Beecher sent to the Willises in May 1829 is a charge of $1.50 for defacing furniture: Sara Willis had carved her initials on a desk with a jackknife on a journey to Guilford with Catharine and Harriet Beecher during one of the school vacations (EP, 69). The total cost of the trip, including board and washing and the charge for defacing the desk, was $10.25. The date of the charges indicates that the trip probably took place between the winter term, which ended in April 1829, and the summer term which began in May. On the trip to Guilford Sara Willis apparently caused considerable trouble. Catharine and Harriet Beecher were probably going to stay with their grandmother Foote, as they had done previously, and in her letter Beecher says of Sara at Guilford: "She was unwilling to stay with my friends at G. tho' I urged it as much as I thought best to do."[28] In a letter to Fanny Fern in 1868 Harriet Beecher Stowe commented: "Do you remember the vacation at Guilford—& your irrepressibility?—The idea that *you* have daughters and—can I believe it—a granddaughter?"[29]

It is interesting that Sara remained with the Beechers during the school vacation instead of going home to Boston. Apparently she spent other vacations at the school as well. Given her reluctance to leave home initially, it would seem that the decision for her not to come home was her parents' and not hers. During one vacation from school, Sara visited her sister Louisa, who was married and living in Stockbridge, Massachusetts. There she met Catharine Maria Sedgwick, whom she remembered as a handsome, distinguished lady, and who was related to Louisa's husband, Louis Dwight (EP, 71).[30] Sedgwick, whose novel *Hope Leslie* was published in 1827, provided an important touchstone for Fern in later years, both as a literary role model and as one of the few creators of strong, rebellious women characters in antebellum American fiction.[31]

Sara did spend some of her vacations in Boston, however. On one vacation in Boston, she called on Catharine Beecher at the home of her father, Lyman Beecher. In 1863 Fanny Fern described the visit and her surprise at finding Beecher's clergyman father to be unlike the dour, joyless clergymen she had been accustomed to:

Attending his daughter's school in Hartford, I had returned home to Boston, to spend my vacation. My teacher, Miss Catharine Beecher, had also returned to her father's house in the same city. One morning I went to call upon her there; for there *are* exceptions to the rule that girls in America consider their teachers in the light of their mortal enemies. I had, of course, often heard of the Doctor, and regarded him with that stand-off-and-awful veneration with which orthodoxy at that time thought it right to impress the young mind as to its clergy. . . .

Inquiring for my beloved teacher, I was invited into the parlor to await her coming. The first object I saw was an old gentleman in his shirt-sleeves, perched on a corner of a table playing on the fiddle. Much to the relief of my seventeen-year-old-bashfulness, he took no notice of me, except by a keen glance, but played on all the same as if I were not present. Who *could* he be? and how funny that he neither stopped playing, nor went out, nor apologized for his shirt-sleeves, nor did anything that etiquette might be supposed to require, even in presence of a very young lady, under such queer circumstances. Presently my teacher entered; no introduction followed, we commenced conversation, and the old gentleman played on. The conversation turning on Nahant, Miss Catharine gave me a glowing description of that celebrated summer resort; upon

which I said to her, "Well—isn't it odd that as long as I have lived, I never
should have seen that place." Down jumped the Doctor (for it was he)
from the table, and approaching me with his fiddle under his arm, laughed
merrily—"ha—ha—as long as *you* have lived you have never seen
Nahant! and pray, my dear, how *very* long may that be?" and back he
went to the table, and resumed his fiddling, never waiting for my answer.
Now this was the first time I had ever seen what I call a *flesh-and-blood
minister*. It was a delicious revelation to me. Perhaps then, thought I, after
all, one *may* laugh and be jolly, all the same as if there were no "ministers" in the world, since the great and good Dr. Beecher can "fiddle!"
(NYL, February 14, 1863)

This visit to the Beecher home gave young Sara Willis a better understanding of Catharine Beecher, who, although she was the daughter of a
clergyman, retained an appreciation of fun and a sense of humor which
allowed her, even in her august role as principal of the school, to laugh at
the harmless exploits of her pupil. Although later in life Catharine Beecher,
like her brother George, who committed suicide, felt that her father had
"ruined her life,"[32] it was enlightening for Sara Willis, whose father was
sternly religious, to see a minister who could let his hair down.

When Sara did have her first vacation at home after many months at the
seminary, she was exuberant. Ethel Parton describes that first visit home
from Hartford:

She swept into the house in a whirlwind of joy, bestowing tumultuous
hugs upon a family who reciprocated gladly, with the one exception of
Brother Nat. That Brother Nat happened to be present was a capsheaf to
her happiness, but when she flung herself upon his neck, laughing and
crying both at once, he fended her off as best he could, protesting in
dismay. "Kiss me if you must, Sarah, but for God's sake don't tumble my
dickey." (EP, 70)

In *Ruth Hall* this incident is told as if it happened when Ruth's brother
visited Ruth at the seminary, the author telescoping this incident into one of
Willis's visits to Hartford, thus conveying in one scene a full impression of
the character she was portraying. This is characteristic of Fanny Fern's style;
she was noted for her brevity and unusual ability to give the whole picture
with a few selected details.

At first when Sara Willis came to Hartford she was known as "Nathaniel
Willis's sister." N. P. Willis, who had gained considerable fame as a poet
while he was still an undergraduate at Yale, had graduated in September
1827 and in the same year had published a collection of his poems as a
book. For four years after graduation, Willis lived at home in Boston, first
editing Samuel Goodrich's popular *The Legendary* and *The Token* in 1828

and 1829 and then publishing his own periodical, the *American Monthly Magazine*, for which he did most of the writing himself.[33]

At Hartford Sara's relationship to her famous brother gave her a certain reflected prestige, particularly when he visited her at the school. Although it is probably exaggerated, the description in *Ruth Hall* of Hyacinth at Ruth's boarding school gives us an idea of what it was like when the worldly and blasé N. P. Willis visited his sister at the seminary:

> He also remarked, that her shoes were too large for her feet, and that her little French apron was "slightly askew;" and told her, whatever else she omitted, to be sure to learn "to waltz." He was then introduced to Madame Moreau, who remarked to Madame Chicchi, her Italian teacher, what a very *distingué* looking person he was; after which he yawned several times, then touched his hat gracefully, praised "the very superior air of the establishment," brushed an imperceptible atom of dust from his beaver, kissed the tips of his fingers to his demonstrative sister, and tiptoed Terpsichoreally over the academic threshold. (RH, 16)

It was not long before the future Fanny Fern gained recognition on her own. At Catharine Beecher's levees she met some of Hartford's notables. Lydia Sigourney, for example, who was at that time a noted writer of prose and verse, sometimes made an appearance at the levees, and Sara also remembered seeing her in her seersucker dress and green sunbonnet working among the pinks and peonies in the garden outside her house in Hartford (EP, 70–71). Sara also met the editor of the local newspaper at one of the levees. Her sayings and compositions had excited notice among her schoolmates and were often passed from hand to hand. In this way the editor had come upon some choice articles to put in his paper. Soon he was coming to the seminary to ask for "Miss Willis's latest," or, if he needed material to fill a column and "Miss Willis" had no new composition at hand, he would come directly to Sara in the schoolroom and, sitting beside her, write down what she dictated as fast as he could write (EP, 70). Sara Willis received no pay for this service. She did not even think of asking for it. It was simply a way of helping an editor. She had often done the same for her father for his publications.

If Sara Willis was good at writing compositions, she was not as proficient in mathematics, a subject that Catharine Beecher had made an important subject in the seminary. This antipathy Sara shared with her brother Nathaniel, who was once suspended from Yale for refusing to memorize certain corollaries in math.[34] In 1827 Catharine Beecher published her own book on arithmetic, which she used in the school and which professed to "give an *explanation* of every *arithmetical process*, and to . . . . make all explanations clear and concise that the pupil may not be prevented from finding the meaning."[35] Harriet Beecher Stowe in one of her letters to Fanny

Fern in the 1860s refers to Sara's compositions, and also to her aversion to arithmetic. She describes Sara as the girl with "laughing light blue eyes—writing always good compositions & fighting off your Arithmetic lessons."[36] Ethel Parton tells us that Sara, years after she left the seminary, sent to her old schoolmate, Betsy, upon the birth of Betsy's first daughter, a blue flannel petticoat worked in a pattern of cubes, circles, and triangles, to thank Betsy for the help she had received from her in geometry during their seminary days (EP, 55).

   In the fall of 1829, at the exhibition that came at the end of the term and for which each student was supposed to prepare a special piece, Sara Willis read a composition she had written, "Suggestions on Arithmetic," which is the only surviving composition from her days at the seminary. She had not herself kept a copy, but many years later, in 1872, one of her schoolmates sent her a copy. The title was a satirical reference to Catharine Beecher's two books, her arithmetic textbook and the report presented to the trustees that year, *Suggestions on Education*. The piece, which Sara read with dramatic effect, was received with great hilarity:

The truth of the matter is, that I have been a persecuted girl ever since my tormentors, in the shape of an uncle and aunt visiting our family, put it into the head of my indulgent parents that their daughter would certainly become a sickly sentimentalist. Something must be speedily done, to curb her imagination, demolish her airy castles; in short, to convert her into a plain, sober, matter-of-fact damsel, without a thought beyond her Murray's Grammar, or Daboll's Arithmetic. All this was wound up with the suggestion, that it would be wise to send me to school without further delay. . . .
   In pursuance of this sage determination, one pleasant morning in May found me, *nolens volens,* on my way to the H.F.S., the principal of which had received orders from my kind relations not to be sparing of anything in the shape of mathematics. . . . I at last became so deeply imbued with the spirit of arithmetic that even my language took coloring from it. . . .
   The dreaded examination day at length arrived. I rose in the morning to make my toilet, when, to my great consternation, my hair, instead of forming itself as usual into flaxen circles, very deliberately erected itself into triangles, angles, and parallelograms all over my head. I set myself to work very philosophically to account for this fact, and discovered that I had curled it with a leaf of my geometry. What could not be cured must be endured, and groaning in spirit that my outward man must needs be sacrificed, I hastened my preparations, and started for school. . . . My meditations were somewhat interrupted by the salutation of a young gentleman whose company, before the days of Euclid and Daboll, was not very disagreeable to me, and whom report had long since tied to my apron strings. However, I then noticed him no more than I would one of

my schoolmates, though the tones of his voice were rather tremulous. Of his many speeches, one in which he protested his warm interest, brought only one word that chimed with my train of thought. "Interest," exclaimed I, starting from my reverie. "What per cent, sir?" "Ma'am!" exclaimed my attendant, in the greatest possible amazement. "How much per cent, sir?" said I, repeating my question. His reply was lost on my ear, save, "Madam, at any rate do not trifle with my feelings." "At any rate, did you say? Then take six per cent; that is the easiest to calculate."

Suddenly I found myself deserted. Why or wherefore, I was too busy to conjecture. I reached school without further adventure, and took my seat in the class to recite; but just as the question was put to me, and while a thousand eyes were levelled at me from all parts of Study Hall, expecting my reply, the whole drift of my friend's conversation at once flashed upon my mind. Amazement seized me, and, covered with confusion, never a syllable could I, for the life of me, utter.

From that day to this I have never opened an arithmetic. (JP, 38–42)

This early composition is important not only because it gives us an idea of the type of satirical writing that was to make Fanny Fern famous, but also because it is indicative of two important aspects of the independent stance that she was to take in her later writing. That a young schoolgirl in 1829 would publicly make fun of her principal's serious concerns and would do so in a format that deliberately mocked the principal's own works indicates, first of all, a remarkable degree of courage and daring in the young Sara Willis, and an ability to defy convention and authority—character traits that would later become the trademark of Fanny Fern. Second, she was able to do so in such a humorous way that, shocking as her essay may have been to the more conventional members of the audience, it made her a great favorite with her classmates and, apparently, with Catharine Beecher herself—just as her later writing, although it was criticized by traditional critics, brought her overwhelming public acclaim.

When Sara Willis was sent to boarding school, her father hoped to make her more seriously religious and more subdued. Zilpah Polly Grant and Catharine Beecher hoped to make her more modest and retiring and to increase her religious commitment. But her schoolmistresses also recognized in her a talent and spirit that her father did not value. She was "The Child Whom Nobody Can Do Anything With" that she wrote about in 1858. "You have too much imagination, you should try to crush it out," she was told, apparently by her father, when she was a child. But, as she realized later, it was that very faculty that later enabled her to lift herself and her children from poverty (NYL, January 23, 1858). It also made her an acerbic and witty commentator on the social scene. And it made her world famous.

The schools that Sara Willis attended were among the best schools available at the time for women. That their teachers accepted the conventional image of woman as submissive and retiring, morally exemplary, and seriously religious is not surprising; a teacher with more radical views would hardly have been able to attract students or financial support for a school. At the same time, however, her teachers possessed the finest and most creative female minds of the period. Zilpah Polly Grant, Mary Lyon, Catharine Beecher—all were innovative and farsighted pioneers in women's education. That they appreciated and encouraged Sara Willis's original and critical thinking, despite their reservations about her behavior and lack of piety, is evidenced by the unconventional exhibition piece that she was permitted to read at the Hartford Female Seminary.

Beecher's conflicting feelings about Sara Willis—her appreciation of her high spirits and brilliant mind, combined with a desire to make her more conventionally passive and subdued—are indicative of the paradoxical nature of Beecher's own concept of the role of women. On the one hand, she herself pursued an independent course and dedicated her life to the education of women. On the other hand, she retained the conventional image of women as passive, subordinate to men in all areas; she opposed political equality for women; and she maintained that her purpose in educating women, in addition to providing new teachers for women, was to train them so that they would grace their domestic station as wives and mothers.[37]

The Hartford Female Seminary was a boarding school, which the young Sara Willis had not wanted, but it had positive results for her: it took her away from the grim creed of her father and it provided her quick mind with challenging ideas. Catharine Beecher never came to share Fanny Fern's radical ideas or to approve of her behavior, just as she did not agree with the ideas of Angelina Grimké. Their defense of political equality for women, for example, was at odds with Beecher's belief that although the moral influence of women was important, women should remain subordinate to male authority. But Beecher's methods were neither oppressive nor repressive. At the Hartford Female Seminary women's minds were stretched and stimulated in an institutionalized setting that revolutionized the concept of education for women. It was a good beginning for the future Fanny Fern.

"Bread-Making and Button-Hole Stitching"

We know these little accidents never happen in novels—where the heroine is always "dressed in white, with a rose-bud in her hair," and lives on blossoms and May dew! . . . But this humdrum life, girls, is another affair, with its washing and ironing and cleaning days, when children expect boxed ears, and visitors picked-up dinners. All the "romance" there is in it, you can put under a three-cent piece!

TF, June 12, 1852

IN 1870 FANNY FERN WROTE that when she had completed her education at the Hartford Female Seminary, she returned to the "bosom of her family" to learn the "Lost Arts" of "bread-making and button-hole stitching" (NYL, February 26, 1870). She was almost twenty years old. Her formal education not only extended beyond that of most young women of the period, but was more extensive than that of any of her five sisters. Moreover, it took place at the most prestigious and most academically advanced institutions available for women in the United States at the time. Why was the young Sara Willis singled out to enjoy such an unusual education? Her brothers were sent to Yale, but they, after all, were boys.

If the future Fanny Fern was favored in this way, it was not because her parents felt she was particularly deserving of an education. It was her father who made these decisions, and his primary concern was the religion of his children. The boys were sent to Yale because their father believed that Harvard was a hotbed of Unitarianism at the time, and Deacon Willis felt that his sons' spiritual life would not be jeopardized at Yale, where the orientation was Congregationalist. Andover was selected rather than Exeter because it was under the wing of the Andover Theological Seminary, which was staunchly Calvinist.[1] His daughters were sent to boarding schools that he knew to be Calvinist in orientation and where he knew there was a heavy religious emphasis. If Sara continued to go to school longer than his other daughters, it was primarily because, unlike her sisters, she had failed to make a religious commitment and he hoped that the religious teachings at the schools would succeed where he had failed in making her more seriously religious.

But Nathaniel Willis had another reason for keeping Sara in school. Partly because of her lack of religious seriousness and partly because of her high spirits, he was uncomfortable in overseeing his rebellious daughter. The other girls he could understand, but Sara was unpredictable; she had a will of her own. In 1870 Fern stated that she was sent to the Hartford Female Seminary "for algebra and safe-keeping," both of which she said she hated (NYL, February 26, 1870). And in her 1829 composition "Suggestions on Arithmetic," she said that she was sent to boarding school to "curb her imagination" and make her into a "plain, sober, matter-of-fact damsel" (JP, 38). But it is her father's comment, reported by James Parton, that is most revealing. Parton noted in his biographical sketch of his wife that after their marriage her father said to him, "How do you manage her? *I* never could" (JP, 32). Deacon Willis regarded his fourth daughter as a "handful." He kept her at boarding school because he did not know what to do with her himself.

When Sara Willis finally came home in 1831, she was brought back into the family to help with domestic chores and to learn the domestic skills she would need as a wife and mother. Her education at the seminaries, no matter how much geometry or chemistry or literature or history she had learned, was regarded as irrelevant to her ultimate station in life. Fern's statement that after leaving the Hartford Female Seminary she went home to learn bread-making and button-hole stitching is an ironic comment on her society's view of her education: most of her contemporaries believed that the "frivolous" part of her education was over and the "real" education was to begin.[2] Even her mentor at the Hartford Female Seminary, Catharine Beecher, maintained that the ultimate goal of a woman's education was to enable her to perform her domestic role more effectively. Sara Willis had been at school until she was twenty; she was to spend the next twenty years wholly in the domestic sphere as "bread-maker and button-hole stitcher" to her father and brothers, then to her first husband, then as a dependent widow with two children, then to her second husband—until in 1851 she left her husband and began a new life as Fanny Fern.

Although Sara Willis had come home to learn domestic skills, she did not always enjoy being domestic. According to her sister Julia, she was often hard to find when she was wanted for extra domestic chores, such as entertaining the clergy, or getting things ready for the female visiting committee, or sewing for charity. Her granddaughter notes, however, that despite her reluctance to do these extra domestic chores, she always responded cheerfully when the requests were made by her mother (EP, 76).

Sometimes Sara would sit sewing with her mother and sisters, along with a seamstress who came in by the day. This employment was a social occasion also, and sometimes the group would laugh heartily over an anecdote told by Sara. Then Julia would call out, "Sarah, stop! You mustn't make Mother laugh like that." The fear was that in her merriment Hannah Willis would prick her finger. If this happened, someone would call for the smelling salts, exclaiming, "Mother's off again," which meant that mother had fainted. Hannah Willis could not stand to see even the tiniest drop of blood. Her work would slip from her fingers and she would fall back in her chair in a dead faint. Her great-granddaughter says that this weakness was a deep source of mortification to her, but she was never able to control it (EP, 77).

The dressmaker who helped the Willis family with its sewing was, according to Ethel Parton, a "sharp-eyed, sharp-chinned, sharp-tongued" "odd little wisp of a woman" who was always eager to know all of the family gossip. One morning she arrived late and, hearing laughter from the sewing room, she could not wait to take off her outer clothes. She ran into the room with her bonnet half off, her shawl dragging on the floor, and one galosh on and one off. "What? What? Who did what?" she called out breathlessly, and this caused so much amusement among the sewers, that the words became a common expression in the Willis family, thereafter used to formulate any type of question (EP, 77).

The dressmaker, who Ethel Parton believes was named Miss Patty, did not "wholly approve" of Sara Willis, although she admitted that she had "a figger it was a joy to fit." Sara, however, wanted too many "fol-de-rols and furbelows" on her dresses, and they meant too much work. Moreover, Sara would run away when Miss Patty tried to show her how to do work that she was not interested in, such as how to seat a man's pants. Consequently, when she had to sew a pair of pants, they were unwearable. When Miss Patty remonstrated with her and said that she would have to learn how to do it properly so that she could make her little boys' trousers when she had children, Sara replied that she did not want any boys and that when she married, she would only have girls. Miss Patty was shocked at this defiance of Providence, and warned, "Mark my words, her first will be a boy!" But when Sara Willis married and had three girls, Miss Patty was flabbergasted. "Sarah Willis getting her way again, in a thing like that," she murmured. "What can the Lord be thinking of!" (NYL, September 11, 1869; EP, 77–78).

Other failures at domestic work also came from not paying attention. Once when Sara was cooking dinner, she seasoned the beef with saleratus instead of salt, making it inedible. This failure came from the fact that she was reading a "too-fascinating" novel at the same time that she was supposed to be cooking. She had kept the novel hidden under her cooking apron, for this was "in a day when novels were forbidden fruit" (NYL, September 11, 1869), being regarded as sinful and worldly in her Calvinist household.

Sara Willis did other chores at home which were not domestic, but she hardly regarded them as "chores." From the time that she was twelve, she had done proofreading for her father's *Recorder* and *Youth's Companion,* and when she was older she wrote copy as well. Like the editor of the Hartford paper, Nathaniel Willis asked Sara or one of his other children to write a paragraph or a longer article when he needed something to fill up a page. It was easy for Sara to dash off an article, and she never thought of receiving pay for it any more than she would have thought of receiving pay for the sewing or cooking she did for her mother (EP, 45). Ironically, whereas the domestic work was regarded by her family and her contemporaries as necessary training for her future career as wife and mother, no one—least of all Sara Willis herself—would have dreamed that this unpaid labor for her father was providing useful training for a future career as a journalist.

Life at home, of course, did not consist only of chores. In 1866 Fanny Fern described the kinds of parties that her family had attended in the 1820s and 1830s. Then, she said, husbands, wives, and children did not have a separate circle of acquaintances. Parties were not formal and elegant. Although she criticized certain aspects of the earlier day (primarily the overemphasis on the frightening, dark side of religion), she preferred the simple "old-fashioned tea parties" to the stiff, formal parties of modern fashion. At dark the parents and the eldest children would go to the party together. Her description provides an interesting view of social activities in New England in the 1830s:

All assembled, the buzz of talk was soon agreeably interrupted by the entrance of a servant bearing a heavily-laden tray of cups and saucers, filled with tea and coffee, cream and sugar. This tray was rested on a table; and the host, rising, requested Rev. Mr.——— to ask a blessing. He did it, and the youngsters, eyeing the cake, wished it had been shorter. So did the girl in charge of the tray. "Blessing" at last over, the tea and coffee were distributed. . . . The men turned their toes in till they met; spread their red silk handkerchiefs over their bony knees, and on that risky, improvised, graceful lap, placed the hot cup of tea, with an awful sense of responsibility, which interfered with the half-finished account of the last "revival." Then came a tray of thinly-sliced bread and butter, delicate and tempting; rich cake, . . . with delicate sandwiches, and tiny tarts.

This ceremony gone through, the young people crawled from the maternal wing, and laughed and talked in corners, as freely and hilariously as if they were not "children of damnation," destined to eternal torment if they did not indorse the creed of their forefathers. Their elders, with satisfied stomachs, and cheerful voices and faces, seemed to have merged the awful "hell," too, for the time being; and nobody would have supposed them capable of bringing children into the world, to be scared through with a claw-footed devil constantly at their backs.

As the evening went on, the buzz and noise increased. The youngsters giggled and pushed about, keeping jealous watch the while, for the nine o'clock tray of goodies, which was to delight their eyes and feast their palates. This tray contained the biggest oranges and apples, the freshest cluster-raisins, and almonds, hickory nuts, three-cornered nuts, filberts and grapes. After this came a tray of preserved quinces, or plums, or peaches, with little pitchers of *real* cream. Then, to wind up, little cunning glasses filled with lemonade, made of *lemons*. (NYL, November 17, 1866)

Ethel Parton tells about some of the games the young people played at these parties. Clap in, Clap out; Going to Jerusalem; Puss in the Corner: these were the quieter games. They also played Blindman's Buff, with "hands clutching, petticoats whisking, squealings and shriekings, and bursts of jolly laughter." And the most popular game was Forfeits, popular because there were the kissing penalties (EP, 80). In an 1864 article, Fern described the ending of this "Old-Fashioned Party." The party ended at ten o'clock. The minister gave a closing prayer and the guests walked to their respective homes—"in those days people had feet and used them" (NYL, December 31, 1864.)

The Willis girls participated in other activities with their various male admirers, activities that did not involve their parents. Sara Willis was attractive and lively and apparently popular with the young men. In 1868 Fanny Fern criticized the fashionable young ladies of the day who complained about their lack of beaux. The lack of beaux in 1868 could have been partly a result of Civil War deaths. But, said Fern, it could also be because they— the ladies—were too expensive; they demanded too much for entertainment. As in the articles about the old-fashioned parties, she contrasts the simple pleasures of her youth with the extravagant formal festivities of fashionable society in the 1860s. These articles are not simply a nostalgic look backward; they reflect the severe criticism of pretentiousness and pomp that characterized Fern's perspective throughout her career:

My dears, *I* never lacked beaux at your age. But a walk in the woods, or in the city either, involved no expense to *my* beaux. I could climb a fence, where there was no gate, or where there *was* either; I was not afraid of dew, or rain, because my dress was simple. My gifts were not diamonds, but flowers, or books. *My* mother would not have allowed me to ride with gentlemen, had they asked me. When they came to spend an evening, our tray of refreshments did not involve a "French cook." So you see, my dears, though I had no silk dresses, I had plenty of beaux, and a gay heart; and I enjoyed a sail with an old sun-bonnet over my curls, or a moon-light ramble, with a merry party, much better than you do "the German" [a dance]; and half an hour was sufficient warning for me "to dress" for any kind of a party—indoors or out—because, unlike *you*, I was not bothered to choose from twenty dresses which to wear. (NYL, August 8, 1868)

A favorite winter activity was the old-fashioned sleigh ride. On January 5, 1861, Fern provided a good description of this pleasurable activity from her New England youth. I quote the article at length because it so clearly expresses the relationships of the young New England couples of the period. It is interesting to note that this daughter of a strict Calvinist home enjoyed outings that included "mulled wine" and even an "unceremonious dance," not to mention some variety of "petting" on the way home:

A sleigh-ride! . . . Six steaming, spanking horses and a driver furry as a polar bear, his nose just visible above the dasher. Two or three dozen merry girls and boys, muffled to their eyes, stowed away with hot bricks under the buffalos. The amicable fight of pairs of lovers for the coveted "back-seat," where are no curious eyes to overlook the young man who, tying his lady-love's tippet under her chin, ties his heart in with it; or tucking the buffalo-robe closer about her shoulders, forgets to remove his arm after the operation. What pleasure, with the warm blood tingling in cheeks beneath eyes that flash like diamonds; what pleasure, when snow-powdered trees, fences and houses, fly past like magic to the merry sound of musical bells,—spelt with and without an -e; what pleasure when the country inn is reached, where your supper was bespoken the day before, and rolling out of your manifold wrappers, you lift to your lips the foaming glasses of hot "mulled wine," of which benighted New York knows not the recipe, and which I too having forgotten, wish somebody would tell me; what pleasure, when we gather round the table, laughing at each other's rosy faces, and discuss the oysters and fowl, and more "mulled wine," till bones and empty glasses alone remain; and the waiter having cleared away the table, we have a good old-fashioned "blind man's buff," or an unceremonious dance in our comfortable winter dresses. What pleasure, when after being deliciously warmed and fed, we pile into the sleigh again, nestling close to the one we like best, and telling the driver to go the longest way home, look up at the stars that never gleamed so brightly, and defy fate ever to make us shed a tear at anything. What pleasure, indeed! Humph—Ask some steady, well-to-do fathers-of-families I *could* name, but *won't*, and see if their eyes don't twinkle, spite of their "responsibilities" and "the panic"! (NYL, January 5, 1861)

In her youth, Sara Willis enjoyed a full social life. She also apparently possessed a healthy libido. Although the mores of the time and of her social class tabooed premarital sexual activity, she clearly was not squeamish about physical contact. The sleigh-ride article suggests that part of the fun of the sleigh ride was the close physical contact between the lovers as the driver took the "longest way home." In 1859 in answer to a correspondent who had asked her what she regarded as permissible behavior among young people, Fanny Fern wrote that although she did not think that young people should be "too exclusively in each other's company," she "would hope that a good night kiss was appetizingly given and taken" (NYL, January 1, 1859).

According to Fern's granddaughter, Deacon Willis was "usually at his genial best" with the young men who called to visit his daughters. Although he yawned and ostentatiously wound the clock when the hour began to get late and the visitor did not leave, he always welcomed the young man heartily. He was greatly amused when he heard that a visiting clergyman had commented that he "would not have believed that any house could be as full of beaux and clergymen as Deacon Willis's" (EP, 82).

Deacon Willis did not always like the young men who called, however. One beau of Mary's he particularly disliked, Ethel Parton tells us, although she does not tell us why. He was "grimly polite and discouraging," but the man persisted. Mary would not end his suit; her father's disapproval made the young man seem all the more romantic. Julia decided to help the matter come to a speedy conclusion. One night as the young man approached the house, Julia went to her room above the front door and dumped a jug of ice cold water on his head. Mary "had hysterics from wrath" and Sara and her mother were nearly hysterical from laughter. But the young man did not call again (EP, 82). Mary was not long without a beau. In August 1831 she married Joseph Jenkins, Jr., who was a friend of her brother Nat's at Andover and Yale. She was not quite eighteen, two years younger than Sara.

Also in the summer of 1831, Fern's brother Nathaniel left Boston to go to New York, where he joined General George P. Morris on the New York Mirror. That fall he embarked for Europe, and for the next five years he lived abroad as correspondent for that paper. Although Willis was more cosmopolitan than the other family members, he joined his father and Sara's teachers in urging her to be more subdued, more retiring, less imaginative. When she was still in her teens, he wrote a poem for her that clearly expressed the concern that she was too "wild," not passive enough to be truly "feminine." The poem, entitled "To My Wild Sis," contains the lines:

> Be thou in thy budding years
> As purely taintless as thy tears—
> Let hallowed thought & simple truth
> Be but the deepen'd hues of youth
> And thou shalt have in future hour,
> A perfect woman's hallowed power—. . .
> But be thou still, thou wayward girl
> A treasure like the ocean pearl
> Whose worth tho' much & pure it be
> Keeps holy shrine beneath the sea.[3]

Sara Willis would not be "still"; not her father nor her teacher nor her brother could make her into the "plain matter-of-fact damsel" who hid her

best self under an ocean of false manners. Willis's poem is significant for
another reason: when read beside the facts of Willis's own life, it points up
the contrasting standards of deportment and sexual behavior for men and
women that Sara Willis's society subscribed to—a double standard that
Fanny Fern was highly critical of in her writings.

Although N. P. Willis urged his sister to be modest and retiring, he himself was criticized by other Bostonians for his social activities and for his
flamboyant dress and manners. While Willis was a bachelor living in Boston, from 1827 to 1831, he led a very active social life that did not conform
to the Calvinist principles of his family. In a series of letters written during
this period to his college friend John B. Van Schaick in Albany, he described
Boston as being "as lively as Christmas," with many parties. In another
letter he wrote, "We are partying it here every night & dissipating all day."
His table was covered with invitations, he said; he had been deprived of
sleep for a week.[4] In February 1829 he founded the *American Monthly,* and
his father, whom Willis described in letters as a "slate and pencil" man,
agreed to attend to the "mechanical" or business side of it if he, N. P. Willis,
signed a contract to abstain from "extravagant living and dissipation" for a
year.[5] Although he signed the contract, Willis apparently continued his life
as before, though not as openly. He attended the theater in secret, and,
although he said that his "bottle green coat" was put away in "lavender,"
he does not seem to have missed out on many parties.[6] On April 29, 1829,
he was excommunicated from the Park Street Church because of his behavior, specifically for "absence from the communion of this church and attendance at the theatre as a spectator."[7]

Willis was not only criticized by church members. He wore conspicuously
expensive clothes and was fond of fast horses. He was also socially ambi-
tious, and his fopperies and affectations brought criticism upon him from all
quarters. He received anonymous letters calling him a "rake" or a "puppy,"
and he was attacked in the newspapers for his "frivolity, his dandyism, and
his conceit."[8] One such attack appeared in a satirical poem by William Joseph Snelling in 1831:

> Muse, shall we not a few brief lines afford
> To give poor Natty P. his meet reward?
> What has he done to be despised by all
> Within whose hands his harmless scribblings fall?
> Why, as in band-box trim he walks the streets,
> Turns up the nose of every man he meets,
> As if it scented carrion? Why of late
> Do all the critics claw his shallow pate?
> True he's a fool. . . .[9]

A social climber, Willis enjoyed the attentions of aristocratic older women; he also lived beyond his means, running up large bills at livery stables and at inns. The most damaging criticism, however, derived from his relationships with women. Although he urged his sister to be "pure" and "taintless," with "hallowed thoughts," he himself was involved in flirtations with numerous respectable young women, and at the same time he was involved in sexual liaisons with other less respectable young women. He wrote to his friend that he could never be satisfied with only one woman, that the thought filled him with "repugnance":

Constancy, like many other virtues, is for the dulls. Who is there that can fill up the broad field of a rioting and indulged imagination? Who can be the "soul of whim & the spirit of variety" always? Can Anna? Can Helen? No!—By the Gods, I do think I should tire of one woman's changes in a month—tire of them as a very boy of his hoop & whistle. I have brought before me, one by one, all the fair women I know, & with the strange power that is given us, imagined them in every degree of possession, from the first kiss to the turn'd back of a morning—and I cannot believe—nay—I cannot *fancy* even, that I should not weary of the brightest.[10]

That Fern was aware of his sentiments is apparent from the similar speech that she puts into the mouth of Hyacinth Ellet, the character who was based on her brother in *Ruth Hall*: "Lord bless me! how immensely tiresome it must be to sit opposite the same face three times a day, three hundred and sixty-five days in a year! I should weary of Venus herself" (RH, 17).

In intimate letters to his friend John B. Van Schaick, Willis revealed the details of his sexual exploits and flirtations. In one letter he tells of his love for Mary Silsbee of Salem, whom he later sought unsuccessfully to marry, while at the same time he brags, "my amour with the sempstress flourishes."[11] In other letters he speaks of his love for Anna Kane, Caroline and Harriet White, Alida Deniston, Miss Bray, Miss Duer, Cleopatra, Anna Bloodgood, and various other society ladies, while at the same time describing sordid back-street affairs such as the one with the unhappy mistress of a general, a young woman whom he "comforted" and who visited him in his rooms dressed in his clothing.[12]

In 1831 Willis became engaged to Mary Benjamin, the sister of Park Benjamin, but the engagement was broken by her family, apparently because they learned of Willis's dissipations. Willis wrote to a friend, "my side scene amours were the cause—though *she* refuses to believe them."[13] Horace Mann was a member of a club that Willis belonged to during these Boston years, and the scandal that surrounded Willis is evident in Mann's reply to

Mary Peabody's letter several years later expressing the hope that Mann would not renew his acquaintance with Willis, whom she regarded as a bad influence. Mann wrote to Peabody in 1836 that Willis's "wickedness must, perforce, remain unpublished, because common depravity has neither organ nor emblem to communicate it." Mann was particularly disgusted because Willis had just written a "diabolitical satire" on Park Benjamin, which, Mann said, would have been bad enough if it had only attacked Benjamin, but it also "stretched" Benjamin's "innocent sister" upon the rack. Mann concluded by saying that he was saved from associating with Willis because Willis had gone back to England, but, he told his fiancée, "your warning is no less friendly, because danger has become impossible."[14]

When Willis left Boston for New York late in the summer of 1831, Boston was glad to see him go, and he felt such hostility toward his critics that he vowed he would never live there again.[15] The *American Monthly* had failed, and when Willis left Boston, he not only left behind the criticism and ridicule of his compatriots, he also left behind three thousand dollars of debts due to the failure of his magazine.

While Sara Willis was criticized for her "imagination" and her vivacity of mind and spirit, then, her brother was engaged in far wilder activities. Their father was angry and distressed at Willis, of course, particularly when Willis was excommunicated from the church. When excommunication was threatened in November of 1828, for example, Willis wrote to his friend that it had created a "bloody bad business here at home."[16] Yet N. P. Willis pursued his course without regard to his father's opinion, and there was no break between the two. He was regarded as a "respectable" young man: he later married an innocent young woman, commenting that he liked the fact that she was so very religious.[17] It must have seemed to Fanny Fern, who later wrote scathingly of the sexual double standard, that her brother wrought with impunity where she was disproportionately censored.

Although Deacon Willis had given up dancing and pretty girls for himself, and although he disapproved of his son's extravagance in his pursuit of women, the deacon liked girls to be pretty, and he was pleased that he had good-looking daughters—except for Julia. Her plainness, in contrast to her sisters, irritated him. She did not have the clear complexion or curly hair of her sisters: she was pale, "her mouth more resolute than smiling, her eyelids often pink from too much reading, her smooth, straight brown hair resistant to all attempts to soften its severity." Deacon Willis was apparently not very subtle in his exhortations to her to improve her appearance, and although she acceded with dutiful filial compliance to all of his attempts to make her more attractive, his attitude must have been hurtful to her. For some time the deacon was determined to make Julia into a harpist; he felt that if she would learn to play the harp she would look feminine and graceful at the instrument. Julia was not at all musical, but it was a long time before Deacon Willis would give up on his idea. His favorite theme was that Julia must do something about her hair; he liked girls with curly hair. "'Look at Lucy's hair—look at Louisa's—look at Sarah's'—he would insist testily. 'If your sisters can fix their hair the way a girl's hair ought to be fixed, so can you.'" Julia did her best, Ethel Parton says: "She gave herself many miserable moments, but to no avail. She remained neither musical nor curly." Although not beautiful, Julia had a good mind and was an "eager and retentive scholar." As an adult she was to write for her father's papers and for her brother's *Home Journal* for forty years; her anonymous book reviews in the latter paper were of particularly high literary quality. However, this talent did not count in Deacon Willis's mind; it would not attract a lover. Julia was never to marry, despite the deacon's attempt to marry her to an elderly widower, a clergyman with three orphaned children who received no encouragement from Julia but pursued his suit because he knew that he had the deacon's approval (EP, 51–53).

Nathaniel Willis's treatment of Julia provides an indication of his character. The deacon was not tolerant of anything in his children that did not coincide with his own definition of them—particularly his daughters. Just as he was insensitive to Julia's feelings in his attempt to make her over, he was insensitive to the feelings of his fourth daughter when as a young girl she did not fit the mold of a passive, obediently religious "sober, matter-of-fact damsel," and later when she defied him and left the abusive husband the deacon had coerced her into marrying. In both instances he was intolerant of her feelings, assuming that he was right and that her opinions did not count. Not as pliant as Julia, Fern refused to change herself to meet his demands, even when he, underestimating her strength of will and perseverance, attempted to starve her into submission by refusing to support her or her children so that she would return to her husband. An understanding of this aspect of his character helps to explain why she was so angry at him that she could satirize him so mercilessly in *Ruth Hall.*

Although Julia had difficulty curling her hair, the other Willis girls did not. All but Julia had natural curls, but the fashion of the day demanded that the curls be specifically defined. All of the girls put their hair in curl papers at night in order to create the sausagelike curls or tendrils that were in fashion. Ethel Parton tells of an incident that reveals Sara's ability to deal with unexpected difficulties at a young age. One morning the Willis family was at prayer. The deacon was in the middle of a long, meandering prayer with the family on their knees before him when a young man unexpectedly came to call. The son of one of the deacon's friends, he had been to sea and, his ship having just docked that morning, he had gone straight to the house on Atkinson Street. When he arrived and found the family in prayer, he dropped to his knees to await the end of the prayer before greeting them. The Willis girls had noted his arrival in consternation: all of their heads were knobby with curl-papers not yet removed from the night before. The papers were not noticeable as long as their heads were bowed in prayer, but

they knew he would see the bristly knobs as soon as the prayer ended. Un-
daunted by the distress this eventuality caused her sisters, Sara quietly and
with unperceived skill removed all of the curl papers from her hair as she
knelt with bowed head. "When at last her sisters were obliged to lift flushed
cheeks and knobbly foreheads from their shielding hands, Sarah raised a
face of seraphic innocence, aureoled in yellow curls" (EP, 53).

Except for Julia, who did not marry, Fanny Fern's sisters all married at a
younger age than she did. Lucy was nineteen, Louisa and Mary seventeen,
and Ellen twenty-one. Sara did not marry until she was almost twenty-six. If
this, too, was a source of irritation to the deacon, his attitude did not hurry
Sara into a marriage she did not want. That some of her admirers were not
to her taste is suggested by the formality of this note, preserved over the
years by an apparently amused Fanny Fern:

My dear Miss Willis:

If nothing transpires to contravene my compliance with your polite request, and it will be my earnest endeavor to prevent such a misfortune, I
shall take great pleasure in presenting myself on Friday evening next,
bringing the volumes with me, and prepared to explain and expatiate
upon their contents to the utmost of my poor ability. With ardent but
respectful admiration, my dear Miss Willis—my dear Miss Sarah—my
dear Sarah (*may* I venture so far?)

I remain ever
Your obedient humble servant,
J. C. A.[18]

That Sara Willis did not marry sooner was not for lack of admirers, her
granddaughter says, but because she did not fall in love. It was not until
May 4, 1837, after living at home for six years, that she married Charles
Harrington Eldredge, a cashier in the Merchants' Bank of Boston and the
son of Dr. Hezekiah and Mary Eldredge of Boston. His family was rigidly
religious, which pleased the deacon, but Charles himself was "of a happy
and buoyant nature," which pleased Sara. Called "Handsome Charlie" by
his friends, Charles, who was one year older than Sara, was particularly
good-looking: "He had a superb athletic figure, over six feet in height, a
fresh, bright complexion, fine clear-cut cameo-like features, large gray eyes,
and abundant dark hair curling at the tips" (EP, 87–88).

The letters that they wrote to each other before their marriage tell us
something of their courtship. They apparently saw each other frequently,
Charles usually stopping at the Atkinson Street house after leaving the bank
in the evening. Of Sara's letters, only one and a fragment of another one
survive. Short, breezy, and humorous, they suggest the style that she was to
develop as Fanny Fern. Charles's letters, of which there are five extant, are
longer. Where her tone is playful, though sincere, his is earnest and labored.

Although most of the letters are not dated, one of the earliest is dated January 23, and was apparently written four months before their wedding. Charles writes modestly and passionately, revealing a respect for Sara's superior writing skills and wit along with a longing for the full physical consumation of their love:

This ominous storm will mar our plans for this evening and therefore as you will be thus rid of one bore I will e'en inflict another upon you in the shape of a note—Oh, that I had your rich and racy wit, your nice perception of the humorous and happy power of delineation. . . . But not having the Promethean fire of genius I must e'en contrive some other way wherewithal to season my dullnes[s] . . . . Therefore in order to interest thee I will deal in affection, but I beg of you do not imagine me comparing you to the weak[;] per contra it is I that lack strength and not thou—strength of intellect I mean[.] [I]n strength of affection I will not yield even to your loving kindness but will hold up mine head and boast me, that I love thee with a passionate earnestness, a depth and strength of affection that language may not paint and thought scarce imagine—if you believe me not take my numberless kisses as an evidence and imagine that if I would thus caress thee when restrained, what rapture would possess me when we are once fairly embarked on the boundless ocean of love with no limit to enjoyment and no restraint but the will—imagine me thine, fully thine by bridal as well as troth, and then paint if thou canst the raptures that follow.[19]

In another letter he continues in the same vein, anticipating eagerly the day when their marriage will release them from the restraints that society had placed on their lovemaking: "Consider yourself kissed a thousand times and loved a thousand times better than kisses or words could express and then you will get some faint inkling of how well I love you and will be able to give a shrewd guess at the number of times I shall kiss you when love has its free course."

On a Saturday morning in April, one month before their wedding, Sara wrote to Charles, whom she calls "Curly Pate." The first part of the letter gives an indication of her jocular manner:

Dear Curly Pate

As you haven't the corners of my mouth to look at just now I suppose you'll be suspicious that I am about to make an "April fool" of you but if you'll excuse an Irish-ism I think I shall wait till *May* before I do that. But to proceed to business—The accompanying note to you from Mrs. Sam Hubbard was sent with *our* notes of invitation. How can you refuse a request penned by the fair hand of one of those young damsels?—Perhaps your sky blue coat and *yaller* pants will be finished[.] Time enough for

you to finish one of them. Give my love to Ichabod and desire him to
hurry.

The second half of this letter suggests that Sara was as interested in the
physical part of their relationship as Charles was. She feels a "stupor" coming over her, she says, in anticipation of his kisses:

How do you do today? *I* feel very nice and bright. I suppose it is because
you are not within kissing distance. I always know when you are coming
for a kind of stupor creeps over me as soon as you turn the corner of this
street. And speaking of that I expect that same stupor to come on about 7
o'clock this evening! (Seriously do you trot round here when you come
from the bank or else I'll put off our wedding another week.) I
believe that's all I have to say except that I think your nose is a nice
straight one & that Mr. Ketchen's[?] ought to be pulled for cutting your
hair so short. Love to your father & mother and a kiss for yourself (if
you'll call & get it to night).

Yours a heap—
Sarah

   Charles, whose position at the bank required him to write most of the
day, said that it was difficult for him to write letters, but Sara refused to
write to him if he did not write to her, and he valued her notes so much that
he wrote as well, often begging her to write to him. He also recognized what
the world was to discover many years later about Fanny Fern: "I pray you
again resume your pen (which next to your tongue is your most effective
weapon)."
   In another letter Charles apologizes that he did not have time to "select an
ornament" for her that morning but says that he is sending up several that
he found at other stores: if she does not like any of them, he says, he will
send her some more in the afternoon and she can select one from among
them. At one point, Charles reveals his ideas on child rearing. In a reference
to Sara's sister Lucy Bumstead, he commented that her child Willis was a
nuisance in church and noted that he did not approve of bringing children to
church so young. His and Sara's children, he says, will not go to church
"until they are old enough to understand the minister and be still and listen."
   The only other surviving letter by Sara is a fragment that gives an indication of her love of freedom and suggests another reason why she delayed
marriage: it was not simply that she did not fall in love, but that she did not
love sufficiently to give up her freedom. Although living at home with Deacon Willis was hardly freedom, she must have seen enough of the lives of
married women, particularly her mother, to see that even the small free-

doms she had as the "deacon's daughter" could be curtailed after marriage, particularly if her husband became less fond and more tyrannical after marriage. In *Ruth Hall,* Ruth thinks on the eve of her wedding: "Would a harsh word ever fall from lips which now breathed only love? Would the step whose lightest footfall now made her heart leap, ever sound in her ear like a death-knell?" (RH, 13). In the following fragment written just before her marriage, Sara describes herself as "chained" and portrays herself as soon to be crouching before her lord like a whipped spaniel—a sad picture indeed for the spirited Sara Willis. Although the fragment is humorously written, it clearly reflects Sara's associations at the time with the concept of marriage, or, as Fanny Fern later said, "what life meant for a woman" (NYL, June 23, 1866). It is interesting that none of Charles's letters project such an image of lost freedom. Sara writes that someone:

tells me that a laughing fashion is much more becoming to me than a melancholy one—Think then what a sacrifice you compel me to make! Well-a-day—I see that my liberty is well nigh gone. Some day before *May* I'll give a spring and run the whole length of my chain for "auld lang syne my dear"—and then I'll crouch down at the feet of my lord & master and be as tame as a whipt spaniel all the rest of the days of the years of my pilgrimage so if you hear a terrible rattling down at the Bank some day you may know that I'm let loose for the last time and am making the best of it—!

When Sara Willis and Charles Eldredge were married in May of 1837, they were a handsome couple. Sara's wedding dress, a piece of which is preserved among her papers in the Sophia Smith Collection at Smith College, was made from fabric purchased in Lyons, France, said to be a reproduction of one of the silks given to Marie Antoinette when she came as a bride to France. It is a pale lavender sheer fabric over white silk, the outer fabric decorated with a delicate lace petal pattern. Many years afterward, Fanny Fern's daughter Ellen met a Mrs. Donnell in Newburyport, who said that she had been with her husband when he purchased the fabric in Lyons. The dress, according to Fern's granddaughter, was a gift of A. T. Stewart, the department store entrepreneur (EP, 90). Also preserved among Fern's papers at Smith are a sample of her wedding lace and her elbow-length white kid wedding gloves, trimmed with lace. The groom's wedding waistcoat was an elegant white satin, brocaded in a thistle-rose-shamrock pattern (EP, 91). This vest is not among Fern's papers at Smith, but her granddaughter reported that it was still in perfect condition in 1939, which indicates that Fanny Fern had preserved it through all of her hardships. How she was able to preserve it is suggested by the incident in *Ruth Hall* when, after the death of Ruth's husband, Mr. Hall demands his son's clothing, and the executor of the estate, cheating Ruth of her legal rights, consents to leave the tearful widow her husband's white satin wedding vest (RH, 78–79).

After the marriage, Sara and Charles moved in with the Eldredges at 18 West Cedar Street in Boston.[20] Apparently this was a serious mistake. In *Ruth Hall,* the young couple also goes to live with his parents at first. Mrs. Hall snoops around her son and new daughter-in-law's room before the bridal couple arrives. "I can't say, though, that I see the need of his being married," she grumbles. "I always mended his socks." And she indicates her jealousy of his new wife: "As to Ruth, I don't know anything about her. Of course she is perfect in *his* eyes. I remember the time when he used to think *me* perfect. I suppose I shall be laid on the shelf now" (RH, 18).

The evidence suggests that this portrait of Mrs. Hall as a possessive mother and jealous mother-in-law is based on the character of Mary Eldredge. Mrs. Eldredge apparently was very possessive of her son, who was the only surviving child of her four children. During their courtship, Charles sometimes was unable to see Sara because he had promised Mary (as he called his mother) to spend the evening with her.[21] One wonders if Charles's father was at home on these evenings (he was still living and well), and if so why he is not mentioned in the letters and why Charles's mother, who was not ill or disabled, required her son's presence.[22]

In an 1852 article by Fern entitled "Self-Conquest," which provides the germ of the situation portrayed in *Ruth Hall,* the servants in the home of a young woman's in-laws comment regarding the new bride: "If she had known as much as you and I do of her husband's mother, she never would have come to live with her. She's a regular old hyena, and if she don't bring the tears into those blue eyes before the honey-moon is over, my name isn't Bridget" (OB, February 28, 1852).

Sara Eldredge's feelings after marriage are suggested by an article she wrote in 1858 for the *New York Ledger.* Entitled "A Few Bridal Thoughts," the article gives us an idea of the sadness she must have felt as a new bride in an alien home. It is also a valuable description of the let-down feeling of a new bride of the 1830s, whose marriage took her away from the full family life and social contacts which had filled her life before marriage and placed her in a new and sometimes inhospitable environment where her life had no occupation but pleasing her husband, and her only meaningful social contact was with her husband—when he was not occupied with business. Fern's "Bridal Thoughts" was particularly significant in a society that geared a woman for no other "career" but marriage and portrayed the single woman as a pitiable figure; she captures the sense of isolation and emptiness that many brides must have felt after marriage in contrast to the euphoria that convention had led them to expect: "When [your husband] is gone off to his business, . . . you sit there in your new dress—how I hate a new dress—looking round on every spick-and-span article about you—missing your brother Tom, who *did* steal your cologne, and whose foot was always in your lap for a missing gaiter button." She goes on to say that she also misses her dimpled baby sister [Ellen], her sister who always borrowed her clothes [Mary], and most of all her mother, whom she wants to run and see. Your mother knows your heart, Fern tells herself; you feel "a choking in your throat" when you see her (NYL, March 13, 1858).

Despite these feelings of sadness, there was also a sense of freedom and independence that came with marriage. In nineteenth-century America a married woman enjoyed certain privileges that a young girl did not. For a young woman from a Calvinist home, one of those privileges was the ability to attend the theater. In an 1871 article in the *New York Ledger* Fern told of how one of the first things she did as a married woman was to attend the theatre, which had been forbidden to her as a sheltered unmarried young woman. "Did I even so much as peep into a theatre till I was a married, independent woman? when the first favor I asked in my new position, was to be taken straight there!" (NYL, January 7, 1871).

As Fern indicates in *Ruth Hall*, however, the freedom and independence that the new wife thinks she has found soon prove to be illusory. When Ruth first enters her in-laws' home as a bride, she rejoices: "How odd it seemed, this new freedom, this being one's own mistress" (RH, 18). The irony of Ruth's comment is apparent to the reader, who has just seen her mother-in-law snooping around Ruth's room and commenting spitefully on the new bride. It is clear that marriage has not brought freedom and independence. Later, when Ruth moves into her own home in the country, she rejoices again in her "new-found freedom" (RH, 28). This time it seems as if she has found it; once again, however, her freedom and independence prove to be an illusion when her husband dies, leaving her in debt, and she realizes that, despite her feeling of independence, she has been dependent on her husband and is now dependent upon her father and father-in-law. In the novel, as in the life of Fanny Fern (and as Fern said many times in her newspaper articles), true independence for a woman only comes with economic independence.

In 1870, after the experience of three marriages and the added experience of earning her own living for almost twenty years, Fern responded to a newspaper writer (whom she sarcastically calls a "modern Solomon") who had urged women to marry if they had the chance; "in so doing," the writer had said, "you will exchange many masters for one." Fern wrote:

"*One* master" is it! What of husband's relatives, who, from the time of the marriage ceremony, set themselves to be "masters?" If not openly, as do many, yet covertly, by insinuations and deplorings, and suggestive head-shakings and eye-rollings, whenever the wife is mentioned. Who but these self-appointed "masters" try to determine in what direction, and for what length of time, the summer jaunt shall be, and advise him, when sick, "to send for one of his own family to nurse him?" Who but they sit in judgment on larder and pocket? . . . Taking it "by and large," my dears, don't flee to matrimony to escape "masters." In other employments you have two advantages: First, wages, second, a change of "masters." (NYL, September 3, 1870)

4

Marriage, Motherhood, and Money

To all these sweet womanly traits in my mother, was added a sound, practical judgment. On one occasion, while visiting me, a law paper was sent for my wifely signature. . . . "Stay! child," said my mother, arresting my hand, "do you know what that paper is about?" "Not I!" was my laughing reply; "but my husband sent it, and on his broad shoulders be the responsibility!" "That is wrong," said she, gravely; "you should never sign any paper without a full understanding of its contents." It seemed to me then that she was over-scrupulous, particularly as I knew she had the same implicit confidence in my husband that I had. I had reason afterward to see the wisdom of her caution.

NSB, 17–18

SARA AND CHARLES'S FIRST CHILD, Mary Stace, was born in 1838, while they were still living with the Eldredges. She was named after Nathaniel Parker Willis's wife, Mary Leighton Stace, whom he had brought back from England in May of 1836. That Sara named her first child after her brother's new wife is a significant indication of her warm feelings toward him at the time. He had written home of his English bride and had expressed the hope that his family would welcome her and love her. Sara's response, naming her daughter after his wife, demonstrates that she was eager to show the welcome and love that he sought for his chosen wife, and it helps to explain why Sara felt so hurt and betrayed when this brother refused to help her in later years.[1]

Fern's 1852 article "The Invalid Wife" in the Boston *Olive Branch* provides a good description of a wife's feelings right after her baby is born when she, according to nineteenth-century upper- and middle-class custom, is confined to bed for several weeks. Although Fern loved children and felt motherhood was an honor and a grave responsibility, she reveals in this article the same undercutting of motherhood that her portrayal of the new bride revealed about marriage; motherhood may be fine, but there are many aspects of it that are not pleasant. Always a realist, Fern could not accept the sugarcoated vision of marriage and motherhood that convention dictated. She begins the article with a quotation: "Every wife needs a good stock of love to start with," and she asserts that one does indeed:

You are upon a sick bed; a little, feeble thing lies upon your arm, that you might crush with one hand. You take those little velvet fingers in yours, close your eyes, and turn your head languidly to the pillow. . . . You wonder if your husband's pudding will be made right, and if Betty will remember to put wine in the sauce, as he likes it. . . . By and by [nurse] comes in,—after staying down long enough to get a refreshing cup of coffee,—and walks up to the bed with a bowl of gruel, tasting it, and then putting the spoon back into the bowl. In the first place, you hate gruel; in the next, you couldn't eat it, if she held a pistol to your head, after that spoon has been in her mouth. . . . Now you hear a dear step on the stairs. It's your Charley! How bright he looks! and what nice fresh air he brings with him from out doors! He parts the bed-curtains, looks in, and pats you on the cheek. You just want to lay your head on his shoulder, and have such a splendid cry! but there sits that old Gorgon of a nurse,—she don't believe in husbands, she don't! You make Charley a free-mason sign to send her down stairs for something. He says,—right out loud,—men are so stupid!—"What did you say, dear?" Of course, you protest you didn't say a word,—never thought of such a thing!—and cuddle your head down to your ruffled pillows, and cry because you don't know what else to do, and because you are weak and weary, and full of care for your family, and don't want to see anybody but "Charley." Nurse says "she shall have you sick," and tells your husband "he'd better go down, and let you go to sleep." Off he goes, wondering what on earth ails you, to cry!— wishes he had nothing to do but lie still, and be waited upon! After dinner he comes in to bid you good-by before he goes to his office,—whistles "Nelly Bly" loud enough to wake up the baby, whom he calls "a comical little concern,"—and puts his dear thoughtless head down to your pillow, at a signal from you, to hear what you have to say. Well, there's no help for it, you cry again, and only say "Dear Charley"; and he laughs, and settles his dickey, and says you are "a nervous little puss," gives you a kiss, lights his cigar at the fire, half strangles the new baby with the first whiff, and takes your heart off with him down street!

And you lie there and eat that gruel! and pick the fuzz all off the blanket, and make faces at the nurse under the sheet, and wish Eve had never ate that apple. (OB, October 2, 1852)

The image that Fern portrays here of the wife confined to her home and helpless before the machinations of others, reduced to picking the fuzz off the blanket, provides a good illustration of the nineteenth-century infantilization of married women, and particularly of new mothers. One thinks of the young mother in Charlotte Perkins Gilman's "The Yellow Wallpaper," whose husband and brother, following the accepted medical practice of the time, prevent her from engaging in any physical or mental activity whatsoever and keep her confined to quarters until she goes mad. Sara Eldredge, however, enlisted her husband's aid; he discharged the nurse, and they faltered through the early weeks together. Fern described the scene in the conclusion to "Our First Nurse," the first article she wrote as an exclusive columnist for the *New York Ledger* in 1856:

Charley paid her, and I was so glad when she went, that I laughed till I cried.

Then we both drew a long breath and sat down and looked at the new baby—*our* baby; and Charley asked me about its little sleeping habits, and I told him, with a shake of the head, that I could not speak definitely on that point; and then we discussed, in a whisper, the respective merits of cribs and cradles . . . and then he drew off his vest and hung it over a chair, and then—out rattled a perfect tempest of half dollars, quarters, shillings, and sixpences, on the hearth! Of course, the baby woke (frightened out of a year's growth) and screamed until it was black in the face. In vain its poor, inexperienced papa kissed it, scratching its little velvet face with his rough whiskers the while! In vain we both walked the floor with it. The fire went out, the lamp went; and just at daybreak it came to us like a revelation, the sarcastic tone of that hateful old nurse, as she said, "Good-bye; I hope you'll get along *comfortably* with the dear baby!"

And so we did. Do you suppose one night's watching was going to quench our love, either for the baby, or for each other? (NYL, January 5, 1856)

Sara and Charles Eldredge did not remain long with the elder Eldredges after their first child was born. On October 30, 1838, Charles Eldredge bought a house in Brighton: "a certain tract of land with the Dwelling House and Barn and all other buildings thereon standing, containing by estimation 15 acres." He paid $5,000 for the property.[2] In 1837 and 1838 Charles Eldredge was listed in the Boston City Directory at the same address as his parents, 18 West Cedar Street in Boston. Since his residence was no longer listed in the Boston City Directory in 1839, we can assume that he and Sara moved to Brighton soon after purchasing the house. The house in Brighton, called Swissdale, provided the basis for the house that Ruth and Harry Hall move into in *Ruth Hall*. Fern described the property thus in an 1856 article in the *New York Ledger*:

Yes, Swissdale was ours! The title deeds were "without a flaw," so lawyer Nix informed us. Ours—the money was paid down that very day. Those glorious old trees were ours; tossing their branches hither and thither, as if oppressed with exuberant animal life. . . . Ours were the broad sloping meadows, dotted with daisies and clover; . . . ours were the dense woods, which skirted it . . . ; ours the rose-tinted and purple anemones; . . . ours the wild rose, fair as fleeting. . . . Ours the hill-side; where creeping myrtle charily hid under the tall grass its cherished blue-eyed blossoms. . . . Ours the bower-crowned, vine-wreathed, hill-summit, whence with rapt vision we drank in that broad expanse of earth, and sea, and sky. (NYL, June 21, 1856)

This article, which begins with such exuberance, is, like *Ruth Hall*, written from the double perspective of the naive and the experienced narrator. Yet, although the article concludes with an awareness of tragedy which, Fern says, underlies our happiest moments (and which makes it impossible so positively to regard anything as "ours"), this section of the article conveys the delight that Sara and Charles Eldredge must have felt when they first moved into their house in the country.

We can get an idea of the inside of the house from *Ruth Hall*. Ruth's mother-in-law comes to inspect the premises, hoping to find fault with Ruth's housekeeping, but she can find no fault with the parlor:

Those long white curtains, looped up so prettily from the open windows, are plain, cheap muslin; but no artist could have disposed their folds more gracefully. The chairs and sofas, also, Ruth covered with her own nimble fingers; the room has the fragrance of a green-house, to be sure; but if you examine the flowers, which are scattered so profusely round, you will find they are *wild* flowers, which Ruth, basket in hand, climbs many a stone fence every morning to gather. (RH, 33–34)

In her newspaper articles, also, Fanny Fern described the kind of interior she liked in a house. She loved beauty, she said, and thought that a house should be bright and cheerful; she did not like houses where the draperies were kept closed in the daytime to protect the furnishings from the sun—making the rooms dark and stuffy. It was good for children, Fern said, to grow up in bright surroundings amid pretty things: a graceful pitcher, a nice vase, a favorite etching, plants in the windows. Such things need not be expensive, she said; in fact, nothing should be so expensive that the sun could not shine upon it or it could not be seen and used every day (NYL, September 3, 1864, June 4, 1859, October 15, 1859). But the house should reflect the taste and individuality of the people who live there. Fern frowned on "house furnishing by proxy," that is, hiring a "professional" to decorate one's house: "The idea of giving an upholsterer an unlimited order to furnish a house for you a-la-mode, and then coolly walking into it, as you would into a great, glaring hotel!" Everything in my house, she said, would be "selected by myself, or—somebody I loved," until "the house was full of things, every one of which had its own little, pleasant home-story" (NYL, December 10, 1859). Fern also felt that rooms should have a lived-in feeling, not the "unsociable" appearance of rooms which were kept only for company: "I confess to liking a home-y parlor—one that looks as if it were used; with a work-basket here, and a book with a folder between the leaves there. . . . a thumb-mark on the door, a few gingerbread crumbs, little worn out shoes" (NYL, December 10, 1870). In 1853 she described her ideal home thus:

Had I a house, there should be no "best room" in it. No upholsterer should exorcise comfort or children, from my door-sill. The free fresh air should be welcome to play through it; the bright glad sunshine to lighten and warm it while fresh mantel flowers should woo us visits from humming-bird and drowsy bee. (MWT, August 27, 1853)

On February 24, 1841, a second daughter was born to Sara and Charles Eldredge. They named her Grace Harrington. Mary was almost three, a little girl with blonde curls and her mother's love of nature. Fern gives us a portrait of Mary in her articles and in the picture of Daisy in *Ruth Hall*. In one of the first articles she wrote, she describes "Little May," who gathers wildflowers with the "dear mother she loved so well." Like Daisy, May allows a yellow caterpillar to crawl on her arm because she loves all creatures:

Seated under the drooping branches of an elm, one bright summer day, sat a fairy child; her rose-tinted cheek resting in the palm of her hand, her deep blue eye fixed on the far-off sky, while her bright, golden hair, on which the sunbeams were playing through the leaves, shone like a glory round her head. (OB, August 30, 1851)

In an article published in 1853, Fern described a similar child, "little Nelly." This article, which corresponds to the picture of Daisy in *Ruth Hall*, suggests Mary's relationship to her father, who looked forward to seeing her "trip down the gravel path to meet him when business hours are over":

It was she who ran to warm his slippers when his horse's feet came prancing down the avenue. It was she who wheeled the armchair to its nice, snug corner; it was she who ran for the dressing-gown; it was she who tucked in the pockets a sly bit of candy, that she had hoarded all day for "poor, tired Papa." It was she who laid her soft hand upon his throbbing temples, when those long, ugly rows of figures at the counting-room, had given him such a cruel head-ache. (LF, 12–13)

Soon after Sara and Charles Eldredge moved to Brighton, Charles's parents moved there also. Hezekiah Eldredge had begun buying property in Brighton in 1833 and by 1838 had acquired a number of parcels of land. In 1839, he, like his son, was no longer listed in the Boston City Directory. As in *Ruth Hall*, the old couple moved to a house in the country to be near their son and his wife.[3]

In *Ruth Hall* the life of Ruth and Harry in their home in the country before the death of their daughter is idyllic except for only one factor: the interfering in-laws. In real life, however, there was another blight upon the young couple's happy existence: the unsuccessful financial dealings of Charles Eldredge. In the novel this is a subtext that does not surface until Harry's death, when Ruth finds herself penniless. And it seems that in real life, too, Sara Eldredge was not aware of the true state of her family's financial affairs until her husband's death. In her marriage, as was the accepted custom in her class and period, money was the man's business; women signed papers if necessary, but left decisions to their husbands and fathers. In fact, the handling of money was thought to be so abhorrent for women that professional women were often paid by checks made out to their husband or father rather than to themselves.[4] A consequence of this convention was that a man was often in a position to invest his own and his wife's money without the knowledge or consent of his wife, and in many cases, to invest it unwisely to the extent of losing it.[5]

Six months after Sara and Charles bought the house in Brighton, Charles obtained a mortgage from a Richard Fay for $4,000. Sarah P. Eldredge signed the agreement to repay the money in five years at six percent interest. Three months later Charles Eldredge obtained an additional mortgage of $3,000 from the Merchants' Bank to be repaid in one year. This agreement was also signed by Sarah P. Eldredge.[6] One wonders why Eldredge needed the money so soon after the purchase of the house. Had he borrowed the money privately to pay for the house, from his father perhaps? Or did he need the money for additional expenses? Another possibility is that he wanted the money to make other investments. His father was continuing to make real estate investments in Brighton, and Charles may have felt this was a good way to make money. On October 10, 1840, Charles purchased approximately twelve acres of land which adjoined his own land. He paid $750 initially, but over the period of the next year he paid an additional $1,000 to six other claimants—which suggests that Charles, who must not have had the title searched adequately to determine that it was clear before making the purchase, was not as careful or astute in his investments as he should have been. Within eight months of the initial purchase, he had sold this land to his father in two parcels for a total of $2,250. That this may have been a transaction necessitated by Charles's lack of funds is suggested by the fact that in August 1841 the Merchants' Bank assigned the $3,000 mortgage on his home (which was to have been paid by July 1840) to his father, Hezekiah Eldredge. The other mortgage, for $4,000, was still outstanding.[7]

At the same time that Sara and Charles were living their blissful—though financially shaky—existence at Swissdale, Charles became involved in another real estate transaction that intensified his financial need. In April 1839 Joseph Jenkins, the father of Sara's brother-in-law Joseph Jenkins, Jr., who was married to her sister Mary, had begun building a large brick structure on property on Tremont Street in Boston, which was to become the Boston Fine Arts Museum. Jenkins ran out of money and credit, and, unable to pay the owner of the land, Elizabeth Deblois, he was threatened with the loss of his investment. After Jenkins had made a number of unsuccessful attempts to obtain the money, he approached Charles Eldredge, who agreed that he would raise the money to purchase the property and complete the edifice.[8]

On August 25, 1840, Eldredge purchased the property from Elizabeth Deblois, paying her almost $6,000 and agreeing to pay her the balance of approximately $15,000 within a year. Sarah P. Eldredge signed her name to the documents. On February 12, 1841, Eldredge paid $1,000 for a triangular piece of property adjoining the larger property. The construction of the building continued, and in April 1841 he took out two $10,000 loans and over the period of the next few years borrowed money from various sources to pay for the property and the construction costs. In the spring of 1841, when the building was completed, Eldredge offered to sell the property to Joseph Jenkins for what it had cost him, retaining a small profit for himself: the agreed-upon profit was $3,500. When Jenkins was unable to raise the money by September 1, 1841, the date agreed upon, Eldredge, for whom the liability had become much greater than Jenkins had originally led him to believe it would, advertised the property for public sale. Jenkins took out an injunction to prevent the sale.

On March 1, 1842, Eldredge, pressed by his creditors and under pressure from the officials at the Merchants' Bank where his involvement with Jenkins's speculation was causing his business reputation to suffer, sold the now-completed museum and surrounding property to David Kimball, treasurer of the Corporation of the New England Museum and Gallery of Fine Arts, for $55,000. Of that sum over $40,000 were in outstanding mortgages in Eldredge's name; the purchaser signed an agreement that he would pay the mortgages and other debts and then pay Charles Eldredge $10,000. Jenkins, crying fraud, filed a bill preventing the sale of the property and brought Eldredge and Kimball to court, maintaining that Eldredge was only acting as his trustee and had no right to sell the property. Eldredge claimed that he was in fact the owner of the property and denied that he had ever been simply a trustee. He said that he originally took over the property with the hope that he could help Jenkins's family, particularly his wife's sister, Mary Jenkins, and that he also sought to make a small profit for himself. But he maintained that it had always been his intention to give any surplus money to Jenkins and his family, not because of any prior agreement but at his own discretion.[9]

The court case lasted from 1842 to 1846, and Justice Joseph Story found in favor of Jenkins and against the defendants, Eldredge and Kimball, concluding that it was not reasonable to suppose that Jenkins would ever have agreed to sign over the property to Eldredge unless it was clear that Eldredge was acting only as his trustee. Eldredge petitioned for a rehearing, maintaining that at the time of the agreement Jenkins's right of ownership had already expired. Eldredge cited contradictory evidence given by Jenkins's witnesses at the Master's hearing regarding the date at which the original agreement was reached, and pointed to evidence that proved that those witnesses, including his brother-in-law, Joseph Jenkins, Jr., who had died in November of 1843, had made false statements about the date. Eldredge's petition was denied. The judge ruled that since the testimony before the Master was without a special order of the court, it could not be admitted, and he also said that he did not wish to malign a dead man (Jenkins, Jr.).

In his petition Eldredge claimed that the decision was unfair and based on perjured evidence and that he would "suffer ruinous loss both of property and reputation." The decision was allowed to stand. Eldredge was ordered to pay court costs and to repay, with interest, all the money he had received from Kimball for rents in addition to the purchase money. In addition, he had contracted other debts and had maintained in his petition that he was in danger of bankruptcy and that the sum he had been awarded would not cover all of his debts and payments.[10] When he died four months later, he was insolvent, leaving Sara an impoverished widow with two children.

What must have been the effect of this long litigation and financial nightmare for Sara and Charles Eldredge? For one thing, family relationships must have been strained. Eldredge had entered into the business originally, he said, because he wanted to help Jenkins's family, particularly his wife's sister. He had come to the aid of Jenkins, Sr., when Jenkins was threatened with foreclosure, and he had assumed a debt of $2,000 that Jenkins, Jr., could not repay.[11] He had taken over the Fine Arts building to help Jenkins when no one else would do so, and he had ultimately gotten into a financial muddle because of it, assuming more than $50,000 dollars in debts and jeopardizing his financial reputation and his position at the Merchants' Bank. Yet Jenkins had done everything to force him to retain the building when he could not do so without declaring bankruptcy, and Jenkins, Jr., he believed, had lied about him in court in order to strengthen his father's claim to the property. Eldredge in his petition claimed that Jenkins was guilty of "unjust and ungrateful conduct."[12] What was the relationship between Sara and her sister Mary while their husbands were involved in this financial name-calling? In later years Sara and Mary and their children were on friendly terms, but for many years the relationship between the two families must have been uncomfortable at the very least.

What of the rest of the Willis family? Did they take sides? One wonders if the family's attitude toward Sara after her first husband died and then toward her when she left her second husband resulted in part from the strain caused by Charles Eldredge's feud with Jenkins. When Eldredge died and left his wife with debts, Nathaniel Willis blamed him, telling the young widow that she wouldn't be in such dire straits if her husband had been a better businessman.[13]

It was unkind and insensitive of her father to criticize Eldredge to his grieving widow, but the evidence suggests that Nathaniel Willis—who, according to his son, was himself a careful businessman[14]—was right. Eldredge took on the museum property when all other speculators regarded it as a very poor risk: Jenkins had approached a number of other businessmen, and they all, upon "mature consideration," had refused to become involved. As the Master of Chancery said in his report, "The nature and hazard of the undertaking were such that the said Eldridge [sic] was the only person in the City of Boston who, with reasonable probability of being successful in the undertaking, could be induced by the Complainant [Jenkins] to render the services required."[15] Eldredge may have been somewhat naive, or perhaps too eager to help his in-laws—or he may have mistakenly thought the venture would provide an easy profit for himself. Whatever his motivations, they were ill-guided, and, as he commented in his petition to the court in 1845, he never would have undertaken the speculation had he "foreseen the difficulties and embarrassments" that it would involve.[16]

What did Sara Eldredge think of the way in which her husband had conducted his affairs? She apparently never criticized him to her relatives, and she seems to have loved and supported him through all of the long ordeal. Although *Ruth Hall* was merciless in its criticism of Fern's father-in-law, brother, brother-in-law, and the newspaper editors who had exploited her, there is no suggestion of criticism of her first husband in her positive portrayal of Harry Hall, who was based on Eldredge, the beloved husband who died in financial ruin, leaving his wife and children without resources. When Hall dies, the author tells us that his hands are folded "over as noble a heart as ever lay cold and still" (RH, 58). In all of the essays of Fanny Fern, who was herself an astute businesswoman, I found only one overt instance of criticism of the husband who mishandles his business affairs and consequently jeopardizes his family's security. In 1861 she questions whether a man should "be called a fond husband and father, who left needlessly to wife and children only the legacy of unpaid debts?" (NYL, August 31, 1861). For the most part, however, Fern's criticism is not primarily of the husband's business sense but of the social situation that put a woman at the mercy of a man's financial bungling. At the very least, Fern notes, a woman should pay attention to what her husband is doing with their money.

Clearly Fanny Fern had learned something from the experience: a wife cannot trust simply to her husband; she must make it her business to participate in decisions that will affect both of them and their children. Ultimately, Fern took this idea even further, maintaining that a woman should be financially independent, either helping to earn the living or at least being capable of doing so if her husband mishandled their money and/or died.

The last two years of the lawsuit were difficult years for Sara Eldredge for another reason also. In less than two years she mourned the deaths of five people who had been very close to her: her young sister, her mother, her daughter, her sister-in-law, and her husband. On February 5, 1844, her sister, Ellen Willis Dennett, died at the age of twenty-two, soon after her newborn baby. On February 20, 1844, Sara wrote to her brother Richard, who was studying music in Germany, to tell him of Ellen's death:

Dear Richard:—Ellen, *our* Ellen, is in Heaven! . . . You have already heard that she lost her babe. About this she mourned incessantly, calling for it to be placed where she could see it as long as it remained in the house. But the *mother* was our chief care, for she was pronounced in great danger, a pleurisy fever having set in. If you know anything about this complaint, you can judge what she must have suffered, as she was already greatly weakened. She was propped up in a sitting posture in the bed, this being the only one in which she could breathe during the whole of her sickness. In a few days, her disease assumed the form of lung fever; a dreadful and incessant cough set in, and her weak and ineffectual attempts to raise the phlegm, with which her lungs were filled, were truly distressing to witness. She occupied the chamber directly over the nursery, where poor mother lay, unable to leave the room, listening, with an ear rendered sensitive by anxiety, to every hurried footstep overhead, and almost dreading to read the countenances of those who had the care of her. Poor Ellen would beg so hard to see her, "Oh! bring my *mother* to me![17]

In after years Fanny Fern said that the name Ellen stood for "all that was loving and sweet and fair." She remembered her sister as a young girl holding her (Fern's) baby: "that lovely summer morning she stood laughing in the door-way, with her sister's curly-headed child upon her shoulder, reaching its dimpled hands up to the roses above its head, and showering the perfumed leaves like incense about her" (NYL, January 14, 1860).

Six weeks after Ellen's death, on March 21, 1844, their mother, Hannah Parker Willis, who had been ill at the time of Ellen's death, died at the age of sixty-two. Fanny Fern referred often to her mother in her newspaper articles, commenting in 1871, a year before her own death, that she had never ceased to miss her (NYL, April 29, 1871). Her 1857 article in the *New York Ledger* provides a fitting eulogy and also gives us a graphic picture of the relationship between the young Willises and their mother, who was almost the only person that Fanny Fern never criticized, even gently, in her otherwise caustic comments on human nature. This article, "Mother's Room," was published twice in the *Ledger*:

Mother's room! How we look back to it in after years, when she who has sanctified it is herself among the sanctified. How well we remember the ample cushioned chair, with its all-embracing arms, none the worse in our eyes for having rocked to sleep so many little forms now scattered far and wide, divided from us, perhaps, by barriers more impassable than the cold, blue sea. Mother's room—where the sun shone in so cheerily upon the flowering plants in the low, old-fashioned window seats, which seemed to bud and blossom at the least touch of her caressing fingers; on which no blight or mildew ever came, no more than on the love which outlived all our childish waywardness, all our childish folly. The cozy sofa upon which childish feet were never forbidden to climb; upon which curly heads could dream, unchidden, the fairy dreams of childhood. The closet which garnered tops, and dolls, and kites, and whips, and toys, and upon whose upper shelf was that infallible, old-fashioned panacea for infancy's aches and pains—brimstone and molasses! The basket, too, where was always the very string we wanted; the light-stand round which we gathered, and threaded needles (would we had threaded thousands more) for eyes dimmed in our service; and the cheerful face that smiled across it such loving thanks. Mother's room! where our matronly feet returned when *we* were mothers; where we lifted our little ones to kiss the wrinkled face, beautiful with its halo of goodness; where we looked on well pleased to see the golden locks we worshipped, mingling lovingly with the silver hairs; where—as the fond grand-mamma produced in charming profusion, cakes and candy for the little pets, we laughingly reminded her of *our* baby days, when she wisely told us such things were "unwholesome"; where *our* baby caps, yellow with time, ferreted from some old bag or closet, were tried on our own babies' heads, and we sat, wondering where the months and years had flown between then and now;—and looking forward, half-sighing, to just such a picture, when we should play what seemed to us now, with our smooth skins, round limbs, and glossy locks, such an impossible part. Mother's room! where we watched beside her patient sick-bed through the long night, gazing hopelessly at the flickering taper, listening to the pain-extended groan, which no human skill, no human love, could avert or relieve; waiting with her for the dawning of that eternal day, seen through a mist of tears, bounded by no night. Mother's room! where the mocking light strayed in through half opened shutters upon her who for the first time was blind to our tears, deaf to our cries—where busy memory could bring back no look, no word, no tone, no act of hers not freighted with God-like love. Alas, alas for us then if turning the tablets, they showed us this long debt of love unappreciated, unpaid. (NYL, August 15, 1857, December 11, 1858)

During the illnesses of her mother and sister, Sara Eldredge spent a great deal of time at the Atkinson Street house, sitting up with the patients and spending several days at a time at the house. During this time the court case in which her husband was involved was pending, and in May of 1844 the judge's decision was handed down—against Charles Eldredge. This was a difficult time for the Eldredges. While Sara was reeling from the deaths of her sister and mother, her husband was struggling to recover his finances, maintain his position at the bank, which was threatened by his involvement in the Jenkins affair, and save his reputation, which had been impugned by Jenkins's cries of fraud. The judge's decision must have been a severe blow. While all of this was going on, Sara had found that she was once again pregnant. Her third child was born on September 20, 1844; Sara named her new daughter after her dead sister, Ellen Willis.

With the birth of the new baby, Sara and Charles attempted to put the tragedies behind them. They continued their idyllic life at Swissdale, while Charles consulted with his attorneys and worked on a lengthy petition asking for a rehearing. Then on March 17, 1845, a new death struck the family: seven-year-old Mary Eldredge died of "brain fever." The description of the death of the child Daisy in *Ruth Hall* suggests the effect the child's death had on her parents. In the 1840s the death of a young child was not an uncommon occurrence in a household. Two months after little Mary's death, Fern's sister Lucy Bumstead's eight-year-old son, Frank, died, and Lucy's three-year-old son, Harry, died in 1847. In 1842 Ralph Waldo Emerson's beloved Waldo died at the age of five. Harriet Beecher Stowe lost her little boy to cholera in 1849 and effectively used the concept of a dead child to provide a bond between the white family, Senator and Mrs. Bird, and the slave woman Eliza in *Uncle Tom's Cabin,* knowing that many of her northern readers would be able to identify with the situation, which to women of her generation seemed a universal experience.[18] In 1871 Fanny Fern wrote an article in response to a letter from a woman who had just lost her child:

I know just how you go about, listening for the little appealing cry that you may nevermore hear; touching listlessly the little useless clothes that you fashioned, with your heart so full of love and hope. I too have done all this. . . . So, as I say, I shall not *reason* with you, now, for that were worse than useless. I only reach out my woman's hand, and clasp yours in sympathy, although we have never and may never meet in this world. (NYL, October 28, 1871)

If the deaths of young children were a common occurrence in the lives of nineteenth-century women, also common were the deaths of the women themselves in childbirth. Ellen had died from the complications of childbirth, and on March 25, 1845, the Willis family suffered another death: N. P. Willis's wife, Mary Stace Willis, died in childbirth at the age of twenty-nine, one week after the death of her namesake, Mary Stace Eldredge.[19] N. P. Willis brought his little daughter, Imogen, to stay with Sara and Charles before taking her with him to England.

In *Ruth Hall* the young couple cannot bear to remain at their house in the country after the death of their daughter because the house and its surroundings contain too many painful memories. Consequently, they sell the house and move back to the city. Sara and Charles Eldredge also sold their country home after Mary's death. However, the death of the child was not the only reason. The principal reason, apparently, was Eldredge's difficult financial situation. The $4,000 mortgage had become due in the summer of 1844, and Eldredge had no money to pay it. With the loss of the lawsuit, he had so many debts that it was impossible to hold on to the house. Very probably, however, the death of Mary lessened the desire of Sara and Charles to struggle to maintain the house. On May 24, 1845, two months after Mary's death, Eldredge sold Swissdale for $7,000. Hezekiah Eldredge, in a move that may have been designed to help his son sell the property, gave the new owner a second mortgage of $2,000. It is also possible that Hezekiah Eldredge helped his son financially by selling off his own land. Between April and October of 1845 Hezekiah Eldredge sold approximately fifteen parcels of his land in Brighton, including the property that his house stood on. In *Ruth Hall* the comments of Ruth's father-in-law suggest that the elder Eldredge did not think his son was wise to sell his property. Mr. Hall complains that he has no patience with Ruth because she had caused her husband to sell the property at a sacrifice "merely" because the memories of her dead child were so painful (RH, 47).

After Mary's death, Sara and Charles moved back to Boston. The elder Eldredges moved to Newton. The Boston City Directory for 1845 lists Charles Eldredge at 5 Cambridge Street in Boston; in 1846 he was at 55 Hancock Street. There is no record that he purchased a house, and he would have had neither money nor credit to do so.

5

"Dark Days"

I wonder who but the "Father of lies," originated this proverb, "Help yourself and then every body else will help you." Isn't it as true as the book of Job that it's just driving nails in your own coffin, to let anybody know you want help? . . . Don't they wrap their warm garments round their well-fed persons, and advise you in a saintly tone "to trust to Providence"? . . . "Help yourself," of course you will (if you have any spirit), but when sickness comes, or dark days, and your wits and nerves are both exhausted, don't place any dependence on this lying proverb!—for the way you'll get humbugged will be more curious than agreeable.

OB, March 13, 1852

CHARLES ELDREDGE'S PETITION WAS DENIED IN MAY OF 1846, but he apparently planned to appeal. Despite his heavy financial loss, Eldredge must have felt that he would be able to recoup. Biographical statements about Fanny Fern by her relatives state that had he not died when he did, he would soon have come into a large sum of money.[1] Perhaps this was too sanguine a view of the matter, but it apparently was his own belief—or at least this must have been what he told Sara, who believed it. Certainly Sara and Charles Eldredge did not noticeably alter their life style. They spent the summer and fall of 1846 at a resort hotel, Sara and the children remaining there during the day and Charles coming out from the city in the evening. It was at this hotel on October 6, 1846, that Charles Eldredge died of typhoid fever. He was thirty-five years old. The circumstances of his death closely resemble those of Harry Hall in *Ruth Hall*. In an early article entitled "Summer Days," Fern gives us a vivid description of their life at the hotel and of Charles's death and its consequences for her. I quote the article at length because it provides, in Fanny Fern's own words, a glimpse of the relationship between her and her first husband, as well as a sense of what their life together must have been like. It also brings us with a characteristic change of tone, to the end of this episode in her life:

A delightful summer we passed, to be sure, at the ——— Hotel, in the quiet village of S———. A collection of prettier women, or more gentlemanly, agreeable men, were never thrown together by the necessity of seeking country quarters in the dog-days. Fashion, by common consent, was laid upon the shelf, and comfort and smiling faces were the natural result. Husbands took the car in the morning for the city, rejoicing in linen coats and pants, and loose neck-ties; while their wives were equally independent till their return, in flowing muslin wrappers, not too dainty for the wear and tear of little climbing feet, fresh from the meadow or wildwood. There were no separate "cliques" or "sets." Nobody knew, or inquired, or cared, whether your great grandfather had his horse shod, or shod horses for other people. The ladies were not afraid of smutting their fingers, or their reputation, if they washed their children's faces; and did not consider it necessary to fasten the door, and close the blinds, when they replaced a missing button on their husband's waistband, or mended a ragged frock.

Plenty of fruit, plenty of fresh, sweet air, plenty of children, and plenty of room for them to play in. A short nap in the afternoon, a little additional care in arranging tumbled ringlets, and in girdling a fresh robe round the waist, and they were all seated, in the cool of the evening, on the long piazza, smiling, happy, and expectant, as the car bell announced the return of their liege lords from the dusty, heated city. It was delightful to see their business faces brighten up, as each fair wife came forward, and relieved them from the little parcels and newspapers they carried in their hands, and smiled a welcome, sweet as the cool, fresh air that fanned their heated foreheads. A cool bath, a clean dickey, and they were presentable at the supper-table, where merry jokes flew round, and city news was discussed between fragrant cups of tea. . . .

It was one harmonious, happy family! Mrs.——— and her husband were the prime ministers of fun and frolic in the establishment. It was she who concocted all the games, and charades, and riddles, that sent our merry shouts ringing far and wide, as we sat in the evening on the long, moonlit piazza. It was she who planned the pic-nics and sails, and drives in the old hay-cart; the berry parties, and romps on the green; and the little cosy suppers in the back parlor. . . . It was she who salted our coffee and sugared our toast; it was she who made puns for us, and wrote verses; . . . it was she who was here, and there, and everywhere, the embodiment of mischief, and fun, and kindness.

[Her husband] was the handsomest man I ever saw— tall, commanding and elegant, with dark blue eyes, a profusion of curling black hair, glittering white teeth, and a form like Apollo's. Mary was so proud of him! She would always watch his eye when she meditated any little piece of roguery, and it was discontinued or perfected as she read its language. He was just the man to appreciate her,—to understand her sensitive, enthusiastic nature,—to know when to check, when to encourage; and it needed but a word, a look; for her whole soul went out to him.

And so the bright summer days sped fleetly on; and now autumn had
come, with its gorgeous beauty, and no one had courage to speak of
breaking up our happy circle; but ah, there came one, with stealthy steps,
who had no such scruples!

———————

The merry shout of the children is hushed in the wide halls; anxious
faces are grouped on the piazza; for in a darkened room above lies Mary's
princely husband, delirious with fever! . . . A fainting, unresisting form is
borne from that chamber of death. Beautiful, as a piece of rare sculpture,
lies the husband!—no traces of pain on lip or brow; the long, heavy
lashes lay upon the marble cheek; the raven locks, damp with the dew of
death, clustered profusely round the noble forehead; those chiselled lips
are gloriously beautiful in their repose! . . . Kind hands are busy with vain
attempts to restore animation to the fainting wife. O, that bitter, bitter
waking! . . . Why should I dwell on the agony of the gentle wife; or tell of
her return to her desolate home in the city; of the disposal of the rare
pictures and statuary collected to grace its walls by the refined taste of its
proprietor; of the necessary disposal of every article of luxury; of her
removal to plain lodgings, where curious people speculated upon her history, and marked her moistened eyes; of the long, interminable, wretched
days; of the wakeful nights, when she lay with her cheek pressed against
the sweet, fatherless child of her love; of her untiring efforts to seek an
honorable, independent support? It is but an every-day history, but—
God knows—its crushing weight of agony is none the less keenly felt by
the sufferer! (OB, May 22, 1852)

When Charles Eldredge died, Sara's father and father-in-law, as she later
said, argued over who would spend the least to support her and her children
(EP, 101). After all of Eldredge's creditors had been satisfied, there was no
money left for his widow, and she found lodgings in a modest boardinghouse for herself and her daughters, who were then two and five years old.
Her father grudgingly gave her a small allowance, which was accompanied
by criticism of her dead husband and constant urgings that she remarry in
order to support herself and her children.[2]

On May 8, 1845, Willis had himself remarried. His new wife was Susan
(Capen) Douglas, the widow of the man who had been his apprentice
printer in Portland. Willis's children had been dismayed that he would
marry so soon after their mother's death, but Willis had bluntly told Lucy,
the eldest, that it was well for a man to marry "lest the Devil tempt him to
do wuss" (EP, 97). Perhaps the fact that he had acquired a new wife helps to
account for his apparently callous treatment of his widowed daughter: his
new wife may not have wanted to take on the responsibility of his daughter's family, and his own remarriage probably made remarriage for Sara

seem to him a logical solution. Moreover, Susan Douglas does seem to have been a no-nonsense type of woman, particularly for her generation: she had Nathaniel Willis sign a prenuptial agreement before they married, and she had her brother, John Capen, superintend her investments throughout her marriage, making certain that the only money that went to Nathaniel Willis were the expenses for her last illness and for her funeral.[3] She does not seem to have been the person to encourage Willis to take on the additional expense of supporting his daughter and her family. One suspects that in real life, however, as *Ruth Hall* implies, had Sara's own mother still been living, her father's attitude toward his widowed daughter would not have been so harsh.[4]

It is significant, however, that Fern eliminated Susan Capen Douglas from the story of *Ruth Hall* and placed the blame wholly on her father, who, in the novel, had not remarried. Willis, as portrayed in the novel, and apparently in fact, was himself somewhat tightfisted. This character trait is commented upon by Ethel Parton (EP, 100) and is referred to in Fern's newspaper articles. Fern also told of specific incidents of stinginess. During her mother's final illness, she said, her father refused to spend the money for the medicine that the doctor has prescribed, and her husband, Eldredge, had to purchase the necessary medicine. Then, after her mother's death, Willis removed the false teeth from his dead wife and sold them.[5]

In a story entitled "A Business Man's Home; or, a Story for Husbands," Fern portrayed family life as it should not be: a father and husband who growls and complains to his wife and never plays with his children, a man who is "incapable of affection for any thing but himself and his money." That the father in the story was based on her own father is suggested by the fact that she inserted in the middle of the story her essay "Mother's Room" and comments that she had made elsewhere about her mother's patience at ill treatment by her husband. At the end of the story, the mother dies, and as she lies dying, her husband continues to complain and refuses to obtain medicine for her. Her married daughter asks her husband, "How can I love or respect my father?" A middle-aged woman visits regularly—just when it is time for the husband to come home from work—and the mother correctly predicts to her astonished daughter (apparently based on Fern herself) that the woman will be her father's wife "when I am scarcely cold."[6]

Implicitly criticizing her father's treatment of herself after her husband's death, Fern, early in her career, wrote articles portraying the ideal father, that is, the father who not only welcomes his destitute children into his home but does so without making them feel the bitterness of their dependence (e.g., OB, March 6, 1852). In 1859 she wrote in "Old Zacharia":

[H]e folded his worse than widowed daughters to his warm, fatherly heart. . . . A few more chairs at the hearth, a few more loaves at the table, that was all. There was enough and to spare in that father's house. That they were poor and desolate built no separating wall between him and them. (NYL, March 5, 1859)

Since there was not room at her father's hearth, Sara Eldredge found lodgings in the boardinghouse of Mr. and Mrs. J. B. Hill at 7 Columbia Street in Boston. William Endicott, who came to live in the house at around the same time, remembered Fanny Fern and her two daughters, to whom he occasionally brought apples and little cakes. Mrs. Hill had been a housekeeper at Brook Farm; her husband and some of the boarders had been Brook Farmers. Endicott tells us in his reminiscences that he paid three dollars a week for room and board for a single room, noting that none of the boarders had very much money.[7]

The young widow attempted to support herself by sewing. As an impoverished seamstress, Sara found herself vulnerable to rough treatment and sexual harassment that she had not experienced as the comfortable wife of Charles Eldredge. In *Ruth Hall* the boardinghouse loungers talk easily about their chances of seducing the pretty widow (RH, 73–74). Fern's 1852 article "Dark Days" is a series of vignettes describing a poor widow who sews for a living to support herself and her child. These two excerpts illustrate the coarse treatment she receives:

"Work done?" said a rough voice; "cause, if you ain't up to the mark you can't have any more. 'No fire, and cold fingers.' Same old story. Business is business; I've no time to talk about your affairs. Women never can look at a thing in a commercial p'int of view. What I want to know is in a nutshell. Is them shirts done or not, young woman?"

"Indeed, there is only one finished, though I have done my best," said Mrs. Grey.

"Well, hand it along; you won't get any more; and sit up to-night and finish the rest, d'ye hear?"

———

"Have you vests that you wish embroidered, sir?" "Y-e-s," said the gentleman (?) addressed, casting a look of admiration at Mrs. Grey.— "Here, James, run out with this money to the bank.—Wish it for yourself, madam?" said he blandly. "Possible? Pity to spoil those blue eyes over such drudgery."

A moment and he was alone. (OB, December 4, 1852)

Living in such reduced circumstances, Sara also found that relatives and friends, many of whom she and her husband had entertained liberally in their home, did not want to see her. Her early articles, as well as *Ruth Hall*, bitterly reflect this ostracism. An 1852 article sarcastically advises that "if a poor wretch—male or female—comes to you for charity, whether allied to you by your own mother, or mother Eve, . . . wish him well, and *turn your back upon him*" (OB, June 5, 1852). An 1853 article describes how when your pocket is empty, you will not be welcome at other people's houses: "They are all in a perspiration lest you should be delivered of a request for their assistance, before they can get rid of you" (OB, June 18, 1853).

Unlike the genteel writers of her day, Fanny Fern took a cynical view of human nature, and her coarse truths were sometimes expressed in coarse language. Impatient with flowery language, especially fatuous moralizing that hid the truth, Fern told the truth as she had experienced it—even if it was not very pretty:

Isn't a "seedy" hat, a threadbare coat, or a patched dress, an effectual shower-bath on old friendships? Haven't people a mortal horror of a sad face and a pitiful story? Don't they on hearing it, instinctively poke their purses into the farthest, most remote corner of their pockets? . . . Ain't they always "engaged" ever after, when you call to see 'em? Ain't they near-sighted when you meet 'em in the street?—and don't they turn short corners to get out of your way? (OB, March 13, 1852)

Fanny Fern had no use for platitudinous proclaimers of "Christian charity"; her experience had shown her that it had few practitioners. An article entitled "Summer Friends" asserts that that poet was a fool who said that if our troubles "could burn upon your brow," people would be eager to help us:

Don't you believe it! They would run from you, as if you had the plague. "Write your brow" with anything else but your "troubles," if you do not wish to be left solus. You have no idea how "good people" will pity you when you tell your doleful ditty! They will "pray for you," give you advice by the bushel, "feel for you"—everywhere but in their pocketbooks; and wind up by telling you to "trust in Providence"; to all of which you feel very much like replying as the old lady did when she found herself spinning down hill in a wagon, "I trusted in Providence till the tackling broke!"

Now, listen to me;—just go to work and hew out a path for yourself; get your head above water, and then snap your fingers in their pharisaical faces! Never ask a favor until you are drawing your last breath; and never forget one. (FL, 290)

The conclusion of this article indicates the road that Fern was herself to follow, that is, one of "self-reliance." Her self-reliance, however, was not based on an abstract philosophy. As the articles indicate, it derived from a realization learned from her own experience.

The bitterness that Sara Eldredge felt at being made to seem a pariah by

her relatives and friends was compounded by her bitterness at the fate that
had caused the deaths of so many of her loved ones. Although her religion
and,her relatives preached submission, she decried the "rapacious grave"
(OB, April 2, 1853). You cannot understand, she told her readers, if you
have never "bent your rebellious knee at God's altar, when your tongue was
dumb to praise Him and your lips refused to kiss the Smiter's rod!" (MWT,
October 9, 1852).

   Unlike her contemporaries Emerson (who carefully hid his pain from the
world and perhaps even from himself, declaring after his brothers, wife, and
five-year-old son died that he had never in his life felt any pain)[8] and Thoreau (who declared that sorrow was only the result of "bad bowels"),[9] Fern
admitted that she felt great anguish. Without affectation, she described in
later years the feelings that so many of us—then and now—have experienced, the immediacy of the pain of memory:

Before me lies a little violet, the forerunner of spring. . . . It should give me
joy, and yet my tears are dropping on its purple leaves.
   Why? Has life been such a holiday to you that your heart never grew
sick at a perfume or a well-remembered song hummed beneath your window, or a form, or a face, which was, and yet was not, which mockingly
touched a chord that for years you had carefully covered over? . . .
   Have you never rushed frantically into a crowd—somewhere, anywhere to be rid of yourself? Did you never laugh and talk so incessantly
and so gaily, that your listeners asked wonderingly and reproachfully,
"Does she ever *think?*" . . . Did you never listen to the tick-tick of your
watch, night after night, with dilated eyes that would not close, with
limbs so weary that you could not change your posture, and lips so
parched you could not even cry, . . . and your brain one vast workshop,
where memory was forging racks, and chains, and screws, and trying
their strength on every quivering nerve?
   There are moments when the heart's cry will *not* be stifled; when the
little child or the blooming girl bounds before you suddenly with *your*
darling's hair, or eyes, or laugh. In a moment the years since she died are
swept away; the years when you tried to do without her; the years you
spelt out letter by letter, "thy will be done," *so* painfully, *so* slowly, and
there you are again at that grave, and the grass has *not* grown over it, and
the cruel earth is still freshly heaped. (NYL, May 8, 1858, May 12, 1866)

   The bitterness and anguish that Sara Eldredge felt at her situation after
her husband died were only intensified by the awareness that she was not
alone; her children shared her sorrow, her poverty, and her friendlessness.
Her early articles reflect this preoccupation. However, she did not simply
write vaguely about sorrow and suffering. Instead she focused on a specific
detail. That detail is usually one with which a mother could identify. In one

early article she recorded the sadness of the mother who sees her young child sleeping on Christmas Eve and knows that she cannot fill the stocking the child has hung out (OB, December 27, 1851). In another, she wrote of the mother who, herself pressed with anguish, hears her four-year-old child sigh among his toys and realizes that the young child has caught the "trick of grief" from her (FL, 47). She also recorded the comment of the child who told her widowed mother that she wished things were as they used to be: "Now . . . you sit up at night till the stars go away, to finish your work, and you step slow and tired, like grandpa" (OB, September 13, 1851, November 15, 1851).

The pictures of poverty and isolation that Fanny Fern so graphically records in her early writing were based on the actual circumstances of her life at that time. Later, when she became prosperous from her writing, her detractors ridiculed the possibility that she had ever really been so poor. But the evidence indicates that she had not exaggerated in her portrayal of her poverty. Her granddaughter, Ethel Parton, when specifically questioned on this point, said that the pictures of poverty were indeed accurate, and cited the testimony of Fern's daughter Ellen, who remembered those days very well, and also of Fern's sister Julia, who was known for her objective honesty.[10] In an 1852 article, "Little Mary's Story," later published as "Thanksgiving Story," Fern described their circumstances during those lean years when there was not enough heat or food and the young child wondered why all the "aunts and uncles and cousins" who used to visit when Papa was alive "*never* come to see us *now*" (MWT, November 20, 1852).

During this time when she was shunned by family and friends, Sara Eldredge found comfort in her children, who, it seemed to her, were the only people she could trust. In 1862 she described the children of a despairing mother as "Angel Comforters": "The soft cheek laid mutely against your own; the timorous velvet hand on the throbbing temples; the pitying eyes. . . . No deceit *there!* no danger of misplaced trust" (NYL, April 19, 1862). In 1857 she wrote in the *New York Ledger* "A Word to Shop-keepers," in which she castigated shopkeepers for treating rudely the poor woman who must count her pennies: "Imagine her with her fatherless, hungry children by her side, plying the needle late into the night, for the pitiful sum of seventy-five cents a week, as I once did." Addressing the shopkeeper who would be cruel to such a woman simply because she cannot afford to purchase expensive merchandise, she writes: "*You* have never . . . leaned with a breaking heart upon a little child, for the comfort and sympathy that you found nowhere else in the wide world beside" (NYL, June 20, 1857).

The latter article is significant as an indication of how Fern became radicalized. It was experiences like these that gave her a lifelong sympathy with working women; she was able to identify with the exploited worker, the poor woman whose experiences she had shared. Similarly, it was the experience of having no one to turn to except her children (and consequently relating to her children as persons and equals) that made her an advocate of what she called "children's rights." Articles like those excerpted above, which, viewed coldly from a twentieth-century perspective, might be dismissed as "sentimental," were based on her own experiences, and those experiences gave rise to some of the strongest statements and most forward-looking arguments for social reform that were penned in her century. She urged educational reforms that today are accepted practice, child-rearing techniques that today are regarded as common sense, and opportunities and rights for women, some of which are still being fought for today.

The most that Sara Eldredge could earn as a seamstress was seventy-five cents a week.[11] Having had a good education, she determined that she could do better as a teacher, and she took the examination to teach in the Boston public schools (JP, 50; EP, 103).[12] *Ruth Hall* contains a satirical description of that exam. In later years Fern said that although the description in the novel was satirical, it was for the most part an accurate representation of the actual exam (EP, 104):[13]

Very respectable were the gentlemen of whom that committee was composed; *respectable* was written all over them, from the crowns of their scholastic heads to the very tips of their polished boots; and correct and methodical as a revised dictionary they sat, with folded hands and spectacle-bestridden noses. . . .

"What is your age?" asked the elder of the inquisitors.
Scratch went the extorted secret on the nib of the reporter's pen!
"Where was you educated?"
"Was Colburn, or Emerson, your teacher's standard for Arithmetic?"
"Did you cipher on slate, or black-board?"
"Did you learn the multiplication table, skipping, or in order?"
"Was you taught Astronomy, or Philosophy, first?"
"Are you accustomed to a quill, or a steel-pen? lines, or blank paper, in writing?"
"Did you use Smith's, or Jones' Writing Book?"
"Did you learn Geography by Maps, or Globes?"
"Globes?" asked Mr. Squizzle, repeating Ruth's answer; "possible?"
"They use Globes at the celebrated Jerrold Institute," remarked Mr. Fizzle.
"Impossible!" retorted Mr. Squizzle, growing plethoric in the face; "Globes, sir, are exploded; no institution of any note uses Globes, sir. I know it."
"And I know you labor under a mistake," said Fizzle, elevating his chin, and folding his arms pugnaciously over his striped vest. "I am acquainted with one of the teachers in that highly-respectable school."
"And I, sir," said Squizzle, "am well acquainted with the Principal,

who is a man of too much science, sir, to use globes, sir, to teach geography, sir." (RH, 100–103)

Sara Eldredge passed the exam, which consisted of an oral and a written section, as well as a mathematical drill. However, lacking the necessary influence, she did not receive an appointment (EP, 105). Her relatives apparently did not help her, although Josiah F. Bumstead, her sister Lucy's husband, was one of the members of the school committee. His attitude can be inferred perhaps from Fern's portrayal of Mr. Millet, the "wooden man" who was also a member of the school committee in *Ruth Hall*. In the novel, the Millets are Ruth's cousins, but they are based on her relatives the Bumsteads. When Fern was widowed, the Bumsteads were living in a fashionable neighborhood on Beacon Street in Boston. Their older children, a daughter, Laura, and a son, Freeman, were at the age of the Millets' children, Leila and John. Like John, Freeman Bumstead became a doctor and moved to New York. Josiah F. Bumstead was a successful merchant who, with his father, had built up a prosperous paper-hanging business. Although the Millets' treatment of Ruth in the novel may be an exaggeration, one suspects that it is based on the Bumsteads' attitude toward Sara Eldredge, whose sudden poverty was an embarrassment to them. Moreover, Josiah F. Bumstead's papers regarding school issues reveal him to be the somewhat pompous, narrow-minded person that Fern satirized in Mr. Millet.[14]

While Sara Eldredge was attempting to support herself by sewing, her father continued to urge her to remarry. Samuel P. Farrington, a widower with two little girls, a Boston merchant at Clark, Sweet and Company and a man whose piety and prosperity Deacon Willis approved of, asked her to marry him. She refused, and the deacon was incensed. He had "no patience with the idea of declining to profit by such a manifest interposition of Providence."[15] Unable to earn enough by sewing to pay her board unaided by her father, and unable to obtain a teaching appointment, Sara capitulated, believing that the marriage would benefit her children. She frankly told Farrington that she did not love him, but he insisted that it did not matter. They were married on January 17, 1849.[16] They went to live at 68 Belknap Street in Boston.[17]

The marriage, according to Fern's daughter Ellen, was a "terrible mistake."[18] Ethel Parton wrote in response to an inquiry about the marriage: "He was a madly jealous man—not merely in the usual sense, but jealous of *all* his wife's friends, male or female; of her popularity; of every interest of any kind outside his own four walls which she might manifest. She attempted an impossible degree of compliance with his whims and tyrannies, until it was obvious that submission was useless—and she was by no means of a submissive temperament! But she tried, because she hated to have her sacrifice a failure."[19] A number of Fanny Fern's articles give hints of what the Farrington marriage was like. "Mary Lee," which is about a woman whose husband is unreasonably jealous, is particularly significant: in this article, the woman does not leave her husband, and, as punishment for her presumed infractions, he tricks her into being committed to an insane asylum (TF, May 8, 1852)—a not uncommon solution to marital difficulties in the mid-nineteenth century, and one Fern returned to in *Ruth Hall*.[20]

Fern's daughter Ellen remembered the extent to which her mother had tried to please her husband, even bending over backward to favor his children at the expense of her own. Once when her mother made dresses for the girls and there were not enough pretty glass buttons to go around, her mother put the glass buttons on her stepdaughters' dresses and plain black ones on her own daughter Ellen's dress (EP, 107). Nothing seemed to please Farrington, however. He set his daughters to spy on their stepmother, and when he came home in the evening he would sit them down and require them to report on her every action (EP, 107).[21]

There is evidence to suggest that, to a certain extent, Farrington's jealousy derived also from his resentment of his wife's superior capabilities. Fern's daughter Ellen describes Farrington as "a very common place man."[22] The Gertrude Dean sections in Fern's novel *Rose Clark* (1856) closely follow the outlines of the Farrington episode in Fern's life. In *Rose Clark*, Stahle, Gertrude's husband, is slower-witted than Gertrude and is jealous of her conversational ability, not wanting her to seem more intelligent or more witty than himself. In order to appease him and to avoid unpleasant scenes at home, Gertrude deliberately suppressed her national volubility, and said very little in company (RC, 242). In "Fanny Ford" (1855), Fern wrote sympathetically of the wife who was forced to handicap herself deliberately so that her husband could seem to be superior when he was not (FF, 122).

In addition to his jealous and abusive behavior, there is reason to believe that Farrington was sexually repulsive to his wife. In *Rose Clark* Gertrude tells us that her second husband's sexual advances filled her with revulsion. Gertrude says that before they were married he said that he loved her and that he would take care of her child, but afterward she realized that he was motivated wholly by lust, and did not care for her or her child:

How can I describe to you my gradual waking up from this delusion? The conviction that came slowly—but surely—that he was a hypocrite, and a gross sensualist. That it was passion, not love, which he felt for me, and that marriage was only the stepping-stone to an else impossible gratification.

Now I understood why that, which, to a delicate mind, would have been an insuperable obstacle to our union [her reluctance], was but a straw in his path. It was not the *soul* of which he desired possession, it was not that which he craved or could appreciate. I was wild with despair. O, the creeping horror with which I listened to his coming footsteps! I sprang from my seat when his footfall announced his approach—not to meet him, as a wife should meet her husband, as I in happier days had met Arthur—but to fly from him—to throw out my arms despairingly for help, and then to sink back into my chair, and nerve myself with a calm voice and shrouded eye to meet his unacceptable caresses.

O, what a fate—and for me! I who had soared with the eagle, to burrow with the mole! . . . To him my disgust was only coyness, and served but as fuel to the flame. . . . I proposed his reading to me, as a reprieve from his caresses. I did not care what, so that his arms were not round my waist, or his lip near mine. (RC, 235–237)

In 1850 Farrington gave up the house on Belknap Street, and they went to live in a boardinghouse at 14 Kneeland Street.[23] In *Rose Clark* Gertrude's husband moves her to a boardinghouse in an attempt to break her will. He treats her cruelly—insulting her in public, withholding money for necessities, spending his evenings out—yet he continues to claim his marital privilege: "Whole days he passed without speaking to me, and yet, at the same time, no inmate of a harem was ever more slavishly subject to the gross appetite of her master" (RC, 245). One does not know to what extent Gertrude's experience parallels Fern's life with Farrington, but, since so much else in Fern's work is known to be based on her own experience, and since it was more likely that a woman writer of the period would diminish rather than invent a sexual experience in her writing, I suspect that, like Gertrude, Sara Farrington found herself in the position of being "used" for sexual purposes with no love—or even affection—on either side (and, in fact, on her side, disgust and eventually loathing).

Ethel Parton tells us that her grandmother endured the situation "as long as self-respect and common prudence permitted, indeed until he reached the point of threatening personal violence" (EP, 107). In January 1851 she left her husband and took her children to the Marlboro Hotel in Boston. She went to see William H. Dennett, who was associated with James Munroe & Company, which is listed in the Boston City Directory as a booksellers and publishing company. Dennett was apparently the brother of her dead sister Ellen's husband, Charles Dennett, whose brother, William H. Dennett, was an attorney and the godfather of Fern's daughter Ellen.[24] He was able to "protect her from molestation by Farrington and to secure from him some provision for her immediate needs" (EP, 108). There is a letter among her papers from her to Thomas Farrington, her husband's brother, dated January 28, 1851:

Sir, I would be obliged to you to send to Mr. Dennett the money you have in your possession from my husband. Any arrangements necessary to be

made will be attended to by my friends without troubling you. Any farther business that you may have with me, I would be obliged to communicate to me in writing to the care of Mr. Dennett, of the firm of Munroe &
Co., Washington St.[25]

Farrington spread slanderous stories about her and had her followed in
an attempt to obtain evidence so that he could divorce her on grounds of
adultery. The men he had hired to follow her were themselves of a suspicious character, and it became apparent that, finding no evidence, Farrington would attempt to fabricate evidence by "staging an apparently
compromising scene." Her lawyer warned her not to go out alone (EP, 108).[26]
Fern's granddaughter tells us that many years afterward she met a man who
had been an acquaintance of Farrington's, who described the man as "a
particularly yellow variety of yellow dog."[27] Farrington continued to spread
stories about his wife, and, although he did not retract them, his brother
did. On January 28, 1851, Thomas Farrington wrote the following letter.
His letter, which remains among Fern's papers, indicates exactly what those
stories were:

I deny ever having used the following words in regard to Mrs. S. P. Farrington, my brother's wife[,] "That Mrs. S. P. Farrington, at other houses
had received visitors, who remained all night, and supposed she did at the
Marlboro." I deny ever having uttered such words or anything like them
and if I ever have uttered words injurious to her character I extremely
regret it, and Mrs. Farrington may rest assured that she will have no
reason to complain for the future of any remarks I may make in regard to
her.[28]

On February 25, 1851, Samuel P. Farrington placed a notice in the Boston Daily Bee indicating that he was no longer responsible for any expenses
of his wife's:

I hereby forbid all persons harboring or trusting my wife, Sarah P. Farrington, on my account, from this date, having made suitable provision
for her support.[29]

Farrington provided her with no further support, and soon thereafter he left
Boston.[30]
    The Willis family was scandalized. Whether or not Sara was guilty of the
things Farrington said she was did not matter to the deacon. It was scandalous for a wife to leave her husband. Moreover, as her granddaughter
said, the mores of the day dictated that no respectable woman would "get
herself talked about" in that way (EP, 109). The nineteenth century tended
to blame the female victim of slander, assuming that she must have done
something to bring it about. Fanny Fern referred often to the failure of the

male members of her family to come to her support when she was slandered by Farrington. She was particularly bitter about the silence of her older brother, N. P. Willis, and of her father, Nathaniel Willis. It is not surprising, perhaps, if Deacon Willis's piety and straitlaced conventionality made him unwilling to come to the support of a daughter who had left her husband. N. P. Willis's failure to come to her defense is more surprising. Not only did he did not share his father's strict religious beliefs, he was currently in the news for his defense of another slandered woman, the wife of the actor Edwin Forrest, against her husband's apparently false accusations of adultery.[31] Moreover, several years before, Willis had almost fought a duel in England because a man had insulted him and his family. "My own honor and that of my family are sacred," Willis wrote at the time.[32]

One reason why Fern's relatives did not come to her defense—and what she apparently believed was the main reason—is suggested in the section of *Rose Clark* that derives from the Farrington marriage. John Stahle, Gertrude's husband, explains to a friend why Gertrude's family did not defend her against his slander:

"I knew I could go to the full length of my rope without any of their interference..In fact, their neglect of her helped me more than any thing else. Every body said I must have been an injured man, and that the stories I had circulated *must* be true about her, or they would certainly have defended and sheltered her. I knew them—I knew it would work just so; that was so much in my favor, you see."

"They liked you, then?" . . .

"Liked me! Humph! They all looked down on me as a vulgar fellow. I was tolerated, and that was all—hardly that."

"I don't understand it, then," said Smith.

"I do, though; if they *defended* her, they would have no excuse for not helping her. It was the cash, you see, the cash! so they preferred siding with me, vulgar as they thought me. I knew them—I knew how it would work before I began." (RC, 347)

In an obvious reference to her own brother's failure to speak out in her defense, Fern wrote of the ideal brother who protects his sister from slander (RC, 348; TF, December 13, 1851). She often expressed disgust at the want of men who would defend their female relatives against slander. In an 1853 article entitled "Men Wanted," for example, she referred to a newspaper story about a woman who, when her male relatives would not come to her defense, took matters into her own hands and shot the man who had slandered her (MWT, September 24, 1853). Fern also wrote bitterly of the slanderer himself, who, she said sarcastically, "displays *manly courage* attacking the reputation of defenceless women" (OB, July 10, 1852). The victim of such slander could not look to other women for support; women, Fern found, were the first to spurn another woman who had been unjustly slandered (OB, August, 16, 1851). And the woman who was most vulnerable to slander was the woman alone who did not have relatives, particularly male relatives, to speak out in her defense.[33]

In the mid-nineteenth century, slander was a convenient weapon that a man could readily wield against a recalcitrant woman. Most women would remain compliant in order to escape such slander, from which there was no defense; once it was said, it was said. As Jean Muir comments in Louisa May Alcott's "Behind a Mask" (1866) about a man who, she says, has attempted to coerce her by threatening her reputation: "a look, a word can tarnish it; a scornful smile, a significant shrug can do me more harm than any blow; for I am a woman—friendless, poor, and at the mercy of his tongue."[34] In E.D.E.N. Southworth's *Hidden Hand* (1859), the intrepid Capitola resorts to fighting a duel herself because no one will defend her against the scurrilous slanders of Craven LeNoir, who, realizing that it is easy to destroy a woman's reputation by innuendo or simply by raising his eyebrows suggestively, attempts to slander her so that he can force her to his will.[35]

In an 1857 article in the *Ledger* Fanny Fern wrote that there was no toil more degrading than a degrading marriage. She urged women who found themselves in such a marriage to leave their husbands:

There are aggravated cases for which the law provides no remedy—from which it affords no protection; . . . hundreds of suffering women bear their chains because they have not courage to face a scandal-loving world. . . . Let a woman who *has the self-sustaining power* quietly take her fate in her own hands, and right herself. Of course she will be misjudged and abused. *It is for her to choose.* . . . These are bold words; but they are needed words—words whose full import I have well considered, and from the responsibility of which I do not shrink. (NYL, October 24, 1857)

They were indeed bold words, but even bolder was the action that preceded them.

If Sara Eldredge had been ostracized as a poor widow, Sara Farrington was even more isolated as the victim of slander and as a woman who had left her husband. The deacon's allowance had ceased when his daughter had remarried, and when she left her husband he refused to resume it. Sara was now without any resources whatsoever except what she could earn herself.

Hezekiah and Mary Eldredge apparently also refused to give monetary assistance to their son's widow and her children.[36] Where Deacon Willis's reluctant charity had been accompanied by recriminations directed at Charles Eldredge for mismanaging his business affairs and for dying at an inopportune time, the Eldredges directed their recriminations at their daughter-in-law, maintaining that if she had no money now, it was due to her own extravagance when she was married to their son (EP, 101). However, they offered to take the children. They wanted to adopt Ellen, the younger, because they felt she could be more easily molded, and they stipulated that they would only take her if her mother would give up all claim to the child and allow them to bring her up according to their own practice (EP, 101). Sara refused. They then offered to give a home to the elder child, Grace, in their home in Newton.

The Eldredges were "excessively rigid" in their ideas on child rearing, and Sara was reluctant to let her daughter go to them, but her finances were such that she felt she could not refuse (EP, 101). She told the child that it would only be until she could earn enough money to come and get her. Grace told of how on the first night, lonely and homesick, she took her candle to go up to her room and turned to kiss her grandmother good night. Her grandmother coldly rebuffed her, saying, "Tut, tut, child! Judas betrayed his master with a kiss."[37] In *Ruth Hall* Fern satirized her in-laws' treatment of her child, and, although the portrayal in the novel is fictionalized, it is valuable in that it gives us an idea of Fern's perspectives on child rearing and how they differed from those of her in-laws, whose methods she portrays as how *not* to bring up children (RH, 129–130, 137–139).

6

The Birth
of Fanny Fern

*Thank Heaven, I can stand alone! Can you? Are you yet at the end of
your life journey? Have you yet stood over the dead body of wife or
child, snatched from you when life was at the flood tide of happiness? . . .
If a woman, did you ever face poverty where luxury had been, and
vainly look hither and thither for the summer friends that you would
never see again till larder and coffer were replenished? Are you sure,
when you boast that you can "stand alone," that you have learned also
how to fall alone?*

NYL, August 26, 1871

HER RELATIVES REFUSING TO HELP TO SUPPORT HER, Sara Eldredge Farrington, without any supplemental allowance, could not afford to live even
in the modest boarding house she had lived in before her remarriage. Instead, she and Ellen found cheaper, less desirable lodgings. It was then that
she decided to try writing for the newspapers. Her father was an editor, and
although he would not help her (he disapproved of and discouraged her
attempts at writing),[1] she had had the experience of writing and reading
proof for his papers. She also remembered how the editor of the Hartford
paper had eagerly printed her articles. She bought an old inkstand at a secondhand shop and determined that she would try to earn her living by writing. In an apostrophe to her inkstand in 1856, when by her writing she had
been enabled to lift herself out of poverty and purchase her own house, she
remembered the attic room in the Brattle Street boardinghouse run by Mr.
and Mrs. Griffin.[2] It was here that she first began to write. This excerpt from
the article gives us an idea of what her life was like in the spring of 1851:

Well, old Ink-stand, what do you think of this? Haven't we got well
through the woods, hey? A few scratches and bruises we have had, to be
sure, but what of that? Didn't you whisper where we should come out,

the first morning I dipped my pen in your sable depths, in the sky-parlor of that hyena-like Mrs. Griffin? With what an eagle glance she discovered that my bonnet-ribbon was undeniably guilty of two distinct washings, and, emboldened by my shilling de laine, and the shabby shoes of little Nell, inquired "if I intended taking slop-work into *her* apartments?" How distinctly I was made to understand that Nell was not to speak above a whisper, or in any way infringe upon the rights of her uncombed, unwashed, unbaptized, uncomfortable little Griffins. Poor little Nell, who clung to my gown with childhood's instinctive appreciation of the hard face and wiry voice of our jailor. With what venom I overheard her inform Mr. Griffin that "they must look sharp for the rent of their sky-parlor, as its tenant lived on bread and milk, and wore her under-clothes rough-dry, because she could not afford to pay for ironing them!" Do you remember *that*, old Ink-stand? And do you remember the morning she informed me, as you and I were busily engaged in our first article, that I must "come and scrub the stairs which led up to my room"; and when I ventured humbly to mention, that this was not spoken of in our agreement, do you remember the Siddons-like air with which she thundered in our astonished ears—"Do it, or tramp!" (NYL, July 19, 1856)

While she was trying to earn money from her writing, Fern and her little daughter lived on meager rations of bread and milk. There was little money for extras. She did not even have the train fare to visit Grace in Newton. She sent Nelly at half-fare in the care of a kind conductor, and once she walked all the way to Newton and back, carrying Nelly most of the distance (EP, 102). One of Fern's early stories tells of how a poor widow took a little girl into a shoe store for a much-needed pair of shoes. Inside the store the weary mother found that she had lost her week's earnings, one dollar. Leaving the store with the child but without the shoes, the mother "feels the warm, confiding clasp of that little hand; she knows a *woman's lot* is before her," and she wishes she could shelter her daughter from the future (OB, June 5, 1852).

That this story was based on an incident in Fern's own life is suggested by a story Fanny Fern told her granddaughter which indicates how precious new shoes were. Fern told how her daughter Ellen (Nelly) had needed new shoes for a long time, but they had not been able to afford to buy any. Finally, after her shoes were badly outgrown and outworn, she had gotten a new pair: "They were cheap flimsy things, but they were new and she was very proud of them." Fern and Ellen were then living in a boardinghouse near Boston Common, and that day, while her mother was busy writing, Nelly, who was seven or eight years old, was allowed to go out and play on Boston Common, where she met some children who told her they had been picking dandelions in the country to sell to the grocer. She decided that she would earn some money for her mother, and she set off for the "country."

Becoming hopelessly lost, she wandered about for hours. Meanwhile, her mother had called the police and a search was on. Eventually, Nelly found her way home, but what she remembered most sadly about the adventure was that her new shoes, the shoes it had been so difficult to obtain, were ruined: "The soles and the uppers of her beautiful new shoes had so nearly parted company that they gaped and flapped as she moved" (EP, 112–113).

After she had a number of articles written, the soon-to-become Fanny Fern took little Ellen by the hand, and, putting the articles into a flat, shabby reticule, she walked the streets, climbing up and down stairs and confronting the rude looks and comments of men who were not accustomed to seeing a woman in the newspaper office. "Many a weary tramp I had," she wrote in later years; "much pride I put in my pocket, and few pennies" (NYL, March 28, 1868, July 8, 1871; EP, 111). She was subjected to an inquisition of personal questions, under which she writhed painfully, but finally, in June of 1851, the Reverend Thomas F. Norris of the Boston *Olive Branch* agreed to purchase one of her articles for fifty cents. He said she would be paid after the article appeared in print. "The Model Husband," a humorous article satirizing male shortcomings, was printed on June 28, 1851.[3] It struck the chord that was to characterize her writing throughout her career: it was written frankly, with no apologies, and from the perspective of a woman. Her first article was published anonymously, over the signature "Clara," and with this introductory paragraph by the editor:

As the following account of a "Model Husband" is from a lady in good position in society, we can but suppose her model husband is the true style of a husband, and what all good married men should be. In looking over our nearly forty years of married life, we find that our good wife has never exacted quite so much of us, but she merely waived her rights, I suppose. (OB, June 28, 1851)

Fern had to call many times for payment, and it was two weeks before she was paid for the article (EP, 111–112; JP, 52). She said that she would have been discouraged but for one thing: the article was copied the next day in a prominent Boston paper.[4] In those days of literary piracy, she received no remuneration for the republication of her article, and it was done without her consent or knowledge, but the fact that a prominent paper had reprinted it was encouraging to her; it meant that the article was good, or at least that there was interest in it.

It was around this time that Fern collected together some sample articles and sent them to her brother, N. P. Willis, who was editor of the *Home Journal* in New York, and a famous poet. In 1846 Willis had married his second wife, the wealthy Cornelia Grinnell. He was known for his willingness to help struggling female writers. Two of his protégés were Grace

Greenwood and Fanny Forrester, whose work he had printed in the *Home Journal* and whose reputations he had promoted. Fern asked his help in placing her articles. Willis refused:

> *Dear Sarah*
>
> I am suffering intensely from tooth-ache, in addition to my other ills, but I will try to answer your letter. New York is the most over-stocked market in the country, for writers, as we get a dozen applications a day from authors who merely wish to have the privilege of seeing themselves in print—writing for vanity only. Besides all the country flock & send here for fame etc. I have tried to find employment for dozens of starving writers, in vain. The Home Journal pays for no contributions, being made up of extract, & so with all the papers, & many magazines.
>
> Your writings show talent, but they are in a style that would only do in Boston. You overstrain the pathetic, and your humor runs into dreadful vulgarity sometimes. I am sorry that any editor knows that a sister of mine wrote some of these which you sent me. In one or two cases they trench very close on indecency. For God's sake, keep clear of that.
>
> The most "broken reed," I know of, to lean upon for a livelihood, is amateur literature. The only chance is with the religious papers, which pay for a certain easily acquired kind of writing. Your education might enable you to do something of this. But in other literature I see no chance for you—unless, indeed, you can get employed by the editors you write for already.
>
> I am sorry that I can write no more encouragingly, but I must speak honestly, & I would not keep you on a mistaken track.
>
> I write in great pain,—you will excuse my abruptness.
>
> *Your affectionate brother*[5]

Angry and hurt, Fanny Fern's first response to her brother's cruel letter was to throw into the fire the poem "To My Wild Sis" that he had written for her years before (EP, 115–116). Before it could be consumed, however, she snatched it from the fire, and it remains today among her papers, charred along the edges, in the envelope that contains Willis's letter. Written on the envelope in Fern's handwriting are the words: "From Nathaniel Parker Willis when I applied for literary employment at the Home Journal office[,] being at the time quite destitute. *My* house having been his child's refuge for months after the death of her mother."[6]

Why did Willis refuse to help his sister? Certainly he could have helped her enormously if he had wanted to. Even if his magazine did not pay contributors, had he been willing to print and/or mention her work in the journal, as he had done for Fanny Forrester and Grace Greenwood, for example, he could have helped to create a market for her writing.[7] One reason that Willis did not help Fern—and the one that he proffers—is that he did not like her writing. Her brusque, ironic style did not suit his more conventional, genteel taste; he preferred delicate, "feminine" writing by women. But this is not sufficient reason to prevent an older brother from helping a needy sister.

Most likely, there were two other and more important reasons why Willis was unwilling to help Fern. First, Willis may have been jealous of his sister's work. She was unquestionably the better writer. When her work was appearing anonymously, N. P. Willis was one of the authors who was thought to be Fanny Fern, and some critics commented that if he was, the works he wrote under the name Fanny Fern were much better than the things he usually wrote.[8] In *Ruth Hall*, Horace Gates comments regarding Ruth's brother Hyacinth that perhaps he wants to stop her from writing because "he wants to be the only genius in the family" (RH, 159).

Probably the main reason Willis did not want to help his sister was because he did not want to tarnish his social standing by becoming associated with her: her poverty and the Farrington scandal made her an embarrassment to him. He apparently wrote a second letter, which has not survived. Fern's granddaughter quotes Willis as saying that Sara had "disgraced the family," and should find a "less obtrusive occupation" (EP, 116). In *Ruth Hall* Ruth's brother Hyacinth writes such a letter to Mrs. Millett, whose family Fern based on her sister Lucy's family, the fashionable Bumsteads. Hyacinth urges Mrs. Millet to try to stop Ruth's writing (RH, 134). Since it was Lucy whom Willis communicated with on the matter, as he makes clear in an 1853 letter to their brother Richard,[9] one suspects that he had written to Lucy, as Hyacinth does to Mrs. Millet, expressing dismay at the idea of their sister writing. By suggesting that she write for the religious papers (which, as he well knew, paid very little), he hoped to keep her in obscurity in Boston. Fern's assessment of her brother's attitude is suggested in the comments of John Walter in *Ruth Hall*:

Mr. Hyacinth Ellet has always had one hobby, namely social position. For that he would sacrifice the dearest friend or nearest relative he had on earth. His sister was once in affluent circumstances, beloved and admired by all who knew her. Hyacinth, at that time, was very friendly, of course; her husband's wine and horses, and his name on change, were things which the extravagant Hyacinth knew how to appreciate.

Hall ('Floy's' husband) was a generous-hearted, impulsive fellow, too noble himself to see through the specious, flimsy veil which covered so corrupt a heart as Hyacinth's. Had he been less trusting, less generous to him, 'Floy' might not have been left so destitute at his death. When that event occurred, Hyacinth's regard for his sister evaporated in a lachrymose obituary notice of Hall in the Irving Magazine. The very day after his death, Hyacinth married Julia Grey, or rather married her fortune. His sister, after seeking in vain to get employment, driven to despair, at last resorted to her pen, and applied to Hyacinth, then the prosperous editor of the Irving Magazine, either to give her employment as a writer, or show her some way to obtain it. At that time, Hyacinth was constantly boasting of the helping hand he had extended to young writers in their extremity. . . . [H]e wrote her a cool, contemptuous, insulting letter, denying her all claim to talent (she had sent him some specimen articles), and advising her to seek some unobtrusive employment (*what* employment he did not trouble himself to name), and then ignored her existence; and this, too, when he was squandering money on "distressed" actresses, etc. (RH, 178–179)

After receiving Willis's letter, Fanny Fern severed relations with him entirely. She did not speak to him for years afterward. Two years later, however, she was in a position to avenge herself upon the man who did not want to see her articles in the New York papers. On June 18, 1853, she published "Apollo Hyacinth" in the New York *Musical World and Times*. It was a satirical sketch of her brother, which provided the basis for the portrait of Hyacinth Ellet in *Ruth Hall*. No longer would anyone think that Fanny Fern was N. P. Willis. When the article appeared, it created a sensation. As the *New York Herald* wrote later, "her sketch of Apollo Hyacinth, which was supposed to be a not too friendly portrait of her brother, the poet journalist, created a fervor greater than any of Macaulay's vivid pictures were capable of creating."[10] At the time that the sketch was published, the identity of Fanny Fern was still unknown to the public in general, although by this time it was known to her brother. New Yorkers had no difficulty recognizing N. P. Willis in the self-centered social climber and dandy portrayed in her sketch:

I am acquainted with Apollo Hyacinth. I have read his prose, and I have read his poetry; and I have cried over both. . . . Should you die to-morrow, Apollo would write a poetical obituary notice of you, which would raise the price of pocket-handkerchiefs; but should your widow call on him in the course of a month, to solicit his patronage to open a school, she would be told "he was out of town," and that it was "quite uncertain when he would return."

Apollo has a large circle of relatives; but his "keenness of perception, and deep love, of the beautiful" are so great, that none of them *exactly* meet his views. His "moral excellence," however, does not prevent his making the most of them. He has a way of dodging them adroitly, when they call for a reciprocation, either in a business or a social way. . . .

Apollo never says an uncivil thing—never; he prides himself on that, as well as on his perfect knowledge of human nature; therefore, his sins are all sins of omission. His tastes are very exquisite, and his nature peculiarly sensitive; consequently, he cannot bear trouble. He will tell you, in his elegant way, that trouble "annoys" him, that it "bores" him; in short, that it unfits him for life—for business; so, should you hear that a friend or relative of his, even a brother or a sister, was in distress, or persecuted in any manner, you could not do Apollo a greater injury (in his estimation) than to inform him of the fact. . . .

Apollo is keenly alive to the advantages of social position (not having always enjoyed them); and so, his Litany reads after this wise: From all questionable, unfashionable, unpresentable, and vulgar persons, Good Lord, deliver us! (MWT, June 18, 1853)

It is interesting to compare Fern's satire of her brother here with Lidian Emerson's satiric "Transcendental Bible," in which she satirizes her husband: "If you have refused all sympathy to the sorrowful, all pity and aid to the sick, all toleration to the infirm of character, if you have condemned the unintellectual and loathed such sinners as have discovered want of intellect by their sin, then are you a perfect specimen of Humanity."[11] It is significant that what Fern satirized in her brother was being preached by Emerson and had become acceptable as part of American individualism. In "Self Reliance," for example, Emerson wrote: "Friend, client, child, sickness, fear, want, charity, all knock at once at thy closet door and say,—'come out unto us.'" But he advised, "keep thy state; come not into their confusion."[12]

The characteristics that Fanny Fern criticized in her brother were commented on by others as well. Another woman who criticized the self-serving aspect of his character was Harriet Martineau, to whom he had presented himself before she left England several years before. In her autobiography, Martineau was very critical of him, particularly of his name-dropping:

While I was preparing for my travels, an acquaintance one day brought a buxom gentleman, whom he introduced to me under the name of Willis. There was something rather engaging in the round face, brisk air, and *enjouement* of the young man; but his conscious dandyism and unparalleled self-complacency spoiled the satisfaction, though they increased the inclination to laugh. Mr. N. P. Willis's plea for coming to see me was his gratification that I was going to America, and his real reason was presently apparent: a desire to increase his consequence in London society by giving apparent proof that he was on intimate terms with every eminent person in America. He placed himself in an attitude of infinite ease, and whipped his little bright boot with a little bright cane, while he ran over the names of all his distinguished countrymen and countrywomen, and declared he should send me letters to them all.

Martineau goes on to say that she was astonished to find when she reached America that Willis had represented her as being a close friend of his, whereas she had only met him once. She also found when she tried to use a few of his letters of introduction that the people to whom they were addressed said they did not know Willis at all.[13] Martineau's impression of Willis as a self-serving social climber and dandy confirms Fern's judgment of him and indicates why her portrait of him was so easily recognized and why so many people were glad to see it. Henry Beers, Willis's biographer, says that, except for Cooper, Willis was the most criticized of American writers, partly because of his literary affectations but also because of what his critics considered his "weaknesses of private character and life."[14]

When her brother refused to help her place her articles, Fanny Fern determined that she would do it herself. In *Ruth Hall*, Ruth's response to her brother's letter is suggestive of what Fern's response must have been: "I *can* do it, I *feel* it, I *will* do it" (RH, 116). An article in the *Saturday Evening Post* in late 1853, based on an interview with Fanny Fern, confirms that her attitude was similar to that portrayed in the novel. The article begins with a quotation from Fern:

"I bowed in despair, but as I thought of my children, I *sprang to my feet*, and vowed that they should have reason to be proud of their mother. . . ." As she said when speaking of the matter [her struggle], with the native fire of more than manly energy kindling in her eye, "I felt that I *would* succeed—and I DID succeed." She was determined to win her way alone, for her children's sake, and to show her independence of those who unnaturally turned away from her in her adversity. (SEP, November 5, 1853)

It was three weeks after "The Model Husband" appeared before the *Olive Branch* published another article of Fern's. On July 19, 1851, "Thoughts on Dress" appeared. Signed "Tabitha," it was a humorous article criticizing men's fashions. Two weeks later, on August 2, two more Tabitha articles appeared. Untitled, the first told the story of an unlucky woman: "I have been unlucky ever since I was born; I was unlucky to have been *born at all*, unluckier still to have been born *a woman*." The second article was entitled "The Model Wife," and unlike the "Model Husband" article, which portrayed what Fern regarded as the ideal husband, it was a sarcastic portrayal of what the ideal wife would *not* be like. The following week, August 9, a new Tabitha article appeared, "Deacons' Daughters and Ministers' Sons," which was a humorous description of some of the incidents from Fanny Fern's own life. On August 16 Tabitha published an article on the Women's Rights Convention in Akron, Ohio, which criticized women—not their desire for rights, but their ill-treatment of each other: "Where is the woman, who, when a sister is unjustly slandered, or spoken against, does not oftener circulate the story than seek to defend or excuse her?"

One explanation of why the Reverend Norris was the first to print Fanny Fern's work is suggested by an editorial he had written that spring. On May 3, 1851, he had written a short description of what he thought newspaper writing should be. His editorial was almost a description of the style that would become Fanny Fern's:

Say it in plain old English, use the most easy words and forms of speech in your power, do not use obsolete or out of the way terms, use no exordium, come directly at what you aim, and give the largest possible number of ideas in the fewest possible number of words. Use no circumlocution, and when you have done, stop; an article is never too short when the writer has comprehended his subject; any verbose additions only take from the force of an article. . . . We beg our contributors all to learn how to say much in a few words. . . . Persons gifted with a concise, forcible, yet graceful and easy style, never fail of success. Daguerrotype your subject, and leave your reader to study the picture. (OB, May 3, 1851)

One does not know if Fern saw this article and was guided by it in her early writing or if, as seems more likely, it was simply a case of Norris's being attracted to her writing because it fit his definition of good writing.

For the first few weeks Fern's articles were humorous, cynical, and ironic. Then she published two articles in a different vein. On August 23 the *Olive Branch* published an article in the "Youth's Department" by "Aunt Emma," which was probably by Fanny Fern, although it is the only article here mentioned that cannot be definitively identified. It was a serious article for children, telling children to be kind to their mothers, but it ended with a humorous story of the writer's brother setting squirrels loose in her room.[15] The following week the article in the "Youth's Department," published with no signature, was "Little May," which was rewritten as "Where is Little Nellie" for Fern's first children's book. It told the story of a little girl who had died, and was apparently based on Fern's daughter Mary. A similar description appears in *Ruth Hall* (RH, 36–37).

The next week, on September 6, 1851, the *Olive Branch* published the first article over the Fanny Fern signature, "The Little Sunbeam." This was published in the "Youth's Department," and told of a little girl who brought the author flowers which reminded her of "happier times." For the first few weeks that Fern used the Fanny Fern signature in the *Olive Branch,* she seems to have used it only for her nonsatirical pieces: on September 20 she published in the "Ladies Department" a piece about three little girls in a flower garden; on September 27 the "Youth's Department" featured "The Young Cook," which was based on an incident in Fern's life; on October 4 "The Ball Room and the Nursery" appeared in the "Ladies Department." In the next two weeks, Fern's pieces, the satirical Caudle article on Bloomers and "A Peep Behind a Curtain," were published over the signature "Olivia Branch." The next two weeks nonsatirical articles appeared over the signature of Fanny Fern. On November 22, however, she published two satirical articles, "An Interesting Husband" and the colloquial "Aunt Charity's Advice to Her Nephew," over the signature of Fanny Fern.

Fern asked the Reverend Norris if he could suggest any other outlets for her articles. He told her of a new weekly that was to begin publication early in November, the Boston *True Flag*. She called on the editor, and he bought several of her articles.[16] Her first article, a long story entitled "The Governess," appeared on November 29, and her articles appeared regularly after that in both periodicals. It was soon after this that she began using the signature Fanny Fern for all of her articles, which suggests that she had become aware of the value of the name. In *Ruth Hall* Mr. Tibbetts of *The Pilgrim* attempts to get Ruth to write for him under a different name, but Ruth refuses, telling him it would be foolish to throw away the reputation she has gained by adopting a different name (RH, 131).

Desperately needing money, Fern offered to write as many articles as the editors would purchase. The editors were willing to purchase several each week, but the editor of the *True Flag* asked her to use a different signature occasionally so that it might not seem as if he had too many articles from one contributor. Consequently, some of her early articles in the *True Flag* appeared over the signature "Olivia."[17] She also was able to sell an article to a monthly periodical for women, *The Mother's Assistant, Young Lady's Friend*. The article, "Maternal Influence," which was published in December 1851 under the name Mrs. S. P. Eldridge [sic], emphasizes the responsibility a mother has and reflects her own feelings at the time, as, weighed down with poverty and bitterness, she strove not to destroy the happiness of her children.[18]

Although Fern's articles in the *Olive Branch* and *True Flag* were sometimes tender and/or somber (and there were more of these early in her career, reflecting her life at the time), for the most part her articles were witty and sometimes outrageous. Reading through the periodicals of the time, it is easy to see why Fanny Fern quickly became so famous. Her articles stand out; they sparkle among the dust of convention and artificiality. Her brusque tone and candid air give the impression that she is saying exactly what she thinks—regardless. One amusing interchange that Fern started attracted a great deal of attention. On December 20, 1851, there appeared in the *Olive Branch* an article signed by Jack Fern, who described himself as a bachelor and said that he probably should get married. Two weeks later, a subscriber wrote in saying she liked the sound of Jack Fern and offered to marry him. She signed herself Eva. Fanny Fern replied:

I'm no more of a "Jack" than *you* are! I'm a poor, long-faced, draggle-skirted, afflicted, down-trodden female; crouching and whimpering my way through the world, like the rest of the sisters. Can't do anything I want to cause it "never'll do." Have to laugh when I feel sober, cry when I'm merry, and be as artificial as a waxdoll, for fear "somebody will say something." Before I was ten years old, I saw what it was all coming to, and the result has fully answered my juvenile expectations. If I had been allowed any *choice* in the matter, I should undoubtedly have been a "Jack." (OB, January 17, 1852)

The next week Eva wrote back saying that she wasn't disappointed: "I love you as Fanny far better than I could as Jack" (OB, January 24, 1852). Fanny Fern answered:

My dear Eva:—Bless your soul, I can't *love a woman!* I had as lief take a dose of physic! . . . Women *never make decent friends to their own sex;* they are always telling each other's secrets, and pulling each other's caps and characters to pieces. . . . Besides . . . you labor under the hallucination that I felt *merry* when I wrote all that nonsense! *Not a bit of it;* it's a way I have, when I can't find a razor handy to cut my throat! (OB, January 31, 1852)

This was a different kind of humor than the readers of the day were accustomed to in women writers. The humor of a Grace Greenwood, for example, was more "feminine": delicate and playful. Fern's was a black humor that was not supposed to exist in women.

The *Olive Branch* was a weekly newspaper, which, as the inscription under the masthead declared, was "Devoted to Christianity, Mutual Rights, Polite Literature, General Intelligence, Agriculture, and the Arts."[19] It was a modest newspaper with a small circulation. During the almost two years that Fanny Fern wrote for the paper, its circulation soared. The letters to the editor during that time indicate great enthusiasm for Fanny Fern's writings. A man wrote from Philadelphia: "I congratulate you upon your recent valuable addition to your corps of correspondents—of course I mean Fanny Fern" (OB, May 8, 1852). A letter from a woman in Salem suggests one reason for Fern's popularity: her frankness made people feel as though they knew her personally, while at the same time she apparently was saying what a lot of people—particularly women—were thinking but would not dare say. The woman wrote that she did not care about Fern's identity: "I know what you are to *me* in the weekly visits of the *Olive Branch*—a kind, loving sister, with a flashing smile that breaks through the drolleries, making me long to shake hands with you" (OB, August 28, 1852). Fern was criticized by conventional critics for being "vulgar," or "indelicate" (e.g., OB, April 19, 1852). But other critics defended her, as, for example, in this editorial from a Virginia paper:

It makes not one iota of difference whether Fanny Fern is a *he* or a *she*, it cannot be denied that she (we call her *she* in virtue of her *nom de plume*,) has written some of the most beautiful fragments and "prose poems" in her piquant off-hand style, to be found in the English language, to say nothing of the dashes of genuine humor which some of them contain. Crusty, crabbed and sour anatomical specimens of editors may say what they please, Fanny Fern is, and will continue a popular writer, for she writes from the *heart*, and it will reach the hearts of those who read. (OB, March 5, 1853)

The *True Flag*, which stated on the masthead only that it was published by Moulton, Elliott and Lincoln, of No. 22 School Street, insisted that its editor remain anonymous. However, his name became apparent later in the feud with the *Olive Branch*, which identified the editor by name as William U. Moulton. The masthead, which featured the title *True Flag* surrounded by leaves and tendrils, was emblazoned with the words *Peace* and *Prosperity* and contained a scroll listing its interests as "Literature, Art, Sciences."[20]

Fern had been paid fifty cents for her first *Olive Branch* article. Later, when she was writing for the *True Flag* as well, she was paid two dollars a column by both newspapers. She wrote two columns for the *Olive Branch* and one column for the *True Flag*. Thus, by the spring of 1852 her earnings were six dollars a week. In order to earn this, she had to write between five and ten articles a week.[21]

The question of the time was, Who *was* Fanny Fern? Almost immediately after first appearing in the *Olive Branch*, Fern's articles were being printed in newspapers all over the country and across the Atlantic. Readers wrote to the *Olive Branch* and the *True Flag*, as well as to other newspapers where her articles had appeared, demanding to know who Fanny Fern was. Norris and Moulton kept her identity a secret, and rumors were rampant. Some felt that she must be a man because of the forthrightness of her articles. One subscriber to the *Olive Branch* wrote a poem, which began:

> Oh mirth-provoking Fanny,
> Pray tell me if you will,
> What sort of a being you really are,
> And whether a Jack or a Jill.
>
> (OB, April 10, 1852)

The *Musical World and Times* wrote: "It was argued, by many, that the writer of such searching, forcible, and, withal, common-sense articles as sometimes came from the unknown pen, must be a man;—the public being unwilling to give femininity credit for the power and courage necessary for their production" (MWT, May 28, 1853).

Fanny Fern was dogged by the press in the way that celebrities are today. She wrote a sarcastic article criticizing the interfering reporter who hides in the newspaper office, follows the author, and then writes a story about her:

Won't it make your book sell? Won't the uninitiated ask, how *you,* J. Neptune Wingay, came to be so *intimately* acquainted with Delilah? and won't you pull up your dickey and elevate your left eyebrow, and look unutterable things?

Should any old-fashioned piece of chivalry question the gentlemanly propriety of your making said sketch without permission, just walk up within an inch of his Charles Grandison nose, and ask him if he supposes that you are going to stop to consider the proprieties of life, where *dollars and cents are concerned?* (OB, April 30, 1853)

There was speculation that Fanny Fern was one of the editors, or N. P. Willis (before her "Apollo Hyacinth" article appeared June 18, 1853), or Harriet Beecher Stowe, Mary A. Denison (who also wrote for the *Olive Branch*), or other well-known writers.[22] Fern's own children were sworn to silence on the subject. Still suffering from the effect of Farrington's slander, Fern had developed an aversion to personal publicity. Her daughter Ellen remembered sitting at the boardinghouse table and listening to the other boarders discuss the new literary light, whose identity they were speculating about, while her mother remained silently drinking her coffee. Fern's children were bursting to tell—but didn't (EP, 118).

The modern reader might wonder why Fern was so concerned about her anonymity. The unwanted publicity she had received from Farrington's slander caused her to be unusually averse to any kind of personal publicity. Her daughter says that she feared publicity so much that when she moved to New York she went by the name of Payson for a while to avoid anyone's knowing who she was.[23] One would also have to ask, if she was going to write under her own name, what name would she have chosen? She stopped using the name Farrington soon after she left her second husband, and she attempted to erase the episode from her life. Legally, she was no longer Sara Eldredge, and, although she used that name for her article in *The Mother's Assistant,* the name of her beloved husband was not perhaps the name to associate with her bitterly satirical articles, particularly since so many of them satirized marriage. Her maiden name was well known in Boston, but her family disapproved of her writing. The logical step was to take a pseudonym. Alliterative, flowery pseudonyms were popular for women writers at the time. They denoted the kind of writing that such writers usually produced: "feminine," delicate, genteel—the kind of women's writing that N. P. Willis liked.[24] When Fanny Fern adopted such a name, she did so partly as a spoof; certainly, for readers of her generation, to see her satirical, staccato prose over such a signature would have been humorous because of its incongruity.

If she was going to pick a plant, why the fern? Why not the honeysuckle, the ivy, or the violet? She tells us that when she was trying to think of a pseudonym, she was reminded of the sweet fern of which her mother was so fond:

I think the reason I selected the name "Fern" was because, when a child, and walking with my mother in the country, she always used to pluck a leaf of it, to place in her bosom, for its sweet odor; and that gloomy morning, when I almost despaired of earning bread for my children, I had been thinking of her, and wishing she were living, that I might lay my head upon her bosom and tell her all my sorrows. (NSB, 7–8)

The fern that her mother liked because of its fragrance was the sweet fern, a low shrub that grows in fields all over New England (EP, 115). A sturdy bush, and particularly tenacious, the sweet fern will grow in sandy soil and windswept locations where more delicate plants cannot survive. It does not have the delicacy of the true fern, with its feathery fronds. Eventually, the name came to be associated with both kinds of fern, but it is significant that Fern was thinking of this sturdy shrub rather than of the delicate feather fern when she conceived of the pseudonym that for the nineteenth century came to epitomize strong-mindedness in women (EP, 115).

Why did she choose the first name Fanny? Her main reason, of course, was to achieve the alliteration. Also, she probably associated the name with Fanny Osgood, the writer she had known whose death she had mourned the year before the name Fanny Fern was born. In 1853, before leaving Boston, she visited Fanny Osgood's grave and wrote a eulogy to her that ironically in later years might have been addressed to Fanny Fern:

Oh God! to be so soon forgotten by all the world! How can even *earth* look so glad, when such a warm, passionate heart lies cold and pulseless! Poor, gifted, forgotten Fanny! She "still lives" in my heart. (MWT, June 4, 1853)[25]

When Fanny Fern first adopted her name, it was as a pseudonym, but, as time passed, she gradually adopted it as her own name. In 1856 she went to court and successfully prevented another author from using the name Fanny Fern, thus establishing once and for all that she had the exclusive right to the name.[26] She was known as Fanny to her friends. Her third husband called her Fanny, and she signed her letters Fanny or Fanny Fern. She only used the name Sara Eldredge and later Sara Parton to sign legal documents. It was as if she had made an identity switch. She was no longer Sara Willis Eldredge Farrington, the domestic woman; she was Fanny Fern, the professional woman. Fern always said that if she had any talent for writing, it was inherited from her mother rather than her father (NSB, 10–13). Symbolically, then, in adopting the name Fern, which she associates with her mother, she had exchanged the male patronym—her father's or her husband's name— for the matrilineal Fern.

7

Columnist and Author

[A] literary life is a tread-mill grind; and it is always that to a married literary woman, even if she be successful; because, to the ordinary labor and cares of all other wives and mothers, she superadds that of her profession. . . . [But if you] pilot your steps safely, all the better for you; for sweet is the bread of independence.

NYL, July 8, 1871

IN THE LATE SUMMER OF 1852, Fanny Fern received in care of the *Olive Branch* a letter from Oliver Dyer, publisher of the New York *Musical World and Times*, asking if the anonymous Fanny Fern would agree to write exclusively for his paper at double her combined earnings from the two Boston papers. Ironically, the editor of his paper was Fern's brother Richard Willis, who had returned from Germany and was living in New York, but who, like the rest of the country, did not know the identity of Fanny Fern. Fern agreed to Dyer's offer, but the Boston editors, who had stolidly refused to raise her salary previously, were so distressed at the thought of losing their star contributor that Dyer released her from the exclusivity of their agreement, and she continued to write for the *Olive Branch* and *True Flag* as well—but with a raise in salary. By the end of 1852 she was earning four dollars a column for two columns in the *Olive Branch* and five dollars for one column in the *True Flag*. This meant thirteen dollars a week, in addition to what she would be paid by Dyer.[1] According to her granddaughter, it was at this point that she was able to obtain better lodgings and bring her daughter Grace home from the Eldredges (EP, 118).

The New York *Musical World and Times*, and soon thereafter the *True Flag*, established a column by Fanny Fern in the fall of 1852. Thus Fern became the first woman newspaper columnist in the United States. Other women—among them, Lydia Maria Child, Jane Cannon Swisshelm, and Margaret Fuller—had been correspondents or editors, but Fern was the first to be a columnist in the twentieth-century sense of the word: a professional journalist paid a salary to write a regular column expressing the author's personal opinions on social and political issues. On September 25, 1852, the

Musical World carried a front-page announcement that Fanny Fern would write exclusively for that paper. Her first column appeared on October 9 under the heading "Fanny Fern's Column." She continued to write a regular column in the *Musical World* for the next year, which suggests that she had signed a contract to write for one year, as Ruth Hall did (RH, 146). Her last original column in the *Musical World* appeared on November 19, 1853.

The *True Flag* began to feature "Fanny Fern's Department" on November 6, 1852, but apparently without the permission of Fanny Fern. For the next few weeks, although the *True Flag* copied Fern's articles from other sources, there were no new Fern articles. Then, on December 11, the *True Flag* announced that Fanny Fern would write a regular column, which indicates that this was when the editor had agreed to raise her salary and the *Musical World* released her from the exclusivity of the agreement. The *Olive Branch* and the *True Flag* argued with each other over who should get the credit for introducing Fern to the public. The *True Flag*, in announcing its new agreement with Fern, wrote:

> Our Fanny is now generally acknowledged to be the most original, piquant, and witty female writer of the day. She sails a rather saucy craft, it is true; she avoids all the currents of commonplace, and at the same time spurns the rocks of absurdity and the quicksands of stupidity, which prove the perdition of all her imitators. . . . We have no hesitation in saying, that in no newspaper of the age will be found anything equal to or approaching "Fanny Fern's Department" in the *True Flag*. She will make it up just as she pleases; and if we don't have a few sharp comments, stinging bits of satire, and witty hits on and at the foibles of the day, each week, we will never prophecy again.

The *Olive Branch* took umbrage at the *True Flag*'s proprietary air, and replied on the same day:

> The *Flag* calls this lady "Our Fanny." Well, we will not complain, so long as Fanny furnishes our paper with the amount of copy we desire. Fanny was first introduced to the great reading public in our columns; and will furnish our readers weekly with a treat from her pen, both on its inside and outside pages. We are glad our neighbors of the *True Flag* have secured contributions from Fanny's pen, but we will assure the readers of the *Olive Branch*, that she is engaged to devote her pen principally to her favorite, the *Olive Branch*.

As Fanny Fern's fortunes improved, her brother, N. P. Willis, found his career on the decline. His health had deteriorated, and for some time he had left the editorial office of the *Home Journal* under the care of an assistant editor. In 1851, 1852, and most of 1853, while Fanny Fern's career was rising, James Parton was in charge of the office. Parton was a young writer who had first claimed Willis's attention by a well-written article on *Jane Eyre*. Parton tells of how he had dropped off the article at Willis's Manhattan house and was delighted to find it printed in the *Home Journal* several weeks later.[2] Willis encouraged him to write pieces from time to time and eventually offered him a job as assistant editor, the post that had been held by Edgar Allen Poe when Willis edited the *Evening Mirror* and later was held by Thomas Bailey Aldrich at the *Home Journal*.

Willis was seldom in the office in 1852. In March of that year, his health having become seriously impaired, he had left on an extended journey to the south, to Bermuda and New Orleans.[3] Parton, who was left in charge of editorial work at the *Home Journal*, had begun to copy Fanny Fern's articles into his paper, as so many other editors were doing. He also published comments praising her writing, and in 1853 published a favorable review of her book.[4] Willis returned from his southern trip in the summer of 1852. His health had not improved, however, and he joined his family in the country, where he began building his new house, Idlewild, on the fifty acres of land on the Hudson that he had purchased two years before. It was not until the late summer or fall of 1853 that he was back in Manhattan at the *Home Journal* office. When Willis returned and learned that Parton had been printing his sister's articles, he demanded that Parton give no more publicity to Fern's work. Parton, who admired Fern's writing and had not known at first that she was Willis's sister, refused to stop printing the articles. Willis became irate, and Parton found himself "assailed with such scarifying language" that he resigned on the spot (JP, 54; EP, 121).[5] In *Ruth Hall* Fern portrays Parton as Horace Gates, who similarly is forbidden to print or to give any publicity to Hyacinth's sister's work (RH, 158–159).

Meanwhile, in Boston, Fanny Fern had been forced to make important decisions regarding her children. Her father-in-law, Hezekiah Eldridge, died on March 14, 1853. He had written in his will that his estate was to go to his wife and to his two granddaughters, *provided* they were brought up by their grandmother:

> I direct her to take and maintain and educate our two grandchildren, the two daughters of Charles H. Eldredge, deceased, provided their mother and father-in-law will let her have them to bring up and educate in that way she thinks best for the children but if their parents will not consent to give them up to their grandmother to be supported and educated as above stated then she is at liberty to do for the children what she pleases to do for them.[6]

Their grandmother apparently chose to do nothing for them. When she died four years later, she left the bulk of her estate to charity.[7] Hezekiah Eldredge's will did provide for the possibility that their mother would refuse to relinquish the children to their grandmother. In that case, the will left for each of them a sum of five thousand dollars, to be invested and to go to them *only after they were married.* If they were unmarried, the income from the sum could be used for their support after they were twenty-one, but the principal was to go to charity after their deaths. If they married before they were twenty-one, they were to receive one thousand dollars of the principal and the remainder when they reached twenty-one.[8]

The effect of this will was to make certain that the Eldredges' daughter-in-law would receive nothing and also to make certain that the children would receive nothing that their mother would have access to. Unless they were handed over to their grandmother, they were not to receive their inheritance until they married—when, Eldredge believed, their husbands would have legal jurisdiction over their money. Had Fanny Fern remained in the difficult financial situation that she was in when this will was written (July 16, 1851), it would have been difficult for her not to relinquish the children entirely, since to refuse to do so would have been to sentence her children to a life of poverty as opposed to a comfortable life and the opportunity for a good education. Eldredge probably thought when he wrote the will that he had his daughter-in-law over the proverbial barrel. Knowing of this will also gives us a better understanding of the impetus that drove Fanny Fern to earn her economic independence; not to do so would have meant losing her children. It is significant that her first article was published at around the time the will was drawn up.

One wonders what motivated the Eldredges to act so cruelly. Since the will is dated mid-1851, I suspect that, considering their strict and pious stance, the Eldredges were infuriated by their daughter-in-law's behavior with respect to Farrington. In *Ruth Hall* Fern portrays Ruth's in-laws as pious hypocrites, very concerned about what other people think and shocked by anything unconventional, such as Ruth's going for a walk in the meadows without her bonnet on, or having a statue of a nude Venus in her home (RH, 35, 38–39). Fern's own family was scandalized when she left her second husband, and they did not support her against the scandalous stories that Farrington circulated. The Eldredges reacted even more strongly: they disinherited her—and her children, too, as long as they remained under her influence. Perhaps the Eldredges believed Farrington's stories; in the will he is acknowledged as the children's "father-in-law" or "parent," although Fern had left him seven months before and he was no longer living in Boston. Whether they actually believed her guilty of promiscuous adultery, as his stories implied, they apparently judged her harshly for leaving her husband and for "getting herself talked about." They did not want her to remain as the guardian of their grandchildren, and they did not want her to receive *anything* from them.

At around the time this will was written Fern sent Grace to live with the Eldredges. When she had begun to earn enough money to keep the two children, she brought Grace home. After Hezekiah Eldredge died, however, Fern sent Grace back to her grandmother, apparently in an attempt to satisfy the conditions of the will and new conditions exacted by Mary Eldredge.

In early 1853, a month or two before Hezekiah Eldredge died, Fern received in care of the *True Flag* a letter from James Cephas Derby of the publishing firm of Derby and Miller in Auburn, New York, a letter which ultimately was to negate the effect of Eldredge's will. Derby was interested in publishing a collection of Fern's newspaper articles. He offered her the sum of one thousand dollars *or* ten cents on each book sold.[9] Fern consulted with Oliver Dyer, and he confirmed her own feelings that it would be better to take the percentage, which, considering the success of the book, turned out to be the right decision. Derby says that Dyer also recommended that Fern, who had received offers from other publishers, have Derby and Miller publish the book because he thought they would do the best job of advertising it.[10] Fern agreed to write the book, and on February 8, 1853, she wrote to Derby and Miller reluctantly telling them her real name:

Gentlemen:

"Fern Leaves from Fanny's Portfolio" is the title of my book. My own name is—(I had much rather be shot than tell! but if I must I must,)
Sara P. Farrington
[I]n revealing it, I trust to your gentlemanly *Honor to keep it strictly secret.* As to "original" matter my engagements are such that it is quite impossible for me to furnish other than my weekly contributions to the different papers for which I am writing (revised of course expressly for your book). I shall send you soon mss. enough for one half or two thirds of the book, pages to be of uniform size, from which you can estimate how much more is needed. In writing to me please address me as heretofore simply by my nom de plume. What do you think of serving my book up in time for Boston & N.Y.'s Trade Sale?—

Yours respectfully,
Fanny Fern[11]

This letter is important for a number of reasons. First of all, Fern's extreme reluctance to reveal her real name, which at this time was still legally Farrington, helps to explain why she chose to write under a pseudonym; the letter suggests that it is the particular name that it is offensive to her to have to tell. Considering how much scandal was attached to the name, and also considering how unhappy she had been since she had borne that name, it is not surprising that she did not want to be known by it. Also important is the very businesslike tone and manner in which Fern apparently conducted her affairs. She does not hesitate to tell the publishers that she cannot provide original matter for them, and she ends the letter with the suggestion that the book be ready in time for the trade sales.

On February 10, 1853, Fern signed a contract with Derby and Miller,[12] and *Fern Leaves from Fanny's Portfolio* was published on June 1, 1853. Its sale was tremendous. Derby and Miller used the newest promotional techniques, advertising the book in newspapers throughout the country. Moreover, since Fanny Fern's articles had been appearing in newspapers all over the country and in England for the past two years, her name was already a household word before the book was even published. In a series of advertisements in October 1853, the publishers claimed that the sales, 46,000 copies in four months, were greater than for any other American book—including *Uncle Tom's Cabin*—at the corresponding time in its publishing history.[13] In 1853 *Fern Leaves* sold 70,000 copies in the United States and 29,000 in England, making it one of the first best-sellers in the country.[14]

Although some reviewers expressed reservations about Fern's "unfeminine" and "vulgar" language, and warned about her "bold masculine expressions,"[15] most of the reviews of *Fern Leaves* were enthusiastic. Her "pictures of love, of beauty, and of suffering" were said to be "equal to the best sketches of Dickens."[16] Her satire was "keen as a razor."[17] James Parton in the *Home Journal* summed up the most significant aspect of her writing—her originality: "Fanny Fern is a voice, not an echo."[18]

In June 1853, after *Fern Leaves* was published and the success of the book was evident, Fanny Fern took the advice James Parton had given her, and traveled to New York. Oliver Dyer introduced her to Parton, and he became her escort as she explored New York (JP, 54–55). Parton tells us that one of the first things she did in New York was to visit the Castle Garden to hear Henriette Sontag in the opera "La Sonnambula" (JP, 55).[19] Beginning with "A Fern Reverie" (later changed to "A Gotham Reverie"), published in the *Olive Branch* on June 18, her articles were written from New York, which indicates that she arrived in New York in early June. "A Fern Reverie" gives us her first impression of New York:

Babel, what a place!—what a dust—what a racket—what a whiz-buzz! What a throng of human beings. "Jew and Gentile, bond and free"; every nation the sun ever shone upon, here represented. What pampered luxury—what squalid misery, on the same *pavé*. (OB, June 18, 1853)

Fern's publisher, J. C. Derby, invited her to visit him at his home in Pennsylvania. Fern responded with the following letter, which is undated but was apparently written in early June soon after she arrived in New York:

Dear Sir:—Your & Mrs. Derby's kind and cordial invitation quite touched my heart (as you know me only through pen and ink). I wonder if you *know* how pleasant it is, this personal interest my publishers take in me? *I like it;* and I like *you;* still I can't come, and I'll tell you why. When I first astonished my brother [Richard Willis] with my sudden appearance in New York, he got up a fraternal frown, because I didn't let him know I

was coming, and because (afterward) I would not come *directly to his
house* with my baby and traps. . . .

I took supper with him at Thomson's on Broadway the other night, and
I know from what he said he is a little *vexed* with me for my obstinacy—.
Well—you see—in such a posture of affairs, if I come to visit *you,
shouldn't I catch it?* So you must come to New York for all I see and call
on me—Won't you?—and meantime believe how much I thank you for
an invitation which it would give me so much *real pleasure* to accept.

I lost my senses at Castle Garden the other night, what with the moon-
light and the music and the glorious expanse of sky—Oh, *wasn't* I a
happy Fanny? I was *too* happy—I didn't know what to do with myself, so
when I got home I *cried!* and then I felt better! I shan't see any thing I like
so well in N.Y., I'm sure of it, though I've many things to see yet—Greenwood Cemetery for one—I shall go there this week. My brother was
charmed because I was so delighted with a little unpretending church
opposite his house—half hidden by ivy and roses—he procured the key
and went in with me and promised to play me a chant on the organ if I
would come there to service some Sunday. I am going to write an article
about it. It is a lovely little place—*way up* near the Crystal Palace. . . .

Just look in the *Musical World and Times* this week, will you, and see
what Dyer has written. Isn't he *keen?* Mr. Miller will tell you about him;
he says more original things in half an hour than I could get off in a year,
and then he's *good* and sincere and *independent* and *dare say* what *he
thinks*—I like *that*; I hate pussy cats![20]

As this letter indicates, Fern had a cordial relationship with her younger
brother Richard Storrs Willis. Willis, who later became known as the composer of the Christmas carol "It Came Upon a Midnight Clear," had been
studying music in Germany for six years. At the time of Fern's struggle, he
had just returned to New York, where he earned a meager living as a musician and music teacher.[21] He became editor of the *Musical World*, and on
September 30, 1852, he married the well-to-do Jessie Cairns, one of his
music pupils. Although Fern did not speak to her brother N. P. Willis, she
held no grudge against Richard. When Oliver Dyer had discovered that
Fanny Fern was his sister, Richard Willis supported the idea of giving her a
forum for her articles, and he wrote favorable comments on her work in the
Musical World and Times. Richard's absence had prevented him from
knowing of her poverty, and, upon his return as an impoverished musician,
he would not have been in a position to help her. She had not applied to him
for help, and he apparently only learned of her poverty after she was no
longer destitute. On May 28, 1853, the *Musical World* printed a long and
very favorable review of *Fern Leaves,* which was probably written by Richard Willis, in which he indicates that he had only recently learned about her
difficulties:

It may be said, without exaggeration, that the success of Fanny Fern has been marvelous; and it has all come from the intrinsic merit of her writings. She has had no adventitious helps. No influence in high places has been exerted in her favor. She has not had the aid of any party, clique, or sect. She has not ridden into popularity upon any hobby. She was evidently unused to writing, when her first articles appeared. She was unknown. She was (as we have since learned) poor and friendless; having been reduced, by unforeseen and overwhelming misfortunes, from affluence to penury. She often wrote her articles as the grey dawn was breaking, after a night's weary watch by the sick couch of those dependent upon her; their only support being the meager pittance received for her early productions. (MWT, May 28, 1853)

After the publication of this review, Richard Willis received a letter from his brother N. P. Willis, expressing dismay that Richard had publicly admitted their sister's poverty. N. P. Willis also denied that she had been poor:

(My brother!) *we* were *not* honored by your publishing the account of her excessive poverty & starving babes, & night watchings, and desertion by friends etc.—*no word of which* (Lucy says) *was in the least true. I,* for one, contributed when money was blood-drops, & when creditors (as now) were screwing "sops" out of my vitals. *You* help'd her. *Lucy* took care that her children never suffer'd. Father did something—did he not? Now, do not let us be thus *gammon'd* out of our respectability and relations, by false pictures authenticated by being given to the world under our own hand & seal.[22]

N. P. Willis was being somewhat disingenuous when he claimed that the family had helped Fern sufficiently, but he apparently did not wish to be criticized for allowing his sister to remain in poverty while he lived comfortably in his new mansion. Richard may have told Fern of N. P. Willis's denial, which would have been an additional impetus to the writing of the "Apollo Hyacinth" article, which appeared two weeks after Willis wrote this letter. She also satirized N. P. Willis's embarrassment in her portrayal of Hyacinth Ellet's discomfort in *Ruth Hall* when a visitor to his estate asks why he did not help his sister (RH, 176–178). In the novel, also, John Millet comments: "It frets Hyacinth to a frenzy to have her [Ruth's] poverty alluded to. He told me that he had taken the most incredible pains to conciliate editors whom he despised, merely to prevent any allusion to it in their columns" (RH, 201).

Fern apparently had left Boston not only because Parton told her she would find more matter for her pen in New York but also because she had been so unhappy in Boston. In *Ruth Hall* Ruth determines to "leave forever a city fraught with such painful associations" (RH, 181). Fern also felt constricted in Boston. She had been persecuted there for her unconventional behavior in leaving her husband and because of his slanderous stories about her. She welcomed the anonymity and less puritanical judgment of New York. Moreover, Moulton of the *True Flag*, angry at having to pay her more money under the threat that she would no longer write for him, apparently threatened to injure her in some way, which threat he carried out in his newspaper columns and in the anonymous *Life and Beauties of Fanny Fern*. Attacking her personally, where, as a nineteenth-century woman she was most vulnerable, Moulton attempted to injure her reputation, portraying her as a flamboyant widow of questionable virtue who lived luxuriously, gaily entertaining men (but no ladies) in her private apartments.[23] In *Ruth Hall*, Mr. Tibbetts, the character who is based on Moulton, threatens to get revenge on Ruth if she discontinues writing for him (RH, 157).

Fern felt more of an allegiance to the elderly Reverend Norris of the *Olive Branch*, who had been the first to publish her work, and she continued to write for him longer than for the *True Flag*. Norris died in December 1853, however. His son, who took over the paper, was critical of Fern after the publication of *Ruth Hall*, but, as is clear from *Ruth Hall*, although Fern was exploited by both papers, it was Moulton of the *True Flag* who was the recipient of her most scathing satire. Fern's last article for the *Olive Branch*, written from New York, contained a letter to Boston, which sums up her criticism of its provinciality:

My Dear Old Boston: You know that you are bigoted, and opinionated, and narrow-minded (and like all who revolve in a two-pint measure), given to meddling with what is lawfully none of your business. (OB, June 25, 1853)

The *Olive Branch*, hopeful that she would continue to write for it, published the following editorial on July 30, 1853:

[Fanny Fern], on receiving her first check for $1500, as her share of profits on the sale of the last 15,000 copies of her book, escaped from our Puritan city to New York, and her pen is nearly idle. We see that a flash pictorial advertises her as being engaged as a regular contributor. This is not a fact. She states to us that at present she does not care to write much for the press, but will write a letter for us and the *Musical World*. For the latter she has written a few articles, but generally not of such a character as would suit the great public for which our paper is intended.(OB, July 30, 1853)

Since most of the readers of the *Olive Branch* were not familiar with the New York *Musical World and Times*, the editor of the *Olive Branch* was safe in implying that Fern was not writing for it regularly and that, in any case, her articles there would not be suitable for the *Olive Branch*. The fact was that she was writing a regular column for the *Musical World*, and that column was being pirated by newspapers everywhere in the country, including the *Olive Branch*. Fern's last original article in the *True Flag* appeared on April 23, 1853. She continued to write for the *Olive Branch* for two more months, her last original article appearing on June 25.

Not only were Fanny Fern's articles pirated by newspapers all over the country and in Great Britain, but her style was imitated everywhere. In October 1852, Fern responded to "Harry Honeysuckle," who was one of her male imitators:

Did you know, my dear "Honeysuckle," that plants sometimes *choke* each other? You'll die of the *Fern-strangle* one of these days, if you don't leave off shooting round a corner at my "model" factory! Don't you suppose *every body else* sees them? and does any but the genuine coin ever get counterfeited, hey? Don't I appreciate the unintentional compliment? "Steal my thunder?" They can't do it, Harry. It has *"my mark"* on it. Every body sees the theft. (OB, October 16, 1852)

In addition to the multitude of Fanny Fern imitators both male and female, a number of fraudulent articles were published under the name Fanny Fern. In April 1853, Fern wrote in the *True Flag* regarding specific articles that had been circulating under her name: "Never wrote one line of the above-named articles, which are traveling round the country, with a host of others like them. The way that illegitimate Ferns are smuggled into my well-regulated family, while my own mental children are kidnapped and baptized by aliens, is very curious to witness" (TF, April 23, 1853).[24] In an article called "Borrowed Light" she satirized the way in which lesser writers copied her work:

Select some popular writer; read over his or her articles carefully; note their peculiarities and fine points, and then copy your model just as closely as possible. Borrow whole sentences, if you like. . . . In choosing your signature, bear in mind that nothing goes down, now-a-days, but *alliteration*. For instance, Delia Daisy, Fanny Foxglove, Harriet Honeysuckle, Lily Laburnum, Paulena Poppy, Minnie Mignonette, Julia Jonquil, Seraphina Sunflower, etc. (TF, April 9, 1853)

During the summer of 1853, Fern and her daughter Ellen lived in a boardinghouse in Manhattan while Fern wrote for the *Musical World*. A look at the articles she wrote then gives us an idea of some of the sites she visited in New York. One of her first stops was the Plymouth Church in Brooklyn, to hear the preaching of Henry Ward Beecher, whom she had known as a young girl at his sister's school in Hartford. She noted that the church was full, and asked herself why so many people came to hear him. She concluded that it was because they could see that his *"heart* is in his work":

> The preacher is remarkable for fertility of imagination, for rare felicity of expression, for his keen perception of the complicated and mysterious workings of the human heart, and for the uncompromising boldness with which he utters his convictions. His earnestness of manner, vehemence of gesture and rapidity of utterance, are, at times electrifying. (MWT, July 2, 1853)[25]

The following week she wrote about boardinghouses (MWT, July 9, 1853). Always interested in the people around her, Fern next wrote an article called "Our Street," which described the people she saw on her street every day (MWT, July 16, 1853). On July 23 she described the opening of the Crystal Palace:

> Such a crowd, such a rush, such confusion I never expect to see again. Equestrians and pedestrians; omnibuses and carriages; soldiers, civilians and *uncivil*-ians; carts and curricles; city exquisites and country non-descripts. . . .
> —Well; it's eleven o'clock, and after several abortive attempts we succeeded in arresting an omnibus, labelled "for the Hippodrome and Crystal Palace." Away we go—dashing through the crowd, regardless of limbs, vehicular or human.
> Broadway is lined, on either side, with a dense throng of questionable looking expectants, waiting "to see the procession." . . . As the eye swept through this magnificent thoroughfare, the rushing vehicles, the swaying, motley multitudes, the gaily dressed ladies, the waving flags and banners which floated over the more public and prominent edifices, presented an ever varying panorama, that was far from being the least attractive and impressive feature of the day. I have often thought when the people come out "to see a sight," that they themselves are far more imposing than what they came to see.
> On entering the Palace, we (my companion and I) found that all the most eligible seats were already occupied, and that what were left were reserved for some man of straw and his wife. . . . We finally resolved on action, seized a couple of boxes of workman's tools, emptied the contents on the floor and converted the boxes into comfortable seats in the most commanding position in the eastern gallery. . . .
> Above us was the lofty stained dome, a most imposing feature;—flags of all nations waved from the latticed balconies; beneath, the jewelled arms of ladies fair gleamed and flashed in the sunlight. . . .
> An hour has passed; our eyes are weary with gazing; still, no President. . . . Another hour has passed. . . . Here he comes, God bless him! You

won't see a sight like that out of America. The representative of a mighty nation—one of the mightiest on earth—receiving the homage of expectant thousands, standing without "star" or "order," or insignia of power other than that with which the Almighty has stamped him. No "life guards," no hedging him in from the people. It is sublime! (MWT, July 23, 1853)[26]

In October an article in the *Home Journal* signed "Silvia" commented that if Fanny Fern had been recognized at the Crystal Palace, she "would have drawn the crowds to her like a magnet"; there would have been more interest in her than in the president or all of the English lords and ladies, said the author.[27]

Fern's next letter to Derby, dated by internal evidence as having been written in late June of 1853, indicates that she was hoping to return to Boston soon to retrieve her daughter Grace:

My dear Sir:

Fanny *does* hope to come, before she dies, to see her kind friends Mr. and Mrs. Derby, but is not able to stay at present, when she has a dear little girl now in the neighborhood of Boston, her eldest child, who is situated in this way. I told you some time since that Mr. Eldredge's parents divided the property between my two little girls: the old gentleman died two months since, making it a condition of them receiving the property that the eldest was still to remain with his wife till her death. The old lady is over eighty and her physicians say cannot live many months. When she dies my child comes to me. That event may happen at any moment, as the old lady is very feeble—in which case I must go directly over to Boston to claim my child, and see that matters are properly arranged.

It was hard work parting from her, for her heart is knit to mine more strongly than children's are ordinarily—by sympathy with me in trial and sorrow. I write her often, for it is very dull for her there. I shall feel unsettled till I get her with me, and fear to move about much at present for that reason. . . .

And now about business—I am so glad my book has done so well. I feel now as though I could lie down to sleep without feeling that it was a waste of time—on waking up in the night thinking over an article for the next morning at the bidding of some Editor. I think you are right about the profitableness of book-writing over this newspaper dribbling—I have been pondering the same thing for some time.[28]

In this letter Fern describes the situation differently than that stated in Hezekiah Eldredge's will. His will had left the matter ultimately to Mary Eldredge, however, and apparently she had told Fern that she would leave the estate to the two girls, provided that Grace remained with her until her

death. Soon after writing the above letter, however, Fern returned to Boston
and brought Grace back to New York. Mary Eldredge was not near death,
as her physicians had predicted, and in fact did not die until October 13,
1857.[29] Fern Leaves had sold so well that Fern must have felt she was safe in
taking the gamble that she could make enough money from her writing so
that she could disregard the Eldredges' money for her children. Fern's jubi-
lation at being able to provide for her children without being dependent on
anyone is reflected in Ruth Hall. After Ruth has retrieved Katy from her
unkind grandmother, she looks at her sleeping children and thinks, "How
sweet to have it in her power to hedge them in with comforts" (RH, 197).
Mary Eldredge rewrote her will on March 17, 1855, after the publication of
Ruth Hall. If she had intended to leave anything to her grandchildren, the
publication of the novel must have changed her mind. At the same time, the
Eldredges' attempt to manipulate Fern by withholding money from her children must have helped to determine Fern's attitude toward them in the
shaping of Ruth Hall.

On August 13, 1853, the Musical World carried instead of a column by
Fanny Fern a letter written by her, which indicated that she was out of
town, apparently at the country estate of J. C. Derby and his family. Since
she now had both of her children with her, she must have returned to New
York with Grace in late July. She wrote from Derby's estate:

Here I am, safe in M., at the hospitable mansion of our big-hearted
friend.—I can't possibly write any thing for you in time for this week's
paper. The children are wearied out, and there's nothing left of me but a
"note of admiration!" Why didn't you tell me about that glorious Hudson? I sat upon deck till one o'clock in the morning, straining my eyes, in
the dim starlight, to catch the outline of some bold bluff, or watching the
boats as they passed us with their many colored lights. Such dear little
nests of houses as are nestled in among the shrubbery! . . . I didn't go to
bed, but sat perched on a table at my stateroom window, from one
o'clock till daylight; consequently, I looked rather black under the eyes, in
the morning.

To-day we have had a hot, dusty ride;—got here late in the afternoon.
J. was alive all over—full of fun—full of kindness, and as proud and
happy as if he were escorting Queen Victoria.—This Pennsylvania is a
great State.

I have a pleasant and commodious suite of rooms, in which I am told to
"do anything I like!" J. crams the children, till their buttons follow Peg-
gotty's, and acts as though he were "walking on thrones"—as your immortal Smith hath it. His wife is a most excellent and admirable woman,
his children smart and lovely—and I'm growing young every minute, to
see poor dark human nature so redeemed. Thank God that I ever saw him
and his. . . .

Our "Iron Horse" crushed the life from out a sweet young child, coming on;—it was so painful a sight to witness. He was only twelve years old—killed instantaneously. . . . I much fear that Judge Lynch will yet summon these "accidental" homocides to a fearful and bloody settlement unless something be done to protect the community. . . . I hardly know what I'm writing. I can scarcely keep my eyes open. In fact, I'm used up with fatigue and kindness. I can't fill the sheet, I'm *so* tired; but I know you'd be disappointed if I didn't write a line. Consider all written, and I will try to get off an article for you in time for next week.

—The children send their love, and so does J. He is up here, setting the dog, the cat and the children all by the ears. (MWT, August 13, 1853)

This letter gives us a sense of the person who was Fanny Fern. We see the accumulation of fatigue that dealing with her personal and business affairs must have wrought; the excitement she felt at new experiences; and the great relief she felt now that her financial and personal difficulties seemed to have been resolved. Yet she was always aware of the tragedies of life, and her letter contains deep regret at the death of the young boy in the railroad accident.

She also includes a postscript, which describes an incident that amused her and tells us something about the methods of her enterprising publisher:

In traveling, one meets with funny things. A boy came into the car with an armful of *Fern Leaves* for sale, thrust a copy into my hand and assured me it was *"the* book of the season—forty thousand already sold!—presses running night and day, but the demand not supplied," etc., etc.

Who wrote it" I asked.

"Fanny Fern," replied the boy.

"Who is she? said I.

"Don't know," said the peripatetic little bookseller. "She's first this person, and then that: now a man, and then a woman; somebody says she's everybody, and everybody says she's *some.*—Here's y'ur *Fern Leaves*, forty thousand sold in sixty days."

I bought a copy. (MWT, August 13, 1853)

On September 6, 1853, Fern signed a contract with Derby and Miller to publish two more books: a children's book, *Little Ferns for Fanny's Little Friends,* and a second adult book, *Fern Leaves from Fanny's Portfolio, Second Series.*[30] Both would be collections of her newspaper articles, with a few new articles written for the books. Through the astuteness of Fern's publishers and/or of Fern herself, the contracts specified that the copyright would be registered in England as well as in the United States, thus preventing piracy of her books. By 1854 the combined sales of the three books totaled 180,000: 132,000 copies in the United States and 48,000 in Great Britain.[31]

In September of 1853, also, Fern learned that Samuel Farrington had obtained a divorce in Chicago, on grounds of desertion. J. C. Derby made the inquiries for her. She probably had asked Derby if Farrington were entitled to the royalties on her book (which he would have been, if he were still legally her husband). One suspects that he turned up or wrote to Fern demanding money as Gertrude Dean's husband, Stahle, attempts to do in *Rose Clark*. In the novel, Gertrude's former husband appears when she is visiting Niagara Falls. It is known that Fern and her daughter Ellen traveled by train to Niagara Falls in the late summer of 1853,[32] which would put Fern's trip to Niagara just before Derby's inquiries about the divorce. This would suggest that the appearance of Stahle at Niagara may have been based on an actual confrontation with Farrington there.

In *Rose Clark* Stahle's friend comments that Gertrude has become quite wealthy:

"I should think it would gall you a little, Stahle, and you so out of pocket."

"It would," said the latter, with another oath, "had I not the way of helping myself to some of it."

"How's that? The law does not allow you to touch her earnings, now you are divorced."

"All women are fools about law matters. She don't know that," sneered Stahle. "She is probably traveling alone, and I will frighten her into it—that's half the battle. . . . Here she is living in clover, going to the Springs, and all that; while I am a poor clerk in a grocery store. . . . I won't stand it; Mrs. Gertrude Dean, as she calls herself, has got to hand over the cash. If I can't ruin her reputation, I'll have some of her money." (RC, 345–346)

If Farrington did present himself to his former wife to ask her for money, she apparently asked Derby to find out if he had any claim upon her. Derby asked his lawyer to investigate the situation, and the lawyer wrote to Derby, sending him a copy of the divorce decree and a letter from the lawyer in Chicago where the divorce was obtained. His reply indicates that Derby's query specifically addressed the issue of whether Farrington was entitled to any of Fern's earnings:

The decree of Divorce is ample and dissolves entirely the marriage between the parties. . . . And the plaintiff can never question the legality of his Divorce or set up at any time hereafter any rights as husband of the defendant either in person or property.[33]

Free of Farrington and free of the Eldredges' claim on her children, Fanny Fern decided to make her permanent home in New York. In October of 1853 Oliver Dyer traveled to Boston. Whether or not Fern went with him is uncertain, but like John Walter in *Ruth Hall*, Dyer apparently sought to promote her reputation in Boston. He visited Moulton and other editors who had printed unkind and untrue allegations regarding Fern's character. Moulton in *The Life and Beauties* says that Fern and "John Walter" (Oliver Dyer) were at the Tremont House in Boston in the summer of 1853, and that "Walter" visited him.[34] We know that Fern went to Boston in late July or early August to retrieve Grace, and this may be the visit that Moulton refers to. In *Ruth Hall* John Walter is with Ruth when she retrieves her daughter from her in-laws.

Fern continued to write for the *Musical World* until November of 1853. On November 5, 1853, the Philadelphia *Saturday Evening Post* announced, "We are authorized to announce a series of articles from one who has rapidly risen very high in popular favor. They will be entitled a 'New Series of Sketches,' by Fanny Fern" (SEP, November 5, 1853). The *Post* described itself as "A Family Newspaper: Neutral in Politics, Devoted to Morality, Pure Literature, Foreign and Domestic News, Agriculture, The Commercial Interest, Science, Art and Amusement." Fern's first article appeared on January 7, 1854. The article was called "Whom Does It Concern?" and it marked the beginning of an intensified concern with social issues. It tells the story of a young girl working as a seamstress for Simon Skinflint. When she asks for more money for her labor, he tells her he can find plenty who will do the work if she won't. "You feminine operatives don't seem to understand trade," he says; "competition is the soul of business." Fern ends with a plea for the day when "thousands of doors, now closed, shall be opened" to provide jobs for women.

Her second article in the *Post*, "Boarding-House Experience," describes the problems of boardinghouses and how the landlords took advantage of the tenants (SEP, January 21, 1854). The following week she wrote "Who Loves a Rainy Day?," which reflects her personal feelings. She portrayed herself glad that it was rainy because that meant no visitors would come, and she could sit around with "loose ringlets and loose dressing-robe," looking at old letters; she ends up looking at a pressed flower, which reminds her of her first husband (SEP, January 28, 1854).

The next few weeks she wrote a series of articles called "Gotham Scribblings," which described sights and people in New York. On March 4 she announced that she was no longer living in a boardinghouse, that she had moved to a hotel, where she enjoyed the "general let-alone-ativeness!" (SEP, March 4, 1854). Her last article in the *Saturday Evening Post* appeared on April 1, 1854.

8

Ruth Hall

*I do not dignify it by the name of "A novel." I am aware that it is
entirely at variance with all set rules for novel-writing. There is no intri-
cate plot; there are no startling developments, no hair-breadth escapes. I
have compressed into one volume what I might have expanded into two
or three. I have avoided long introductions and descriptions, and have
entered unceremoniously and unannounced, into people's houses.*

Ruth Hall, *Preface*

FANNY FERN'S ARTICLES STOPPED APPEARING in the *Saturday Evening Post*
in April 1854 because on February 16 of that year she had signed an agreement with Mason Brothers to write a novel. The contract with the publishing company stipulated that she would do no other literary work while
working on the novel:

Whereas the said Mrs. Eldredge intends to prepare a volume for the said
Mason Brothers to publish; and whereas the said Mason Brothers intend
to use extraordinary exertions to promote the sale thereof, so as, if possible, to make it exceed the sale of any previous work, and will, moreover,
use every means in their power to attain that end, Therefore:
   The said Mrs. Eldredge agrees to write and prepare for the press a novel
or tale to be comprised in a duodecimo volume of about four hundred
pages, the title of which shall be hereafter determined. . . .
   It is further agreed that this volume shall be prepared as soon as circumstances will permit, and that the said Mrs. Eldredge shall not prepare,
or aid in preparing, any other work until this shall have been issued—
with the exception of the Second Series of *Fern Leaves,* now in course of
publication.[1]

   Mason Brothers apparently asked Fern to abstain from any other literary
activity partly because they wanted to bring out the book as quickly as
possible. There was an intense demand for anything that Fanny Fern could
write. Moreover, for some time, there had been comments in the press expressing the hope that Fern would write a novel.[2] In fact, according to her

granddaughter, she wrote the book in response to the demands of the publishers.[3] One reason given for her shift in publishers (and the one proffered by her former publisher, J. C. Derby) was that Oliver Dyer, who had become her financial and legal advisor, had become affiliated with the firm.[4] More significant, however, is the fact that Mason Brothers agreed to pay her fifteen cents for each book sold—which was a substantial increase over the ten cents per book that Derby and Miller had paid her for her previous books.[5] However, the publishers' guarantee to "use extraordinary exertions to promote the sale" of the book "to make it exceed the sale of any previous work" was the most noteworthy clause in the contract. In effect, Mason Brothers were promising to make the book a best-seller, even before the manuscript had been written, solely on the basis of Fanny Fern's name—an indication of how popular she had become in just two and a half years.

When Fern finished the novel *Ruth Hall* nine months later, Mason Brothers launched a mammoth advertising campaign. The Masons' campaign made readers aware of the book, but the novel succeeded because of intrinsic qualities which today still draw readers to *Ruth Hall*. The principal reason for the long-lasting appeal of Fern's novel was her ability to write outside the conventions of the time. It was her refusal to be bound by the restrictions of conventional femininity that drew criticism down upon her; yet it is this very defiance of convention that gives *Ruth Hall* its strength. A British review of *Fern Leaves* in 1853 praised Fern's work because she was "totally without that affectation of extreme propriety which is popularly attributed to the ladies of the New World."[6] And Nathaniel Hawthorne, also writing from abroad, wrote to his publisher in February 1855 that after reading *Ruth Hall* he wanted to qualify his earlier criticism of the "damned mob of scribbling women":

In my last, I recollect, I bestowed some vituperation on female authors. I have since been reading "Ruth Hall"; and I must say I enjoyed it a good deal. The woman writes as if the devil was in her; and that is the only condition under which a woman ever writes anything worth reading. Generally women write like emasculated men, and are only distinguished from male authors by greater feebleness and folly; but when they throw off the restraints of decency, and come before the public stark naked, as it were—then their books are sure to possess character and value. Can you tell me anything about this Fanny Fern? If you meet her, I wish you would let her know how much I admire her.[7]

Although critics have been eager to quote Hawthorne's comments on "scribbling women" (so much so that the phrase has become a part of our national literary vocabulary), they have been puzzled by his comments on Fanny Fern.[8] The statement itself is quite clear. Hawthorne was saying that women writers were hampered by conventions imposed by society and that

those restrictions prevented them from writing as powerfully as they otherwise could have. The strength of *Ruth Hall*, he believed, was possible exactly because Fanny Fern had thrown off the straitjacket of convention,
which, he said, was the only way a woman could write anything worth-
while.

Moreover, Hawthorne felt, there was substance to what she wrote. Somewhat later, when he had learned who Fanny Fern was, he wrote to another
correspondent:

Certainly not an exhibition to please Nat Willis nor one to suit the finikin,
this spectacle of Fanny Fern in little more than her bare bones, her heart
pulsating visibly and indecently in its cage of ribs. Still, there are ribs and
there is a heart. Here is not merely silk and suavity and surface. (EP, 128)

Fanny Fern's defiance of convention also enabled her in *Ruth Hall* to
write one of the few examples of the female *kunstlerroman* published in
nineteenth-century America.[9] Although the *kunstlerroman*, a novel chronicling the development of the artist, was a popular means of expression
among male writers, women writers found it difficult to portray a serious
female artist in a society that denied women the right to an existence separate from the home sphere. The tragedies inherent in this situation are powerfully portrayed by Elizabeth Stuart Phelps in *The Story of Avis* (1877),
which chronicles the resultant failure of the artist. Fern's Ruth Hall (who
was called "Ruthless Hall" by Fern's contemporary, Grace Greenwood)[10]
succeeds as a professional writer, but, although she maintains her love for
her children, she only becomes successful as a writer when she is no longer a
wife.

Before we examine the literary and cultural significance of the novel,
however, let us look at two important aspects of its publication: the publisher's campaign and the critics' reaction to *Ruth Hall*.

The Publishers

In mid-November 1854, Mason Brothers launched their advertising campaign, inundating the newspapers with advertisements.[11] One suspects that
the projected advertising campaign was another reason why they did not
want Fern to work on other material while she was writing the book: they
did not want to spend a great deal of money on advertising if it was going to
benefit another publisher. The Masons' advertising campaign is significant
as one of the first examples of modern advertising methods in America.
They not only advertised heavily in newspapers and magazines across the
country, they also attempted to create a need, and to create a public image
of the book.

In the weeks prior to the book's publication, the Masons' advertisements made bold predictions, asserting that Fern's book was "destined to make a sensation" and would surpass "any other work whatever."[12] On December 11, the day the book had been scheduled to be released, they announced that they had decided to delay its publication until December 14, when the second edition came out, because the demand was so great that they could not meet it. In the weeks after the novel appeared, the Masons printed extracts from favorable reviews calling the book "brilliant," "a work of genius." Included in these extracts were several that made the claim the Masons had stressed since the beginning of the campaign: the book was "destined to be one of the most popular works ever issued from an American press."[13] On December 18 the publishers inserted a notice in the newspapers stating that the first two editions were already exhausted, and that even though they were turning out the third edition at fifteen hundred copies a day, they were still not able to keep up with the demand.[14]

On December 23 the Masons began a series of advertisements that responded to the critics who had insisted on reading the book as autobiography. Pointing out that the author had not said the story was true, and that the publishers had not even hinted that it was, they referred to claims that Hyacinth was "the chronicler of Idlewild" (N. P. Willis), and, without denying them, noted that the fault lay with the critics if they recognized a certain person in an unflattering portrait.[15] Of course, this oblique reference to N. P. Willis succeeded in introducing into national papers the suggestion that Fern's book did, in fact, pillory the famous author, and consequently created more interest in the book.

On December 25, the Masons took an action that was to call even more attention to Fern's novel. Responding to an unfavorable review of *Ruth Hall* which had claimed that "almost any educated girl" could write such a book, the Masons offered to award $10,000 to every " 'well educated' girl (or other person for that matter) who will furnish us for publication the manuscript of a tale equal to *Ruth Hall*."[16]

That Fanny Fern's name was already well known to the public made Mason Brothers' task easier, of course. And then on December 30, 1854, something happened that, although catastrophic for Fern personally, dramatically increased the sale of the book. In the first of a series of spiteful articles, the editor of the *True Flag*, William U. Moulton, angered by his loss of Fanny Fern's columns and incensed at her unflattering portrait of him in *Ruth Hall* as Mr. Tibbetts of *The Pilgrim*, revealed the carefully guarded secret of her identity. Having written the book in the belief that her incognita was safe, Fern had based the story of Ruth Hall on her own life, using real models for many characters, who, though fictionalized, were easily recognizable once her identity was known. Sales of *Ruth Hall* climbed to 70,000. The book became a roman à clef, with readers particularly eager to see the author's portrait of her famous brother, Nathaniel Parker Willis, as Hyacinth Ellet.

Without attempting to deny the *True Flag*'s identification of Fanny Fern as Sara Willis (and astute enough to know how to profit from the additional publicity), the Masons continued to advertise the book widely, quoting from favorable reviews and making the claim that *Ruth Hall* was "the most successful American book." In the first two months since its publication, they said, *Ruth Hall* had sold more copies than any other American book within the same period. In an indirect reference to *Uncle Tom's Cabin*, the Masons noted that for its success *Ruth Hall* "derived no interest or popularity" from political questions of the day.[17] In other advertisements, the success of *Ruth Hall* was compared to that of *Uncle Tom's Cabin* and other successful novels, and Fanny Fern was compared to Dickens. Other innovative advertising techniques included printing one sentence over and over between other book advertisements in the newspapers: "*Ruth Hall*, Fanny Fern's first novel, has proved the most successful romance."[18]

The Critics

The critical response to *Ruth Hall* was extensive. The novel was reviewed in newspapers and magazines throughout the United States and in England, and the following year it was translated into German and French.[19] Stores advertised the "Ruth Hall bonnet, in elegant black gauze" (EP, 131). The composer [Louis] Jullien wrote "The Ruth Hall Schottische," and the sheet music was published in March of 1855 and dedicated to Fanny Fern, with a lithograph of a young woman on the cover who very much resembled Fanny Fern. In May of 1855 a popular song entitled "Little Daisy" was written by G. F. Wurzel and published by Firth, Pond & Co. Advertisements for the song, based on the character from *Ruth Hall*, began appearing in *The New York Times* and the *New York Tribune* on May 11.

Although the widespread notice of her novel and the controversy surrounding its autobiographical character helped to boost sales, the critics were not kind to Fanny Fern. The reviewers—even those who praised other aspects of the novel—castigated Fern for her "unfeminine" writing, her immodest "self-love," and her "unfilial" portrayal of her father, brother, brother-in-law, and in-laws. It is clear that much of this criticism derived specifically from the fact that Fanny Fern was a woman. *The New York Times* declared that if she had been a man, the revenge that she sought in satirizing her relatives would have been excusable, but in a "suffering woman" it was reprehensible:

If Fanny Fern were a man,—a man who believed that the gratification of revenge were a proper occupation for one who has been abused, and that those who have injured us are fair game, *Ruth Hall* would be a natural and excusable book. But we confess that we cannot understand how a

delicate, suffering woman can hunt down even her persecutors so remorselessly. We cannot think so highly of [such] an author's womanly gentle-
ness. (*New York Times*, December 20, 1854)

The *New York Tribune* lamented the "unfeminine" character of Fern's
satire and ended with the hope that her next work would be "characterized
by the womanly charities which it is one of the noblest functions of feminine
genius to illustrate" (December 16, 1854). The *London Atlas* expressed a
similar hope. Commenting that, if he had not known the autobiographical
character of the work, he would have praised it, the reviewer instead said
that it was an "exhibition of wayward ambition, bad taste, and obtuse
moral perception, such as we regret to find in any female writer." Implying
that it was only because the writer was female that he deplored these qualities in the work, the reviewer recommended that she follow a "more womanly and modest course in her future works."[20] In a scathing review of the
novel, *Putnam's Monthly* said that *Ruth Hall* was "overflowing with an
unfemininely bitter wrath and spite."[21] The *Protestant Episcopal Quarterly
Review*, in a long and very critical review, said that Fern was not properly
"decorous" or "womanly."[22] The London *Albion* asserted that the book
was not "creditable to the female head and heart."[23]

Not only was Fern criticized in general for not being properly feminine,
she was criticized for other "sins" that derived from her failure to behave as
a woman was supposed to behave in the 1850s. Many of the critics of *Ruth
Hall* focused specifically on what they regarded as Fern's "self-love." In an
age in which a man could say, "I celebrate myself" (Whitman's *Leaves of
Grass* was published in the same year as *Ruth Hall*), a woman was expected
to remain modest and selfless. In *Ruth Hall* the author applauds Ruth for
her accomplishments: Ruth rescues herself and her children from poverty
and, by her own self-reliance, manages to attain wealth and fame. Because
she applauded the accomplishments of a character who was based on herself
and her own experiences, Fern was criticized for "self-praise," "self-exalta-
tion," and "self-love."[24]

The other—and, according to her critics, the most serious—sin that Fern
was guilty of was that she was perceived as unfilial: she had dared to criticize and satirize her relatives—particularly her male relatives. The novel
was called "abominable," "monstrous," "eminently evil in its tendencies
and teachings."[25] *The New York Times*, in its review, included a warning to
other girls to beware of Ruth Hall, "lest they come to consider the Fifth
Commandment a humbug." The *True Flag* in its bitterly critical review of
the novel summed up this criticism with the exclamation, "O, Goneril! O,
Regan!"[26]

The primary reason behind this violent reaction to Fern's satirical portraits of her male relatives probably was the one openly stated by the New
Orleans *Crescent City* in a review of *Ruth Hall* in January of 1855: "As we

wish no sister of ours, nor no female relative to show toward us, the ferocity she has displayed toward her nearest relatives we take occasion to censure this book that might initiate such a possibility."[27]

The threat to male self-esteem of Fanny Fern's "ferocity" can be further seen in the vituperative pseudobiography that appeared anonymously in March 1855. The author of *The Life and Beauties of Fanny Fern* was apparently William Moulton.[28] The book contained the articles already printed in the *True Flag*, along with other criticism, and a selection of Fern's most satirical and unconventional articles, which, the author pointed out, had been left out of *Fern Leaves*, but which he erroneously believed would discredit her in the eyes of the public. The book was a vindictive attempt to injure Fanny Fern's reputation and was filled with innuendoes and false statements designed to cast doubts on her morals, her character, and her integrity.

In a mock review of her own book in 1857, Fern satirized the stereotypical male criticism of her work:

We have never seen Fanny Fern, nor do we desire to do so. We imagine her, from her writings, to be a muscular, black-browed, grenadier-looking female, who would be more at home in a boxing gallery than in a parlor—a vociferous, demonstrative, strong-minded horror,—a woman only by virtue of her dress. . . . Thank heaven! there are still women who *are* women—who know the place Heaven assigned them, and keep it. . . . Thank heaven! there are women writers who do not disturb our complacence or serenity; whose books lull one to sleep like a strain of gentle music; who excite no antagonism, or angry feeling. . . . We regret to be obliged to speak thus of a lady's book: it gives us great pleasure, when we can do so conscientiously, to pat lady writers on the head. (NYL, October 10, 1857)

The female critics, however, were no kinder to Fern. Of the female critics who are known to have commented on *Ruth Hall*, only one reviewed the book itself; the others focused on criticism of the author. The most stinging comments were by "a talented woman," whose anonymous review in the *Olive Branch* criticized Fern for being irreverent, unfilial, unfeminine, and guilty of too much self-esteem. Even more petty than the male critics, this "talented woman" added that she personally knew someone who had known Fern when she was married to her first husband and she knew for a fact that she, Fanny Fern, was a "poor housekeeper."[29] Caroline Healey Dall, writing in the suffragette journal *The Una*, censured Fern for her satirical treatment of her relatives; if it was true that they had treated her cruelly, said Dall, Fern should have exercised a "noble self-restraint" and kept silent. Moreover, Dall insisted that Fern had not told the truth about herself, which only proved "how unfit any woman is to write her own life when it has been a succession of passionate struggles against circumstances." Her *Fern Leaves,* Dall said, was "full of smart 'manly' wit and the sarcasm of a soured soul." Dall said that she had kept Fern's children's book from her own little ones so that they would not be "taught to take bitter views of men and things, to question the motives of their fellow-men."[30]

Sarah Josepha Hale, the editor of *Godey's Lady's Book,* refused to review the novel at all because of Fern's satirical treatment of her relatives. She said she did not want to interfere in family affairs (it is significant that Fern's brother, N. P. Willis, was a frequent contributor to the journal). Previously she had warned Fern not to go beyond the bounds of feminine propriety.[31] Although Hale supported education for women, she endorsed the image of woman as selfless and submissive. This image is explicitly stated in a story she published in 1850, "Woman's Rights." A young woman named Fanny is verbally abused and struck by her father, but she meekly bows her head in acceptance, and, as the author tells us, does not defy him, for *he is her father:* "Fanny is learning a lesson of self-denial, of patience; and though it may seem an unenviable right to you to be able to 'bless them that curse you,' we must think of 'the great reward' which Fanny will obtain in heaven."[32] Clearly, Fanny Fern was a deviant for not bowing her head in silence and reverence in the face of ill-treatment by her male relatives.

Ellen Louise Chandler, who wrote for the *True Flag* at the same time as Fern, was jealous of Fern's popularity. Although she urged her publishers to use the same advertising techniques as Fern's publishers, she spitefully complained about Fern's "vulgarity" and unladylike expression, which, she reported, a lady friend said caused a "pain at her heart, that any lady should so far forget herself." In October of 1854 she predicted somewhat hopefully, "Poor Fanny! . . . her day is done."[33] In August 1855 Chandler married William Moulton. Given her hostile attitude toward Fern, it is possible that she encouraged Moulton's publication of the vindictive *Life and Beauties.*

In her newspaper articles, Fern satirized the backbiting and jealousy that characterized the female critics. Women, she said, are seldom friends to each other: "Just cross the track once of some female friend (?) either in love or literature. Hornets and nettles! the way you'll get demolished!" (OB, July 3, 1852). In an 1856 article she described a woman who probably was either Ellen Chandler Moulton or the "S" who reviewed *Ruth Hall* in the *Olive Branch:*

There was Miss Moses, *proper* Miss Moses, who had been for a year or more writing for the *Scribetown Gazette,* when I commenced. How delighted she was at my advent— . . . —what an interest she took in my progress. *She* never tried to keep my articles out of the paper (benevolent soul!) "lest they should injure its reputation"—not she; . . . she never,

when she found one containing an attack on me (written at her own suggestion) marked it with a double row of ink marks, and laid it on a conspicuous place on the editor's table—not she. She *liked* my articles—
liked them so well, that, on several occasions, she appropriated whole
sentences and paragraphs; omitting (probably through forgetfulness) to
make the necessary quotation marks! Dove-like Miss Moses! I think I see
her now looking as though she was ready to be translated (which, by the
way, her works never have been). Pious Miss Moses . . . ; she tried hard to
extinguish me, but success makes me magnanimous. I forgive her. (NYL,
May 3, 1856)

Throughout all of the blistering criticism, Fanny Fern, the writer and public woman, never faltered. But for Sara Willis Eldredge Farrington, the private person, the criticism was devastating. Many years later she wrote:

And how I *did* cry if an editor reviewed *me* personally, instead of my
book, in his book notices. How I used to wish I were Tom Hyer, or Jack
Sayers, or some high and mighty muscular pugilist, to make mincemeat of
the coward, who wouldn't have dared to "hit one of his own size" in that
sneaking fashion. (NYL, November 26, 1864)

Fanny Fern's satiric portrayal of her relatives also caused tension between
her and members of her family. This, however, she had expected. According
to her granddaughter, when Fanny Fern was writing *Ruth Hall* she had
known that those satirized would be annoyed, and, because of the wrongs
she felt she had suffered at their hands, she derived satisfaction from being
able to revenge herself in this way (EP, 129–130). As the *New York Atlas*
commented, the book, like Lady Bulwer's attack on her husband, was "designed to avenge insults, indignities, and outrage.[34] Fern's father-in-law had
died before she wrote the book, but her mother-in-law's reaction was to
rewrite her will.[35] Her brother N. P. Willis was the one most offended by the
novel, but Fern had severed relations with him in 1851. Although Willis did
not reply publicly to Fern's satiric portrayal of him in *Ruth Hall*, there is an
oblique answer to his sister in his comments in the January 13, 1855, issue
of the *Home Journal:* "I think we have passed a year without the saying of
an unkind word. . . . Answers to the malignity and injustice which are never
without new shapes, have been sometimes difficult to forebear—but we
have foreborne them."
    Fern's brother Richard Willis, who does not appear in *Ruth Hall* and with
whom she was on amicable terms, apparently did not like her portrayal of
their father in the novel, and in an article in the *Musical World and Times* he
wrote kind words about their father and reprinted N. P. Willis's poem "To
My Aged Father"—in an apparent attempt to counteract Fern's portrayal
(MWT, January 13, 1855, January 20, 1855). He did not discontinue his

friendly relations with his sister, however, and in later years characterized her as a "woman with a great heart."[36] When Richard Willis's wife died in 1858, Fern was at the funeral. It was at this funeral that she spoke to N. P. Willis for the first time in seven years (NYL, June 5, 1858). Although she was never to resume friendly relations with N. P. Willis,[37] her relations with the rest of the family were only "temporarily strained," and after a time her father was able to regard *Ruth Hall* "without rancor," accepting the book as fiction (EP, 130). That her sister Lucy, whose family had been satirized in the Millets, did not break off relations with Fern is apparent in letters from her to Fern's daughter Ellen.[38] And Fern's sisters Mary and Julia, who are not portrayed in *Ruth Hall*, both remained on friendly terms with her.[39]

Despite all of the public criticism of Fanny Fern, and although there were few wholly favorable reviews, there were reviewers who found much to praise in the book. Even reviewers who lamented Fern's unfeminine or unfilial writing were able to see merit in the book. An aspect of the novel that was most frequently praised was Fern's original style. *The New York Times* commented that the book was "written in the same lively, dashing, unaffected style" as her articles.[40] The *New York Tribune* noted that her "style has the abruptness, audacity, and defiance of conventional rules, which mark the genius of the author."[41] The *Hartford Courant* asserted that her style was original: "the style is Fanny Fern's, and resembles that of no other."[42] The other aspects of Fern's novel that were praised were her humor, her "powerful satire," and her "insight into character."[43] As the comments about Fanny Fern's writing style indicate, *Ruth Hall* was, more than anything else, very readable. *Graham's Magazine*, responding to *The Life and Beauties of Fanny Fern*, commented that although it was clear the anonymous author had intended to condemn Fern by his publication of what he regarded as her too-spicy articles, the book did not make the reviewer like her any less; her work, he said, made "uncommonly lively reading," combining "in merry union the most extraordinary and startling incongruities on record."[44] The readers of *Ruth Hall* were not simply East Coast literati who might be titillated by the amusement caused in Boston and New York literary circles by Fern's satiric treatment of her brother. A. B. Cooke and Company, the Chicago booksellers that distributed books to Iowa, Wisconsin, Minnesota, Indiana, Kansas, Michigan, and Illinois, reported in October 1856 that it had sold 15,000 copies of Fern's works, including *Ruth Hall*, during the same time period in which it had sold 3,000 copes of Longfellow's *Hiawatha* and 3,000 copies of Macaulay's *England*.[45]

Readers of Fern's day, whether or not they were familiar with the specific people that Fern satirized in the novel, and even if they thought the author "unwomanly," found the book very funny. What won readers to the book were Fern's humor, her "condensed and vigorous style," her understanding of human nature, and her ability to portray real people and recognizable situations. The success of Fern's novel lay in its familiarity and her skill at

portraying with deft strokes people from every walk of life. Despite the
critics' stern criticism of the author, the readers of Fern's novel, like the
readers of her newspaper columns, laughed along with her as she ridiculed
the cruel, the pompous, the hypocritical, and the pretentious.

The Novel

When conservative critics reacted violently to Ruth Hall, they did so with
reason: it was a revolutionary book. They did not, however, criticize it on
its own terms but focused instead on issues connected with the author's
identity as a woman; in writing such a book, she had deviated from the role
prescribed for women at the time. Ruth Hall was attacked on five counts:
the author's lack of femininity in seeking revenge (a woman was expected to
be gentle and submissive); her self-portrayal in heroic terms (a woman was
supposed to be selfless and self-effacing); her failure to show filial piety
because she criticized her father, brother, and in-laws (a woman must be
respectful of and deferential toward her male relatives); her vulgarity (a
woman should never be lacking in female delicacy); and her sacrilege in
satirizing devout people (the crowning glory of any woman was her religious piety and respect for religion).

These criticisms were all directed at the author, not the book. Although
the critics were right in seeing the danger of these unconventional qualities
in a woman (without them, Fanny Fern could never have written Ruth
Hall), by focusing on them they missed the book's revolutionary message.
The real threat posed by the novel was its insistence that a woman should be
independent. And, for Fanny Fern, true independence could come only with
financial freedom. The role of American individualist, she was saying (contrary to popular thought at the time), should not be reserved for male Americans only; women too could be self-reliant and self-sufficient.

The term revolutionary clearly does not apply here to a radical change in
the economic structure of society, but rather to a rearrangement of the
power alignments associated with the control of wealth. Fanny Fern did not
question the basis of capitalism, although she was critical of its abuses and
satirized the selfishness of an uncontrolled individualism. With her awareness of social injustice, moreover, she knew that self-reliance would not
always work. She had seen too many people—particularly working women
—struggling against impossible odds. She felt a kinship with suffering humanity and believed that society had a responsibility to help "life's unfortu-
nates."

Ruth Hall was a revolutionary book because it threatened to subvert the
male-dominated power structure of society by suggesting that women get
some money for themselves. Fern realized that the hierarchical structure
that she and other women had been conditioned to believe was fixed by God

and Nature was, in fact, a construct, that is, a power system constructed by, and designed to preserve the power of, those in power.[46] Fern's novel can be read as a portrayal of the Derridaean dismantling of the first principle.[47] Ruth Hall discovers the thread that permits the "dissemination" or unsewing of the whole patriarchal structure that has created the binary opposition of men and women and would keep her—and other women—in subjugation. The thread that will pull down, or deconstruct, this political structure is the economic enabling of women. Economics is the key—not the economics of class (although it is interesting that Fern's novel appeared during the period in which Karl Marx was working on *Das Kapital*)[48]—but the economics of gender. To the criticism directed at a woman sculptor who had received a federal commission, Fern replied in the *New York Ledger* on April 10, 1869: "I would like to ask, amid the crowd of lobbying *men*, whose paws are in the national basket, after the loaves and fishes—should not this little woman's cunning white hand have slily drawn some out?"

For Fanny Fern, then, financial independence, even more than the vote, was the key to women's rights:

When you can, achieve financial independence. Freedom from subjection may be gotten by the fruits of your own labors, and by your own efforts you can learn to conquer yourselves. When you have done all this, you may rightfully demand—even the right to vote, as vote you certainly will some day.[49]

Thus Fern's "Modern Old Maid" does not live with her married sister and tend her nine children. Instead, she supports herself:

She teaches, or she lectures, or she writes books, or poems, or she is a book-keeper, or she sets type, or she does anything but hang on to the skirts of somebody else's husband. . . . She lives in a nice house, earned by herself, . . . and has a bank-book and dividends. (NYL, June 5, 1869)

Her widows are equally self-reliant. Even in her works for children, she insists on the necessity for female independence. In "Cicely Hunt," published in *Little Ferns for Fanny's Little Friends* in 1853, Cicely and her mother refuse to accept a friend's offer to help them further than to get them started; after that, "they supported *themselves*" (LF, 206).

The career of Ruth Hall—and incidentally of Fanny Fern herself—provided a rare role model for nineteenth-century women: the example of a woman who had achieved financial independence solely on her own. Fern realized that not every woman could have the opportunity or the ability to succeed, but, as she stated in her preface, she saw her novel as a means of providing hope an inspiration for women all over America. *Ruth Hall* was far more than the momentary aberration of an individual woman; it was a call to arms to women everywhere, for whom the conventional formula for feminine success—submissive dependency—had not worked.

Ruth Hall is nearly unique in that, unlike other nineteenth-century American novels in which an impoverished woman is forced to support herself, it does not end with the heroine's marriage and the renunciation of her career. In many novels, a woman might find she is quite able to support herself, but this is seen as only a temporary measure. At the end of the novel, the woman finds a husband and gives up her career for what she and the author and society see as her true calling: submerging herself in love and marriage.

The principal attribute of nineteenth-century American woman's fiction is its portrayal of a heroine who, although she may not engage in the heroic activities of Catharine Sedgwick's spirited protagonist in Hope Leslie (1827), is nevertheless a strong, independent central character. Ruth Hall follows this tradition, but also diverges from it in three important respects.

First, Fanny Fern takes her heroine farther into independence than any other heroine of the period. Hester Prynne in The Scarlet Letter (1850) is, like Ruth Hall, totally self-sustaining to the end of the novel, but Fanny Fern does not have the ambivalence toward her character's self-assertion that Hawthorne has. In many novels written by women, the heroine is spirited and self-sustaining, sometimes self-supporting for a time, but even the most aggressively independent heroine of all these novels, the lively Capitola in E.D.E.N. Southworth's Hidden Hand (1859), marries at the end of the novel. Similarly, Fleda Ringgen in Susan Warner's Queechy (1852) and Edna Earl in Augusta Jane Evans's St. Elmo (1866) support themselves with admirable grit and determination, but at the conclusion of the novels they give up their economic independence. In these novels marriage is seen as a refuge from the world, and the heroine is rescued from the necessity of supporting herself. As St. Elmo says to Edna in the last chapter of Evans's novel:

To-day I snap the fetters of your literary bondage. There shall be no more books written! No more study, no more toil, no more anxiety, no more heartaches! And that dear public you love so well, must even help itself, and whistle for a new pet. You belong solely to me now, and I shall take care of the life you nearly destroyed in your inordinate ambition.[50]

All of these heroines are quite young when they begin to support themselves, and the implication is that they have not come to their true vocation until they marry.[51] Ruth Hall, however, has already tried love and marriage, and although for her it was good while it lasted, it did not last. Ruth realizes that she cannot depend on others; even a loving husband can die. Her goal becomes independence, and Fanny Fern portrays this as a necessary and desirable goal for women, just as Americans already believed it was a necessary and desirable goal for men.

Second, Fanny Fern's heroine diverges from the norm in mid-nineteenth-century woman's fiction in the scope of her power. As Nina Baym points out in *Woman's Fiction*, the heroine traditionally manages, in the course of the novels, to gain power and control over her environment.[52] Although she might "belong" to her husband, as St. Elmo said, he would look to her for moral and spiritual guidance, and she would rule the domestic sphere. These novels celebrate the home values of love and harmony over the pragmatic values of the marketplace; their heroines build domestic strongholds where those superior feminine values can prevail. Since the home was seen as a training center for the world, as Baym notes, to grant the heroine the home was to give her considerable power.[53] Jane Tompkins describes the process thus in *Sensational Designs:* "The sentimental novelist elaborated a myth that gave women the central position of power and authority in their culture.[54]

Like the heroines of these novels, Ruth Hall gains power and control over her environment, but her influence extends into the world outside the home. The domestic values of love and harmony which seem to be extolled at the beginning of the novel gradually give way to a cynical realism as the heroine evolves from a trusting innocent, who accepts the feminine role imposed on her by her culture, into a hardheaded businesswoman who forges her own identity. *Ruth Hall* begins with the heroine's acceptance of what French psychoanalyst Jacques Lacan defines as the "symbolic order." Ruth has been brought up to accept the teachings of a male-dominated society inculcated in her by her father, her brother, her teachers, even her peers. As Lacan would describe the process, she has developed her identity through a series of exterior signifiers or contacts with the world outside the self, while the principle of the phallus, or "transcendental signifier," governs the way in which she sees herself and her role in society.[55] However, when she goes outside her usual sphere, she redefines herself through contact with another "Other": friends and relatives who are no longer friendly, exploitive editors, appreciative readers, and finally an editor and a publisher who place a high economic value on her work.

Instead of retreating from the marketplace into a domestic paradise, as is the case in so many nineteenth-century novels by women, Ruth leaves a domestic paradise—which proves to be a fool's paradise—enters the competitive male world, and prevails in it. Although Ruth retains her deep attachment to her children and keeps the feminine values of love and harmony, she discovers that by themselves these values are worthless; they must be joined to a realistic understanding of the world outside the home. She learns that if she is to survive, she cannot retreat from the unpleasantness of a moneyed society, but must adapt herself to it.

Finally, Fanny Fern's portrayal of her heroine departs from most woman's fiction in her encouragement of self-assertion as a positive virtue. In many women's novels self-assertion is depicted as a character flaw.

Although the heroine is strong, she has to learn to curb her will and suppress her anger, rebellion, or defiance—all the qualities that spur Ruth Hall on to success. Whereas Ellen Montgomery in Susan Warner's *The Wide, Wide World* (1851) and Gertrude Flint in Maria Cummins's *The Lamplighter* (1854) are successful because they are able to conquer the self, Ruth's success is possible only through her assertion of the self. Once she enters the male world of competition, she needs that individualistic self-assertion American society encouraged in men. Religion, too, is used differently in Fern's novel. In *The Wide, Wide World* and *The Lamplighter*, religion helps the heroine to gain a victory over self. But Ruth Hall finds in religion the encouragement she needs to continue her struggle for independence in defiance of her male relatives (RH, 123).

Since economic independence for women is a central concept in *Ruth Hall*, it will be useful to trace Fern's development of the theme, both in her protagonist's career and in the novel's important subplots. At the beginning of the story, Ruth Hall is dependent upon her father, and when she marries she rejoices in her "new freedom." But her in-laws infringe upon this freedom until, moving away from them, she rejoices again in her "new-found freedom" in her own home. Still, she is dependent upon her husband, and she discovers to what extent when he dies and she is unable to support herself. She remains dependent—this time upon her father and father-in-law—until, stung by her father's grudging charity, she decides to try writing for the newspapers: "She would so gladly support herself, so cheerfully toil day and night, if need be, could she only win an independence" (RH, 115). Then, rebuffed by her brother when she asks for his help, she determines to succeed on her own: "I *can* do it, I *feel* it, I *will* do it" (RH, 116). The three successive "I" clauses emphasize her self-assertion. Her goal throughout the rest of the novel is to maintain that course, and the author describes Ruth metaphorically as a ship "steering with straining sides, and a heart of oak, for the nearing port of Independence" (RH, 133).

Ruth Hall tramps the streets and endures rudeness and hardship, but her eye is always on her goal. She has no time even for romance, and her success at the end of the novel is marked not by the acquisition of a husband but by the acquisition of ten thousand dollars in bank stock—a very American ending (paralleling that of *Tom Sawyer*, for example), but not one for a nineteenth-century novel with a female protagonist.

The struggle for independence is counterpointed by the very different stories of two other women in the novel: the comic history of Mrs. Skiddy and the tragedy of Mary Leon. Mrs. Skiddy, whose husband deserts her to go to California, successfully manages her own business for a year, and when he finally writes and asks her to send him the passage money to come home, she looks at her purse filled with "her own honest earnings," and hisses through her teeth, "like ten thousand serpents, the word 'N—e—v—e—r!'" (RH, 109). By itself, the story of Mrs. Skiddy—based on an earlier article,

"Family Jars"—is an amusing anecdote. But within the context of the novel, it provides an important touchstone for Ruth and the reader.

Mrs. Skiddy, although a comic figure, is clearly better off than Mary Leon, Ruth's alter ego. We are told that Ruth did not have many female friends, but from the beginning she feels a kinship with Mary Leon, who, like her, despises such "air bubbles" as the "common female employments and recreations." Mrs. Leon is a passionate, intelligent woman. Her husband, however, does not regard her as a person, but simply as a possession. He buys her fine clothes and jewels, but, as she tells Ruth, "they, equally with myself, are necessary appendages to Mr. Leon's establishment" (RH, 51). When he tires of her, he has her committed to an insane asylum, where she dies alone, like other women there, "forgotten by the world and him in whose service her bloom had withered, insane—only in that her love had outlived his patience" (RH, 109). The story of Mary Leon, who had warned Ruth that a woman should not marry only for economic security, is based on Fern's earlier article "Mary Lee" (TF, May 8, 1852). Mary Lee's husband was patterned after Fern's second husband in what was a marriage of convenience. But Ruth, with Mary Leon's tragic fate as an example, will not seek economic support in a second marriage; instead she determines to support herself.

If *Ruth Hall* was a revolutionary book in its major theme, stylistically it also departed radically from nineteenth-century popular fiction. It begins as a sentimental novel: a young girl, mistreated by her family, finds a strong, protective male figure. Guided by religion and the beauty of nature, she endures countless trials, including the death of a beloved child. In the first part of the novel, the prose often takes on the sentimental rhetoric of the period: such phrases as "death's dark wing," "most blessed of all hours," "velvet cheek nestled up to as velvet a bosom," "the bounteous Giver" remind us that the novel was written in the mid-nineteenth century. Yet after Ruth's husband dies and she is thrust out on her own, these phrases disappear, and Fanny Fern consistently uses the sharp staccato prose that characterized her satirical newspaper articles. The earlier prose reflects the young heroine's state of mind—innocent and trusting in her idyllic bower—whereas the later writing conforms to her disillusionment and realistic determination to succeed on her own.

Despite this clear stylistic shift, however, the book from the beginning shows its resistance to convention. First of all, marriage, which is the culmination of the action in many novels, here takes place at the opening. Like Hester Prynne, Ruth is already married when the major action takes place; the title of the novel is her married name. Also, a cynical undertone constantly undercuts the sentiment. In the first chapter, on the eve of her wedding, Ruth is thinking not of the happiness before her, but of possible disillusionment: "Would the step whose lightest footfall now made her heart leap, ever sound in her ear like a death-knell?" But, most important, the tone of the novel shifts constantly and suddenly; each description of Ruth's early happiness is immediately undercut by a satirical scene portraying the other characters' sour comments or unfeeling behavior. Early in the story Ruth's marriage is seen through the selfish eyes of her dilettante brother Hyacinth, and her happiness in her new home is prefaced by her jealous mother-in-law's interior monologue. Her joy at her first child's birth is balanced against her in-laws' cynical attitude and against the portrait of her unctuous, profiteering baby nurse. Even the deaths in the novel are not presented in purely sentimental terms; Ruth's sorrow is only one factor amid the coarse, hypocritical, or mercenary comments and actions of the other characters. When Ruth lies prostrate after her husband's death, for example, her brother thinks: "Somebody ought to tell her, when she comes to, that her hair is parted unevenly and needs brushing badly" (58). Thus each time the author seems to indulge in a tender description of family life or death, the reader is immediately snapped back to a harsher reality by an opposing scene. It is almost as if the first part of the book were written from two points of view: the perspective of the young Ruth and that of the cynical realist, Fanny Fern (or the disillusioned Ruth Hall indirectly commenting on her own prior innocence). With Ruth's growing disillusionment, the realistic and satirical scenes gradually increase in number and length until they finally take over the book.

Fanny Fern's strength did not lie in the creation of fully developed characters of great psychological depth and emotional intensity. Ruth Hall herself is the only complex character. But Fern's genius for observation enabled her to capture her characters' personalities with very specific details of gesture and expression. She put this talent to good use in her satirical portrayals in *Ruth Hall.* Hyacinth Ellet, the Halls, the Millets (particularly the "wooden man"), Ruth's father, and the minor characters that appear on the scene— the mantua maker, the boardinghouse loungers, Mrs. Waters, the editors Tibbetts and Lescom—are skillfully drawn portraits that simultaneously create a character and make a social comment.

Significantly, Fanny Fern, unlike less sensitive writers who made minority groups and the uneducated classes the butt of their humor, always directed her satire at pretentiousness and pomp. Her sympathy is with decent people, whatever their race, religion, or social status. Robert Bonner described her as "one of the most democratic and catholic of women" (NYL, February 16, 1856).[56] The sympathetic characters in Ruth Hall—other than Ruth herself, her children, Mary Leon, John Walter, and Horace Gates—are the black servants, Irish laborers, simple farm women, Johnny Galt, and the "unhonored" firemen. Although her relatives and former friends never visit Ruth in her poverty, the farm boy Johnny Galt brings her apples and a bouquet of flowers. And Ruth's inhuman treatment by her cousins, the Millets, is contrasted with the sympathetic attitude of their servants—black and white—who provide a kind of choric comment on their employers' cruelty. These sympathies are apparent throughout Fern's writing, from the 1852 article "The Model Grandmamma," which states that one of her characteristics is that she does not teach her grandchildren racial prejudice (OB, August 7, 1852), to the 1872 article "Theological Nuts" (NYL, February 10, 1872), which criticizes doctrinaire clergymen and urges tolerance and understanding of other religions.

Fanny Fern's sympathy for common people carries over into the abundance of detail from everyday life. In this regard her writing is linked most clearly to other novels written by women at mid-century. We read about where Ruth Hall lives and shops, where she keeps her milk, the cost of a train ticket to visit Katy at the Halls, her interviews with the editors, the letters she receives, the phrenological exam, the chores and specific delights of child raising. We are not simply told that she becomes wealthy and famous; we follow her chronicle step by step. By integrating the demands of everyday life and relationships with the details of Ruth's individual struggle, Fanny Fern combines the realism of woman's fiction with the self-determining theme of the American male writers of the period.

Finally, an important aspect of Fanny Fern's style is its terseness. The novel is written in a brisk, offhand style that includes the vernacular when necessary and, except in the early sections, seldom reaches for effect. Fern wrote more dialogue than description and was particularly effective in her use of understatement. At the end of Chapter 3, for example, Ruth, in her bedroom after her marriage, looks around and sees her husband's things in "unrebuked proximity" to her own. The author says simply, "Ruth liked it."

At times, however, the novel, with its short chapters and lack of transition between them, seems to carry terseness too far. Fern won fame for her short newspaper sketches, and at first glance the novel seems to be simply a succession of independent sketches. Once one understands Fern's method, however, one can see that the short chapters and lack of transition clearly contribute to the novel's effectiveness. First, the constant shifts in tone that are so important in the first part of the book are possible primarily because of the abrupt chapter breaks. Second, several seemingly unrelated chapters presented in rapid succession are used to provide different aspects of the same point. When Ruth becomes poor, for instance, the cumulative effect of chapters 35 to 51 provides an effective picture of the treatment she will receive in her newly vulnerable position: the Halls and her father haggle about who will pay for her support; the boardinghouse loungers plan an assault on the unprotected widow; Tom Develin takes advantage of her ignorance of the law; two women friends will not call because they do not wish to be seen in such a poor neighborhood; and the Millets, her cousins, refuse to help her. This accumulation of cruelty and selfishness is relieved only by a short section in the middle: Chapter 42 portrays the sympathy of the Millets' servants, and Chapter 43 brings the apples and bouquet of Johnny Galt.

The structure of the chapters also enables Fanny Fern to order the events without commenting overtly on the action. She juxtaposes chapters that comment on each other, either by contrast, as in the case of the satirical scenes following the sentimental scenes, or by reinforcement and clarification, as in the portrayal of the hotel fire toward the end of the novel. The fire is given minimal description and seems to function principally to praise the firemen. Fern's position vis-à-vis the firemen is not without significance, however, when we realize that the representative of the American common man in the popular literature of the late 1840s derived from the figure of the fireman, who came to be associated with the "republicanism of the streets."[57] Sandwiched between the references to the fire and the noble firemen are four chapters depicting respectively the Millets, Mrs. Hall, Mr. Ellet, and Tom Develin—all "good" people by society's standards—and their various reactions to Ruth's success. By juxtaposing these chapters with the story of Johnny Galt, who unselfishly has just saved Ruth from the fire, and whose simple flowers and basket of apples "saved her life" in another way when she was shunned by everyone else, Fern indirectly comments on the selfishness of the other characters and on the relative values of social class and human worth.

The fire also has an important relationship to the major theme of the novel, functioning as an ironic comment on the nineteenth-century reader's expectations that so unconventional a heroine would surely be punished, perhaps even killed, by the censorious author. This latter was the fate of Mark Twain's transgressing heroine, Laura Hawkins, in *The Gilded Age* (1873), for example, and of Cooper's self-assertive heroines, Isabella, Cora, and Judith, in *The Spy* (1821), *The Last of the Mohicans* (1826), and *The Deerslayer* (1846). Fanny Fern, however, refuses to censor Ruth, and in order to make her position wholly clear, allows her triumphant heroine to survive a major catastrophe unscathed. This aspect of the novel is particularly significant if looked at in conjunction with a novel that was published the previous year and may have provided the inspiration for the name of Fern's protagonist: *Ruth*, by the English novelist Elizabeth Gaskell, was published in 1853. It was highly criticized because of Gaskell's sympathetic treatment of a "fallen woman." Because of the controversy and publicity surrounding this novel, it is certain that Fern was at least familiar with the story and may have had it in her mind when she was writing *Ruth Hall* in 1854. Gaskell's Ruth is a young seamstress and orphan who is seduced and then abandoned by a young aristocrat. With the help of two kind samaritans, she raises her son, educates herself, and manages to earn her own living. At the end of the novel, however, this estimable young woman dies of typhoid. Readers who had praised the book were appalled. "Why should she die?" protested Charlotte Brontë.[58] Fern, who in her newspaper columns criticized the author who killed off a female character because the author "didn't know what else to do with her" (NYL, April 20, 1861), must have asked herself the same question; and her Ruth does not die.

As Fern said in her preface, *Ruth Hall* is "at variance with all set rules for novel writing": there are no "startling developments," no transitions (she "enters unceremoniously and unannounced into people's houses"), and no long passages of "description." In some ways *Ruth Hall* seems disconnected and too spare in its development of plot and character. But with her talents as a writer of short, pointed newspaper articles, Fanny Fern ordered the short chapters into a well-structured contrapuntal pattern. Writing from her own experience and developing her revolutionary theme with characteristic sharpness and vitality, she created in *Ruth Hall* an original and effective novel of extraordinary power.

Ruth Hall *and the American Dream*

In the mid-nineteenth century the economic double standard—assertive men in the marketplace and dependent women in the home—was accepted by both men and women, novelists and readers. In the popular novel the male individualist succeeded because of his independence, self-reliance, and self-assertion. In Horatio Alger's *Ragged Dick* (1866), for example, Dick is "manly and self-reliant." Alger writes of his hero: "He knew that he had only himself to depend on, and he determined to make the most of himself,—a resolution which is the secret of success in nine cases out of ten."[59] The success that Alger is talking about, of course, is monetary success. That he is not directing his advice to young girls as well as to young boys would have been understood by all of his readers. Not only are the self-reliant protagonists always male, but the public knew that their maleness was made essential within the construct of the novel—to the extent that women writers found it almost impossible to envision the female protagonist as the same self-reliant hero.

In *Ruth Hall* Fern's female protagonist demonstrates all of the qualities of the male individualist as she climbs the ladder of success to fulfill the American Dream. Unlike the male individualists, however, Ruth Hall and her creator, Fanny Fern, who succeeded in the same way, receive not praise and encouragement but blame and criticism for their "unfeminine," "unwomanly," and "vulgar" success. Ruth's relatives offer no assistance, and, in fact, attempt to impede her progress. Her father, father-in-law, and cousin, all of whom are prominent citizens, not only will not help her financially but will not even use their influence or recommendation to help her obtain a teaching position. Her brother, Hyacinth Ellet, a successful New York editor, refuses to help her find a market for her newspaper articles, and when he discovers that she is succeeding without his assistance, he tries to stop her from writing (RH, 134). The editors for whom she writes exploit her because she is a woman, and when she asks for more money, they use her status as a woman to denigrate her. "Just like a woman," they say; "women are never satisfied" (RH, 131, 147).

In her struggle to attain and portray female success, Fanny Fern was herself subjected to gender-specific criticism, as is apparent from the critics' comments quoted earlier in this chapter. In February 1855 the editor of the *New York Ledger* noted that a woman writer who wrote under the pseudonym of Minnie Myrtle (Nancy Johnson) had criticized Fanny Fern explicitly and precisely because Fern had succeeded on her own: " 'I have made my fortune in the world, and taken care of myself, and thanks to nobody,' is not a boast I should care to make," wrote Minnie Myrtle, echoing the sentiments of most of her contemporaries (NYL, February 17, 1855).

Faced with comments like these, Fern was impatient with her society's double standard of financial success, and wrote on June 8, 1861:

There are few people who speak approbatively of a woman who has a smart business talent or capability. No matter how isolated or destitute her condition, the majority would consider it more "feminine" would she unobtrusively gather up her thimble, and, retiring into some out-of-the-way place, gradually scoop out her coffin with it, than to develop that smart turn for business which would lift her at once out of her troubles; and which, in a man so situated, would be applauded as exceedingly praiseworthy. (NYL, June 8, 1861)

In all of the criticism of *Ruth Hall*, not one conventional reviewer praised *Ruth Hall* or Fanny Fern for the phenomenon that made the novel unique: its triumphant portrayal of female success. Despite the fact that novels about self-made men were commonly viewed as expressions of the promise of the American Dream, critics did not recognize this same message in *Ruth Hall*. Clearly, the pride of accomplishment that was a given in any man's chronicle of his triumph over American economic adversity was not expected or condoned in a woman; women were expected to be self*less*, not self-assertive; passive, not aggressive; and deferential to, not critical of, men.

The only American review of *Ruth Hall* that I have been able to find that recognized and praised the novel as a female success story is Elizabeth Cady Stanton's review in the suffragette paper *The Una*. Stanton wrote: "The great lesson taught in *Ruth Hall* is that God has given to woman sufficient brain and muscle to work out her own destiny unaided and alone." Stanton also decried the critics who focused on Fern's satire, noting, "if her pictures are not pleasing ones, it seems to me the censure more justly belongs to the living subjects." To emphasize her meaning, Stanton pointed out that no one accused a mulatto slave of "filial irreverence" if he or she told of the cruelty and injustice of his or her white father or brother—indicating that, unlike other reviewers, Stanton did not find it irreverent for Fern to criticize male relatives who deserved censure. Stanton was critical of the reviewers whose focus on this ostensibly "unfeminine" characteristic of the author caused them to miss the more important point of the book: the female success story.[60]

The male reviewers—and the conventional female reviewers—were unable to see the significance of Fern's novel within the context of American individualism because they did not associate women with individualism. *Harper's New Monthly Magazine* expressed a common feeling in its complaint that the novel lacked significance because, unlike other private histories, it contained no "universal meaning" in its story.[61] Since the "universal" in American individualism was essentially male, American critics could see in *Ruth Hall* only the *particular*: the story of one woman and the character of the author of the book. This focus on the particular resulted in an obsession with the personality of the author and the extent to which she had deviated from the conventional feminine role. The other result of this focus on the particular was that the critics were unable to see the story's significance. The *Southern Quarterly* complained of the novel's "littleness," for example, maintaining that there was no interest in "conversations between mothers and children, and enemies and patrons, such as you cannot escape in a morning's business and an evening's visit." The reviewer also found little of interest in the literary career of a woman: "She is nothing but a woman who has perpetrated a book; as if that astonishing merit, like the birth of a child, was the crowning feat of her existence."[62] Since the self-made American was perceived as inherently male, both in American culture and American fiction, critics were unable to place Fern's novel in that tradition and consequently missed the point of the novel.

That it was not so difficult for critics to see the message of American individualism in a book that told of the story of a man's success in America is apparent in a notice of a book that, ironically, was published in the same month and by the same publisher as Fern's *Ruth Hall*, and was written by the man who in a year was to become Fern's husband. In December 1854 James Parton published his first biography, *The Life of Horace Greeley*. The book was well reviewed, and although it was not as successful commercially as Fern's novel, it marked the beginning of Parton's distinguished career as a biographer. In reviewing the book, the reviewer for *Peterson's Magazine* wrote in February 1855: "The chief purpose of the narrative is to prove, by a well known example, that perseverance and talent is sure of its reward, at least in America. The work will do good."[63]

There is a certain irony in the fact that this comment could so easily apply also to *Ruth Hall*, whose author, like Horace Greeley, was born in 1811, and whose career also was in journalism. It might have been said of Fanny Fern and Horace Greeley that *both* proved that perseverance and talent are sure of their reward, at least in America. Although the critics of the time could easily see Greeley's life as exemplary of the American success myth, they could not see the same pattern in *Ruth Hall*.

Moreover, except for Elizabeth Cady Stanton, the critics could not say of *Ruth Hall* as *Peterson's Magazine* could say of the Greeley biography, "The work will do good." Instead, they castigated the author for being "unfeminine." Yet Fanny Fern herself hoped that her novel would "do good." She hoped that it would help to give women the courage to depend on themselves. As she wrote in the preface to her novel, "I cherish the hope that . . . it may fan into flame, in some tried heart, the fading embers of hope, well-nigh extinguished by wintry fortune and summer friends." It was her hope that women as well as men could profit from her chronicle of one woman's struggle against and triumph over adversity.

Robert Bonner
and James Parton

*How provoking! What is breakfast without the morning paper? . . . Oh,
here comes Mr. Pax with one—good soul—he has been out in his slippers, and bought one; now I shall find out all about everything. . . . No,
I shan't either; may I be kissed if Pax has not sat down to read that
paper himself, instead of giving it to me. . . . Perhaps he is going to read
it aloud to me. . . . No, he isn't either; he means to devour the whole of it
solus. . . .*
  "Pax! what is there interesting in that paper?" . . .
  "Nothing, my dear, absolutely nothing."
  *Humph! wonder if it takes a man a whole hour to read "nothing."
Now, do you suppose I whined about that? cried till my eyes looked as
though they were bound with pink tape? Not I. I just sat down and
wrote an article about it for the "Weekly Monopolizer."*
                                              (NYL, March 22, 1856)

THE YEARS 1855 AND 1856 marked the pinnacle of Fanny Fern's success.
During that period she might be said to have experienced what a twentieth-
century American woman journalist once called "having it all."[1] Fern had
become the most highly paid newspaper writer in the United States; she
wrote a second best-selling novel; she signed an exclusive contract with the
New York Ledger to write a weekly column, thus helping to ensure the
spectacular success of that paper and a generous regular income for herself;
she married a man eleven years younger than she, whom she found both
physically and intellectually compatible; and she purchased her own house.

  After the astounding success of *Ruth Hall* and the two volumes of *Fern
Leaves,* Fanny Fern, whose name had already become a household word
through her newspaper columns, became what today would be called a "hot
commodity." Neither the term nor the phenomenon had yet come into use.
It was left to Robert Bonner, the enterprising editor of the *New York Ledger,*
to discover the sales value of celebrity names.

Robert Bonner

Robert Bonner, who had emigrated from northern Ireland in 1839 at the age of fifteen, first worked as an apprentice printer on the staff of the *Hartford Courant*. In 1844 he came to New York, where he worked as a printer for a small businessman's journal, *The Merchants' Ledger and Statistical Review*. In 1851 the paper was seriously in debt, and Bonner acquired it for a small sum. He gradually changed the commercial format of the paper, substituting literary matter, and changing the name to the *New York Ledger*. He began by lowering the price of the weekly to three cents a copy, thus ensuring that it would be available to the widest possible audience.

While insisting that the *Ledger* would be a family paper (he said he would not print anything that he would not want to read aloud to his children),[2] Bonner managed to obtain an unusual variety of material: sensational serialized novels; poetry; political, historical, and literary essays; news stories; and articles of social criticism. Bonner advertised the *Ledger* as a "good family paper," which, he said, did not mean that it was innocuous, only that it was not vile: "Some editors seem to imagine that the harmlessness of a paper is in exact ratio to its stupidity; but that is a mistake; a stupid paper is only less injurious than a vile one. Human nature is active, analytic, investigating, and it must have something vital to feed upon" (NYL, January 12, 1856).

Bonner's statement is particularly interesting if viewed from within the cultural context of the period. Beginning in the 1830s Americans had been producing a voluminous popular literature that combined prurient sexuality and violence.[3] Bonner was able to succeed without pandering to the public's taste for sadomasochistic gore and pornography, while at the same time resisting the blandness imposed by conventional piety and puritanical morality. Maintaining the standards of a "family" paper but seeking out material that was entertaining and provocative as well as material that was enlightening and informative, he was able to produce a paper that was of vital interest to the widest reading public. The key was variety. The heading on the first page read: "Devoted to choice literature, romance, the news, and commerce." Within a short time, Bonner had transformed the journal from an obscure commercial paper to the most widely circulated paper of the day: when Bonner bought it in 1851 the circulation was 2,500; by 1860 the circulation was 400,000.[4]

When Bonner was working as a printer for the old *Ledger*, the editor occasionally asked him to write short articles, and once, as an experiment, he signed the name of a famous theologian to his article. He noted how much more attention was paid to the article which bore the name of a famous person, and this experiment was to provide him with the idea that later made him famous.[5] At a time when most of the material in American magazines and newspapers was anonymous or was pirated from British journals, Bonner evolved the idea of printing only original, signed material. First he asked Lydia Sigourney to write poetry for the *Ledger*. Then, early in the spring of 1855, after the success of *Fern Leaves* and *Ruth Hall* had made the name Fanny Fern even better known than it already was, Bonner approached Fern and offered her twenty-five dollars a column to write a story for the *Ledger*. Fern, who had decided that writing books was more profitable and less tension-provoking than being a columnist, thanked Bonner but told him that she did not plan to do any more writing for the newspapers. He offered her fifty dollars a column. When she still refused, he offered her seventy-five dollars. Again she refused. However, Bonner was determined to obtain a story from Fern, and he offered her the unprecedented sum of a hundred dollars a column. Impressed by his pluck and determination, Fern accepted his offer and agreed to write a serialized story.[6] Bonner announced his coup in the May 19, 1855, edition of *The Ledger:*

GREAT ATTRACTION!

NEW STORY FOR THE LEDGER

by

FANNY FERN!

GREAT PLANS FOR THE FUTURE

. . . . . It gives us pleasure to state that the most popular authoress in this or in any other country—

FANNY FERN

is now engaged in writing a Tale for the *Ledger,* the publication of which we will commence about the first of June. For this production we have to pay by far the highest price that has ever been paid by any newspaper publisher to any author.

The literary world was already abuzz with rumors about the unparalleled offer, and on May 19 Bonner quoted the reaction of the New York *Evening Mirror:* "We certainly do not know which to admire most, the ability and perseverance of the lady in making a reputation that commands such unheard-of remuneration for the labors of her pen, or the enterprise of the publisher who pays for it. Such a price for newspaper writing is certainly unprecedented." Although the editor of the *Mirror* quoted the rumored price of a hundred dollars a column, Bonner did not confirm it; he simply said, "The *Mirror* has not underrated it." It was not until June 2, the week

before the first installment of the story appeared, that Bonner confirmed the
price he had paid. In response to the avalanche of questions and rumors, he
printed an affidavit stating that he had indeed agreed to pay Fern a hundred
dollars a column for her story. He noted that the columns were not contracted, but would be the regular length, in the large *Ledger* type. He also
printed a statement by Oliver Dyer, who had drawn up the contract and
who affirmed that Bonner's statement was true.

Fanny Fern's hundred-dollar-a-column story, "Fanny Ford," began appearing in the *Ledger* on June 9, 1855, occupying four and a quarter columns on the front page of the *Ledger*. On June 16 the story filled three and a
half columns on page one. Bonner wrote at the top of the page:

> We give you in this number of the *Ledger* the second installment of
> FANNY FERN'S GREAT STORY. . . . [The story] has done much better
> than we anticipated, and notwithstanding the immense outlay, we know
> enough of the success with which it has already met, to warrant us in
> expressing the belief that *it will pay us three times over!* What have the
> timid, old-fogy, behind-the-age editors, who thought we were "insane" in
> making the costly arrangement with FANNY, to say now?

"Fanny Ford" ran for several weeks, and Fern is said to have received one
thousand dollars for the story: one hundred dollars a column.[7] This made
her the most highly paid newspaper writer of the time.

The acquisition of "Fanny Ford" proved to be so successful for the *Ledger*
that Bonner determined that he would obtain Fern's services as an exclusive
columnist. For her part, Fern had come to like and respect Bonner, so that
when he approached her with the offer of an exclusive contract to write a
weekly article for the *Ledger*, she agreed. She was to be paid twenty-five
dollars a week to write a regular weekly article, the length of which was to
be determined by herself.[8] On December 29, 1855, Bonner announced:

NEW ARRANGEMENT WITH FANNY FERN

> . . . A new agreement with FANNY FERN for a new series of her spirited,
> lively, dashing, unrivalled sketches. We will have a complete Sketch from
> her brilliant and popular pen every week during the entire year. Her ef-
> forts will be devoted exclusively to the LEDGER, *as she will write for no
> other paper!*

Fern's first article appeared on January 5, 1856. She continued to write for
the *Ledger* regularly—without missing a week—for the rest of her life. Her
last article was published on October 12, 1872, two days after her death.

When Fanny Fern began writing for the *Ledger*, her identity was already
known, but readers were eager for any information they could find out

about her. Pressed by his readers to give a description of Fanny Fern, Robert Bonner wrote in the February 16, 1856, edition of the *Ledger:*

Who can describe the Indescribable? Suppose we were to say that Fanny Fern is tall, superbly formed, of graceful carriage, and bright, blooming countenance; that her hair is golden-brown, of silken texture, rippled with glossy curls; that her dress, always inexpensive, is yet worn with so much taste, and is so well displayed by her fine person, as to convey the impression that she must be on the free-list at Stewart's; that she possesses, in a word, that assemblage of graces which invests a person with the composite and indefinable charm designated by the word *style;*—if we were to say this, and much more than this, should we have described Fanny Fern? By no means. . . . There is about her a magnetic *something* which defies description.

Within a year after Fern began writing for the *Ledger,* its circulation had increased by over 100,000 subscribers. Satisfied that his strategy was successful, Bonner proceeded to acquire other celebrities at equally high prices. In 1856 and 1857 he engaged adventure novelists E.D.E.N. Southworth and Sylvanus Cobb, Jr., to write exclusively for his paper. He signed a five-year contract with Southworth, agreeing to pay her a regular salary of forty dollars a week. Southworth, who, despite her success, had been treated shabbily at the *Saturday Evening Post,* continued to write for Bonner for the rest of her life, her salary increasing over the years and continuing whether she was sick or well, writing or not.[9] A prolific writer, she provided Bonner's paper with tales of passion and adventure; her most famous was *The Hidden Hand,* which Bonner serialized three times.

Sylvanus Cobb, Jr., who was lured away from the *The Flag of Our Union* and signed a five-year contract with Bonner for fifty dollars a week, continued to write for Bonner for thirty years. The first novel that he published in the *Ledger* was *The Gunmaker of Moscow,* which began on April 19, 1856. Although it was not published in book form until after Cobb's death, it was also serialized three times and was one of the most popular works of the 1850s.[10] In June 1856 Bonner heralded the success of the *Ledger* with a hundred-gun salute in City Hall Park.[11] By the fall of 1856, the circulation of the *Ledger* had reached 180,000 (NYL, December 6, 1856), the highest circulation ever reached by any American paper at the time, and continued to climb to a peak of 400,000.

Bonner continued to seek out celebrity writers. He paid Henry Ward Beecher, the charismatic preacher of Plymouth Church and brother of Harriet Beecher Stowe, thirty thousand dollars to write a novel, *Norwood.* He paid Whittier one thousand dollars for a poem, Longfellow three thousand dollars, and Alfred Tennyson five thousand dollars for a poem. Charles Dickens received five thousand dollars for a story, "Hunted Down," the only Dickens story published first in the United States. Bonner also obtained a series of articles by Edward Everett, a former president of Harvard, by offering to pay ten thousand dollars to the Mount Vernon Fund to obtain George Washington's birthplace as a national museum. Everett, who otherwise would not have written for a popular paper like the *Ledger*, agreed to the proposal, and when he had finished the series he found that he liked and respected Bonner so much that he continued to write for the *Ledger* until his death.[12] Bonner also obtained articles by college presidents, senators, and members of the clergy. Louisa May Alcott, James Parton, John G. Saxe, Horace Greeley, T. S. Arthur, William Cullen Bryant, Harriet Beecher Stowe, and Alice and Phoebe Cary were among the other well-known authors who wrote for the *Ledger*.

The principal reason for Bonner's ability to obtain celebrity writers was, of course, his willingness to pay high prices for their material. However, his ability to hold on to his regular writers was due not only to the high prices but also to his fairness to and cordial treatment of his writers, all of whom came to regard him not only as a publisher but as a warm friend. Writers like Southworth, Cobb, and Fern, who had exclusive contracts with the *Ledger*, all staunchly refused to be lured away by offers of higher pay.[13] Alice Cary once commented that Bonner had the ability "of gathering together not only the best writers in the varied departments of literature, but of holding them together as one family."[14] An 1870 history of twenty years among New York businessmen described Bonner as a " 'square,' manly, generous, high-minded" man, who "has the confidence of all who do business with him; a true friend."[15] Mary Noel, in her study of American magazines, pointed out that his business ability "involved little gestures of kindness, as well as liberality of pay."[16]

In the years that she wrote for the *Ledger*, Fanny Fern was the recipient of Bonner's "little gestures of kindness." On a number of occasions, and for no particular reason, Bonner sent her an extra check. Southworth was indebted to Bonner for similar kindnesses, such as extra checks for herself as well as help for her son.[17] On September 14, 1856, after Fern had been writing for the *Ledger* for nine months, she wrote to thank Bonner for one of his acts of kindness: "Thank you! Your note made my eyes swim. I know no other man who would have done so liberal and generous an action, and done it so delicately. You have added a warmth to my heart, and a point to my pen, which time can neither blunt nor chill, as my column in the *Ledger* shall show" (NYL, November 9, 1872). These acts of kindness contributed to the loyalty that Bonner's writers felt toward him and, as Fern's comment reveals, motivated his writers to do their best for the *Ledger*.

That Bonner's acts of kindness continued throughout her career is evident from a letter from Bonner. Fern had mentioned in her article that week that she had been writing for the *Ledger* for fourteen years. Bonner's letter is indicative of his discretion and concern:

Can it be possible that it is as long as that? . . . I enclose a check to remind you of the event; no, not exactly a present, for you might not like to receive it that way; but as compensation for some anonymous paragraphs which I want you to write for the *Ledger* whenever you feel like it. . . . If you should send me no more than five during the next year or two, I'll be satisfied; and if you should send me fifty, I'll take them just the same. (JP, 66)

On January 25, 1870, when, unknown to all but her immediate family, she was ill with what was to be a terminal cancer, she wrote to thank Bonner again: "How did you know that I was blue and discouraged, and had been crying all day because there was so much in the future to do, and I had so little strength left to do it? I am so *very down* when I *am* down! It was just one of your felicitous impulses to *feel* that I was blue without *knowing* it. Thank you for the gift and the generosity that prompts it" (NYL, November 9, 1872).

The acquisition of celebrity writers was one reason for Bonner's success. The other reason for his success was his advertising strategy. Bonner eliminated all advertising in his own paper when he took over the *Ledger*. At the same time, he inaugurated a new era in American advertising, using innovative and hitherto unheard-of methods, and paying out thousands of dollars each year to advertise his paper. His methods included purchasing a whole page in a newspaper only to print one or two sentences over and over, for example, "Fanny Fern writes only for the *New York Ledger*." He bought space in rival newspapers to print the first installment of one of his serialized novels, ending with the injunction that the readers would find the rest of the novel in the *New York Ledger*. His most outrageous feat of advertising was the purchase of all eight pages of the May 6, 1858, *New York Herald* and of the May 13, 1858, *New York Times* to advertise the *Ledger*. On the days that this advertisement appeared, the *Herald* and the *Times* contained sixteen pages, eight of which were Bonner's advertisement.[18] He also created amusing advertisements using famous people to endorse the *Ledger*. The first of these advertisements appeared in March 1856 in all the leading papers, and purported to be a conversation between Lord Palmerston, the British prime minister, and President Buchanan:

Lord Palmerston is said to have remarked to Mr. Buchanan (although we scarcely credit it) when matters looked squalliest between England and the United States: "My dear Buch, there is one reason why I should exceedingly dislike a rupture between our respective Governments, and that is this: I should be deprived of my *New York Ledger*. I could give up Central America and the other points but the *Ledger* I must have—especially now that Fanny Fern writes for it exclusively."

James Parton

On January 12, 1856, the *Ledger* announced: "We have the honor of announcing that our gifted contributor, Mrs. Sara Payson Eldredge (so renowned and admired as Fanny Fern), was married on Saturday the 5th, to Mr. James Parton, well known in literary circles as the author of *The Life of Horace Greeley.*"

James Parton, who was the prototype of Horace Gates in *Ruth Hall,* was born in 1822 in Canterbury, England. In 1827 his widowed mother brought her four children to the United States. After working as a teacher in Philadelphia and New York, Parton began writing for the newspapers. His first article was an assessment of *Jane Eyre,* proving that the author was a woman and not a man: he found in the book "the vehement, nervous, impetuous force of a great woman," rather than the "placid strength of a great man."[19] In 1852 Parton became assistant editor at the *Home Journal,* and, due to N. P. Willis's ill health, was in charge of the office during the early period of Fern's career. He admired Fern's writing, and, not knowing that she was Willis's sister, Parton, like most of the editors around the country, reprinted her articles in his paper. At one point he received a poem from a reader and sent it to Fern in care of one of the Boston papers for which she wrote. He appended a note to the then anonymous author:

Dear Unknown: New York is the place for you. You will find subjects here starting up in your path wherever you go. Come! Come! come! (JP, 54)

Parton later said that he did not know whether his note helped to effect her removal to New York, but a few weeks after he had sent it, Oliver Dyer informed him that Fern was in New York and offered to introduce him to her. This was in July of 1853, and Parton notes that it soon became part of his "daily occupation to show her the sights of this metropolis" (JP, 54–55). For the next two and a half years Parton was Fern's constant escort. In the fall of 1853 Parton resigned from the *Home Journal* apparently because of Willis's insistence that he (Parton) stop printing Fern's articles.

Early the next year Parton was having dinner in the fashionable Dietz Restaurant on Barclay Street, and sitting next to him were the Masons—Lowell, Jr., and Daniel—of the publishing firm Mason Brothers. At dinner, Parton mentioned that a biography of Horace Greeley would make a good book, and soon afterward the Masons asked him if he would write such a book. On March 3, 1854, the Masons signed a contract with him, providing him with an advance of fifteen dollars a week to work on the book for a year. One suspects that Fern, who had signed a contract with the Masons on February 16, 1854, to publish *Ruth Hall,* was instrumental in influencing the publishing firm to make this offer to Parton, who at the time was an untried author. His book was published in December 1854, at the same time as *Ruth Hall*. During the following year Parton wrote for various papers, principally *Life Illustrated*. Later he was to become a contributor to the *New York Ledger*, the *North American Review*, and the *Atlantic Monthly*. He went on to write a number of distinguished biographies, including a renowned biography of Andrew Jackson, and has been called the "father of modern biography."[20] His method, which was innovative at the time, marked him as one of the first modern biographers: he used anecdote and incident to bring his subject alive, and he included negative as well as positive characteristics so that his subject emerged as recognizably human.

The diary of Thomas Butler Gunn, who was a newspaper writer and illustrator, provides us with some interesting insights into the life of Fern and Parton in 1855 and during the early years of their marriage.[21] Gunn first met Parton on August 17, 1855. At this time Parton had known Fern for two years. Gunn subsequently visited Parton in his boardinghouse on Waverly Place, where they began collaborating on a book. On August 20 he described Parton: "He is a thin, gentlemanly, earnest looking young man, of no small intellect, and worth." On September 7 he mentioned that he and Parton talked of many things, "Washington Irving, Willis, 'Fanny Fern,' men, nationality, and books." In the earlier references to Fern in his diary, Gunn always put her name in quotation marks. Later, however, as he came to know her by that name and no other, he eliminated the quotation marks.

On August 25 Gunn was invited to spend the first of many evenings with Parton's relatives, the Edwardses, at 745 Broadway near Washington Square. Sarah Edwards, who was Parton's mother's sister, had been a governess in the home of George Edwards, and when his wife died, she had married him. On November 8, 1855, after William Thackeray's third lecture in New York, Gunn spent the evening with Parton, and they spoke of Fanny Fern, whom Gunn had seen with Parton at the first lecture, but whom he was not to meet until after she was married to Parton. The conventional Gunn, who preferred retiring women, apparently was not prepared to like Fern. He commented about her in words that were later inked out, and called *Ruth Hall* a "bad-hearted book." Parton, he said, "spoke of the Willis blood as being bad, but of her, with a leniency springing from personal intimacy." On December 6, Gunn noted that he had passed Parton and Fanny Fern on the street, commenting, she "has just produced another of her bad-hearted books" (*Rose Clark*).

On January 5, 1856, the day of the wedding, Gunn wrote that he stopped at Parton's to drop off an article for the book they were working on. Parton met him at the door, but apparently did not say anything about his impending wedding. Gunn did not find out about the marriage until January 7, when he reported it without comment: "Sol returning from down town tells that Parton is married to 'Fanny Fern.' It occurred on Saturday afternoon or evening."

At other times in his diary Gunn speculates about why James Parton married Fanny Fern. When he is in a friendly mood, he assumes that Parton is in love with Fern and she with him and that they respect and admire each other; when he is feeling unfriendly, he ascribes Parton's proposal to sexual passion and/or a desire to get ahead.

It is clear from Gunn's diary that the relationship between Fern and Parton involved a healthy physical relationship.[22] Although the fastidious Gunn was uncomfortable to see Fern and Parton demonstrate a frank physical interest in each other, the reader who is familiar with the horror that Fern felt at the unwanted embraces of her second husband can only be glad that she and Parton were sexually compatible. They also apparently both felt a strong attraction to and respect for one other's intellect and integrity. Parton had admired Fern's writing long before he knew who she was, and she wrote admiringly of his work. They both had a horror of sham and pretense, and each liked the straightforward common sense of the other. And probably not insignificant was their mutual dislike of N. P. Willis. That Parton did not respect Willis is clear from his refusal to write a biography of him because he felt that he could not write anything positive about his brother-in-law.[23] Moreover, Willis, whom Fern satirized in *Ruth Hall* as a name-dropping social climber and dandy, represented ideas that were antithetical to Fern's and Parton's lifelong struggle for social justice and empathy for the less privileged members of society. Willis's *Home Journal*, which survives as the upscale periodical *Town and Country*, was dedicated to the "beautiful," and, as Willis wrote in 1855, the "one purpose" of his journal was "*the keeping open of a bridge of human sympathy and kindly feeling between the upper classes in cities and the country at large*" [his italics].[24]

Parton's feelings about Willis are probably reflected in the comments of Horace Gates in *Ruth Hall* about Hyacinth Ellet. Gates complains that Ellet takes the credit for articles he (Gates) has written while paying him "principally in fine speeches." Gates also complains about Hyacinth's editorial methods. Because Hyacinth does not want to offend southern subscribers, for example, the word *slave* is tabooed from the columns of the paper and books like "Uncle Sam's Log House" are not reviewed. Hyacinth orders Gates to give favorable reviews to books by people who have been or can be useful to Hyacinth—regardless of the quality of the book. Gates comments:

That is the way it is done. Mutual admiration society—bah! I wish *I* had a paper. Wouldn't I call things by their right names? Would I know any sex in books? Would I praise a book because a woman wrote it? Would I abuse it for the same reason? Would I say, as one of our most able editors said long since to his reviewer, "cut it up root and branch; what right have these women to set themselves up for authors, and reap literary laurels?" . . . Would I have my tongue or my pen tied in any way by policy, or interest, or clicque-ism? No—sir! (RH, 158–161)

That Fern put these words—which reflect her own ideas—into the mouth of Horace Gates, whom she based on James Parton, suggests that Fern and Parton shared similar attitudes not only toward N. P. Willis but toward editorial practices in general. On February 14, 1857, Fern satirized Willis's *Home Journal* as the *Foam Journal*, calling it "Fashion's High Priest." In an article entitled "No-Newspaper Day," published on August 4, 1860, she tells how distressing the newspaperless holidays are to both of them, and reveals not only an important shared aspect of her life with Parton but also their common attitude toward the press:

I have never seen any person who fully sympathized with me on conduct so reprehensible, save the partner of my coffee and pillow, and let me add of my morning paper. There *may* be married people who do not read the morning paper. Smith and I know them not. . . . It is not too much to say that newspapers are one of our strongest points of sympathy; that it is our meat and drink to praise and abuse them together; that we often in imagination mutually edit a model newspaper, which shall have for its motto, "Speak the truth, and shame the devil."

On the day of their wedding and before the ceremony, Fern and Parton signed a prenuptial agreement, witnessed by Oliver Dyer, who was named as trustee and attorney:

Whereas the said Sara has and ownes [sic] certain property consisting of Funds invested and to be invested, Stock in Bank or corporate institutions, the Copyright of and to Books & publications, Contracts and other effects and interests; and has children by her former Marriage, to whom she is desirous of being able at any time hereafter to confer benefits out of her said property in such mode and manner as to her shall seem proper. . . . [T]he said James the party aforesaid of the second part hereby covenants and agrees to and with the said Sara, the party aforesaid of the first part, that from thenceforth and after the said contemplated marriage shall have taken place, the said Sara shall have, hold, possess, own, manage, use, control, and enjoy her said property, and each and every part and parcel thereof, and the income, profits, interest, dividends and payments accruing and to accrue, due or to become due therefrom, and the proceeds thereof including any other increased or substituted property or securities which in the management or transmutation of said property or of any part thereof, may arise therefrom and including any and all property which may hereafter arise or accrue to her by reason of any new works which may be prepared by her, as her separate Estate and as if she were unmarried with full power and authority to apply or dispose of the same.[25]

The terms of this agreement thus permitted Fern to marry without risking the loss of her assets, which, according to the law at the time, would have belonged wholly to her husband.[26] After having experienced the powerlessness that derived from dependency upon men—husband, father, brother, brother-in-law, and father-in-law—Fern was careful to include in the agreement the stipulation that she and only she would have control over her money and that she would have the power to use that money for the benefit of her children in any way that she wished. One of the problems in her second marriage was that her husband withheld funds from her for her own and her children's necessities in order to force her to his will. Similarly, when she left him, her father withheld funds in the attempt to force her to return to her husband, and her father-in-law wrote his will in such a way that his money would be withheld from her children unless Fern agreed to give them up. Fern had seen how the male control of money could be used to assert power over women, and she had found how powerless a woman was without money.

After signing the prenuptial agreement, the couple, with Oliver Dyer, traveled to Hoboken, New Jersey, where the ceremony was performed at five o'clock in the afternoon by the Reverend Isaac Stryker, pastor of the First Presbyterian Church.[27] They could not have picked a worse day for the trip. On January 5, 1856, Fanny Fern's and James Parton's wedding day, a terrific snowstorm blanketed the Northeast. Fern and Parton must have found it difficult to return from New Jersey after the ceremony. The storm, which was said to be the worst snowstorm in seventy years, had by early evening shut down most railroad and omnibus lines and water traffic, and by midnight all traffic into and within the city was at a standstill.[28] Gunn wrote on January 5: "This morning a heavy and continuous snow storm set in, far exceeding anything I have yet seen. All the rest of the day and night it lasted, and a wild night it proved." The next day he wrote: "Sunday. New York a half buried city, areas full, windows half hidden, carts covered and streets impassable."

On January 9, 1856, Gunn attended a party to celebrate the marriage:

In the evening to the Delancy House, corner of Broadway and Waverly Place, there to visit Parton and his wife, in accordance with an invitation I had through Haney. The night was piercingly cold, my mustache all ice hidden in five seconds after my stepping forth. The snow carnival in operation, and sleigh bells jingling along Broadway. The apartments occupied by the newly wed pair are at the top of the hotel, four stories up. She resided there before; he has quitted his old Waverly Place room. The hotel is a stylish one, servants about in the landing places, gas and warmth every where. I found the company—consisting of Mr. and Mrs. P., a daughter of the latter's [Grace], Colonel Forbes, and Haney (who had preceded me by half an hour,) assembled in a neatly furnished room, with new desk, sofa, a rocking chair or so, and adjoining it an alcove where was a bed. We soon however adjourned into another room, more luxuriously fitted up. A neat open stove wherein a fire was blazing bonnily kept up a pleasant warmth. There were oil portraits (I guess of "Fanny's" two children), and everything was very snug and tasty. And now to pay respects to the goddess herself after describing the shrine. Haney sat at her right side, on the sofa, I in easy chair at her left, Parton near me, and Forbes, in his plain gray suit, and look of a true gentleman-aristocrat-republican-soldier, opposite. "Fanny Fern" is, I suppose, upwards of 35, has fairish brown hair worn protruding out rather pretentiously, bright-ish eyes and a high color (which may be natural). . . . She was gaily attired now, having on a brown satin dress, with more than one ring on her fingers. Her frock was cut *rather* low in front. She talked with much ani-mation. . . . The evening was a great success. Parton looked pale, and wore gorgeous slippers. She called him "Jem" or "Jemmy," he addressing her as "Fanny." There was considerable rallying on the suddenness of the match, she taking the occasion to intimate that it must not be considered as affecting his bachelor friendships. We partook of milk punch and ev-erybody talked. "Fanny's" daughter [Grace] is a tall grown-girl, nearly as high as her mother. She said nothing, standing listening. After an hour or so we came away, rather gladsomely, Haney convinced "the match wasn't so bad" after all, and talking laudation of matrimony.

One notes that Gunn underestimated Fern's age; she was forty-four at the time. Parton was thirty-three, and Gunn would be thirty the following month. On January 26 Gunn reports that he visited Parton and Fern in their new quarters at "the Waverley House, lower down on Broadway." He re-cords frequent visits to the Waverley House, stopping in almost every other day. On Thursday, February 14, for example, he writes: "To Parton's. There spent the evening. She 'Fanny Fern' talks very freely, telling all sorts of little domestic details (and inventing some) about her husband." On Sun-day, March 17, he writes: "To the Waverley in the evening & had a long, pleasant talk with Parton & his wife." On Wednesday, March 27, he writes:

Evening to Parton's, and there till 10 1/2. Fanny certainly talks with greater freedom than I have ever heard before from the lips of a woman. She not only puts "Jim" in the *Ledger* from week to week as "Mr. Pax" but tells one all sorts of things about him, quizzing and fudging most enormously.

Soon after their marriage, on January 19, 1856, Fern had published in the *Ledger* an article entitled "The Last Bachelor Hours of Tom Pax," which portrayed Parton as an eager but nervous bridegroom. More revealing is her portrayal of "Tom Pax's" realization of what it is like to be married to a writer. On February 9, 1856, she published in the *Ledger* "Tom Pax's Con-jugal Soliloquy":

Mrs. Pax is an authoress. I knew it when I married her. I liked the idea.
I had not tried it then. I had not a clear idea what it was to have one's wife
belong to the public. I thought marriage was marriage, brains not ex-
cepted. I was mistaken. Mrs. Pax is very kind: I don't wish to say that she
is not. Very obliging: I would not have you think the contrary; but when I
put my arm round Mrs. Pax's waist, and say, "Mary, I love you," she
smiles in an absent, moonlight-kind of a way, and says, "Yes, to-day is
Wednesday, is it not? I must write an article for 'The Weekly Monopolizer' to-day." . . .

Mrs. Pax opens her writing desk; it is one I gave her; takes some delicate buff note-paper; I gave her that, too; dips her gold pen (my gift) into
the inkstand, and writes—writes till eleven o'clock. Eleven! and I, her
husband, Tom Pax, sit there and wait for her. . . .

Not that I am *complaining* of Mrs. Pax, not at all; not that I don't like
my wife to be an authoress; I do. To be sure I can't say that I knew *exactly*
what it involved. I did not know, for instance, that the Press in speaking
of her by her *nom-de-plume* would call her "OUR Julia," but I would not
have you think I object to her being literary. On the contrary, I am not
sure that I do not rather like it; but I ask the Editor of "The Weekly
Monopolizer," as a man—as a Christian—as a husband—if he thinks it
right—if it is doing as he would be done by—to monopolize my wife's
thoughts as early as five o'clock in the morning?

Although one does not know how accurate this portrayal of Parton is,
Fern's tendency to write from her own experience suggests that the article
does reflect Parton's mixed emotions. On the one hand, he apparently liked
the idea of being married to a successful writer: he was a literary person
himself, and Gunn had noted in his diary that he admired success (November 20, 1855). On the other hand, as Fern's choice of the name *The Weekly
Monopolizer* for the *New York Ledger* indicates, it must have been difficult
for him to overcome the expectations of a nineteenth-century husband that,
as Fern said elsewhere, his wife would exist wholly for him. In "The Tear of
a Wife," for example, she wrote that a husband "wants to be *considered* the
source of your happiness, . . . your mind *never* being supposed to be occupied with any other subject than himself" (OB, August 28, 1852).

In a *Ledger* column in March 1856, describing various well-known
people that she saw as she walked down Broadway, Fern provided this description of James Parton:

And there is Mr. James Parton, author of the *Life of Horace Greeley*,
whom I occasionally meet. Jim is five feet ten inches, and modest—wears
his hair long, and don't believe in the devil—has written more good anonymous articles now floating unbaptized through newspaperdom (on both
sides of the water), than any other man, save himself, would suffer to go

unclaimed. Jim believes in Carlyle and lager bier—can write a book better than he can tie a cravat; though since his late marriage I am pleased to observe a wonderful improvement in this respect. It is my belief, that Jim is destined by steady progress, to eclipse many a man who has shot up like a rocket, and who will fizzle out and come down like a stick. (NYL, March 29, 1856)

Fern's comment here that Parton did not "believe in the devil" refers to Parton's stance as an unbeliever. Although Fern had herself eschewed the rigid Calvinist teachings of her father and criticized hypocritical and doctrinaire religion, she maintained a belief in the basic teachings of Christianity. Parton, however, had rebelled against his mother's stern creed, and his refusal to hold religious services in his school in Philadelphia had led to the breakup of the school. He regarded religion as a source of bigotry and refused to acknowledge the divinity of God. On November 15, 1857, Gunn tells of a visit to Henry Ward Beecher's church with Fern, Parton, and other friends, "Parton quietly rampant with wrath at *being* in church." Parton was to maintain his atheism throughout their marriage.[29]

Gunn's March 27, 1856, diary entry includes a reference to Fern's dressing in men's clothing:

[Fanny Fern] told personally of her dressing up in *his* clothes yester evening, and *how she looked* (rather minutely), and how "they wished *I* had come in." She put on my hat too, and talked of the privilege accorded by it. It's all very innocent perhaps, and a stranger oughtn't to object, but I wonder *Parton* likes it. *Does* he?

Here Gunn touches on a theme that was a dominant one in Fern's writings: the power that was accorded to people on the basis of gender; her metaphorical way of expressing it was to refer to the power accorded to the wearer of a "hat" (as opposed to a "bonnet"). This is also the first known reference to Fern's dressing up in men's clothes, which she was to write about two years later in the *Ledger*.

On May 10, 1856, the *Ledger* printed a notice that Fern's daughter had taken first prize in a seminary uptown. At this time Grace was fifteen; several years later she too would be writing for the *Ledger*. In the spring of 1856 Gunn stopped at the Waverley regularly on Saturday evenings. In June 1856 he described a typical evening there with Parton, Fern, Walt Whitman, Oliver Dyer (whom he identifies as the John Walter of *Ruth Hall*), Fern's daughters, and other guests. This gives us a good description of Fern and her daughters at this time:

Fanny's eldest daughter, Grace (Eldredge) will be reading. She is a tall, fair-haired girl of 16 or so, with an innocentish face,—very fond of reading.

Nelly, the younger, is fair and fat. . . . Fanny has been a handsomish woman, and looks well now but haggard. She is light haired, and when animated her face flushes. . . . Parton appears very fond of her.

In June 1856 Gunn noted, "Parton and his wife have just moved to Brooklyn, where *she* has bought a house." Fern's elation at being able to buy her own house is reflected in her July 19 article, "My Old Ink-Stand and I." On July 26 she wrote about the happiness she derived from having *closets*, which were not usually available in hotel rooms or boardinghouses; on August 9 she wrote about the benefits of living in Brooklyn, which was cleaner and greener than Manhattan. On July 5 Gunn visited Parton and Fern in the new house at 33 Oxford Street:

The house is a pleasant, handsome one, situated behind Washington Park, from the avenues of which you have a noble view of the city of New York. "Fanny" gave me a pleasant welcome and showed me over the house, and then Parton came in. Some fellow in Philadelphia has published a cookery book attaching Fanny Fern's *nomme de plume* to it, and both Parton and his wife were in a freeze about it. Oliver Dyer goes to Philadelphia to-morrow with an injunction, they have, to day, procured. We supped in the front basement, with Fanny's daughters.

The book that Gunn mentions was a cookbook published by William Fleming. On Friday, July 14, Parton and Fern appeared in court in Philadelphia before Judge Kane. At that time a married woman could not legally bring suit in her name alone, and Fern was fortunate that her husband was in agreement with her; the suit was brought in both their names. Fern was able to stop the author from using her name, and published an article in the *Ledger* describing her triumphant fight. Henceforth, the name Fanny Fern was to be hers alone:

Issue a book, and put my name to it! Mine? A *man* to do such a thing! . . . "What am I going to do about it?" Why, get an injunction served on the honorable publisher, to be sure. What is the use of laws if they were not made for my use? . . . "Fanny Fern is not my name, is it?" Let me tell you, that if I originated it as a *nom de plume*, I have as much right to the sole possession of it, as I have to the one I was baptised by. . . . Are bonnets to be trampled on by boots? Judge Kane says No. . . . Listen! All you who wear (blue) bonnets; and down on your grateful knees to me, for unfurling the banner of Women's (scribblers) Rights. (NYL, August 2, 1856)

For the next three years Gunn described frequent visits to the house on Oxford Street, where he spent pleasant afternoons or evenings, sometimes staying overnight. On May 9, 1858, he wrote: "These Brooklyn visits are my true holidays. To know how much I value them I have but to think how I should miss them were I deprived of the pleasure." Gunn tells of the other visitors, of playing whist and fortune-telling games, talking, laughing, throwing snowballs, going out for walks, and to the circus, and listening to Fern tell "capital stories over the breakfast table, which she ought to write out under the title of 'Schooldays of an Incorrigible girl.' "[30]

IO

❧

Walt Whitman

Because a man is a "genius," must one endorse [unspeakable] things and write them down as "eccentricities" inseparable from it and to be lightly passed over? Must intellect necessarily *be at variance with principle? . . . I do hold that he is to be held as accountable for his errors as the most ordinary farmer's boy who is unable to spell the name of the plow which he guides.*

(NYL, June 4, 1864)

WHEN FANNY FERN AND WALT WHITMAN MET EARLY IN 1856, she was, at forty-four, the author of four very successful books and the highest-paid newspaper writer of the time. The thirty-six-year-old Whitman, on the other hand, was an unemployed newspaper writer and housebuilder who, the year before, had published at his own expense a slim volume of poetry, of which few copies had been sold. The meeting was fortunate for Whitman. During the year that they were friends, Fern was to exercise all of her influence—and it was considerable—on his behalf.

Whitman was probably familiar with Fern's work before he met her, and he may have taken the idea for the title and cover design of *Leaves of Grass* from Fern's first book, *Fern Leaves from Fanny's Portfolio,* published in 1853.[1] Both books were bound in dark green cloth with gold lettering and decorated with tendrils intertwined on the cover and spine, with a triple-lined border stamped in gold. Whitman's book was larger, however, in keeping with the magnitude of his claims, or, as has been suggested, to allow for the easier printing of the unusually long lines in his poetry.[2] The immediate fate of the two books was dramatically different. Whereas *Fern Leaves* sold fifty thousand copies in six months, *Leaves of Grass* sold fewer than ten copies.[3] The history of the two books since then has been different also, but in reverse: whereas *Leaves of Grass* has been reprinted many times since Whitman first brought it out and is known throughout the world, *Fern Leaves,* until recently, had not been reprinted since the period of its original fame and is little known today.[4]

It cannot be said that either Fern or Whitman was influenced by the other or that one was the disciple of the other. Rather, theirs was a literary friendship that grew out of their apparently common attitudes and beliefs. In her newspaper columns, Fanny Fern was an outspoken critic of sham and pretense, and a firm believer in the democratic man and woman. She eschewed stilted, artificial language and abhorred hypocrisy and the superficial dandies of her time—both male and female—and apparently thought that she had found in Walt Whitman, the man and his work, the kind of unpretentious honesty that she extolled in her columns.

The Fern-Whitman friendship ended in mid-1857 when Whitman failed to repay two hundred dollars that he had borrowed from Fern's husband, James Parton. Angered by the apparent disingenuousness of Whitman's promises, Fern and Parton pursued the matter, and their lawyer collected certain goods from Whitman in lieu of cash.[5] Whitman harbored no ill will toward Parton, commenting favorably on Parton's *Life of Aaron Burr* in his paper the following year. Instead, he blamed Fanny Fern. When questioned about the debt by Horace Traubel years later, Whitman was vague:

There were other elements in the story—venom, jealousies, opacities: they played a big part: and, if I may say it, women: a woman certainly— maybe women: they kept alive what I felt James Parton would have let die.[6]

In later years, Whitman's defenders used this quotation and its obscure reference to a woman's "jealousies" to support the contention that Fanny Fern was in love with Whitman, and that, spurned by him, she had urged Parton to pursue the debt.[7]

The innuendoes of Whitman's defenders are not only without foundation, they are offensive to any student of Fern's works. They imply that Fanny Fern could not have—perhaps that no woman could have—appreciated Whitman's poems unless she was in love with him, and contrarily that no woman would have a reason to become angry with him unless she was a woman scorned. The implication is that Fanny Fern is not to be treated seriously as a critic of literature or as a person.

Whitman scholars have made two serious errors in writing of this episode in Whitman's life. First, they have not read Fern's work and thus, like Fred Lewis Pattee in 1940, they have dismissed her as a writer of "sentimental pap," unworthy to be discussed as an intellectual equal of Walt Whitman.[8] And second, assuming this to be true, they have accepted Whitman's friends' hints that Fern must have been in love with Whitman as the only explanation for her appreciation of his work and her later hostility toward him.[9]

Early in 1856 James Parton introduced his new wife to Walt Whitman. Fern reflected her impression of Whitman in a column she wrote on April 19 in the *New York Ledger* as part of a series of columns describing New York celebrities, "Peeps from under a Parasol." After deftly sketching such New Yorkers as Charles A. Dana, Henry Ward Beecher, P. T. Barnum, her husband, James Parton, the actors John Lester and Laura Keene, Horace Greeley, and herself, she included in the third column in the series this sketch of Walt Whitman:

And speaking of books, here comes Walt Whitman, author of *Leaves of Grass*, which, by the way, I have not yet read. His shirt collar is turned off from his muscular throat, and his shoulders are thrown back as if even in that fine, ample chest of his, his lungs had not sufficient play-room. Mark his voice! high—deep—and clear, as a clarion note. In the most crowded thoroughfare, one would turn instinctively on hearing it, to seek out its owner. Such a voice is a gift as rare as it is priceless. A fig for phrenology! Let me hear the *voice* of a man or a woman and I will tell you the stuff its owners are made of. (NYL, April 19, 1856)

In order to understand the perspective from which this was written, it is useful to compare it to Fern's sketch of Bayard Taylor earlier in the series:

Now I don't suppose Bayard is to blame for being a *pretty* man, or for looking so nice and bandbox-y. But if some public benefactor *would* tumble his hair and shirt collar and tie his cravat in a loose sailor knot; and if Bayard himself *would* open that little three-cent mouth of his a l-i-t-t-l-e wider when he lectures, it would take a load off my mind. (NYL, March 29, 1856)

To interpret Fern's appreciative description of Whitman as indicative that she had "cast her eye on Walt in a cherishing way,"[10] as so many Whitman scholars have concluded, can only be done if the passage is taken out of context—out of the context of the series in which it is only one short sketch among many, and out of the context of Fern's career, where it is simply an example of the kind of person that she preferred. Throughout her writing career she criticized the fashion-conscious "smirking fops and brainless belles" (NYL, November 12, 1853) and advocated practical dress and good health habits. Typical of her attitude is the following passage from an 1867 article entitled "Fashionable Invalidism," in which she urged men and women to live active, healthy lives: "How I rejoice in a man or woman with a chest; who can look the sun in the eye, and step off as if they had not wooden legs" (NYL, July 27, 1867).

With this attitude, it is not surprising that Fanny Fern liked Walt Whitman, whose deliberately casual dress and robust good health must have been a refreshing contrast to the mincing dandies she criticized in her column. Nor is it surprising that Whitman responded to Fern's down-to-earth manner. He said that he "liked her better than any woman,"[11] and he visited her and her husband regularly, first at the Waverley House in Manhattan where they lived after their marriage and then at the house on Oxford Street in Brooklyn that Fern bought in June 1856. Of course it,is possible that since Whitman worked very hard as his own public relations man,[12] he may also have been motivated by the hope that Fern and Parton could be useful to him. When Samuel Wells began to divest himself of *Leaves of Grass* because of what he called "certain objectionable passages" in the second edition, he wrote to Whitman on June 7, 1856, that Fern's and Parton's publishers, Mason Brothers, were "rich and enterprizing," and suggested that Whitman get them to publish his book.[13] Moreover, Whitman could not have been unaware of the power of the *New York Ledger* as a publicity tool. In August 1856 he wrote a character sketch of Robert Bonner, editor of the *Ledger*. In an article much like Fern's earlier "Peeps from under a Parasol," describing people he saw on the street, he called Bonner the "hero of unheard-of and tremendous advertising," and lauded the *Ledger* as a "gorgeous and unprecedented sheet."[14]

Not only might Whitman have perceived that Fern herself could be useful to him, but her home was a good place to meet other potentially useful journalists and writers. Fern had a wide circle of literary friends, and although she did not like to attend fashionable evening parties, she regularly entertained these friends in her home.[15]

It is clear, then, that Whitman had much to gain from his friendship with Fanny Fern. However, despite Whitman's "lifelong maneuvering for publicity,"[16] it is unlikely that, given his high opinion of friendship, he would have pursued his friendship with Fern if he had not also genuinely liked her. He was a frequent visitor, and he seems to have enjoyed himself while in her company. Thomas Butler Gunn's diary entries for 1856 and 1857 provide a revealing picture of the relationship between Whitman and Fern. Gunn, who records first meeting Whitman at the Partons' in May 1856, notes that Whitman subsequently called on him, that he liked him "immensely," and says that he "must put him in pen and ink hereafter."[17] If Whitman was looking for literary contacts at Fern's and Parton's, he certainly did not waste any time following up on Gunn, and Gunn did soon thereafter publish a pen-and-ink sketch of Whitman.

The following June 1856 entry from Gunn's diary answers some important questions about the friendship between Whitman and Fern:

I used, as wont to drop in at the Waverley on Saturday nights, always finding Walt Whitman there, and sometimes Oliver Dyer. . . . Walt Whitman is six feet high, nearer forty than thirty, I should say, very much sun-burned and rough handed. He is broad in proportion to his height, has a short, partially grey beard and mustache, and a neck as brown as a berry. His face is very manly and placid. He wears a wide brimmed low crowned felt hat, a rough, loose coat, striped shirt (with perceptible red flannel one under it), no vest, loose short pants, and big thick boots. Thus accoutered I find him lounging on the sofa beside Fanny Fern, his legs reposing on a stool or chair. . . . Parton seated in an arm chair, in short, brown, loose in-doors coat, white pants and low shiny shoes, listens, leaning forwards to Walt's talk. . . . Dyer will probably be sitting 'tother side of Fanny. . . . Parton appears very fond of her (He, however, isn't jealous of Walt's kissing her, which he always does on quitting.) Walt talks *well*—but occasionally too much, being led by the interest with which his remarks are received into monopolizing the converse. I, as a rule, would prefer to play listener, yet it is a violation of good taste to find yourself constrained to become one. And nobody wishes to become a bucket to be pumped into, let the stream be ever so nutritious.[18]

This diary entry tells us three important facts: first, that Whitman was a regular visitor at Fern's and Parton's; second, that he was at his ease there; and third, that rather than Fanny Fern being "sweet" on Whitman, as Whitman scholars have asserted, it seems to have been he who played up to her.[19]

On April 21, 1856, after reading the first edition of *Leaves of Grass*, Fern wrote Whitman a note telling him her opinion of it:

"Leaves of Grass"

You are *delicious!* May my right hand wither if I don't tell the world before another week, what *one* woman thinks of you.

"Walt"? "what *I* assume, *you* shall assume!" Some one evening this week you are to spend with Jemmy [James Parton] & me— Wednesday?—say.

Yours truly,
Fanny Fern[20]

This note has been used as evidence for the rumor spread by Whitman's friends that Fern was in love with Whitman. However, this interpretation is only possible if one misreads the beginning of the letter to mean that she is calling *Whitman* "delicious." It is clear from the manuscript copy that at the beginning of the letter when she says, "You are delicious," she is addressing not Walt Whitman but *Leaves of Grass*. The word "You" comes on the next line immediately after "Leaves of Grass," which is clearly the salutation. Moreover, this is the same expression she uses in the first paragraph of her review of *Leaves of Grass*, again addressing the book. Fern had already told the world what she thought of Whitman in her *Ledger* column of April 19, so that when she says she will tell the world "what *one* woman thinks of you," the "you" again refers to *Leaves of Grass*.

Whatever Whitman's later attitude toward Fanny Fern, the receipt of this letter must have pleased him greatly. Fanny Fern, the most popular newspaper columnist in America, whose words in the *Ledger* reached more homes than any other journalist's, had promised to praise in print his obscure *Leaves of Grass*. That Whitman kept this little note, although he burned so many other letters and papers, indicates how much it meant to him.

Fanny Fern kept her promise, and on May 10, 1856, the *Ledger* printed her review praising *Leaves of Grass*:

"Leaves of Grass"
Well baptized: fresh, hardy and grown for the masses. Not more welcome is their natural type to the winter-bound, bed-ridden, and spring-emancipated invalid. "Leaves of Grass" thou art unspeakably delicious, after the forced, stiff, Parnassian exotics for which our admiration has been vainly challenged.

Walt Whitman, the effeminate world needed thee. The timidest soul whose wings ever drooped with discouragement, could not choose but rise on thy strong pinions. . . .

Walt Whitman, the world needed a "Native American" of thorough, out-and-out breed—enamored of *women* not *ladies, men* not *gentlemen;* something beside a mere Catholic-hating Know-Nothing; it needed a man who dared speak out his strong, honest thoughts, in the face of pusillanimous, toadeying, republican aristocracy; dictionary-men, hypocrites, cliques and creeds; it needed a large-hearted, untainted, self-reliant, fearless son of the Stars and Stripes, who disdains to sell his birthright for a mess of pottage. . . .

Fresh *Leaves of Grass!* not submitted by the self-reliant author to the fingering of any publisher's critic, to be arranged, rearranged and disarranged to his circumscribed liking, till they hung limp, tame, spiritless, and scentless. No. It were a spectacle worth seeing, this glorious Native American, who, when the daily labor of chisel and plane was over, himself, with toil-hardened fingers, handled the types to print the pages which wise and good men have since delighted to endorse and to honor. Small critics, whose contracted vision could see no beauty, strength, or grace, in these "Leaves," have long ago repented that they so hastily wrote themselves down shallow by such a premature confession. Where an Emerson, and a Howitt have commended, my woman's voice of praise may not avail; but happiness was born a twin, and so I would fain share with others the unmingled delight which these "Leaves" have given me.

I say unmingled; I am not unaware that the charge of coarseness and sensuality has been affixed to them. My moral constitution may be hopelessly tainted—or too sound to be tainted, as the critic wills—but I confess that I extract no poison from these "Leaves"—to me they have brought only healing. Let him who can do so, shroud the eyes of the nursing babe lest it should see its mother's breast. . . .

Sensual? Let him who would affix this stigma upon "Leaves of Grass," write upon his heart, in letters of fire, these noble words of its author:

> "In woman I see the bearer of the great fruit, which is immortality
> .... The good thereof is not tasted by *roues*, and never can be. ..."

I close the extracts from these "Leaves," which it were easy to multiply, for one is more puzzled what to leave unculled, than what to gather, with the following sentiments; for which, and for all the good things included between the covers of his book, Mr. Whitman will please accept the cordial grasp of a woman's hand:

> "The wife—and she is not one jot less than the husband.
> The daughter—and she is just as good as the son,
> The mother—and she is every bit as much as the father."
> (NYL, May 10, 1856)

Fanny Fern was the first woman to praise *Leaves of Grass* in print—and the only woman to do so for many years. Her review was daring and courageous, written at a time when few men were willing to praise Whitman's work publicly. And even those who did so would probably have agreed with Charles Eliot Norton that they "would be sorry to know that any woman had looked into it past the title-page."[21] Even the favorable reviewers had qualified their praise with reservations about Whitman's coarseness and indecent language. But it was typical of Fanny Fern to "tell the world" what she thought regardless of the opinions of others. In her columns she spoke out on religion, prostitution, venereal disease, divorce; why not speak out on *Leaves of Grass?* The editor of the *Ledger* was willing to print her controversial opinions, though sometimes he made editorial comments on them, and, in the case of her review of Whitman, he subtly qualified her review by printing on the same page an earlier sentimental article, "Little Benny," whose maternal theme demonstrated that Fanny Fern was not "unwomanly" despite her questionable views on *Leaves of Grass.*

Why did Fern respond so favorably to Whitman's book? Anyone who has read her work has no difficulty answering this question. As Emerson said, he read other books only to see his own thoughts.[22] What Fanny Fern found in *Leaves of Grass* were her own thoughts. Each of the six major points for which she praises *Leaves of Grass* has its counterpart in her own writings.

First of all, the language of *Leaves of Grass* is not stiff and artificial. Fern's own writing had been criticized as vulgar because she did not use the delicate language expected of women writers. It is no wonder that Fern welcomed the freshness and frankness of *Leaves of Grass.*

The second point she addressed was the bold strength that she saw in the writer. For some time Fern had lamented the hypocritical timidity of "milk and water" men. In 1853, after seeing a "Men Wanted," sign in a shop window, she commented: "Well, they have been 'wanted' for some time, but the article is not in the market, although there are plenty of spurious imitations" (MWT, September 24, 1853). And early that year, on seeing "The Bearded Woman," she wrote: "As if *that* was a curiosity! I can see legions of them any day . . . lisping and mincing aimless through creation, on their patent leather toes, behind a dickey and a moustache. . . . these bewhiskered, bescented, be-cravatted, be-jewelled, be-everlastingly-despised Lilliputian dandies" (MWT, May 7, 1853). The world, as Fern saw it, had become "effeminate." It needed a strong man like Whitman, "enamored of *women* not *ladies, men* not *gentlemen.*"

A third point that Fern commented on was the fearless individualism and self-reliance of Whitman's *Leaves of Grass.* Fern was particularly critical of writers who were simply imitators, and in 1853 her article "Borrowed Light" satirized the writers who lacked the courage or were too lazy to "take the trouble to light a torch of their own" (TF, April 9, 1853). Throughout her writing career, also, Fern urged individualism in all areas for both men and women. She detested conformity: "One may even do a worse thing than to be 'odd.' One may be untrue to one's self, or a mere echo of others, which is to me the alpha and omega of disgustingness. Heaven save us from colorless characters, what else soever it inflicts upon us: people who don't know what they think till they ask somebody" (NYL, April 8, 1871).

The fourth point that Fern makes is to praise Whitman's democratic ideal. Fern wrote all her life as a friend of the working man and woman, urging reform and putting herself in the place of the shopgirl, the house-maid, the factory worker, even the prostitute. Always critical of the Mrs. Grundys who looked down on the less fortunate, Fern wrote with great understanding of the conditions of poverty and the human dignity of all people. Like Whitman, she would not "call one greater or one smaller." Thus at the end of the Civil War, she wrote: "*My* history of the War . . . shall record, not the deeds of our Commanders and Generals, noble and great as they were . . . but *my* history shall preserve for the descendants of those who fought for our flag, the noble deeds of our *privates,* who shared the danger but missed glory" (NYL, February 15, 1868).

The fifth point that Fern addressed—and the most difficult one for a woman of her period to discuss—was Whitman's "undraped" portrayal of sex and the human body. She welcomed it, she said, because it was a true picture of sex as it should be: honest and open love, not the prurient sex of the roué and the woman he defiles because he regards her as worthless. This was a subject Fern wrote on many times, often in relation to the spread of venereal disease and the creation of genetically defective children. In 1858 she wrote in the *Ledger:* "Let every man look upon every woman, whatsoever her rank or condition, as a sister whom his manhood is bound to protect . . . and let every woman turn the cold shoulder to any man of her acquaintance, how polished soever he may be, who would degrade her sex" (NYL, July 17, 1858).

Finally, after calling attention to the beauty of some of the images projected by Whitman's words, Fern concluded her review with an appreciation of Whitman's apparent extension of the democratic ideal to women: "the wife—and she is not one jot less than the husband." This was the underlying theme of all of Fern's work. It is not surprising that, believing that she saw her principal ideas reflected in *Leaves of Grass,* she should have responded to it so favorably. On this point, however, she was mistaken, and her mistaken estimate of *Leaves of Grass*—and of Walt Whitman—on this question of the role of women goes a long way toward explaining the falling-out between them later.

In many ways, Whitman might seem to be advocating a new and fairer attitude toward women. He made a point of speaking to both men and women: "The Female equally with the Male I sing."[23] And, breaking with the tradition that regarded women as natural invalids, he admired the strong, physically active woman. In "Democratic Vistas," he urged that women be raised to be the "robust equals" of men.[24] And in "Specimen Days," he wrote of his disappointment with the women of the West. He had hoped they would be strong and vital like the men, but they were as "dyspeptic-looking" as their eastern sisters.[25] He also recognized the sexual nature of women, which the sexual double standard of his time did not grant to "respectable" women.

If one analyzes Whitman's attitude, however, it becomes clear that, except for this emphasis on woman's physical nature, his conception of women differs little from the conventional one.[26] First of all, although he insists that he is talking to women as well as to men, he does not see woman as the doer, the individualist that he is writing about. In "Children of Adam," Whitman describes the female and then the male. The words he uses to describe the male are the conventional ones: *action, power, defiance, pride, knowledge.* The female is passive and yielding, acted upon, not acting. Whitman concludes with this image: "See the bent head and arms folded over the breast, the Female I see."[27]

Even the robustness that Whitman liked in women is part of this conventional picture. For Whitman, the significance of woman lies in her biological function. Thus, even when he praises woman, it is only in her role as mother:

> I am the poet of the woman the same as the man,
> And I say it is as great to be a woman as to be a man,
> And I say there is nothing greater than the mother of men.[28]

At first this seems to be a recognition of woman as a person in her own right. But Whitman undercuts the independent image of woman by telling us that woman's greatest function is to be a mother—of men. What about her value for herself, one might ask. And if she is to be a mother, why not a mother of daughters? At other times, Whitman does mention daughters as well as sons, but it is clear that the value of the daughter is the same as the value of her mother—her potential motherhood. When Whitman insists that women are important, too, he means that they are important as breeders of men. If we are to have strong, vital men, they must have strong, vital mothers.

For Whitman, motherhood was the most important function of women. Although in his later works there are occasional references to some future idyllic time when women might be "even practical and political deciders with men,"[29] Whitman apparently could not conceive of such a time as a reality, and the overwhelming effect of his work is to entrench women even further in the traditional role—which Whitman portrays as both beautiful and necessary for his democratic vision. In "Democratic Vistas" Whitman writes of women's "divine maternity" and cites as the ideal woman "the perfect human mother."[30] For Whitman, woman does not exist for herself, and she is nothing without a man:

A woman waits for me, she contains all, nothing is lacking,
Yet all were lacking if sex were lacking, or if the moisture of the right man were lacking.[31]

The opinions that Whitman expressed editorially during his journalistic career confirm the limited conception of women that emerges from his poetry. Although there are articles in which, like Fanny Fern, Whitman sympathized with the plight of poor working women,[32] unlike Fern, he did not urge the expansion of career and educational opportunities that would make women less vulnerable to economic exploitation. In fact, he specifically opposed education for women on the basis that women did not need to be educated to become good wives and mothers.[33] And whereas Fern consistently deplored the unfair wage differential between men and women in the same occupation, Whitman, in writing on the low salaries of teachers, for example, advocated an across-the-board raise for all teachers, but saw nothing wrong with the unequal pay scale for male and female teachers.[34] He could praise Margaret Fuller's *Papers on Literature and Art*,[35] but unlike Fern, who urged that women read as much as possible to broaden their minds, Whitman feared unlimited reading among women and blamed female infidelity on the "evil influence of French and British literature."[36] He could support an isolated issue like the Wisconsin action on married women's property rights,[37] but he did not support women's suffrage or any activity in which women were "unfemininely" assertive. He had no objection, he said, if women interested themselves in politics, as long as they

retained their "mildness" and did not "violate the rules of decorum."[38] Like
Fern, Whitman advocated good health for women and criticized such fashions as tight lacing, but unlike Fern, he did so primarily because of his concern with woman's role as wife and mother. Poor health, he said, prevents a
woman from being cheerful in the "conjugal relation," and tight lacing can
make a woman unfit to be a wife and mother.[39]

Charles Eldridge, who was a close friend of Whitman and a member of
the circle that met almost nightly with Whitman at the O'Connors' house in
Washington in the 1860s and 1870s, described Whitman as "one of the
most conservative of men." Of Whitman's attitude toward women as revealed in these conversations, Eldridge wrote:

> I have never heard him give any countenance to the contentions of the
> "Woman's Rights" people; thought they were a namby-pamby lot as a
> whole, and he did not believe that woman suffrage would do any particu-
> lar good. Susan B. Anthony was far from his ideal of a "fierce athletic
> girl." He delighted in the company of old-fashioned women, mothers of
> large families preferred, who did not talk about literature and reforms.[40]

Over the years, since Fanny Fern first praised *Leaves of Grass*, many
women who have read and responded favorably to Whitman's poetry have
been impressed by his portrayal of women. However, as Whitman's relationship with Fanny Fern makes abundantly clear, this response is, in fact, a
cruel joke on the women who felt that Whitman offered equal recognition
of the sexes. The cruelty lies in the promise unfulfilled: although he was
unusual in his day for recognizing woman's physical nature, he never regarded her as a doer in the way that he did man; he never saw woman as a
person independent of her relation to man.

Fanny Fern's conception of women was very different. In 1859 she described the "coming woman":

> Heaven forbid the coming woman should not have warm blood in her
> veins, quick to rush to her cheek, or tingle at her fingers' ends when her
> heart is astir. No, the coming woman shall be no cold, angular, flat-
> chested, narrow-shouldered, skimpy, sharp-visaged Betsey, but she shall
> be a bright-eyed, full-chested, broad-shouldered, large-souled, intellectual
> being; able to walk, able to eat, able to fulfill her maternal destiny, and
> able—if it so please God—to go to her grave happy, self-poised and se-
> rene, though unwedded. (NYL, February 12, 1859)

This sounds like a Whitman woman: robust and strong, able to have children. But there are important differences. Fern's coming woman will be
"intellectual," and she is a significant person even if she remains unwed-
ded—even if she is never seen in relation to a man. Despite the claims made

1.   Nathaniel Willis,
Fanny Fern's father, 1827.
By permission of the Houghton Library,
Harvard University.

2.   Hannah Parker Willis,
Fanny Fern's mother, c. 1831.
Painting by Chester Harding.
From the collection of
Mr. and Mrs. Edward William Carter.

3.   Sara Payson Willis, Fanny Fern as a young woman.
Painting by E. D. Marchant.

4.   Nathaniel Parker Willis,
Fanny Fern's brother.
From the collection of James Parton II.

5.   Richard Storrs Willis,
Fanny Fern's brother.
By permission of the Houghton Library,
Harvard University.

6.   Ellen Willis Dennett,
Fanny Fern's sister, 1844.
Charcoal Drawing by Francis Alexander.
The National Portrait Gallery,
Smithsonian Institution.

7. Hartford Female Seminary. Stowe-Day Foundation, Hartford, Connecticut.

8. Catharine Beecher, 1860, founder of the Hartford Female Seminary. The Schlesinger Library, Radcliffe College.

9.   Charles Harrington Eldredge,
Fanny Fern's first husband.
Painting by Albert Gallatin Hoit.
From the collection of
James Parton II.

10.   Grace Harrington Eldredge,
Fanny Fern's daughter, c. 1842.
Painting by Francis Alexander.
From the collection of
James Parton II.

11.   J. C. Derby, publisher of Fanny Fern's first book.

12.   Robert Bonner, editor of the *New York Ledger*.

13.   Lithograph from the sheet music for the "Ruth Hall Schottische," by Jullien, published March 1855.

14.   James Parton, Fanny Fern's third husband, c. 1855.
By permission of the Houghton Library, Harvard University.

15. Sketch of Walt Whitman by Thomas Butler Gunn, 1856. Missouri Historical Society.

16. Fanny Fern's house from 1859 to 1872, 303 East Eighteenth Street, Manhattan. Photograph by Margaret Rustemian.

17.   Grace Eldredge Thomson, Fanny Fern's daughter, 1862.
Sophia Smith Collection, Smith College.

18. Ellen Willis Eldredge, Fanny Fern's daughter, c. 1870.
Sophia Smith Collection, Smith College.

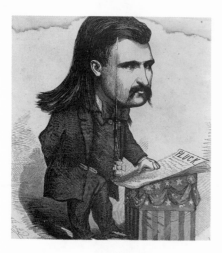

19.   Mortimer Thomson (Doesticks),
Grace's husband, 1859.
Sketch by Thomas Nast.
Missouri Historical Society.

20.   Harriet Beecher Stowe
and Henry Ward Beecher, 1868.
J. Gurney and Son Photographers.
Sophia Smith Collection, Smith College.

Sara Willis Parton —

Copied from a
"picture that little Nelly drew"
of her Mother; described by her
sister Grace as "a very bad likeness —
yet funnily like, too, in some respects."

21.   Sketch of Fanny Fern by her daughter Ellen, c. 1860.
Sophia Smith Collection, Smith College.

23.   Grace Ethel Thomson, Fanny Fern's granddaughter, c. 1868. By permission
of the Houghton Library, Harvard University.

22.   (*opposite*) Fanny Fern, c. 1868. From the collection of James Parton II.

24. (*next page*)   Fanny Fern's grave in the Mount Auburn Cemetery, Cambridge,
Massachusetts.
Photograph by Christina Kiely.

by some Whitman scholars on this point,[41] it should be clear that the individualist that Whitman celebrated was a man. For Whitman, woman was always the "other," not, as she was for Fanny Fern, an individual, a person in her own right.

Given this misunderstanding of each other's attitudes toward women, it is not surprising that the next episode in the Fern-Whitman friendship took the form that it did. After Fern's review of *Leaves of Grass*, the friendship between them continued. She apparently did not like certain passages in the second edition of *Leaves of Grass*, but there was no break because of it. Some time late in 1856 or early 1857, however, Whitman borrowed two hundred dollars from James Parton and signed a short-term note claiming that he would soon be receiving money for a literary project. There is no evidence to indicate exactly when Whitman borrowed the money, but the note was due on approximately February 3, 1857. If the note was for six months, then the loan was made in early August 1856, which was a month before Whitman published the second edition of *Leaves of Grass*, and this may have been the literary project that he spoke of. If so, then he was being disingenuous to say that he expected a large sum of money from it, considering the dearth of sales of the first edition.

On February 15, 1857, Thomas Butler Gunn records in his diary that he had visited Fern and Parton and was told that Whitman had failed to meet the note, "since which something like twelve days has elapsed." Gunn adds, "It would appear there's reason for suspecting the great 'Kosmos' to be a great scoundrel." On February 22 Gunn reports that Whitman had called on Parton and "appears *shuffling*." Parton, says Gunn, is going to sue. Gunn indicates that he felt that Parton, who was always "enthusiastic about human nature," had been fooled by Whitman, and notes that he himself, although originally cynical, had been "carried away by *his* [Parton's] judgement of Walt Whitman, despite my own thoughts."

After this incident, Gunn apparently did not have a high opinion of Whitman. On January 17, 1859, after seeing Whitman in the street, he wondered:

How does that man—a unique character in his way—live? He has a mother, an industrious brother, and one idiotic. I suppose the second maintains the family. Then, too, there is or was some middle aged Philadelphia lady, a widow of indifferent character, who admired him and whom he spunged from. And Parton's $200 might have sufficed to let him "loaf and be at his ease" for a long time.

And on July 29, 1860, Gunn reported: "Walt Whitman is voted mean [at Pfaff's beer cellar] as he never stands drinks or pays for his own if it's possible to avoid it."

Fern and Parton insisted on repayment of the debt, James Parton having specifically told Whitman at the time of the loan that the money was a sum he had saved for a trip to New Orleans to research his forthcoming biography of Andrew Jackson.[42] They did not sue, but their friend Oliver Dyer, who was a friend of Whitman also, offered to try to settle the dispute.[43] He arranged to meet Whitman at his house, where he agreed to take a painting and some books in payment of the debt. In 1869 Whitman explained the arrangement in a letter to William Douglas O'Connor, giving the date as June 17, 1857, and enclosing the receipt.[44]

In a letter to William Sloane Kennedy in 1897, replying to his questions about the debt, Ethel Parton, Fanny Fern's granddaughter, made it clear why Fern and Parton were disturbed by Whitman's behavior: "The offense was not merely an unpaid debt which the debtor for any unforeseen reason could not pay"; had that been the case, "Whitman would have received only consideration, sympathy, and absolute silence." The problem, she said, was that Whitman had obtained the loan under false pretenses, "solemnly and repeatedly" assuring Parton that he would soon have the money from a literary project he was completing. When the loan was not repaid, and the date for payment several times put off, Parton investigated Whitman's tale and found that it was wholly untrue. At this point, he put the matter in the hands of Oliver Dyer.[45]

Upon first hearing this story, William Sloane Kennedy, one of Whitman's staunchest supporters, indignantly defended Whitman. Just how determined he and other supporters were to defend Whitman at any cost is apparent from his comments on what Ethel Parton said regarding Dyer's visit to Whitman. She had written:

We both [she and Fern's daughter Ellen] have a very distinct impression that the lawyer friend, when he went in search of Whitman, found him in bed, and his mother scrubbing the floor; and that he also encountered a brother who was a carpenter, and who told him that W.W. had always been lazy, and untrustful, and apt to lump down upon his relatives.[46]

Kennedy commented:

One is glad to have a good laugh at this point of the little tragedy. No doubt the brothers of Jesus & Socrates (if he had any) thought them both lazy loafers & humbugs, & no doubt Mary & Xantippe scrubbed many a floor (I hope they did it well & left no dirt in corners) while the son & husband were toiling for humanity at large.[47]

That Whitman had assumed the stature of a god or demigod in the eyes of cultists is an indication of why they would be so eager to blame Fanny Fern.[48] Grasping at straws and at the hints of an anonymous friend that Fern was in love with Whitman, his supporters sought to portray the situation as the case of a woman scorned because this would explain Fern's and Parton's hostility and exonerate Whitman. However, the only source for this rumor seems to have been Ellen O'Connor,[49] the wife of William Douglas O'Connor, and her credibility is complicated by the possibility that for years she was herself in love with Whitman.[50] James Parton's later comments indicate no ire regarding his wife's behavior, but only indignation that Whitman could have been such a scoundrel as to have no scruples about inventing an "entire fabrication" in order to borrow money that he had no intention of repaying. According to Ethel Parton, Parton "never ceased to resent what seemed to him so peculiarly base an extortion under false pretenses."[51] Fern's and Parton's friendship with Walt Whitman ended with the symbolic burning of *Leaves of Grass* in their fireplace.[52] Both Fanny Fern and James Parton believed that they had been "victimized" by a man who was not what he pretended to be.[53]

When the Partons insisted that Whitman make good his debt, Whitman's reaction was to strike out at Fanny Fern. This he did in his July 9, 1857, article in the *Brooklyn Daily Times*, in which he vindictively disparaged Fanny Fern three weeks after his goods were collected by Dyer. In an editorial arguing against the establishment of free academies for girls similar to the ones for boys, he wrote:

The majority of people do not want their daughters to be trained to become authoresses and poets; but only that they may receive sufficient education to serve as the basis of life-long improvement and self-cultivation, and which will qualify them to become good and intelligent wives and mothers. . . . We want a race of men and women turned out from our schools, not of pedants and blue-stockings. One genuine woman is worth a dozen Fanny Ferns; and to make a woman a credit to her sex and an adornment to society, no further education is necessary.[54]

Whitman scholars have interpreted this to be a disparagement of Fern's writing, which they have characterized as sentimental.[55] But, in fact, it is a criticism of women who are *more* intellectual, rather than less. What Whitman is saying here is that we need earth mothers, not intelligent women like Fanny Fern. Perhaps the implication is that intelligent women are too assertive; they might even be strong enough and smart enough to insist that you pay your debts.

Fern was in Philadelphia when Whitman's cowardly attack appeared in the *Brooklyn Times*, but in later years she never retaliated in kind—that is, she never mentioned Whitman by name in her column. Perhaps, to a man as publicity hungry as Whitman was, this was the worst punishment of all. But in three columns, Fern did make references that are unmistakably to Whitman. These columns help us to understand her attitude toward him.

On April 3, 1858, she wrote in the *Ledger* in a column entitled "On Voices and Beards":

> I once believed in voices as indicative of character; it makes me laugh now to think of it. I was cured of it by a fellow who looked born to express physically "the dignity of human nature." I believe that is the fashionable phrase. Dignity! there's where the laugh comes in; dignity—in a leviathan of muscle and flesh, crawling lazily out of bed at twelve noon to live the rest of the day by borrowing of anybody who could be bamboozled into believing that honesty, honor and manliness were represented in his deep, rich, sympathetic voice—his stock in trade, which it would be next to impossible to associate with cowardice or dishonor! . . . The dollars that fellow has borrowed on that voice, the drinks he has swallowed on the strength of it, not to mention the strength of the drinks! the oysters he has eaten by virtue of it, and the rides and invitations he has got!—all by those frank, hearty, jolly, musical tones, which it would puzzle a Shylock to resist. No, I believe no more in voices.

In her "Peeps" column in 1856, Fern had commented on Whitman's voice and added, "Let me hear the *voice* of a man or woman and I will tell you the stuff its owners are made of." In this article two years later, she confesses that she was taken in by the voice. The man that she had thought was a superior man is, she now believes, a lazy charlatan, who takes advantage of other people in order to get what he can out of them. Fern obviously felt not scorned, but used.

That Fanny Fern's reaction to Whitman's behavior did not derive from the ulterior motive of a spurned love, as Whitman's defenders have insinuated, is clear from the fact that she held this opinion of such behavior before she even met Whitman. In *Rose Clark,* published in December 1855, for example, she satirizes in Tom Finels the type of poet who lives wholly off other people. Finels obtains free dinners, free steamboat rides, even presents, and rationalizes his parasitical existence with Whitmanesque references to "the sovereignty of the individual" (RC, 321, 354, 355). Given this opinion of poetic spongers, it is not surprising that Fern reacted as she did when she concluded that Whitman was guilty of such behavior. By the summer of 1857 she was determined not to give Whitman any further publicity. The article "Look Aloft" was prefaced by a quotation from Whitman's poetry when it originally appeared in the *Ledger* on July 5, 1856, but when it was published in her book *Fresh Leaves* in September 1857, the Whitman quotation had been eliminated. Similarly, the paragraph describing Whitman in her "Peeps" series was deleted when the articles were published in *Fresh Leaves.* And her review of *Leaves of Grass* was never reprinted in any of her collections.

On September 24, 1864, Fern wrote an article in the *Ledger* called "In Debt," which makes very clear her opinion of Whitman's behavior with respect to the loan:

How can a man eat, drink, sleep and be jolly under the pressure of debt. Perhaps one of the meanest of these dainty fellows' tricks is to victimize a *friend* who may be supposed to have scruples about refusing monetary compliance, or about reminding the creditor of his protracted forgetfulness of the sum due. Yes—there *is* one lower depth of meanness yet, and that is, when the friend is a woman who, if she be not too smart, may be generally conveniently put off with well-framed excuses, or, at all events be supposed to be too "refined" and "delicate" to press so unromantic a theme. Fortunately, all women are *not* "fools." . . . It is comforting when such an one without compromising her womanly dignity handsomely compels as a man might and would do, immediate restitution, or the alternative penalty.

This article suggests that Whitman had counted on Parton's "scruples about refusing monetary compliance" and on Fern's feminine "delicacy" not "to press so unromantic a theme" as a debt. But Fanny Fern was nobody's "fool," not even Walt Whitman's. She was a practical woman who had learned to take care of herself and to stand up for herself. As she said in 1856 after successfully taking a man to court who had fraudulently published a book in her name, women have got to stand up for their rights (NYL, August 2, 1856).

The final reference to Whitman in Fanny Fern's column appeared in the *Ledger* on October 28, 1865, in an article on "Unprincipled Talent":

He really did not *mean* to incur debts he could not pay, but he never could keep a cent of money, and he had never the resolution to face those to whom his money was due; but why mention such *little* foibles? How remember them when reading his splendid, etc., etc. . . . A fig for such a genius! Give me in preference the man who *can* face those he owes, with the hard-earned money in his rough palm, though he never read, or owned, a book in all his toilsome life . . . before him whose verses or whose writings are quoted the world over, and who yet lets any foolish friend who will, pay for the clothes he wears, or for the food he eats because, forsooth, "he can never keep a penny." . . . Genius forsooth! I have yet to learn that when the ten commandments were written, "geniuses" were counted out.

This article provides the key to an important difference between Fern and Whitman. Although they both urged self-realization and self-reliance, although they both were literary people dedicated to their art, Whitman was in the end concerned primarily with Walt Whitman, while Fern was concerned also with the people around her. No matter how much she complained about the distractions that interfered with her work as a writer, she could not conceive of individual concerns taking priority over people. That is what she could not forgive in Whitman; genius was no excuse for treating friends shabbily.

Whitman was probably right: it probably was Fanny Fern who insisted that he repay the debt. He had underestimated her. His bitterness arose from his having found out too late that she was not the passive, voiceless woman that he wrote about. And she realized that she had overestimated him, having believed him to be possessed of the "candor" that he celebrated in *Leaves of Grass*. Nor was he the advocate of women that she had thought him to be.

Had Whitman read carefully the note that Fern sent him on April 21, 1856, he would not have made the mistake that he did about her. Quoting from *Leaves of Grass* the lines, "What I assume you shall assume," she wrote, "What *I* assume, *you* shall assume!" The significance is in her italics. By italicizing the words that she did, she pointed out to him that they could have the reverse meaning as well—that she, too, was the self, the "I" of the poem. Like Margaret Fuller in her resistance to Emerson's overwhelming attempt to absorb her personality into his own,[56] Fern refused to be the passive other of the poem.

In the context of this situation, there is something very sad about Fern's concluding statement in her review of *Leaves of Grass*, where she asked Whitman to accept the "cordial grasp of a woman's hand." She extended her hand in friendship, but Whitman, although he seemed to portray woman as the equal of man, did not regard her in this light. And his defenders—with his encouragement—turned an honest friendship between them into a sorry tale of unrequited love.

The irony of this aborted friendship is that, although Whitman's name lives on, the name of Fanny Fern—so well known in her own day—in the twentieth century had until recently only been heard in reference to Walt Whitman. Fanny Fern, who insisted that women should be regarded as individuals in their own right, came to be known only in relation to a man. It was Whitman's picture of woman that survived.

The question is, Why has Whitman been remembered when Fern for so many years was not even a memory? There are many reasons. Whitman's own lifelong search for publicity and his devoted disciples who turned the man into a myth during his own lifetime—these are two reasons. In contrast, Fanny Fern shunned personal publicity, and after her death her family, in seeking to counteract the unfavorable publicity spread by such sources as the author of *The Life and Beauties,* preferred to foster the image of her as a domestic woman. The literary value of their work is not comparable, perhaps. Whitman was a journalist, but it is as a poet that he is remembered; Fern's major contribution was as a journalist. Yet in their respective fields both were remarkable. Fanny Fern's frank satire, down-to-earth language, and sharp prose were as unique in her field at the time as Whitman's poetry was in his. Both were innovators who opened the doors to a new tradition in literature.[57]

But there is one major difference between the work of Fanny Fern and Walt Whitman, a difference inherent in the metaphors suggested by the titles of their two books, *Fern Leaves* and *Leaves of Grass.* The titles are similar, but they are also different—and the difference is significant. Although Fern was thinking of the shrub fern when she first determined upon her pseudonym, the name came to be associated with the feathery fern. Such ferns grow only in hidden, shady nooks; grass grows in the open sunlight. Fern's message was couched in socially acceptable language and imagery, but the message itself was indeed radical. Fanny Fern was projecting a message that was radically un-American at the time: individualism for women. The year before Fern began to write, James Fenimore Cooper wrote of the ideal woman: "a kind, gentle, affectionate, thoughtful creature, whose heart is so full of you, there is no room in it for herself."[58] This was the credo of nineteenth-century Americans; it was heresy for Fanny Fern to insist that a woman could exist *for herself.*

Fern's message to women was the opposite of Whitman's for women. She insisted that woman existed for herself alone, not merely as wife or mother in relation to man. This is the underlying theme of her newspaper articles, and the theme of *Ruth Hall.* The difference between Fern's and Whitman's messages can be described as the politics of subversion versus the politics of celebration. Like the ferns in the title of her first book, Fern's message, if it was to flourish in her day, had to be kept in the shade of acceptable language and imagery. Whitman, however, used language and imagery that were daring in his day, but his message to and celebration of the American male were not new; they were simply a restatement of that individualism articulated by Emerson which had long been the cornerstone of American culture. His message, therefore, like the grass in his title, could grow and flourish in sunny soil.

It is this difference that helps to explain the disappearance of Fanny Fern from American literature, and the simultaneous growth of Walt Whitman's reputation. Once Whitman's language and imagery were found to be acceptable, his message was no threat; Fern's message, on the other hand, was transgressive, and once her columns stopped appearing after her death, there was no one in the literary establishment—except, as was proper, her husband—willing to champion her. She was popular in her day because the people—mostly women—who read her caustic, thought-provoking barbs at men and institutions responded overwhelmingly in her favor. But her admirers were ordinary people, not literary Brahmins. Who among her supporters—the factory women, the shopgirls, the overworked farm wives, the tired mothers—had the knowledge or the time to create a Fanny Fern cult, to ensure that her works were printed and reprinted, to bring her un-American message to succeeding generations?

II

Famous and Infamous

Not long since a lady friend of mine [Fern herself] wrote a book. In it she made use of the expression—"Nobody could be more astonished than I to find myself famous." Whereupon comes a shower of abuse for that which her critic styles disgusting egotism. . . . [W]e think that when a lady has had a mud-scow and a hand-cart, a steamboat and a hotel, a perfume and a score of babies, not to mention tobacco and music, named for her; and when she is told what her name is, wherever she goes, till she is sick of the sound of it, that she does not earn for herself a boxed ear when she couples with it the word "famous."

NYL, December 10, 1864

ALTHOUGH FERN ENJOYED THE MONETARY AND EMOTIONAL REWARDS that came with fame—primarily the ability to maintain her independence—her success was bought at a tremendous personal cost to herself: many people were not kind to the woman who flouted convention. Her frankness and her satirical treatment of sacrosanct institutions, coupled with her success itself (particularly her refusal to be coy or "feminine" in expressing false modesty about her success), caused conventional people to regard her as improper and unfeminine.[1] She was criticized for even acknowledging that she was famous. Her comment that she had found herself famous, which was simply the truth, was regarded as immodest in a woman, whereas such a statement from a man who had similarly "found himself famous" was hardly criticized—and in fact the statement is an echo of Lord Byron's comment about himself after the publication of *Childe Harold's Pilgrimage*.[2]

Fanny Fern's fame was to cause her much pain and annoyance in her personal life. Some of the disagreeable results of her fame derived from the constant probing of the public: celebrity hunters followed her on the streets, pointing her out and rudely staring at her and commenting on her appearance; men pretended familiarity with her; souvenir hunters tried to get into her house; and autograph hunters harassed her with constant requests for autographs. Fern's annoyance at these results of her celebrity is reflected in her response to one autograph hunter who had solicited her and James Parton's autographs in 1868. The single sheet of paper contains only the date and the words "With pleasure, James Parton; Without pleasure, Fanny Fern."[3]

These annoyances were minor, however, compared to the pain inflicted by sniping criticism and gossip. In his diary Gunn notes that women were particularly critical of Fanny Fern. On March 24, 1856, he describes their attitude:

How especially *down upon* "Fanny Fern" all the women appear to be. There's an amount of respectable rancour manifested, though in the gentlest and most incidental manner by Mrs. E. (Parton's aunt) on the subject of the marriage, which is quite edifying. As for Mrs. Levison, she can't keep her tongue from open abuse when "Fanny" is mentioned.

These comments reflect the criticism that Fanny Fern received for attempting to free herself of some of the oppressive restrictions of conventional femininity, and also for her success itself. Moreover, she had not been able to escape the effects of the scandal spread by Farrington, which was resurrected in the hostile book *The Life and Beauties of Fanny Fern*, published anonymously by the spiteful editor of the *True Flag* early in 1855. Hinting of sexual indiscretions and portraying Fern as a colorful adventuress, the anonymous author caused Fern so much pain that, given the emphasis on retiring womanhood that the century demanded, it is a mark of Fern's unusual courage that she did not wholly withdraw from public life, which would have meant giving up her writing and her career.

For many years these scandals haunted Fern. She tried to dissociate herself from the Farrington name and did not include reference to her second marriage in any of her official biographical sketches. In 1858 James Parton wrote to the editors of a proposed dictionary of authors, who had asked Fern about some facts relating to her background:

The name *Farrington* is wrong, and it would be in the highest degree offensive to the Lady, and to all her friends, to have it used in connection with her. *Since she has been a writer that has not been her name.* However you may choose to alter the enclosed article, I *beg* that the name Farrington may *not* be seen in it. The work entitled, The Life and Beauties of Fanny Fern, is not authentic—was published by an enemy—has no right to exist.[4]

Fern's response to the publication of *The Life and Beauties* is reflected in a letter she wrote to the editor of the New Bedford *Mercury* on 31 January, 1855, regarding its announcement of the forthcoming *Life and Beauties*. The fact that the original letter contains many ink blottings, which are not usual in Fern's writing, suggests that it was written in great emotion:

I feel called upon, in justice to the public as well as to myself, to state that the work referred to will *not* "appear under my own guaranty,"— that I have never authorized it,—that I have never been consulted with regard to it,—that I am, and always have been, opposed to any such work (my life having been a humble one, in no ways of any interest, or concern to the public), & that for any "sketch of Fanny Fern" which has yet appeared, I am not responsible. I am inclined to think the volume above referred to is merely a catch-penny affair, from the fact that it is claimed that *"it will contain many original articles written in my earlier years."* I certainly never have written anything worth publishing which has not already been given to the public in *Fern Leaves* (first & second series), in "Little Ferns," & "Ruth Hall."

In this connection, it may not be inappropriate to say with respect to the multifarious and contradictory rumors concerning me, which have gone through the press, that I have neither time nor inclination to chase them round.

To those who have cheered me by friendly commendations, or aided me by severe, but gentlemanly criticism, I return my sincere thanks; to those who have seen fit persistently to misrepresent & malign me, I decline replying.[5]

Robert Bonner was attempting to counter the kind of criticism deriving from the Farrington stories and *The Life and Beauties* when he included in his description of Fern praise of her as a loving mother and wife: "Few, perhaps, would infer from her writings that, attractive as she is in company, she is nowhere so engaging as at home. *There,* indeed, she shines" (NYL, February 16, 1856). This was not simply the conventional kudo to the domestic role of women, but a deliberate attempt to counter the cruel gossip that was circulating among the scandal-loving public. Bonner's comments indicate how Fern was personally affected by the gossip:

She appreciates honesty and true merit, though clothed in homespun, and abhors superficiality and hypocrisy however dazzlingly arrayed. These qualities of mind, together with the malignity and cruelty with which some women and more men have causelessly persecuted her, occasion her to avoid general society and to exercise great caution in making acquaintances. (NYL, February 16, 1856)

The result of this malignity and Fern's resulting caution was that at this time she had few friends and did not have any close female friends. Her staunch friends—the people who championed and protected her against spiteful and malicious tongues—were men: Oliver Dyer, Robert Bonner, James Parton. Of course, as men, they could afford to champion her; they did not risk tarnishing their own reputations as women did. However, one could never make a friend of a woman, Fern wrote; they were always too eager to tear each other down.[6] Considering her lifelong dedication to the cause of women's rights and her defense of women against the tyranny of men, it is a sad comment on the realities of her society that, aside from her daughters (and her deceased mother), her experience made it impossible for her to perceive women as her friends.

If Fern's female critics were cruel, neither could she count on men to come to her defense. Her unconventional writings and behavior and the scandal deriving from the Farrington stories and *The Life and Beauties* (both of which were originated by men) made her vulnerable to sexual innuendo. Gunn had refused to meet her before she was married to Parton because he had assumed that she was "base and unwomanly like her writings."[7] He assumed that she had a colorful sexual history, asserting that she probably was sleeping with Oliver Dyer and also with James Parton before her marriage. He wondered why Parton did not simply keep her as his mistress instead of marrying her; most men, he said, would have preferred that to "marriage with a divorced woman and one of inenviable notoriety."[8] His friends also talked loosely about Fern. Jesse Haney, when he was angry at her, claimed to Gunn that she had made advances to him. Ed Cahill, who was notorious for his drinking and dissipation and was angry at Fern for having told Mrs. Edwards about his dissipation (he was interested in one of the Edwards daughters, and when Mrs. Edwards learned of his dissipations, she no longer welcomed him at the house), told Gunn that he could have slept with Fern if he had wanted to. Gunn, who was very moralistic and conventional in his views of women, was shocked at Fern's uninhibited behavior in other areas and consequently concluded that these unfounded rumors must be true.[9] Noting how cruel the women were, he commented: "It is proper that women are merciless toward the impure of their own sex."[10] And he concluded that Fern probably attacked women because "they instinctively know what *she is*."[11]

In order to assess Gunn's judgment, one needs to understand the kind of behavior that he censured in Fern: she wrote articles criticizing conventional oppressions of women, she talked about a French novel that she had been reading, she sat on Parton's lap, she mentioned that she missed her husband when he was absent, she occasionally made risqué humorous comments, she hinted at her sexual desires, and she had been known to dress in her husband's clothes.[12] These facts of her behavior which, to a modern reader only serve to humanize her and provide an indication of a healthy libido, a sense of humor, and a critical mind, were to conventional men and women of Fern's day indications of impropriety and immorality.

This personal criticism was not confined to Fern's personal life. As we saw in the previous chapters, reviewers of her books often indulged in personal criticism instead of focusing on the merits of the book. It was after one of these particularly malicious and devastating attacks that James Parton

asked Fanny Fern to marry him. Harriet Spofford, who was a friend of
James Parton in later years, believed that Parton asked Fern to marry him
"for the sake of affording her protection at a time when she was undergoing
some painful injustice."[13] Whether this was one of Parton's motives, marriage in the mid-nineteenth century was perceived as a means of "protection" for erring or slandered women. In *Isa,* for example, the 1852 novel by
Caroline Chesebro', a woman who is in danger of being "lost" because of
her irreligious and immoral ideas is offered "salvation" by an elderly admirer who seeks to protect her by marrying her.[14] If, in addition to their
many points in common, Parton was also motivated by a desire to protect
Fern by aligning himself with her, she may also have been glad of the support. In any case, family stories indicate that Parton's proposal came at a
time when Fern was depressed because of malicious talk and personally
hostile reviews. Ethel Parton, Fern's granddaughter, describes the scene:

> He chanced to come upon her one day in one of her darkest . . . moods. . . .
> She was seated before her desk, weeping, her arms across a half-written
> manuscript and her head upon her arms. Caught thus off guard, she was
> persuadable. By the time she was fully comforted, she found herself en-
> gaged to be married. (EP, 141)

During this turbulent time, there were other consolations. One came in
the form of a letter from Catharine Beecher, Fern's principal many years
before at the Hartford Female Seminary:

> *My dear Sarah:*
>   Do you remember when Mrs. Dr. Strong used to complain that you
> were a favorite & that "Miss Beecher always like those that plagued her
> most"?
>   This being so—& as you have "plagued me" lately considerably I want
> to see you *of course*—I hear *"the other side"* only, and I want to hear
> *your side.*
>   I am "at home" for you any morning before 11 and any evening after 6
> until Thursday. I hope to see you before I leave. (EP, 140)

Ethel Parton tells us that Fern did go to see Beecher and did tell her side of
the story.
    One aspect of Fern's behavior in the 1850s that was particularly shocking
to her contemporaries was her campaign in favor of men's dress for women.
Gunn had commented in March 1856 that Fern told him of dressing in
Parton's clothes, and during 1858 he reported that Fern, as well as her
daughter Grace, experimented with male dress. On June 23, 1858, Gunn
says that Fern had gone into New York in Parton's clothes, and Grace "had
ventured on a wild promenade a la Amazon, in Brooklyn." On August 19

Grace showed him a picture of herself in male costume wearing a Scotch cap that she intended to give to her sister for her birthday. In July Gunn writes:

Went over to Parton's on Sunday, the 18th. The Thompsons and Wells there in the evening. Grace with her hair cut short, her mother in similar tress. This they did to facilitate a visit to New York one night dressed *a la Amazon,* in company with Parton. A very unwise business, not to speak of the delicacy of it. It might have produced unpleasant consequences, for going into a saloon—Florence's, or some such place—the disguise didn't deceive some man present (probably a policeman in regular attendance) and he, stepping up to Parton, told him that "he'd better take them gals away, or he might get into trouble!!!" So they had to avail themselves of a passing omnibus and *cut.* Another adventure Fanny told with great gusto. She got into a street weighing machine, to ascertain her weight, and not taking her feet from the ground, the proprietor caught hold of her leg to hold it up! In the Brooklyn cars Grace forgot herself and addressed her mamma as "mother"! They were recognized by some neighbor, who mentioned the circumstance to others.

Although Gunn found it shocking, Fern and Parton regarded it, first of all, as an amusing adventure, but also as a serious statement concerning the limited rights of women; the encumbrances of female dress at the time were clearly symbolic of and an addition to the repressive condition of women. And—what angered Fern more than anything else—it was illegal for a woman to presume to dress in the comfortable and more practical attire that men wore. One article in which Fern addressed this subject was published on October 8, 1859, "Was She a Heroine, or a Criminal?" In response to a news item about a woman who had been arrested for wearing men's clothes in order to make a living, Fern defended the woman and angrily commented that as long as women are paid one-third the wages of men, it should not be surprising if a woman wished "she had been born a man" (NYL, October 8, 1859).

Fern's position on the dress issue is made clear in the articles she published in the *Ledger* on July 10 and 17, 1858, describing how she dressed in her husband's clothes and went out for a walk with him in the evening:

Here I have been sitting twiddling the morning paper between my fingers this half hour, reflecting upon the following paragraph in it: "Emma Wilson was arrested yesterday for wearing man's apparel." Now, why this should be an actionable offense is past my finding out, or where's the harm in it, I am as much at a loss to see. . . .
Everybody knows what an everlasting drizzle of rain we have had lately, but nobody but a woman, and a woman who lives on fresh air and

out-door exercise, knows the thraldom of taking her daily walk through a
three weeks' rain, with skirts to hold up, and umbrella to hold down, and
puddles to skip over, and gutters to walk round, and all the time in a
fright lest, in an unguarded moment, her calves should become visible to
some of those rainy-day philanthropists who are interested in the public
study of female anatomy.

One evening, after a long rainy day of scribbling, . . . I stood at the
window, looking at the slanting, persistent rain, and took my resolve:
"*I'll do it*," said I, audibly, planting my slipper upon the carpet. "Do
what?" asked Mr. Fern, looking up from a big book. "Put on a suit of
your clothes and take a tramp with you," was the answer. "You dare
not," was the rejoinder; "you are a little coward, only saucy on paper." It
was the work of a moment, with such a challenge, to fly up stairs and
overhaul my philosopher's wardrobe. . . .

Well, Mr. Fern seized his hat, and out we went together. "Fanny," said
he, "you must not take my arm; you are a fellow." "True," said I. "I
forgot; and you must not help me over puddles, as you did just now, and
do, for mercy's sake, stop laughing. There, there goes your hat—I mean
my hat; confound the wind! and down comes my hair; lucky 'tis dark,
isn't it?" But oh, the delicious freedom of that walk; after we were well
started! No skirts to hold up, or to draggle their wet folds against my
ankles; no stifling vail flapping in my face, and blinding my eyes; no umbrella to turn inside out, but instead, the cool rain driving slap into my
face, and the resurrectionized blood coursing through my veins, and tingling in my cheeks.

. . . .To be able to step over the ferry-boat chain when you are in a
distracted hurry, like any other fellow, without waiting for that tedious
unhooking process, and quietly to enjoy your triumph over scores of im-
patient-waiting crushed petticoats behind you; to taste that nice lager
beer "on draught"; to pick up contraband bits of science in a Medical
Museum, forbidden to crinoline, and hold conversations with intelligent
men, who supposing you to be a man, consequently talk sense to you.
That is worth while. . . .

I want to do such a quantity of "improper" things, that there is not the
slightest real harm in doing. I want to see and know a thousand things
which are forbidden to flounces—custom only can tell why—I can't. I
want the free use of my ankles, for this summer at least, to take a journey;
I want to climb and wade, and tramp about, without giving a thought to
my clothes; without carrying about with me a long procession of trunks
and boxes. . . . I want to run my fingers through my cropped hair some
fine morning without the bore of dressing it; put on some sort of loose
blouse affair—it must be pretty, though—and a pair of Turkish trousers—*not* Bloomers—and a cap, or hat—and start; nary a trunk—
"nary" a bandbox. Wouldn't that be fine? But propriety scowls and says,

"ain't you ashamed of yourself, Fanny Fern?" *Yes I am,* Miss Nancy. I *am* ashamed of myself, that I haven't the courage to carry out what would be eminently convenient, and right, and proper.

Reading Fern's account of her feelings in these two articles is particularly saddening if the account is read in conjunction with Gunn's attitude and the hostility of her peers—particularly the women. Fern's yearning is so reasonable and so understandable today; western women reading these words now have grown up taking for granted the right to wear trousers and can walk with the freedom that was denied Fern. If we are to understand the significance of Fern's courageous stance on the issues of her day, it is important to read Fern's words, and, knowing how she was regarded by her more conventional peers, to feel with her the "delicious freedom of that walk."

Another aspect of Fern's behavior that shocked many of her contemporaries was her open admiration of the male form. If Whitman's references to the body and bodily functions were shocking to Americans, similar comments by an American woman were even more shocking; moreover, such comments helped to confirm the unsavory picture that had been painted of Fanny Fern by such works as *The Life and Beauties:* a "respectable" woman, her critics concluded, would not write so. American women in the mid-nineteenth century were expected to be reticent and modest—to the extent of appearing to take no interest in sex or to have little awareness of the male body. Fern made it clear in her writings that she was not only aware of what men's bodies looked like but also admired an attractive male body. Such frankness was unsettling to men and suggested to women that Fern was no "true woman." As in her review of Whitman's *Leaves of Grass,* however, Fern argued in favor of honesty, maintaining that healthy admiration of the opposite sex was preferable to sneaking innuendo. After a trip to Philadelphia in 1857, for example, she wrote of some of the men she saw there:

I thank every well-made man who passes me with well-knit limbs and expanded chest, encased in nice linen, and a coat he can breathe in; yes— why not? do you purse up your mouth at this? do you say it was not *proper* for me to have said this? I hate the word proper. . . . Out upon proper! So I say again, I like to see a well-made man—made—not by the tailor—but by the Almighty. I glory in his luxuriant beard; in his firm step; in his deep, rich voice; in his bright, falcon eye. I thank him for being handsome, and letting me see him. (NYL, July 25, 1858)

Given her unconventionality, James Parton's relatives apparently were not happy about his marriage to Fern, and, unlike Catharine Beecher, they were not interested in hearing her side of the story. She was not regarded as a "proper" woman by the Edwards ladies. For this reason, she was reluctant to visit their home. Although they were civil to her, they were not warm, and, even worse, they talked maliciously about her behind her back. Their comments were reported to her by others, and Parton himself told her how they felt. In March 1859 Gunn speculated about the reasons for Mrs. Edwards' hostility: "Mrs. Edwards *detests* her, I am sure, first on account of her writings, secondly, because Jim married her—doing it on the sly. . . . Thirdly, because they are and must be, in in this life, at least, radically antagonistic."

Parton's relatives were also unkind about Fern's daughters, whom they regarded as unladylike. Fern tried to bring up her daughters without the repressive restrictions that young girls of her period were under. Although she apparently was careful that they maintain a high level of conduct with respect to moral or compromising issues (for example, she would not permit her seventeen-year-old daughter, Grace, to become intimate with a woman who was not married to the man she was living with),[15] Fern permitted her daughters to speak and act with fewer inhibitions than did traditional young ladies of the period. The resulting freedom in their behavior brought them criticism from more conventional women. For example, when Fern bought a new house in 1859, Sally Edwards asked Fern's daughter Grace about the size of the drawing room. Grace excitedly told her that it was big enough to turn somersaults in. The Edwards girls (and Gunn) were shocked that Grace would even mention such unseemly behavior.[16]

Gunn comments that Ann Edwards, Mr. Edwards's daughter from his previous marriage, disliked Fern, apparently because she had expected to marry James Parton herself, and Mrs. Edwards also resented Fern for interfering with her matchmaking. Parton's mother, Mrs. Pillow, who had remarried, was also unhappy about the marriage.[17] In March 1859, at the time that Gunn was making many of these observations about the hostile attitude of Parton's relatives toward her, Fern wrote an article in the *Ledger* which sums up her criticism of the hypocrisy and backbiting attitudes that she found to be prevalent among contemporary women. "Amiable creatures are women," she says sarcastically; they will nudge each other to look at a "sister woman, . . . while recapitulating within ear-shot all the contemptible gossip which weak-minded, empty-headed women are so fond of retailing." Women, she avers, also sarcastically, would "never say of an authoress, oh yes, she has talent, but *I* prefer the domestic virtues; as if a combination of the two were necessarily impossible, or as if the speaker had the personal knowledge which qualified her to pronounce on that individual case" (NYL, March 12, 1859).

Each year the Edwards family held a Christmas party at their home at 745 Broadway. In December of 1856 and 1857, neither Fern nor Parton was present at the Christmas party because Fern was not welcome and Parton would not go without her. On the evening of December 25, 1858, however, Parton and Fern, with her two daughters, attended the Christmas party

along with approximately forty guests. Some of the guests put on a performance that had been elaborately prepared for with scenery and a jocularly
printed program. The program included the names of James Parton, "Histo-
rian of the Day and Member of the College of Perfect Bricks," and "Mrs.
Parton, a Brick-ess and authoress of an elegant work entitled "Grace and
Ella." It is not without significance that Fern is listed in the program as wife
and mother and not under her professional name. The play was followed by
"charades, dances, healths, speech making, 'musical honors' and papa Edwards['] famous punch."[18]

The most hostile of Parton's relatives was his sister, Mary Parton Rogers,
who from the first did not like Fern. When she first met Fern at the Edwards's Christmas party in 1858, she ran from the room and burst into
tears, she said, because she was so upset at seeing her.[19] Fern's relationship
with her sister-in-law, always strained, was injured further by two incidents.

The first occurred in 1859, when Fern and Parton visited the Rogerses at
their home in Rochester. Fern, who had felt Mary Rogers's hostility when
she had seen her at the Edwards home in New York, was not comfortable
about the visit, but she hoped that it would help to smooth out relations
between the families. Mary Rogers, however, wanted to effect a rupture
between Parton and Fern, whose marriage she refused to accept. During the
visit, she persuaded Parton to go out with her, leaving Fern to spend the day
alone. The next day, when the indignant Fern went for a walk with her
husband, she called his sister "an ill-tempered skeleton." Parton was offended at her criticism of his sister and told Mary Rogers what Fern had
said. Mary Rogers complained to her husband, and the irate Rogers, who
was apparently a short-tempered man, told Fern to leave the house immediately and attempted to keep her away from Parton. Fern tried to go upstairs, but Rogers threw himself at her as she clung to the stair rail in terror,
calling out for "Jim." Parton came out of his room and found Rogers trying
to push her down the stairs and screaming insults at her. Her arm was
bruised where Rogers had taken hold of her. Rogers called out to Parton
that she didn't have any feeling for him, that he should send her away.
Aghast at the scene, Parton replied that she had "slept in his arms," and
Fern and Parton immediately left the house to return to New York. Mary
Rogers told Gunn later that she hated Fern, and insisted that the marriage
never should have taken place. Rogers said that there was only one word in
the English language to describe Fern, and that word was "Bitch." Gunn
concluded that whatever had caused the situation, the Rogerses had not
acted "judiciously, nor was it altogether in the right."[20] In any case, Fern did
not visit the Rogerses again. When Parton wanted to visit his sister, he went
alone.

The second incident occurred in the summer of 1859. Mary Rogers wrote
a letter to Parton, and Parton read aloud some "agreeable portions of the
letter" to his wife. Fern, pleased with the letter and apparently believing

Mary Rogers's hostility had abated, decided to answer it. She obtained the letter from Parton's pocket and found to her distress that the parts that he had not read to her were highly insulting. On August 6, 1859, she published an article in the *Ledger* deriving from her relationship with her in-laws:

> Since the world began, there probably never was a marriage of which *somebody* did not "disapprove." That somebody, and everybody, has a perfect right to an opinion on such a subject, nobody doubts. But how far you prove your greater love for "Tom," by whispering round "confidentially" your fore-ordained determination not to believe that "that woman" can ever make him happy, is a question. Poor fellow! and *she* of all people in the world; the very last woman *you* would have selected; which of course is sure to get to Tom's wife's ears. . . .
>
> Broad philanthropists! Tom can surely be happy in no way but *theirs*. They love him so much better than *"that* woman" possibly can. Poor "Tom!" He looked so poorly last time they saw him. *Her* fault, of course. They knew it would be just so. Didn't they say so from the first? Poor Tom! such a sacrifice. It is unaccountable how he can like her. For the matter of that, they never *will* believe he does (and they might add, he sha'n't if we can help it). And so, when they see him, they inquire with a churchyard air, "Is he well?" "Is anything the matter?" "Ah, you needn't tell us; *we* know how it is; poor Tom—we know you *try* to bear up under it. Come and see *us*. We will love you. You never will find *us* changed."
>
> No. That's the worst of it! No hope of *their* changing. Bless their souls. How lucky "Tom" has somebody to tell him what a "sacrifice he has made," or he never would find it out! Well, it is astonishing that such people don't see that this is the last way to convince any person with common sense, that they are better qualified to be installed guardians of "Tom's" happiness than *"that* woman."

This article gives us an idea of Fern's relationship with her in-laws and their attitude toward the unconventional woman that James Parton had married. She referred specifically to his sister, Mary Rogers, whose hostile comments she had read in the letter, but she apparently felt the hostility of his mother and the Edwards family as well. On the same date that this article appeared, Gunn wrote in his diary in response to Fern's article:

> She really shows pretty shrewd intuition of her adversaries' opinions, but is a tremendous fool to publish to all the *Ledger* readers the fact that her husband's relatives detest her. How the Bostonians must chuckle over it! And how delightful for Jim! There's something to be said on Fanny's side of the question too . . . . Mrs. Edwards had a dislike to her from the outset. And I believe Jim himself has let Fanny know how she is regarded. He's just the man to be guilty of such a piece of candor.

Gunn apparently believed that Fern had summed up the situation accurately—if unwisely—and, since he was a frequent visitor in the Edwards house, he was in a good position to assess the accuracy of Fern's portrayal of their attitude toward her. On August 10, 1860, he gives this description of Mary Rogers, who apparently had also had a falling out with Sally Edwards:

She is a little, clever woman, with much of her brother's tendency to extremes of opinion and sentiment, but in her it is *feminized* into narrowness. If she dislikes anybody, she can see nothing but evil in them, and being a clever, shrewd woman, can put that dislike into sharp sentences. Withal she never doubts but that she is actuated by the highest motives, or distrusts her own infallibility. Jim she thinks highly of, taking command of him, and consistently hating Fanny for doing the same. When she visited them in New York she was all affection to her brother's wife, after the feminine fashion; when she returned to Rochester, she wrote that celebrated letter which produced a tremendous rumpus and was replied to by Fanny in the *Ledger*. Mrs. R. had advised her brother to overhaul his "Katherine and Petruchio" and to act on the latter's example.

Fern and Parton also attended the Christmas party at the Edwards home in 1859. However, this party followed the fiasco at the Rogerses' and Mary Rogers's letter, as well as Fern's article in the *Ledger*; although the Rogerses were not present, the Pillows were present, and the former had apparently told them and the Edwards family their version of the incident. Thus, although Fern and her daughters attended the party, they were even less comfortable than before. There was a performance, as there had been the previous year, and dancing, but Fern and her daughters did not join in. Gunn describes the scene: "The three sat in a row, both before and when the chairs were placed for the audience, Mrs. Thomson beside Fanny, and Mrs. Edwards, civil, hospitable, but not exceeding it one jot, to the party." Neither Fern not Grace danced. Ellen, however, danced with Jack Edwards, but clearly felt the animosity of the gathering. Gunn writes:

"Ella" danced with honest Jack, looking particularly nosey and contemptuous of the better people among whom she moved. I am pretty sure she felt all her mother's bad blood rising, in her wish to imply silent enmity to the family who cannot but detest the woman, and who, when she forces her undesired company upon them, knows pretty surely that it is only because she *can't* keep Jim away and prefers accompanying him.

Later in the evening Jesse Haney read a poem about the various guests, including a verse about Fern and her daughters. Gunn writes:

Haney's poem, an immense success, the healths of the persons alluded to being drunk in order as they appeared, with three cheers each, sometimes more. (Fanny's obtained none, indeed the verse was introduced at the last moment, lumping her and party together; a mere compliment of Haney's designed to prevent their remarking about what might have looked like a marked omission.)

After this uncomfortable evening, Fern attempted to mend the breach between the families by inviting the Edwards family to tea. The "tea-fight," as Gunn calls it in his diary, took place on January 13, 1860, and was on the surface a "very pleasant evening." Gunn writes on January 14: "Mr. and Mrs. Edwards, the three girls, Haney, Welles and the Thomsons constituted the company. They talked, supped, had punch, music and the girls sang a song or two, against their liking." The undercurrents of hostility must have been apparent to Fanny Fern, however. Gunn tells us that on January 16 when he visited the Edwardses, "the girls [were] imitating and ridiculing Fan."

All of this criticism from Parton's friends and relatives could not help but cause friction in the relationship between Fern and Parton. Fern was critical of Parton for allowing his relatives to speak critically of her, and Parton was hot-tempered in his reply. On December 13, 1856, Fern wrote in her *Ledger* column: "Has *he* any call to be a husband, who permits his own relatives, in his hearing, to speak disrespectfully or censoriously of his wife?" Julius Ward wrote of Parton: "In early life he had an extremely quick temper; he could not argue his case without getting into a heat; but such was his control of himself by the time he had reached middle life that this tendency to fly into a passion had passed away, and he could master himself with ease."[21] Gunn notes that Parton had a "lurid spark of wrath in him" and mentions several occasions when he believes arguments had taken place between Fern and Parton, although he apparently never witnessed one.[22] Certainly Fanny Fern was not a woman to be easily overruled. As she wrote in 1853 before she met Parton: "Just imagine ME, Fanny, sitting down on a cricket in the corner, with my forefinger in my mouth, looking out the sides of my eyes, and waiting till that man got ready to speak to me! You can see at once it would be—be—. Well, the amount of it is, *I shouldn't do it!*" (OB, April 9, 1853). On September 27, 1856, nine months after her marriage, Fern wrote in a *Ledger* article entitled "Crotchets," in which she describes herself, "Am I to be forced—by anybody—at any time, to do anything? I trow not." Gunn's solution was one that James Parton did not follow. At one point Gunn, exasperated with Fern's independent behavior, asserted: "Were I Jim, I'd horsewhip her until she prayed for mercy."[23]

James Parton's relatives having continued to make clear their dislike of Fern, she did not often visit them, and, knowing that they would talk about her behind her back, she resented his spending much time with them. On

Tuesday, October 30, 1860, Parton spent the evening at the Edwardses, returning home very late. Fern apparently was upset, and the next morning there was an argument, with Fern becoming very distraught. Later, when Fern was out, Parton packed his suitcase and, without saying where he was going, took the train to Rochester to his sister's. After his arrival, Parton wrote to Fern telling her where he was. Fern left immediately for Rochester, and, arriving at a hotel, she sent word to Parton at the Rogers house asking him to join her. As we saw earlier, the Rogerses were determined to cause a separation between Parton and Fern, and when the messenger arrived, Rogers did not inform Parton of his arrival, but told the messenger that Parton had gone to bed. The next morning, however, Fern hired a carriage and drove to the Rogers house, where she stayed three days in Parton's room, he bringing her up her meals. On the fourth day they came down to dinner, and then they went back to New York together.[24] According to Gunn, Mary Rogers was furious that Parton had gone home with his wife, regarding it as a "deplorable triumph on Fanny's part." She told Gunn that Fern was "the worst woman in every way in the world" and refused to admit that she and Parton loved each other.[25]

On Christmas 1860 Fern and her daughters did not attend the Christmas party at the Edwards home. Thomas Butler Gunn was not there either, apparently being on a writing assignment in the South. However, he received letters describing the events, and he recorded the information in his diary. Sally Edwards commented ironically on the absence of Fern and her daughters, as well as the Thomsons:

Mrs. Jim did not permit the light of her countenance to dazzle our optics on this occasion, nor did any of that brilliant circle honor us, but Jim himself and Mr. Welles. Our distress at this cutting slight was keen, as you may imagine, but with almost supernatural self-control we managed to swallow our agitated feelings and received our guests with astonishing equanimity considering.[26]

Eliza Edwards wrote that Fern "did a headache at Mrs. Thomson's after dinner."[27] Although Eliza implies that the headache may have been feigned, one suspects that whether it was or not, Fern was probably reluctant to attend the Christmas party after the unpleasant and distressing hostility apparent at the previous year's party and after the embarrassing altercation at the Rogers home the month before. They had apparently all planned to go, and Parton had written a poem for the occasion. The party was a small one, but included the usual performance. Although Parton attended the party without Fern or her daughters, his poem constitutes a kind of statement of allegiance. Parton's poem contains this verse about his wife:

> What next? To whom shall now your poet turn?
> The rhyme decides 't must be the Lady Fern. . . .
> This lady, though I had the luck to win her,
> All the world some property claims in her.
> I don't complain! Though all the world's she be,
> The exchange is fair—she's all the world to me!
> Respecting this famed authoress, my mate,
> I merely wish to night some facts to state,
> Her stockings do not show a tinge of blue,
> And as to mine, they're all attended to;
> Punctually, she has the mutton on,
> Religiously, she sews shirt-buttons on.
> Some wives when crossed, husband both and cub lick,
> She silent sits and gives it to the public.[28]

In this poem Parton tells his relatives that he will stick by his wife, and incidentally points out that, despite what they think, she is a good wife, that is, sufficiently domestic.

Although attempts were made to heal the breach between Fern and Parton's relatives, they never came to accept her, and, for her part, she remained aloof.[29] That Parton's relatives never became kind to Fern is apparent from a letter her daughter, Ellen, wrote from Newburyport, Massachusetts, to Robert Bonner after her mother was dead. Parton's cousins were coming to Newburyport, she said, and she did not want to see them: "You know how Jim's relatives treated mother. . . . It seems cruel [to bring them here] when I have told Jim that I can never associate with my mother's detractors." She asked Bonner's advice concerning the "best and most dignified thing for my mother's daughter to do?"[30]

Ethel Parton, Fern's granddaughter, tells us that if there was dissension during the early years of the marriage, it was owing to the coming together of two very strong personalities, but that the marriage soon resolved itself into a union of mutual respect and affection (EP, 142). Moreover, Parton, unlike his relatives, apparently was not bothered by the unconventional. His own ideas on social issues, for example, were very forward looking, and his religious ideas were definitely not orthodox. In 1864 he wrote in a letter to Charles Eliot Norton, who had asked him to write an article on John Jay, that he wanted instead to do something on the unconventional Voltaire, whom he found more interesting than Jay. He characterized Jay as "too respectable": "It is impossible for me to consider the Jays of this world in a serious light, being myself constitutionally a loafer, and having no taste for the Respectable. To me the faults of a Franklin are more pleasing than the virtues of a Jay."[31] In his poem at the Edwards's Christmas party, Parton had told his relatives that his wife sewed on his buttons and prepared his dinners as a good domestic wife should do, and perhaps he himself was pleased that this was so; however, it is clear that what he admired about Fanny Fern was not her conventional domesticity, but her unconventionality. As he had said admiringly of her writings in 1853 before he had even met her, Fanny Fern was "a voice, not an echo."[32]

Fern admired the same quality in Parton. She was critical of his being too "easy" sometimes, however, particularly as we have seen in his failure at first to stand up to his relatives. Parton, although he could be outspoken and uncompromising in matters of principle, did not like confrontation in his personal life. Fern criticized this trait in one of her articles, noting that the problem with people who avoid confrontation is that someone else has to bear the brunt of the problems caused by their unwillingness to face up to an unpleasant situation (NYL, December 14, 1867). In the early years of their marriage, Fern had to take on this role vis-à-vis Parton's relatives. However, the statement of allegiance contained in Parton's Christmas poem in 1860 must have made his position clear. Except for this early dissension owing to the hostility of Parton's relatives, Fern and Parton were able to tolerate each other's differences of opinion with equanimity. And for the most part, their ideas were in accord; they both were lifelong supporters of social justice and humanitarian ideals.

In spite of the criticism Fern received from friends and strangers, relatives and book critics, she continued to write her weekly column, she published numerous collections of her articles, she remained married to James Parton, she bought herself a house, first at 33 Oxford Street in Brooklyn, and then, in 1859, at 303 East Eighteenth Street in Manhattan, and she did not alter her behavior or change her ideas about women's rights. As time passed and her reputation as wife and mother and then grandmother overcame the adventuress label, the rumors were laid to rest, and the name Fanny Fern was associated with wit and social justice more than it was with scandal.

12

"Fanny Ford"
and *Rose Clark*

*We are tired . . . of the piled-up horrors with which some novelists
bait for readers. Anybody can introduce a ghost or a bloody head; it
takes genius, and that of the very highest order, to make what are called
"common-place" events and persons interesting.*

NYL, April 20, 1861

IN ADDITION TO *Ruth Hall* Fanny Fern wrote two other works of long fiction, "Fanny Ford," the hundred-dollar-a-column novella that was serialized in the *Ledger* in the summer of 1855, and *Rose Clark*, a novel
published in December of 1855.

"Fanny Ford"

"Fanny Ford: A Story of Everyday Life" began publication on June 9,
1855, occupying four and a half columns on the front page of the *Ledger*. In
1856 it was translated into German and published in Pesth and Leipzig in a
volume also containing *Ruth Hall*, and in 1857 it was published as part of
the collection *Fresh Leaves*.

In the novella, the wealthy Jacob Ford had been the owner of a sweatshop
that exploited poor seamstresses, and his wife, Lucy, who had been one of
the seamstresses, feels that his money is ill-gotten; her fears are confirmed
early in the story by a fortune-teller who prophecies "retribution." Soon
after this, their daughter Mary's fiancé, Percy Lee, is imprisoned for embez-
zlement, and the shock throws Mary into a stuporlike state of depression. In
prison Percy attacks a man named Scraggs, who accuses Percy of having
seduced Mary. News of this rumor is brought to Mary, who sinks further
into depression. Jacob is so distraught at the condition of his daughter that
he is unable to concentrate on his business, and the Fords lose all of their
money. Jacob dies, leaving Lucy to care for the feeble Mary.

At this point, Tom Shaw, a rival of Percy's, marries Mary in order to spite Percy. Lucy, who is penniless, allows the marriage to take place; Mary offers no resistance. Shaw soon tires of Mary and takes up with his former mistress. Mary dies when her daughter is born, and Lucy stays at Shaw's home to look after little Fanny, whose father takes no interest in her. Shaw brings his mistress to live in the house, and later he dies in a drunken fall down the stairs. The mistress evicts Lucy and Fanny, who have no possessions but the painting of Mary, Fanny's mother. Lucy works as a seamstress to support the two of them, and one day Percy Lee, who has been released from prison and is working as a peddler, stops at their house. He sees the painting and realizes that Fanny is Mary's daughter, but he does not tell them who he is.

Percy Lee visits the house whenever he is selling wares in the neighborhood, and when Lucy dies, he arranges to have the child brought up and educated while he travels to build up his business. When she is grown up, he returns, and they marry. Their wedding day is darkened by the death of Scraggs on the church steps. Seeking vengeance for the beating he had received from Percy, Scraggs had whipped himself into a drunken frenzy with the intention of telling Fanny that Percy was a jailbird who had murdered her mother. His accidental death while wrestling with a policeman on the church steps prevents him from destroying the couple's happiness, but effectively destroys the possibility of an unmixed fairy-tale ending for the story.

The story, which spans eighteen years in less than a hundred pages, uses the same abbreviated style and sudden scene shifts that Fern had developed in *Ruth Hall*. The chapters are slightly longer, averaging four and a third pages, and there are no sudden shifts of tone as there are in *Ruth Hall*. The tone throughout is world-weary, often cynical, undercutting the conventional language and stereotyped situations of the sentimental story. In the first chapter, the narrator sets the tone, commenting that the love of Percy and Mary is first love, "before distrust has chilled, or selfishness blighted, or . . . worldiness evaporated the heart's dew." Though the lovers are blind to "care and sorrow" now, they will find that once this early love is past, everything in life is "stale." The voice of the narrator makes clear that, though her characters may fall in love or sentimentalize, she knows that, as one of the characters says, "If you own a heart, it is best to hide it, unless you want it trampled on" (FF, 115–116, 200).

It is not only the tone of the story that provides the reader with an indication that the story is not the simple one it at first seems. A careful reader will find sewn into the fabric of the story innumerable threads of "differance,"[1] which point to a subversive subtext in this ostensibly sentimental tale. The reader who is familiar with Fern's work cannot help but realize that if Mary had married Percy Lee, she would have become Mary Lee—which is the name of the woman in Fern's 1852 article whose husband tired of her and had her committed to an insane asylum to get rid of her (TF, May 8, 1852).

The sketch "Mary Lee" provided the basis for the tragic story of Mary Leon in *Ruth Hall*. This association, coupled with the cynical comment in the first chapter and the ironic undertone throughout the story, indicates the extent to which Fern's story provides a critique of conventional love stories and of marriage itself.

An understanding of this theme helps to explain why some of the characters seem to be turned inside out. The "heroine," Mary Ford, is beautiful and good, but she turns into a zombie—the passive heroine carried to its grotesque extreme. The "hero," Percy Lee, is handsome and kind, but he is a crook. Jacob Ford is a loving father, but he is a cruel exploiter—even murderer—of poor seamstresses. Fern's portrayal of these characters suggests that such duality is not uncommon in life; that in romanticized stories, perhaps, it is simply hidden from us.

An unusual aspect of Fern's fiction is her technique of characterization. Particularly effective in the story is the introduction of numerous short scenes and dialogues between minor characters. One function of these dialogues is to provide a comment on the action. Except for an occasional comment from the author, like the one about first love, Fern relies upon these scenes to shape the theme. For example, the draymen reflect the public attitude toward Percy's arrest; Miss Snip's callous do-goodedness points up the cruel attitude of the "good" people toward a woman who has been slandered; Mrs. Jones and the Reverend Parish's conversation highlights the horror of Tom Shaw's marriage to Mary; the Irish servants' comments about Tom Shaw reveal the despicableness of his behavior; and the conversations between Zekiel and John Pray, the tailor, underscore Jacob Ford's criminal treatment of his employees. It is in these quick characterizations, such as she used in her newspaper articles, that Fern excels.

Fern uses this same technique in portraying her main characters. She portrays each of them in a series of vignettes. Their characters are suggested, not developed. Fanny Ford is a child until the end of the story. She appears in a series of isolated scenes or pictures. We see her as a very young child looking out the window of her dark attic at the children and the dog playing in the fountain; we see her touching her father's face as he lies dead at the bottom of the stairs; we see her being reprimanded by Mrs. Quip for picking flowers on Sunday; we see her walking along the road with the peddler; we see her as a young girl talking to a friend in boarding school; we see her on her wedding day. Some of these images are very vivid, and although they do not give us the connectedness that is necessary for full character development, they enable Fern to develop her theme with great precision.

The most interesting character in the story is Lucy Ford, the mother of Mary and grandmother of Fanny. She is more fully developed than the other characters, and she has the strength and flexibility that Mary lacks. Moreover, as a mature character, she has an interest and a complexity that the child Fanny does not have.

The story begins with Lucy reminding her husband of the tainted source of their money:

"It was lonesome enough, Jacob, stitching in that gloomy old garret. I often used to think how dreadful it would be to be sick and die there alone, as poor Hetty Carr did. It was a pity, Jacob, you did not pay her more, and she so weakly, too. Often she would sit up all night, sewing, with that dreadful cough racking her."

"Tut—tut—wife," said Jacob; "she was not much of a seamstress; you always had a soft heart, Lucy, and were easily imposed upon by a whining story."

"It was too true, Jacob; and she had been dead a whole day before any one found it out; then, as she had no friends, she was buried at the expense of the city, and the coffin they brought was too short for her, and they crowded her poor thin limbs into it, and carried her away in the poor's hearse. Sometimes, Jacob, I get very gloomy when I think of this, and look upon our own beautiful darling; and, sometimes, Jacob—you won't be angry with me?" asked the good woman, coaxingly, as she laid her hand upon his arm—"sometimes I've thought our money would never do us any good."

"Pshaw!" exclaimed Jacob, impatiently shaking off his wife's hand; "pshaw, Lucy, you are like all other women, weak and supersititious. A man must look out for number one. Small profits a body would make to conduct business on your principles. Grab all you can, keep all you get, is every body's motto; why should I set up to be wiser than my neighbors?"

Lucy Ford sighed. A wife is very apt to be convinced by her husband's reasoning, if she loves him; and perhaps Lucy might have been, had she not herself known what it was to sit stitching day after day in her garret, till her young brain reeled, and her heart grew faint and sick, or lain in her little bed, too weary even to sleep, listening to the dull rain as it pattered on the skylight, and wishing she were dead. (FF, 117–118)

In this passage is a thread that the reader who knows something of Fern's life will find particularly significant. Fern, who had herself experienced the suffering of the exploited seamstresses, similarly refused to be convinced by the faulty reasoning of the patriarchal culture, which idealized marriage and insisted upon seeing woman as safely under the protection of man. Fern's experience had shown her that this was a false picture; that women could not always rely upon men and that marriage was not ideal.

Throughout the story, when the other characters falter or fall, Lucy has the strength to carry on. When Jacob dies, she takes care of Mary. When Mary dies, she takes on the care of Fanny, working long hours sewing to support them. She is fortunate that the man she sews for, a former employee of her husband's, has vowed not to treat his seamstresses as unfairly as Ford did.

This criticism of society's treatment of seamstresses, whose hard struggle Fern had shared, indicates another aspect of the story: its social criticism. Not only does Fern point out the plight of underpaid seamstresses, she portrays the need for prison reform, the need for improved child-rearing and educational methods, the causes of prostitution, the disparity between the haves and the have-nots, the wastefulness of the fashion-conscious, and the injustices in the marriage relationship. All of these are issues that figure prominently in her newspaper columns. In "Fanny Ford" they are presented as part of the action, however. As we have seen, the slave wages paid to seamstresses at the time are an integral part of the story. The need for prison reform becomes clear in the scenes of Percy Lee in prison: the disgusting food, the sorry accommodations for the sick, the cells even at noonday too dark for the prisoners to read the Bibles that had been philanthropically placed in every one, the crushing punishment of "The Douche."

Fern's social criticism is most effective in her creation of dialogue, as in this conversation between a visitor and the keeper in the prison room where Percy works:

"Bah! how these fuzzy bits of lint and flax fly about the room; my throat and nose are full. I should think this would kill a fellow off before long."

"It does," said the keeper, coolly.

"And what's that horrible smell? Faugh—it makes me sick."

"That?" Oh, that's the oil used in the machinery."

"Why the fury don't you ventilate, then? asked [the visitor], thinking more of his *own* lungs than the prisoners', adding, with a laugh, as he recollected himself, "I don't suppose the Governor of your State is particular on that p'int." (FF, 133–137, 169–171)

Another example of Fern's social criticism is her ideas on child-rearing and educational methods. Her ideas on education are apparent in the contrast between the narrow views of Mrs. Quip and the progressive methods of Mrs. Chubbs, who, Fern says sarcastically, would have been "turned out of office by any MODERN school committee" (FF, 188–190, 196–197). Fern also uses dialogue to develop her ideas on child rearing. Of particular interest is the dialogue between two farmers who are neighbors of Lucy Ford: Farmer Rice tells his neighbor that scolding a boy all the time will "discourage any lad, such a constant growling and pecking. . . . If you lace up natur too tight, she'll bust out somewhere" (FF, 148–151).

A final consideration is Fern's portrayal of the marriage relationship. "God pity her," she writes of the woman "who, with a great soul, indissolubly bound, must walk ever backward with a mantle (alas! all too transparent), to cover her husband's mental nakedness!" (FF, 122). In *Woman in the Nineteenth Century*, Margaret Fuller wrote: "What woman needs is . . . as a soul to live freely and unimpeded, to unfold such powers as were given her."[2] Fern here depicts the tragedy of the woman who has a "great soul," which should be expanded to the fullest; instead, linked to a man of meager intellect, she must try to hide his deficiencies and "walk backward" to submerge her own superiority lest he and society condemn her. This apparently was one of the causes of Farrington's jealousy: not only was he jealous of Fern's friendships with others and of her dead husband's memory, he was jealous of *her*—her person, her intellect, her conversation—and she learned to be constantly on the watch lest she seem more talented than he.

It is this revelation from the perspective of the "other" in "Fanny Ford" that constitutes the subversive subtext of Fern's story. We hear the voice of the female "other"—the wife, the mother, the grandmother, the seamstress. Fern's perspective is that of the "other," the woman no longer silenced, raising her voice—sometimes obliquely, sometimes overtly—in criticism of the patriarchal givens. Lucy Ford criticizes her husband's treatment of the seamstresses; she is stronger than he as well as morally superior. By itself, this portrayal of a strong and long-suffering woman is not inconsistent with the sentimental theme of many women's novels. It only becomes significant in relation to the many oblique references and seemingly unimportant details that point to the author's critique of marriage and of male authority: Scraggs's death on the church steps on Fanny Ford's wedding day; the author's cynical tone; the associations of the name Mary Lee; the duality of the main characters; the presentation of the seamstresses' point of view; the use of dialogue as social commentary; and the wife's revelation of how she must hide her own talents in order to allow her husband to appear superior. It is not without significance that the titular character is not even referred to by the name of her father; although her mother was legally married to Tom Shaw, Fanny Ford is known by the name of her mother. Ostensibly a story of tragedy overcome, ending in a happy marriage, "Fanny Ford" contains so many elements of "differance" that, when the story is deconstructed in this way, with particular attention to Fern's life and work, as well as to the details of the text, the subtext overpowers the text, providing a pungent critique of the marriage convention and phallogocentrism, or the male-dominated ideology of the central culture.

Rose Clark

If "Fanny Ford" provides a suggestion of one of the problems in the Farrington marriage, *Rose Clark* provides a detailed description of several of those problems. The autobiographical *Ruth Hall* closely followed the events in Fern's life, but with one very important omission: her second marriage. The circumstances surrounding that marriage are introduced into her second novel. Both novels are, of course, fictionalized accounts, and cannot be read as literal histories of Fern's experiences. However, enough is known of Fern's life from her newspaper columns and other sources to indicate that the events in *Ruth Hall* and the description of Gertrude's marriage in *Rose Clark* are based on Fern's life and follow the basic outline of her experiences.

Before we look at other aspects of *Rose Clark*, then, let us examine the novel for its description of the disastrous second marriage of Gertrude Dean. After the death of a loving first husband (who dies in October, as did Charles Eldredge), Gertrude, like Sara Eldredge, marries a man she does not love in order to support herself and her child. Like Samuel Farrington, he is a widower with two children; Gertrude, like Fern, believes him to be a good man. Like Samuel Farrington, Gertrude's husband, John Stahle, is ostentatiously pious, but after their marriage she finds him to be a "hypocrite, and a gross sensualist." She is disgusted with him and finds him sexually repulsive. Like Sara Eldredge, however, she resolves to do her duty as his wife and as the stepmother of his two children. But Stahle is jealous of her. He hears others comment on her superiority, wondering how "such a fellow" as Stahle managed to get such a superior wife. Gertrude describes him to Rose:

He was under-sized, with a pale complexion, and light brown beard. He wore his hair long, and parted on the left temple, its sleek, shining look, giving him a meek appearance; his lips were thin, and, in a woman, would have been called shrewish; this tell-tale feature he dexterously concealed with his beard. I have never seen such a mouth since, that I have not shuddered; his eyes were a pale gray, and were always averted in talking, as if he feared his secret thoughts might shine through them. He appeared to great disadvantage in company, both from his inferior personal appearance and his total inability to sustain a conversation on any subject. Of this he seemed to be unaware until we appeared in company together. I soon found that the monosyllabic system to which he was necessarily confined, it would be necessary for me also to adopt, when addressed. (RC, 241–242)

We know that Farrington was similarly jealous of Fern, and one suspects that this very detailed description is an accurate description of him. Increasingly jealous and apparently angered by Gertrude's reluctance to sleep with him (although as a wife she is forced to comply), Stahle breaks up housekeeping, sending his children to a relative and taking Gertrude and her son to a boardinghouse. We can only hypothesize concerning this aspect of the Farrington marriage, but the evidence suggests that, like Gertrude, Sara Farrington found herself married to a man whom she did not respect and whom she found sexually repulsive. We also know that Farrington moved her into a boardinghouse and that, like Stahle, he refused to allow her any money. One wonders how much of Stahle's behavior in the boardinghouse parallels Farrington's: Stahle makes clear to the landlady that she is not to wait upon his wife; he also allows the landlady and the men in the house to think that his wife would welcome the attentions of other men—believing that in her desperate need (since he will give her no money) she will gladly turn to other men. Gertrude, however, does not fall into this trap, and manages to subsist in her humiliating position.

Gertrude tells of specific incidents that revealed the "pettiness of Stahle's revenge." On one occasion she had stepped on a needle. He refused to help her or to obtain medical assistance. On another occasion her son was hit by a carriage. Stahle refused to obtain medical help for the child, remaining away from home that day and all night as well, while the penniless Gertrude attempted to nurse her injured son by herself (RC, 247–250).

These two incidents underscore the vulnerability of the economically dependent woman, who, without assistance from the man she is dependent upon, cannot purchase necessities for herself or for her child. Whether the incidents are based on actual events in Fern's marriage to Farrington, they are important as evidence of Fern's growing realization of the need for economic independence for women. Another event that Gertrude tells of provides a further comment on marriage. When she returns home one day she finds that Stahle has opened her private writing desk and is going through its contents, including the letters from her first husband. When she takes them from him, declaring that they are hers, he replies: "The law says you can have nothing that is not mine" (RC, 251).

After this incident, Stahle begins to stay away from home nights and eventually leaves her, moving out of the state. Wishing to protect himself, however, he does not want to give her any evidence for legal complaint. He writes to her regularly, fraudulent letters which on the surface ask her to join him—but without her son and in the company of his brother, who had "uttered the foulest slanders" about her. "Every letter," she says, "was legally worded," but "was so managed as to render compliance with it impossible, had I desired to rejoin a man who had done, and was still covertly doing, all in his power to injure my good name" (RC, 253). Meanwhile, Stahle and his brother continue to slander Gertrude, making insinuations of sexual irregularity. Gertrude describes the result of these slanders, which not only cut her off from family and friends, who failed to come to her defense because they did not want to have to support her, but also made it difficult for her to find employment: "Men stared insolently at me in the street; women cast self-righteous scornful glances; 'friends' worse than foes, were emboldened by *his* villainy to subject themselves to a withering repulse from her who sought to earn her *honest* bread. . . . Even blood relatives have been known to circulate what they knew to be a slander to cover their own parsimony" (RC, 253–254).

The outlines of this story closely parallel Fern's experience with Farrington, who, anxious to preserve his own religious reputation, attempted to drive his wife into indiscretions that would enable him to get a divorce, cutting off her money and, with his brother, spreading slanders about her from which her family and friends did not defend her. In January 1851 Fern left him, taking her children to a hotel; Farrington left Massachusetts, writing her fraudulent letters and eventually settling in Chicago, where he obtained a divorce in 1853 on the grounds of desertion. The principal difference is that in the novel Gertrude does not leave her husband; one suspects that Fern, remembering how violently she had been condemned for leaving her husband—regardless of the circumstances—changed the facts hoping to make Gertrude a sympathetic character.

Eventually Gertrude is able to support herself and her son by painting. Later, when she has become wealthy and famous, Stahle, who has divorced her, reappears with the intention of getting money from her. Deeming her ignorant of the law and still vulnerable to his threats, he plans to intimidate her into sharing her wealth with him. "All women are fools about law matters," he says (RC, 345). However, Gertrude's newfound brother appears and threatens to give him a beating, and Stahle, who, Fern says, is a coward like all "woman slanderers," retires, tail-between-legs (RC, 346–348). In this scene it is clear that Fern is writing what she wished had been a conclusion to her own second marriage—that a protective brother had stood up for her before Farrington. Even more important, as the lawyer's letter in the Sophia Smith Collection makes clear, Fern had informed herself of the facts regarding Farrington's rights to her property after the divorce. It is probable that Farrington, like Stahle, attempted to get money from his former wife soon after she became wealthy and famous as Fanny Fern. Armed with the letter from J. C. Derby's attorney and a copy of the divorce decree, however, Fern was herself prepared to send him packing.[3]

Rose Clark is not only valuable as an exposé of Fern's second marriage. It is also interesting as a novel. Of particular interest are the novel's structure, theme, and style, and Fern's satiric portrayal of character and event.

The principal criticism of *Rose Clark* as a novel is that it relies too much on coincidence: John Perry happens to meet his long-lost sister Gertrude in New Orleans; Vincent happens to stop at Mrs. Bond's where Rose had lived; Stahle happens to come to Niagara when Gertrude is there; John Perry happens to meet Vincent in Boston. Primarily because of this reliance on coincidence, the plot strains the reader's credulity. Fern was aware of this problem and, foreseeing criticism, attempted to answer it within the novel in Gertrude's comment in Chapter 68 with respect to Vincent's story: "His history is so singular that in a novel it would be stigmatized as incredible, overdrawn, and absurd; in truth, a novelist who would not subject himself to such charges must not too closely follow Nature" (RC, 405).

Although this explanation hardly justifies the heavy reliance on coincidence in *Rose Clark,* it is interesting as an indication of Fern's awareness of the extent to which she was exceeding the probable in the novel. One wonders if she was consciously parodying the improbable plots of many popular sensation novels. Certainly, despite this heavy reliance on coincidence, the novel focuses not on the sensational but on the everyday problems of ordinary people. As the reviewer for *Harper's* wrote in December of 1855, "The plot of the story is of an unpretending character, free from extravagant incidents and artificial complications."[4] And as Fern said, she did not feel that a writer should rely for interest upon the spectacular or the supernatural. She found sufficient interest in the ordinary people who make up society, and, as she demonstrates in *Ruth Hall* and *Rose Clark*, one can find hair-raising cruelties in the ordinary, the law-abiding, even the avowedly pious. In the Halls' treatment of Ruth, Mrs. Markham's and Aunt Dolly's treatment of Rose (and of everyone else in their power), Stahle's treatment of Gertrude, Fern's powerful satire demonstrates that evil is not found solely in the criminal and the macabre. It forms a very real part of the commonplace.

The other principal criticism of *Rose Clark* is that the multiple events and swift scene changes create a structural disconnectedness in the novel. Although the introduction of numerous characters and the many scene changes give rise to charges of disconnectedness, there is an unusual symmetry to *Rose Clark*. First of all, the story begins and ends with a six-year-old child's confrontation by Mrs. Markham, the cruel matron of the orphanage. In the first chapter, six-year-old Rose, who has been newly orphaned, enters the orphanage where for the next several years she is to be victimized by Mrs. Markham. Mrs. Markham has absolute power over the children in the orphanage. Because of her drive for wealth and power, and through her machinations and clever manipulation of one of the trustees, she is able to exercise that power for evil, destroying the lives and spirit of the children in her charge. In the last chapter Rose's six-year-old son Charley sees what appears to be a bundle of rags in the gutter and with the help of his parents rescues the dying Mrs. Markham, who begs for mercy. The difference in the scenes and the characters' respective power and the use they make of it comment on the action that takes place between the two scenes.

Also significant is the novel's form. *Rose Clark*, which covers sixteen years and takes place in a number of totally different settings, is structured like a five-act play. Act I (chapters 1–18) encompasses Rose's childhood and covers the scenes in the orphanage and in Aunt Dolly's home. It ends with the death of the minister's baby and Aunt Dolly's callous comment, which ironically foreshadows Dolly's own child's death. Considerable time has passed before Act II (chapters 19–31) begins with the reappearance of Rose as a young mother at Mrs. Bond's and Dolly's (now Mrs. Howe). This act ends with the death of Dolly's baby. Act III (chapters 32–48) begins with Rose on shipboard on her way to New Orleans to search for the absent Vincent, whom she believes to be her husband, but who others tell her—and who the reader also believes—is a fraud. After the scenes on shipboard, the rest of Act III takes place in New Orleans, where Rose meets Gertrude, John Perry, and the mother of the other—evil—Vincent. The act ends when Anne Cooper, the vindictive housekeeper at Mrs. Vincent's, tells Rose's landlady that Rose is an unwed mother and Rose is evicted. Act IV (chapters 49–58) takes place primarily at Niagara Falls. The first chapter in Act IV focuses on the servants' talk in the kitchen, firmly grounding the action in the present and indicating that the retribution will be sure and swift. In this act Mrs. Markham is found out, Stahle is driven off, and the act ends with the violent death of the cruel and selfish Dolly Howe lying alone and friendless in the police station. Act V (chapters 59–71) takes place in Boston. John Perry meets Vincent, and, overcoming the temptation to withhold the information from Rose, whom he wants to marry, leads Vincent to Rose and little Charley for a happy reunion. The middle of the act portrays the peaceful death of the good Mrs. Bond, loved and respected by all who knew her, in contrast to the violent and lonely death of Dolly Howe. The final act ends with the retributive death of the power-seeking Mrs. Markham, who ends her life in the gutter.

It will be apparent that all of the acts end with a death, except the central act, Act III, which ends with the sisterly embrace of Rose and Gertrude *and* the "Satanic laugh" of Anne Cooper, who is the principal evil character in the book who does not meet retributive justice at the end of the novel. That Fern ends the central chapter with this woman's vindictive speech rather than with the embrace of the two female protagonists undercuts the sisterliness of their embrace; in fact, Gertrude is urging Rose to marry her brother and thus become her sister-in-law, which, however well-intentioned, is, to Rose, an abhorrent idea. Moreover, since Anne Cooper is never punished, to end the central act with her "Satanic laugh" undercuts the faith in a beneficent universe that is contained in the ostensible happy ending. Fern has deliberately constructed a novel with an apparently symmetrical design. Built into this ordered structure, however, is an overarching disconnectedness that implicitly questions the order and provides an important indication that the religious ending is not the whole story; that the order implicit in such an ending is an ideal, not an accurate assessment of the experiences related in the book.

It is a mistake to interpret the wish-fulfillment ending as a reflection of Fern's vision of human experience. The novel ends with the injunction that "God is Just," and the events of the story presumably prove that good will be rewarded and evil punished: the good Rose is rewarded in the end, while the evil Dolly Howe and Mrs. Markham are more than amply punished. This is a simplistic interpretation of a complex novel, however. Although Rose appears to be portrayed seriously, it is clear that Fern is spoofing the sentimental portrayal of the "good" heroine in her portrayal of the innocent Rose: she uses expressions and situations that elsewhere she criticized and satirized. For example, she calls Rose an innocent maiden of "sixteen summers," which was an expression that she explicitly criticized in her newspaper articles (NYL, April 28, 1860).

Moreover, the Gertrude Dean story undercuts the credibility of the Rose Clark story. As we saw in the discussion of *Ruth Hall*, what seems like disconnectedness in the novel is a carefully constructed contrapuntal pattern designed to illustrate the protagonist's gradual evolution of self and the consequent deconstruction of the cultural order that had previously defined it. Fern uses a different technique in *Rose Clark*, but the same principle is at work. Instead of following the development of one protagonist, in *Rose Clark* Fern introduces two female protagonists, one of which (Gertrude) provides the principal means by which the reader can deconstruct the cultural order represented by the story of the other female protagonist (Rose) and explicitly stated at the end of the novel. The Gertrude Dean story, which derives from Fern's own experience, provides a significant element of "differance" and points the way to the ultimate dismantling of the text. Just as *Ruth Hall* was told from the point of view of the innocent, domestic Ruth at the beginning of the novel and the experienced businesswoman Ruth later on, with the narrator undercutting the sentimental by juxtaposing it with the satirical throughout the novel, there are similarly two points of view in *Rose Clark*—Rose's and Gertrude's—juxtaposed against the satirical and sentimental scenes presented by the narrative voice. Rose remains trusting and faithful to the long-absent Vincent, despite the overwhelming evidence indicating he is false. Gertrude, on the other hand, tells her brother: "Men are so gross and unspiritual, John, so wedded to making money and promiscuous love, so selfish and unchivalric; of course there are occasionally glorious exceptions, but who would be foolish enough to wade through leagues of brambles, and briars, to find perchance one flower?" (RC, 283). The reader discovers at the end that, despite all of the evidence that seemed to point to the contrary, Vincent is that "one flower" and Rose was right to believe in him. On the other hand, he could just as easily have been the other Vincent, who had deserted the young woman whom he had tricked into a false marriage—which is what everyone but Rose believes her Vincent is guilty of.

Other evidence in the novel indicates that Gertrude's cynicism outweighs Rose's faith. One important clue is the names of the male characters: just as there are two Vincents, who might be said to be mirror images of each other, it is not accidental that four of the principal male characters are named John. John Perry is a good man; John Stahle is a bad man; John Howe is a weak man; and John Grey is a bad man who reforms. "John" is Fern's everyman: bad and good, weak and strong—in other words, human. The repeated use of the name John connects the different stories and makes the men all a part of the human condition. In *Rose Clark* Fern gives us her vision of life as it is and life as it should be. As she said in an 1857 article, she was annoyed sometimes by the "microscopic spectacles" that she said had been "mounted on my nose by the hypocrites I have known," and that ever came between her and her inclination to love or trust in humankind (NYL, August 1, 1857). She might have struggled against the cynicism of a Gertrude, but she never attained the faith of a Rose.

In order to understand Fern's point of view in this novel, however, one needs to look closely at Fern's portrayal of the other characters. *Rose Clark* contains a veritable gallery of characters, the most interesting of which are treated satirically. The first part of the novel in which Fern portrays the cruelty of Mrs. Markham and Aunt Dolly is by far the strongest section of the book. The realism of these scenes is striking: the pale children standing at attention, Mrs. Markham maneuvering with Mr. Balch, Aunt Dolly jealously cutting off Rose's hair, or refusing to give her her mother's thimble, or bruising her arm. After Dolly marries John Howe, the scenes between the Howes are reminiscent of those between the Halls in *Ruth Hall*, humorously satirical and vividly portrayed. Also well done is Fern's satire of Dolly Howe as a fashion-conscious, pretentious woman, made a fool of by the parasitical poet Tom Finels. Particularly interesting is the satirical treatment of the unregenerate Finels himself, whose letters provide an ironic comment on the action, throwing into question the conventional piety of the narrative voice. These characterizations are far more numerous and more vivid than the portrayals of "good" people, and cannot help but undercut the affirmative ending of the novel.

All of these elements of "differance" help to deconstruct the metaphor of the beneficent universe, or "transcendental signified," that is represented by the novel's conventional ending.[5] The optimistic belief in a metaphysical order that Fern's contemporaries were happy to see in *Rose Clark* is thrown into question by the discontinuities in the text and the discordant realities that Fern portrays. Although Fern herself maintained a belief in a divine Being, and found comfort in the idea of immortality, this novel is consistent with her rejection of any system of closure that idealized or romanticized reality.

When *Rose Clark* appeared, some of the critics were kinder to Fern than they had been after the appearance of *Ruth Hall*. In fact, it seems clear that Fern wrote *Rose Clark* partly to vindicate herself before the harsh criticism that had been heaped upon her after her previous novel. After the publication of *Ruth Hall*, Fern had been criticized so widely that the conclusion of the public was that no "true woman" could write such a book. In writing *Rose Clark* Fern set out to show the public that despite her outspoken opinions on marriage and women's rights, and in spite of her satirical treatment of her relatives, she was essentially a "true woman." That she did not recant in her insistence on independence and even economic independence for women is clear from her inclusion of the Gertrude Dean sections in the novel. Similarly, her satirical treatment of her second husband in *Rose Clark* reveals that she did not recant in response to the outcry against her for her criticism of her male relatives in *Ruth Hall.*

The *New York Tribune,* which had complained about the character of Ruth Hall, called Rose Clark "the most attractive character" Fanny Fern had created.[6] *The New York Times,* which criticized every other aspect of *Rose Clark,* declared that the sweet Rose was the "only character in the book at all real."[7] And the *Boston Daily Bee* said that "a more beautiful character than Rose herself does not exist in English literature."[8] Not only were the critics fond of the gentle Rose, they liked what they perceived to be the religious message of the book—that a trust in a beneficent God will bring its own reward—and the gentler, more charitable tone. The New York *Mirror* praised the "general tone and sentiment of the book," and noted that the book "inculcates a philanthropy as wide as the world, and a charity that reaches to the honest depths of human degradation and suffering."[9] The *Boston Daily Bee* acclaimed the "noble" purpose of the book.[10] And *Harper's New Monthly Magazine* predicted that *Rose Clark* "in tone and temper will be deemed a marked improvement on 'Ruth Hall.'"[11] This latter was, of course, what Fern had hoped.

Although today's readers will perhaps find *Rose Clark's* religious assertions intrusive and its heroine, Rose, less interesting and less credible than the strong-minded Gertrude Dean or Ruth Hall, it was these aspects of the book that caused many critics to hail it as Fern's "best work to date" and "ten times better than *Ruth Hall.*"[12] Fern knew what the critics wanted from a woman writer, yet, fortunately for her readers—her contemporary readers and the readers of today—she could not wholly write pap. As Herman Melville said when his works were not selling, "What I feel most moved to write, that is banned. . . . Yet altogether write the *other* way, I cannot."[13] Fern's problem was different from Melville's: his works did not sell, whereas she was criticized for being unwomanly. As a woman she was expected to be religious and affirmative; she was not supposed to be angry or satirical or to know about the dark side of life. In her 1857 essay "Facts for Unjust Critics," she cited appreciatively the comment of Charlotte Brontë, who was similarly frustrated by the critics' standards for women writers: "I wish all reviewers believed me to be a man; they would be more just to me. They will, I know, keep measuring me by some standard of what they deem becoming to my sex; where I am not what they consider graceful, they will condemn me" (NYL, June 13, 1857).[14]

To understand the climate in which Fern was writing, one needs to look at the comments that critics were making about women writers who were perceived as having exceeded the bounds of feminine propriety. It is clear from these comments that American society at the time had very rigid requirements for women and for women novelists. Caroline Chesebro's *Isa* (1852) was criticized as "painful—shocking—we might add disgusting."[15] E.D.E.N. Southworth was criticized because in her adventure novel, *The*

Curse of Clifton (1853), she had "rushed out of her sphere," writing about violence instead of "good and pleasant things" and her "every-day sentiments" as a woman.[16] E. Marion Stephens was criticized for a "recklessness of propriety" in her 1855 novel, *Hagar the Martyr*; the reviewer said that a woman's name on the title page should be a guarantee against "gross faults of principle."[17] And an article in *The Living Age* in 1864 declared that women should not "understand the meannesses of the world" which were necessary for great writing; any woman who attempted to do so would have to do so "by a defeminizing process."[18] In *Rose Clark* Fern sought to prove that although she was independent and aware of as well as critical of society's wrongs, she had not been "defeminized." The modern reader tempted to ask "why did she bother?" has only to remember the anguish she suffered in her personal as well as her public life because of the gossip and scandal to which her writing made her vulnerable. To many Americans at the time, her "strong-minded" writing only seemed to confirm the scandal spread by Farrington and the author of *The Life and Beauties*.

As a literary work, *Rose Clark* served a dual function: its religious tone and gentle heroine demonstrated that Fanny Fern was at heart a "true woman," while at the same time its portrayal of the Gertrude Dean story reiterated Fern's criticism of society's restricted role for women. The novel also served a purpose in Fern's personal life. The Gertrude Dean story told Fern's side of the story of her second marriage. A not unimportant result of this aspect of the novel was the element of revenge. Just as *Ruth Hall* was Fern's revenge on her brother and father, Fern must have felt some satisfaction in knowing that in *Rose Clark* she had evened the score with Samuel Farrington.

The Mason Brothers used many of the same advertising techniques with *Rose Clark* that they had used so successfully with *Ruth Hall*. They began advertising in late November, comparing the two novels and suggesting that *Rose Clark* might even be better than *Ruth Hall*. Successive advertisements quoted from favorable reviews, and then, on December 6, the publication day, Mason Brothers announced that twelve thousand copies had already been ordered in advance of publication. In this advertisement Mason Brothers commented that unfavorable reviews of such a successful book are often motivated by jealousy—the critic is often the author of an unsuccessful book—and suggested that this was the explanation for the unfavorable review in the *New York Times*.[19] There are no sales figures available to make a final comparison with the sales of *Ruth Hall*, but contemporary sources reported that *Rose Clark* "also met with success."[20]

Although some reviewers responded positively to Fern's portrayal of Rose and took the novel at face value as a work with a noble purpose, other reviewers focused on the less gentle aspects of the novel. In its scathing review of *Rose Clark*, *The New York Times* criticized most vehemently those aspects of the novel that a modern reader finds most appealing: the satirical portrayals of Mrs. Markham and Aunt Dolly and Fern's use of down-to-earth language. Pronouncing the novel a "failure," the reviewer expressed disgust with a woman writer who would attempt to portray ordinary members of society as such despicable people and who would use words that are not "delicate." *Rose Clark*, the reviewer asserted, "contains a superfluity of painful incident and passages so exaggerated as to be extremely unnatural." Maintaining that characters like Mrs. Markham and Aunt Dolly were too monstrous to be real, the reviewer continued:

There is another character, Gertrude, whose adventures occupy a large portion of the volume, who is also anything but akin to reality. [She] is a strong-minded woman—"drawn mild"—a victim, of course, to marital tyranny, self-boasted as the incarnation of purity, but, while telling her story to a female friend, using such suggestive language as this, "Whole days he (the husband) passed without speaking to me, and yet, at the same time, no inmate of a harem was ever more slavishly subject to the gross appetite of her master." This high-bred Gertrude is made to speak of a child as "this little piece of quicksilver *squirming* around her," and the use of this word is not a mere slip of the pen, for we have it more than once. The wit (and delicacy) of the book may be judged from a description of a "pompous city autocrat, all dignity and shirt collar, following his *abdomen* and the waiter."[21]

This review helps us to understand what Fern was up against. It was not enough that she concluded her novel with a religious affirmation and made her titular heroine sweet and gentle; in order to meet the requirements for women writers of critics like the *Times* reviewer she would have had to water down all of her characters and have them, as well as the narrator, speak in carefully guarded euphemisms. The most revealing aspect of this review, however, is its denunciation of a woman for mentioning—even to a female friend—the horror of being used sexually by a husband who degraded and mistreated her and for whom she felt neither love nor respect.

After reviews like this one, it is not surprising that Fern wrote no more long works of fiction. Reading a review like the one from the *Times*, which criticized everything that she must have known was most successful in the novel—her pungent satire, her deft characterization, and her candid portrayal of Gertrude's marriage—Fern no longer desired to seek a future as a novelist. In the 1850s the boundaries for women novelists were too tightly drawn. During the remainder of her career, Fern would be outspoken and satirical—but in the essay; in a sense she had invented the form, and the boundaries were her own.

13

❧❦

"A Practical Bluestocking"

Is my article for the Ledger *ready? No sir, . . . it is NOT! Have I not been beset, since I left my bed this morning, with cook, chambermaid and sempstress? Have not butcher, baker, and grocer been tweaking that area-bell unceasingly, about matters which must be referred to my unpostponable decision? . . . Is not my head as woolly inside as out, with . . . the settling of the thousand and one little matters which take up, and* must *take up, the precious morning hours, which, alas! show for nothing, and yet which no housekeeper may dodge, even with her coffin or a prospective article for the* Ledger *in sight?*

NYL, October 26, 1861

DURING ALL THE TIME THAT FANNY FERN WAS WRITING a regular column for the *Ledger* she was also wife, mother, and then grandmother. She attempted to set aside the mornings for her writing. But, as the opening quotation suggests, these precious morning hours were often intruded upon by the demands of the household. Nevertheless she managed to write her weekly columns and also to publish six more collections of her articles.

From January 5, 1856, the day her first regular column appeared in the *New York Ledger,* to October 12, 1872, two days after her death, Fanny Fern's column appeared every week in the *Ledger,* without fail. Grace Greenwood commented on this amazing feat in her biographical sketch of Fern in 1868.[1] Certainly Fern's disciplined production was different from that of her contemporary Margaret Fuller, of whom Horace Greeley commented that when she was writing for the *Tribune,* her articles were always late, "a day after the fair."[2]

While maintaining her career as a writer, Fern simultaneously had demands upon her time deriving principally from three other areas: domestic, social, and personal. In order to understand the significance of her achievement, it will be useful to look at her life in the late 1850s with respect to these areas.

Domestic

Fern wrote a number of articles about the difficulties women faced in attempting to write and maintain a household as well. A look at some of those articles can give us an idea of the pressures that Fern felt. In her 1854 "Mrs. Adolphus Smith Sporting the Blue Stocking," she portrayed a woman attempting to write amid the chaos of family life.³ "Soliloquy of a Literary Housekeeper," published on May 16, 1857, reflects Fern's attitude toward the requisites of housekeeping and female dress in the mid-nineteenth century. Clearly, the added responsibility of writing created other priorities, and the practical Fern rebelled against being the slave to home and fashion that her age demanded:

"Spring cleaning!" Oh misery! Ceilings to be whitewashed, walls to be cleaned, paint to be scoured, carpets to be taken up, shaken, put down again. . . . [C]hildren's last summer clothes to be inspected. . . . When is that book of mine to get written I'd like to know. . . . Must I turn my house topsy-turvy, and inside out, once a year, because my grandmother did, and send my MSS. flying to the four winds, for this traditionary "spring cleaning?" Spring fiddlestick! Must I buy up all Broadway to be made into dresses, because all New York women go fashion-mad? What's the use of having a house, if you can't do as you like in it? What is the use of being an authoress, if you can't indulge in the luxury of a shabby bonnet, or a comfortable old dress? . . . "There goes Lily Larkspur, the authoress, in that everlasting old black silk." Well—what's the use of being well off, if you can't wear old clothes? . . . Give me good health—the morning for writing, and no interruptions, plenty of fresh air afterwards and an old gown to enjoy it in and you may mince along in your peacock dry-goods, till your soul is as shrivelled as your body.

However, in those days before the advent of ready-made dresses, Fern said in an 1861 article, it was impossible for a woman *not* to give "a great part of her 'thoughts and attention' to dress." In this article, entitled "Plain Thoughts in Plain Words," Fern described the process necessary for a woman to acquire a dress: first she had to visit numerous stores to find the right fabric; next other stores must be visited for the thread and buttons; if ornamental trimming was needed and colors were to be matched, "the labor is doubled"; then she would need to cut and fit the dress herself or find a dressmaker—a difficult task in itself; and she would need to try the dress on a half-dozen times before it was satisfactorily fitted (NYL, March 23, 1861).

Like the woman in Elizabeth Stuart Phelps's "The Angel over the Right Shoulder" (1852), who found it impossible to have two hours to herself, most women writers, Fern said, are "liable to perpetual interruption, which can neither be foreseen nor prevented":

Sometimes I look at it on the ridiculous side. I see parentheses in *Uncle Tom's Cabin* and *Jane Eyre* and *Shirley*, where the authors stated, that here they stopped to wash the ink spots from their fingers; or to make bread or put kindling in the oven preparatory to it, while the celestial spark stood in abeyance. Sometimes "stopped to wash baby" might have been inserted on the margin opposite some interrupted pathetic passage, or "a pair of little breeches here demands attention"; or "a person who had nothing to say has just left, after taking two hours of my best time to say it"; or "the grocer or butcher, having failed to send supplies, I here stopped to go and inquire into it," or "little Bobby having the stomach ache, I had to leave here to get some hot peppermint." . . .

I should like an edition of famous books with truth-telling margins like these inserted. It would be funny reading to everybody but the authors, to whom indeed it would be "no joke." (NYL, May 8, 1869)

Although to the woman writer the infringements of household responsibilities were "no joke," Fern was able to portray the humor of such a harassing situation. In a comic article in the *Ledger* on April 4, 1868, Fern portrayed herself as "A Maniac Authoress," who forgets people's names and faces, forgets how much the fare was on the omnibus, forgets to take her change, and forgets to pay for an item in a store. When asked if she is going mad, she says, "The solution of all this is, that I write for the *New York Ledger*. That I have a new book in press, that the proofs are sent to snarl me up late in the evening. . . . That I have had sickness in the house for six weeks. That I am housekeeper. . . . [A]nd that I have a little duck of a grandchild, who every hour or two wants me 'to tell her a story *new* and *true*.' Am I excused?"

Despite the difficulties Fern encountered, she persisted with her career. A number of factors enabled her to do so. First of all, her mind was always working, gaining material for columns in everyday experiences and observations. Moreover, she was an avid newspaper reader, and as she was reading the newspapers in the morning, she was filing away in her mind more material for future columns. Another factor that enabled her to continue her career throughout all the interruptions of domestic life was her apparent ability to use spare moments productively. In an 1864 article entitled "Those Few Minutes," she described the way a person can make good use of time. "Executive people," she said, "are chary of the precious flying moments." Those moments can mean "much in the course of a life-time to those who carefully husband them":

Those "few minutes" may make all the difference between an educated and an uneducated person. . . . Those "few minutes," carefully improved as they occur, have filled libraries with profound and choice volumes; those "few minutes," saved for mental cultivation, have enabled men, and

women too, to shed over a life of toil a brightness which made even monotonous duty a delight. Such can ill afford to be robbed of them by those
unable to appreciate their value. Like the infinitesimal gold scrapings of
the mint, they may not be purloined, or carelessly brushed away by idle
fingers; but conscientiously gathered up and accounted for; to be molten
and stamped with thought, then distributed to bless mankind. (NYL, February 27, 1864)

Also important was the fact that Fern wrote with great facility and with a
sure hand. Robert Bonner once commented in the *Ledger* that he never cut
or altered a line of any of Fanny Fern's articles (NYL, March 14, 1857).
James Parton describes how she wrote her articles when he first knew her:

Her writings never seemed to cost her any effort. She would sit down at
the desk at that period of her life, and dip the pen in the ink, and bring it
in close contact with the paper, before she knew what she was going to
write about, and, having thought of a subject, she would write with the
utmost rapidity to the very end without a pause.
I believe, however, that she had usually reflected upon several subjects
beforehand. At a late period I know that she did; for I have heard her say,
a hundred times, that she did her thinking early in the morning, while she
was arranging her hair. (JP, 55–56)

Parton also notes that he found among her papers a packet labeled "Pious
Cant," which contained paragraphs taken from newspapers (JP, 70). Many
of her articles were written in reaction to such paragraphs, and she apparently collected them over the years to provide herself with ideas for
columns.
Fern did not see her writing and household tasks as incompatible. In "A
Practical Blue Stocking," in the *Olive Branch* on August 2, 1852, she portrayed a woman who converts a man who has been adamantly opposed to
women writing; he is amazed to see how well she can maintain a household
and be a successful writer at the same time. Fern criticized the woman writer
who felt everyday household chores were beneath her. In the article "Bogus
Intellect" she asserted that although she would "indignantly deny" that a
woman was "born with a gridiron around her neck," that is, that she was
born for housework and housework alone, she repudiated the idea that
household duties were beneath any woman:

Because a woman can appreciate a good book, or even write one or talk
or think intelligently, is she not to be a breezy, stirring, wide-awake, effi-
cient, thorough, capable housekeeper? Is she not to be a soulful wife and a
loving, judicious mother? Is she to disdain to comb a little tumbled head,
or to wash a pair of sticky little paws, or to mend a rent in a pinafore or a

little pair of trousers? I tell you there's a false ring about women who talk that way. No woman of true intellect ever felt such duties *beneath* her. She may like much better to read an interesting book, or write out her own thoughts when she feels the inspiration, than to be *much* employed this way, but she will never, never disdain it, and she will faithfully stand at her post if there can be no responsible relief-guard. (NYL, December 30, 1865)

When Fanny Fern began to write she did so because she needed the money. Driven by poverty and by the terms of her father-in-law's will, she desperately needed to earn money not only to feed and clothe herself and her children, but ultimately—and this was probably the strongest motivation—so that she would not have to give up her children. The question is, why did Fanny Fern continue her career throughout her life, long after she no longer needed the money and even after she remarried? This would not be a question today, perhaps, but for an American woman of the mid-nineteenth century, it was very much a question. In most novels of the period, the woman who supports herself when she is single gratefully gives up her career as soon as she is married. The "true woman" of the period was modestly and "femininely" dependent. Fern would not have had the problems she had with her society if she had simply retired into married anonymity. But she did not. Why she did not is clear from her articles.

First of all, Fern believed that writing was a natural talent that should not be stifled. In an early article in the *Olive Branch* on February 2, 1853, "A Chapter on Literary Women," a woman writer comments in response to the question, Why do women write?:

Because they can't help it. . . . Why does a bird carol? There is that in such a soul that will not be pent up,—that must find voice and expression; a heaven-kindled spark, that is unquenchable; an earnest, soaring spirit, whose wings cannot be earth-clipped.

Fern also believed that writing provided an outlet for ideas and emotions that women could not otherwise give utterance to, but which it was unhealthy to repress. In her own case, her column provided her with a useful forum in which she could have the last word on any number of subjects. On August 10, 1867, Fern wrote in the *New York Ledger* an article called "The Women of 1867," in which she explained the value of writing to women:

A woman who wrote used to be considered a sort of monster. At this day it is difficult to find one who does not write, or has not written, or who has not, at least, a strong desire to do so. Gridirons and darning-needles are getting monotonous. A part of their time the women of to-day are content to devote to their consideration when necessary; but you will rarely find one—at least among women who *think*—who does not silently rebel against allowing them a monopoly. . . . It is not *safe* for the women of 1867 to shut down so much that cries out for sympathy and expression, because life is such a maelstrom of business or folly, or both, that those to whom they have bound themselves, body and soul, recognize only the needs of the former. . . .

I say to such women: Write! Rescue a part of each week at least for reading, and putting down on paper, for your own private benefit, your thoughts and feelings. Not for the *world's* eye, unless you choose, but to lift yourselves out of the dead-level of your lives; to keep off inanition; to lessen the number who are yearly added to our lunatic asylums from the ranks of the misappreciated, unhappy womanhood, narrowed by lives made up of details.

For Fern, then, writing was not only a means to earning a living and a talent that needed to be expressed; writing was also therapeutic. Writing, whether it was done professionally or simply in a private journal, could provide women with a necessary outlet for their ideas and feelings, an "escape valve," as Fern says in *Ruth Hall*. This conception of writing helps to explain Ruth Hall's comment to her daughter, who asks if she too will write when she grows up: "God forbid," says Ruth, thinking of the hard circumstances that drove her to write. "No happy woman ever writes" (RH, 175).

Certainly when Fern began to write, she was writing out of her unhappiness and desperation. That this was no longer her motivation by the time that she married James Parton is evident from the fact that she included in the prenuptial agreement the assumption that she would continue to write after her marriage; the agreement specifies that she will possess separately, "as if she were unmarried," all of the income deriving from her writing, "and including all property which may hereafter arise or accrue to her by reason of any new works which may be prepared by her."[4]

It is this prenuptial agreement that provides the key to Fern's major motivation in continuing her career: she wanted to maintain her independence. In order to understand how Fern conceived of marriage for a literary woman, and how the maintenance of her independence was associated with her writing, it will be interesting to look at an article that she published in *Galaxy* magazine in 1867, "A Literary Couple." Since her exclusive agreement with Robert Bonner prevented her from publishing elsewhere under the name Fanny Fern, this article was published under the name Mrs. James Parton. It reveals a woman who refused to give up her independence and her individuality when she married; in Fern's mind, the two were interdependent, and it was through her writing that she felt she was able to maintain them:

My name is Pamela—Pamela Penfeather. I am literary. So is my husband. . . . My gift is inherited—my father was an editor. I came into the world wrapped in a proof-sheet. When I was no taller than an editor's table, I used to paste newspapers in their envelopes for the mail. When proof-readers were scarce, I read the proofs. Older, when contributors were wanting, or exorbitant in their demands, I furnished articles. When letters or MSS. of awful chirography came, I translated the heathenish characters. With the eye of an eagle, I ran over a pile of exchanges as high as my head, and pounced upon anything that concerned "our office." I mention these little items, to show you my qualifications for a literary man's wife. Also, that you may understand why I did not, when I married, bury myself in Penfeather's shirt-fronts, or crush myself under his household gridiron. On the contrary, I remarked to him on our wedding day, "Penfeather, although matrimonially we are one, literarily we are two. Marrying me, you didn't marry my pen. That is going still to wag on in single blessedness. Your divine afflatus is one thing; mine is another." This was agreed upon in that halcyon hour.

But you know what man is, and what his promises are. If you don't, I hope you never may. It was not long before Penfeather came nosing round my writing desk, which, I trust to goodness, is not so dusty as he insists on keeping his; and peeping over my conjugal shoulder, which you will agree was treating me more like a wife than an individual, remarked: "Pamela, I wish you would leave out that sentence"; pointing to my most cherished idea. . . .

"Penfeather," said I, rising and sitting down on his lap, to make sure of him till I got through, "Penfeather, have you forgotten our agreement?" . . . When the storm comes, I shall stand and take it like a woman; and you need not consider it necessary to be on hand with your umbrella."[5]

Fern insisted on independence—the independence to earn her own living and the independence to write her own thoughts. Her writing gave her the individuality that she felt would have been submerged in a traditional marriage. As she indicates in this article, the terms "wife" and "individual" are not synonymous. One might compare this concept with that of Emily Dickinson, for whom the two were also opposed: in her poem "I'm Wife," for example, the fact of being "wife" is described as a "soft Eclipse" which has "finished" the independence of the single state.[6]

The *Galaxy* article also gives a good picture of how Fern functioned as part of a literary couple, that is, how Fern and Parton maintained literary independence, yet were able to come together "matrimonially," as Fern says, in love and sympathy:

Whenever we talk to each other, we always preface our remarks by saying, Now, Pamela, or Now Penfeather, I am talking *article;* so don't steal it for the "Indian Chronicle" or the "Weekly Gazette"; honor bright, now! no filching—this is *my* thunder! This gives spice to what would otherwise degenerate into stupid matrimonialities. . . .

But when that autocrat inkstand undertakes to lay down rules as to hours for retiring, singly or together, and more than all, when it insists that friendly conversation shall be suspended as soon as the gas is turned off, lest to-morrow's "article" be damaged, why then I feel impelled emphatically to remind Penfeather that though literarily we are two, matrimonially we are one.

"A Literary Couple" concludes with a section written presumably from the point of view of the author's husband. It provides an update on their life together, echoing the article Fern wrote soon after her marriage, "Tom Pax's Conjugal Soliloquy," but also describing the relationship as it had developed in the eleven years since that article was written:

Jove! what it is to have a literary wife. I thought when I married one it would be so charming to have a companion who could understand literary labor and its necessities. Never was a poor devil so mistaken. She interrupts me in my writing, on as trivial pretences as if she herself were not the authoress of half a dozen books. A funny story she has heard from some woman, and wants to tell me. A greenback she has torn and wants me to tinker together. . . . An editorial in the morning paper she wishes to read to me, which she says won't hold water. . . .

This is not all. When my wife, Pamela, has done writing, her head is on fire, her cheeks burn, and she is wild for the fresh air and a long walk to cool herself down. Now, when I have done writing I want to lie off and smoke. The idea of exercising is perfectly disgusting. . . .

Again, I thought it would be so delightful to have a wife who had an opinion of her own on every subject, who read and thought for herself, and was not a mere echo. By Jove! I've changed my mind on that point, too. Pamela is the most insatiate gobbler of newspapers. She wants to know the political pros and cons of everything. She digs into isms and ologies in the most helter-skelter fashion. She rushes round into primary schools, and Magdalen asylums, and houses of correction, and pokes into tenement-houses, and station-houses, and prisons, and wants me to right every existing abuse before tea. . . .

Then—what sacredness is there about a man's literary wife? Do people address her as *Mrs.* Penfeather? Not at all. It is, There goes Pamela, and How dy'e do Pamela? and Have you read Pamela's book, or article. Every whipper-snapper writes letters to her; and who knows what she answers? She has requests for her autograph, and her picture, and a lock of her hair, till she gets so confoundedly inflated that no matrimonial cord will hold her down. She has piles of correspondence, both before and since her marriage. Yes, sir, *since!* . . .

For what purpose that intense creature, Mrs. Penfeather, was created, I shall never know. She wants a man's freedom, and independence of expression, and action, and yet a bigger baby never warmed its pug nose against a mother's bosom. It is most extraordinary. Alas! she is so stormy, and I so adore repose.

At the idea of Pamela and repose, I laugh hysterically!

This is Fern's projection of Parton's opinion of her. She was well aware of the difficulties that her career created, yet she apparently never thought of giving it up. Fanny Fern wanted the "freedom and independence" that society accorded to a man. She accepted the responsibilities that came to her as a woman, but struggled against the artificial restrictions that her culture placed on women. Her experience showed her that life for a woman must be a constant battle to maintain the self. "Fight it," she said of the oppression that surrounded all women (NYL, August 10, 1867). With this determination, Fern's life could not be one of repose.

Social

Another aspect of Fern's life in the 1850s involved people and events outside the domestic circle. On April 26, 1856, for example, she wrote about going to see the launching of the ship *Adriatic*. Other activities included visits to the opera, which Fern sometimes enjoyed, but which she more often criticized (NYL, November 13, 1858, December 1, 1866), lectures, and art galleries. On February 8, 1859, Gunn reports that Fern, Parton, and Grace were at a lecture by Lola Montez, "On the Wits and Women of Paris." On October 31, 1857, Fern wrote of seeing Rosa Bonheur's controversial painting *The Horse Fair*, which now hangs in the Metropolitan Museum in New York:

Women should cheer that one of them has painted it. And men should be magnanimous for once and not whisper "Quite good—for a woman." It would make the reputation of any man. There are few masculine pencils equal to the production of a horse like that superb fellow in the foreground. The very sight of him makes my blood leap like the sound of a trumpet. . . . That adorable creature—a spirited horse—is second only to a shapely, manly man; and so the fair artist seems to think; for she has done full justice to the muscles and sinews of their stalwart riders.

Fern had suffered so much from unwanted publicity that she did not like to attend large social functions where she would be stared at. She preferred small, friendly gatherings. In her articles, she satirized the pomp and shallowness of large social functions, the principal purpose of which was display. On May 8, 1858, she wrote of a charity fete that she attended at the Crystal Palace, commenting on the horrors of fashionable dress. On March 27, 1869, she wrote in the *Ledger* an article on "A Fashionable Dinner Party":

> Perhaps the lady who gives the dinner-party would really prefer a plain dinner with her friend Mrs. Jones, than all the elaborate dinners she is in the habit of giving and attending; but her husband likes wines and French cookery, and would consider anything else a poor compliment to a guest; and so there's an end.
>
> And now, what are these fine dinners? Just this: a pleasant gleam of silver and china; a lovely disposition of fruit and flowers; a great deal of dress, or undress, on the part of the ladies; much swallow-tail, and an exquisite bit of cravat and kid-glove, on the part of the gentlemen. Brains—as the gods please; but always a procession of dishes, marched on and marshalled off, for the requisite number of tedious hours. . . .
>
> Everybody there feels just as you do. Everybody would like to creep into some quiet corner, and be let alone, till the process of digestion has had a chance.
>
> Instead—they throw a too transparent enthusiasm into the inquiry, "How's your mother?" . . . Then may a good Providence put it into the distracted brain of the hostess to set some maiden a-foul of the piano!
>
> Oh, but that is blessed! no matter what she plays, how hard she thumps, or how loud she screeches. . . . And this is a "dinner-party." For this men and women empty their purses, and fill their decanters and wardrobes, and merge their brains in their stomachs, and—are in the fashion!
>
> Better is a leg of mutton and caper-sauce, and much lively talk, whensoever and wheresoever a friend, with or without an invitation, cares enough about you and yours with impromptu friendship to "drop in." Best clothes, best dishes, best wine, best parlors!—what are they, with rare exceptions, but extinguishers of wit and wisdom and digestion and geniality.

Although Fern resented interruptions during the time she had set aside for writing, and although she did not enjoy large, formal functions, she did enjoy having visitors and small gatherings in her home. Fern was known as a particularly lively conversationalist. An article in the *Boston Chronicle* entitled "Fanny Fern at Home," written by a visitor to her home, describes her as "the brightest and most entertaining of hostesses. She carries the vivacity of her writing into her manner, and is witty and sprightly to a degree that drives younger women quite wild with envy. She is an inimitable story-teller, and has very fine powers of mimicry."[7] Another writer characterized her as a "rapid and interesting talker."[8] Thomas Butler Gunn commented also on her story-telling skills, portraying her as the vivacious center of conversation. Although for the most part Gunn enjoyed these conversations, his dislike of the unconventional in women caused him to criticize Fern for not being more "femininely" retiring and withdrawn in conversation. He criticized her for being "self-centered" and for acting on the "Steerforth principle—desire of shining, of applause." Gunn's perspective is explained in his further comment regarding Fern's behavior in company: "No man could live happily with her who strove for—not the mastery—but an equal platform."[9]

Although the diary of Thomas Butler Gunn is clearly biased against the principle of equality that Fern stood for, it is useful for its glimpses of some of the visitors to Fern's home during those early years on the *Ledger*. As we saw in a previous chapter, during the first year of Fern's marriage to Parton, Walt Whitman was one of the visitors to her home. Gunn's diary indicates that Oliver Dyer was also a frequent visitor, both as friend and as legal advisor. It was he who, in the fall of 1852, as publisher of the *New York Musical World and Times,* had sought out the anonymous Fanny Fern in care of the Boston papers for which she wrote. He witnessed her contract with the Masons in 1854, and he was a witness to her marriage to James Parton and to the prenuptial agreement, being named trustee in the latter. He acted for Fern in her suit against the man who attempted to publish a book using her name, and he acted for Parton in the Whitman suit. Gunn did not like Dyer and became particularly hostile about him in mid-1857 when Robert Bonner refused to publish Fern's favorable review of Gunn's book, *The Physiology of New York Boarding Houses,* in the *Ledger* because Dyer had called Bonner's attention to the book's criticism of Sylvanus Cobb, Jr.; Bonner would not print a review of a book that was insulting to one of his writers.[10]

Fern, however, regarded Dyer as a trusted friend, as is clear from her portrayal of him as John Walter in *Ruth Hall.* Some readers of *Ruth Hall* have mistakenly concluded that Ruth will marry John Walter,[11] but there is no suggestion of a romance between them. Fern makes clear that Walter is already married and that there is no disharmony between him and his wife. He discusses Floy with his wife, and when he helps Ruth rescue her daughter from the Halls, he is accompanied by his wife's brother (RH, 140, 185). Ruth looks upon Walter as an elder brother, whose advice and support she appreciates (RH, 143–144). Like Walter, Dyer was married, and, although Gunn's conventional attitude led him to suspect the unconventional Fern of sexual irregularities with Dyer,[12] there is no evidence to suggest that this was more than Gunn's imagination. Since so much else in *Ruth Hall* derives explicitly from Fern's own experience, it seems likely that the details about John Walter derive from Oliver Dyer; that is, that Dyer discussed Fanny

Fern with his wife and that he, too, was accompanied by his brother-in-law
when he helped Fern to bring her daughter from Boston. Fern was apparently on friendly terms with Dyer's family; on December 24, 1858, Gunn
mentions that Grace was taking some Christmas gifts to Dyer's children.

Another frequent visitor was Jesse Haney, who had been a student of
James Parton's in Philadelphia. If Dyer was first of all a friend of Fanny
Fern, Haney was primarily a friend of James Parton. Gunn tells us that
Haney idolized Parton, and indicates that although Parton apparently
liked Haney, the relationship was one-sided.[13] A newspaper writer and editor, Haney often stayed overnight at 33 Oxford Street along with Gunn,
"tossing for choice of bed or sofa."[14] Haney later married Martha Edwards,
Parton's cousin. Other visitors included Frederick Perkins of *Life Illustrated*
and the *Tribune*, who was the nephew of Harriet Beecher Stowe, and later
the father of Charlotte Perkins Gilman.[15]

A particularly interesting visitor to Fern's home was Louisa Matilda
Jacobs, the daughter of Harriet Jacobs, the author of *Incidents in the Life of
a Slave Girl* (1861), who had escaped from slavery in North Carolina in
1842 after being concealed for seven years in her grandmother's house. She
had two children, one of whom was Louisa. Louisa Jacobs lived in Fern's
home from July 1856 to April 1858. On his first visit to 33 Oxford Street,
on July 5, 1856, Gunn mentions the presence at dinner of a "handsome but
silent young lady." On July 17 Gunn identifies the woman as a "Miss
Jacobs," whose mother had "been a slave down south." Gunn describes her
thus:

The girl is handsome possessing a . . . delicately shaped acquiline nose,
and hair of such a deep, lustrous, silky black that I have *never* seen its
equal. To see the sunlight rest upon it was to marvel that hair could be so
lovely. No painting or words could do justice to it. Her complexion is of a
warm, sunny tint, such as you might fancy proper to an Italian girl, her
eyes full and modest, her face clear and perfectly proportioned, her manner reserved. One would never suspect the existence of negro blood in
her. I was told that she had been highly educated, but was conscious of
the prejudice against her birth here—as how should she escape knowing
it?

The next mention of "Miss Jacobs" occurs on August 1, when Gunn gives
her first name and describes her along with Fern's daughter, Grace. At this
time, Grace was fifteen; Louisa Matilda Jacobs was in her early twenties:

The girls, Grace (Fanny's daughter) and Louisa Jacobs, form an exquisite
contrast. Grace with her fair, bright, light brown hair in long curls, innocent and pleasant maiden face, heighth [heather] and pink summer dress;
and the other with her lustrous silky black hair worn madonna wise,

warm complexion and white dress presented quite a picture. We talked
and played guessing proverbs.

It is not until May 23, 1858, however, that Gunn identifies Louisa
Jacobs's mother as "Hattie" and tells her story:

The story is a tragic and touching one, illustrative of the far-reaching
wrongs inflicted by "the sum of all villanies," Slavery. The woman was a
slave, young and good-looking. Her owner pursued her lustfully, she de-
testing the man, and this, in conjunction with his wife's jealousy, made
the slave-girl's life a hell. She was flogged and ill-used. A relative, some
old woman, her mother or aunt kept her concealed in a hiding-place prepared for her, a sort of hutch in a loft, and here, with her spine bent into a
hoop she lived six or seven years, finally escaping to the North. The Willis
family—N.P.'s first *English* wife received her, her price and that of her
children was paid. These were born to her by a white man, now a member
of Congress. She liked him and gave herself up to the lover of her choice
rather than her brutal owner. The incipient M.P. like a true American
never cared a jot for his slave mistress or her children by him.

Gunn's comments indicate that Jacobs had told Fern her story; she had
even told Fern who was the father of her children, although Jacobs was
embarrassed by the fact and was reluctant to speak of it.[16] That Fern never
once referred to Jacobs's story in all of her years as a columnist indicates
how much she respected the confidence. On March 16, 1859, Gunn comments that Fern had told him that she felt a special obligation to Harriet
Jacobs, who, she said, was one of the few people who stuck by her when
others did not. When Jacobs escaped to the North, she worked as a nurse-
maid in the home of Fern's brother Nathaniel P. Willis. She never told Willis
her story, and did not trust him—with reason, apparently; he was a southern sympathizer whom Fern satirized for his fence-sitting before and during
the Civil War.[17] Jacobs did, however, confide in Willis's two successive
wives and apparently told Fern her history. She probably knew Fern during
the times that she (Jacobs) was living in Boston between 1844 and 1849 and
perhaps during her flights to New England in 1851 and 1852.[18] Jacobs was
working as a seamstress in Boston at the time of Fern's first husband's death
(October 1846), and she returned to New England after Fern had left her
second husband (January 1851) and was shunned by her family and friends.
    In a letter to Amy Post in March [1857], Jacobs says that Louisa is work-
ing as a governess to a twelve-year-old girl on Long Island.[19] Fern's younger
daughter, Ellen (Nelly), had turned twelve on September 20, 1856, and
Jacobs's letter apparently refers to Louisa's position in Fern's home. Fern,
however, did not identify Louisa Jacobs as a governess when speaking to her
guests, and one suspects that the position was a manufactured one, that is, a

way of providing a home for Harriet Jacobs's daughter. Gunn was apparently unaware of Louisa Jacobs's presumed position; he describes her simply as a houseguest, whereas he identifies other employees (for example, Ferdinand Ulric, the German music teacher) by their positions. It is clear from Gunn's diary that Louisa entered into all of the social activities of the family during the time that she was living in the house—talking, dining, playing games, going for walks, visiting neighbors. Gunn portrays her as a friend of Grace, and indicates that she is perceived as a marriage candidate for the eligible bachelors who visit the house, himself included. On August 21, 1856, he mentions going to a circus with the family and other guests, and writes "I squired Miss J." On Sunday September 1, Gunn writes:

> After supper we took a walk, myself squiring Grace and Miss Louisa. A capital, pleasant, frank girl is Grace, possessing withal a smack of her mother, in her liking for exaggerated remarks on folks. The handsome Creole is graver, more thoughtful. I am mistaken if there is not an amiable intention on the part of "Fanny Fern" to abet my falling in love with Miss J.—indeed the self sufficient donkey Dyer blurted out some stupid attempt at jocular allusion to such a presumption! It's very kind of 'em. May the girl—kind and handsome as she is—find a good husband elsewhere.

On December 8 Gunn writes that he has mentioned this "little good natured match-making project" to the young woman he writes to back in England and whom he hopes eventually to marry. He vows he will only marry an Englishwoman.

On June 21, 1857, Gunn comments that Louisa Jacobs and Grace are at Idlewild, which was N. P. Willis's estate on the Hudson, where Harriet Jacobs worked. It is interesting that although Fern did not speak to her brother, her daughter visited his home with the daughter of his servant. On August 9, 1857, Gunn comments that Louisa is in Boston. On April 1, 1858, he says that she has returned to Idlewild, and on April 22, 1858, he writes, "Miss Jacobs is in Boston *en permanence* or for a year or so, to learn a trade—dressmaking or appertaining to it."[20]

On May 23, 1858, Gunn describes Louisa again and discusses her position as a marriage candidate.

> This girl, Louisa Jacobs is intelligent and handsome. I have sketched her heretofore but will do it now more minutely. No European would suspect the African blood in her veins; probably she would be considered a trifle Jewish. (Most likely the *name* was selected for that purpose.) . . . The girl has a sweet, soft, contralto voice, was kind, modest and self respective, and I do believe would make any man a good, loving wife. I've never seen any *one* white American girl whom I'd have chosen in preference. . . .

Well, this girl can never be married and admitted into society on this side of the Atlantic. . . . They thought Ed Wells was affected towards her, and Haney told me that "it might have been" but for her origin. Had I loved such a girl, that shouldn't have stopped me, nor all the Americans in this unchristian sham-republic.

Here, as elsewhere in his diary, Gunn, who was English, is harshly critical of Americans. His speculation about the name Jacobs is interesting; however, it is not accurate: the name was the name of Harriet Jacobs's father.

One other visitor to Fern's home during the 1850s deserves mention. Mortimer Thomson, who was known by his pseudonym, "Q. K. Philander Doesticks, P.B.," was a humorist who had gained considerable attention with his newspaper writings and the publication of a collection of his writings in 1855 and a satire based on Longfellow's *Hiawatha* in 1856.[21] Known to his friends simply as "Doesticks," Thomson was married to Anna Van Cleve on October 24, 1857. They lived with Thomson's mother in Brooklyn, within walking distance of Fern's home on Oxford Street. Fern's daughter Grace was a friend of Thomson's wife, who was known as "Nanny" or "Chips." In 1858 Parton wrote to Mrs. Van Cleve requesting information for his biography of Andrew Jackson, and Fern included news of Mrs. Van Cleve's daughter: "I keep a motherly watch over her," Fern said; "your rosy girl is as rosy as ever. I sometimes hear her romping in my parlor with mine."[22] Fern and Parton, and Fern's daughters, visited the Thomsons, and the Thomsons—Mortimer, his mother, his wife, and sometimes his brother Clifford—were frequent visitors at Fern's home. Gunn describes one of these visits on Grace's seventeenth birthday, February 24, 1858: "We played games of the forfeit character, with more or less osculatory results, then at 10, to the basement and supper. Pickled oysters, cakes, confectionaries, beer and cider. Songs and speech-making. Cahill & Haney read poems. . . . My song a great success. Everybody amusing and jolly. The Thomsons off by 12. Haney to bed on the parlor sofa, I on one in Jim's room, Cahill in the adjoining apartment."

On January 5, 1858, Gunn had similarly reported that he had paid a visit to the Thomsons:

Parton and the Ferns arrived, Miss Jacobs with 'em. Burlesque acrobatic feats by Ed Wells and Cahill; "Shadow Buff" by the company; dance *a la* caclenca by Wells, in ballet costume, songs, music and "fox and geese," with more gambols than I can set down. The feature of the night was "Doesticks' " wife—in male costume. She went up stairs and dressed herself in a suit of his clothes and came down in them, being introduced as a boy. I can't describe how exceedingly pretty she looked—how *very* exceedingly pretty. Especially when the girls, Grace and Miss J., *would* take off her coat and vest, leaving her in dark pants, clean white shirt with broad lay-down collar, neckerchief tied sailor-fashion and pretty brown boots. In this costume she continued all the remainder of the evening, taking part in the "Fox and Geese," during which her hair came down. She looked so pretty and so innocent that nobody could think it immodest for a second. *Nor was it!*

One suspects that Fern and her daughter were influential in introducing Doesticks's wife to the idea of trying on men's clothes. Although Gunn was shocked at the behavior of Fern and Grace when they dressed in men's clothes, he apparently found that of Doesticks's wife acceptable—even pleasing. The difference, of course, was that they went outside the house in male dress, whereas Anna Thomson was only play-acting in her home.

On July 12, 1856, in an article in the *Ledger* entitled "Summer Travel," Fern wrote about the possibility of going out of the city during the summer. She concluded that she would only go if she could go incognita "in masculine attire," with no dresses to look after and the "liberty to go where she liked without being stared at or questioned," with "nobody nudging somebody, to inquire why Miss Spinks the authoress wore her hair in curls instead of plaits."

In June of 1857 Fern and Parton were in Philadelphia, where they visited Colonel Thomas Fitzgerald, the editor of the Philadelphia *City Item*. Fern wrote about the trip in the *Ledger*, praising Philadelphia as a more pleasant place to live than New York: the streets were cleaner, there were no beggars, and the ladies' dresses were more sensible. She also noted that Philadelphia had small, affordable houses for working people and hoped that such could be built in New York, commenting that we each need "a little snuggery of one's own—where one may cry, or laugh, or sneeze, without asking leave" (NYL, July 11, July 18, July 25, August 1, 1857).

During the stay in the hotel, Fern accidentally broke the pitcher in her room. Always thinking of the vulnerability of the working woman, she reported the breakage to the management, "lest the chambermaid should suffer." Upon receiving her bill, however, Fern was angry to find that the management had charged her, not only for the pitcher, but for the whole set. She said that she felt like breaking the whole set if she was going to be charged for it anyway (NYL, July 25, 1857). The incident was widely commented on by Fern watchers, who embroidered the story to include her smashing the rest of the crockery set. This story was told and retold so often that in 1868 when Grace Greenwood was writing her biographical sketch of Fern, Greenwood wrote to Fern to ask if it were true or not.[23]

It was very hot in New York in the summer. Fern's August 15, 1857, article describing "A Hot Day" is a valuable description of what it must have been like during a city heat wave in the days of long skirts and multiple petticoats—and no air conditioning or even electric fans:

Not a breath of air stirring, and mine almost gone. Fans enough, but no
nerve to wield 'em. . . . Chairs hot; sofa hotter, beds hottest. . . . Every
thing sticky, and flabby, and limpsey. Can't read; can't sew; can't write;
can't talk; can't walk; can't even sleep. . . . "Lady down stairs wishes to
see me?" In the name of Adam and Eve, take all my dresses off the pegs
and show her—but never believe I'd be so mad as to get into them for any
body living.

The above article is a good example of the kind of writing that earned Fern
criticism from conventional critics. Her suggestion that she was sitting
around in her underwear—or less—would not have been acceptable writing
from a "lady."

Beginning in 1857, Fern and Parton left the city for several weeks each
summer. These trips not only provided them with the opportunity to get out
of the city during the hottest part of the summer, but also provided Fern
with additional material for her columns. Her columns continued while she
was away, and as she had done during her visit to Philadelphia, she wrote
penetratingly on the people, places, and events that she encountered in her
travels. On August 9, 1857, Gunn comments that "the family are meditat-
ing a week at the Cattskills, probably going on Wednesday." Leaving on
August 12, Fern and Parton, with Grace and Ellen, remained two to three
weeks in the mountains. Gunn noted on September 20 that they were back
in Brooklyn. Fern wrote about their trip in the *Ledger:* the stagecoach ride
up the mountain was "purgatorial," she said, but, once arrived, the view
from the mountain was magnificent. Moreover, the accommodations at
the hotel, with its common dining room and parlor, were interesting in
themselves:

It is well for people from different parts of the country to rub off their
local angles by collision. It is well for those of opposite temperaments and
habits of thought, to look each other mentally in the face. (NYL, September 12, September 19, September 26, October 3, 1857)

In July 1858 Fern and Parton went with Grace on a Canadian and eastern
tour. Fern's younger daughter Ellen stayed with the Thomsons. Gunn mentions that he had visited Fern and Parton on July 18, shortly before they
were to leave on tour. Fern wrote several articles in the *Ledger* about the
tour. The first place they visited was Saratoga, as Fern said, only to see "the
place itself," not the fashionable "peacocks" in it. Then, after a few rainy
days at Lake George, they traveled by steamer across Lake Champlain and
by train to Montreal and Quebec, where Fern was surprised to find the *New
York Ledger*. On the return trip they stopped in Portland, where Fern explored the streets, attempting to find the house in which she was born (NYL

September 4, September 11, September 18, September 25, October 2, 1858). They returned to New York in the middle of August. Gunn visited on August 15 and reported that "both Fanny and Grace had got bad colds in Canada, especially the former, inasmuch that she coughed very much."

Personal

In addition to the interruptions of domestic life and the diversions of social life, Fern was also subjected to the distractions of her personal life. Like Margaret Fuller and many other women of the period, she was prone to severe headaches, which, it seems clear, were in part the result of the constrictions that society put on women.[24] On March 21, 1857, Fern describes the severity of her headache:

> Now I am in for it, with one of my unappeasable headaches. Don't talk to me of doctors; . . . nothing on earth will stop it. . . . I suppose every body in the house to-day will put on their creakingest shoes; and every body will go up and down stairs humming all the tunes they ever heard, especially those I most dislike; and I suppose . . . all the little boys in the neighborhood, bless their little restless souls, will play duets on tin-pans and tin-kettles; . . . and I suppose that unhappy dog confined over in that four-square-feet yard, will howl more deliriously than ever; . . . and I've no doubt there will be "proof" to read to-day, and that that pertinacious and stentorian rag-man will lumber past on his crazy old cart. . . . There goes my head again—I should think a string of fire-crackers was fastened to each hair.

On May 7, 1859, Fern notes that one could not say "only" when referring to a headache:

> If ever the word *only* was an impertinence, it is so in this case. It is very well for you to be philosophical about it—you, who never endured it; . . . who never felt the blood rush to the top of your cranium, as if it were on a wager to force up your scalp; you, who never carried your head on your shoulders as if it were some dainty bit of porcelain, which, in a fatal moment, might receive some annihilating smash. . . . Perhaps you never sat and talked calmly, when you were so agonized with pain that the little red spot on each cheek seemed to send out phosphorescent sparks of fire beneath your eyes, or sat and wrote, till the letters mingled in one confused mass, and your pen, inkstand and paper seemed dancing a jig before you. . . . You never smiled, with sad faithlessness, at the "unfailing recipes," which kind hearted people sympathizing offered you for a thing

which you felt was fixed as the Eternal decrees,—which a chance word or sudden disagreeableness might in a moment bring on.

Despite these occasional headaches, Fern was otherwise an unusually healthy woman, and she did not allow the headaches to interfere with her life. Up until the last years of her life, when she was becoming progressively incapacitated by her final illness, she was remarkably energetic. "Who will care for you?" Harry Hall cries out to Ruth as he is dying (RH, 57), but Ruth, like Fanny Fern, finds that she has reserves of energy within herself and discovers that she can care for herself. James Parton wrote of Fern after her death: "She was endowed with a constitution so abounding in vitality that, at fifty-five, her step was as elastic, and her general health as sound as they had ever been" (JP, 71). On August 1, 1857, at the age of forty-six, Fern wrote about herself:

It must be time I was feeling venerable; but how is a woman to feel venerable, who catches herself jumping down three stairs at a time? who never can lie-a-bed a minute after sunrise, and who never feels tired, or cold, or solemn? How is a woman to feel venerable who likes a frolic better than a sermon? It is all nonsense. That feeling comes with grey hair, and my hair *won't* turn grey.

Ten years later, in an article entitled "Fashionable Invalidism," Fern criticized women's lack of exercise and poor diet and wrote about her own good health and energy:

I hope to live to see the time when it will be considered a *disgrace* to be sick. . . . Those who *inherit* sickly constitutions have my sincerest pity. . . . But a woman who laces so tightly that she breathes only by a rare accident; . . . who lies in bed till noon, never exercises, and complains of "total want of appetite" save for pastry and pickles, is simply a disgusting nuisance. . . . Heavens! I am fifty-five, and I feel half the time as if I were just made. . . . I have a water-proof cloak and no diamonds. I like a nice bit of beefsteak and a glass of ale, and anybody else who wants it may eat pap. I go to bed at ten, and get up at six. I dash out in the rain, because it feels good on my face. I don't care for my clothes, but I *will* be well; and after I am buried, I warn you, don't let any fresh air or sunlight down on my coffin, if you don't want me to get up. (NYL, July 27, 1867)

Although Fern was herself unusually healthy and vigorous, Parton was not. On several occasions, Gunn comments on Parton's ill health, noting on November 11, 1860, that all of his family had a "consumptive tendency."

Parton was not consumptive, but he did suffer from headaches and indigestion, and many of his letters refer to his ill health.[25] Although Fern never directly expressed annoyance at her husband's chronic ill health, it was another factor that she had to deal with in her personal life. Perhaps this was one of the factors in her mind when she wrote sardonically, a year and a half after their marriage, "Man that is born of a woman is—very troublesome!"[26]

Other personal matters included a possible pregnancy in 1857. On August 22, 1857, soon after Fern had described herself as liking "a frolic better than a sermon," she published in the *Ledger* an article called "What Shall We Name the Baby?" which speaks as though a new baby was on the way. Fern says that she will not name the new child after the little daughter she lost in 1845: "Mary? Not so, my little ones; have you forgotten the headstone in the churchyard, with that name upon it, and the little sister who lies beneath it? The new baby is welcome, but call her not Mary; there can be but one Mary. *Her* spirit voice still calls me 'Mother.' " Since Fern had no further children, she either had a miscarriage later in 1857, or she was mistaken in believing she was pregnant.[27]

Also distressing to Fern were the deaths in 1858 of two young women in childbirth. In April 1858 Fern's brother Richard's wife died after the birth of her third child. Jessie Cairns Willis was thirty-one years old. Fern wrote about the death in the *Musical World,* and her article was published in the *Ledger* on June 6, 1858, Bonner explaining that, although she had an exclusive contract with the *Ledger,* it was "proper" that this article should have been published first in her brother's paper. Fern's article was addressed to the three little girls who were left motherless and to the father, Richard Willis, who was trying to crush his own sorrow that he might alleviate theirs.

Nor did the happy activities with the Thomsons last very long. On December 23, 1858, Gunn records in his diary: "Doesticks' wife—Doesticks' pretty, good, kind, innocent, little wife is *dead*. It occurred yesterday, twelve hours after she had given birth to a son." The following day Gunn attended the funeral with Fern, Grace, and Ellen. They told him of the events:

Fanny was sent for between three and four in the morning. . . . When she arrived at the house a doctor was there, Mort drenched through with rain and misery, and poor "Chips" suffering horribly. Fanny took charge of her, stayed by her till all was over. The convulsions were dreadful—in her agony she bit through her lips and tongue. . . . Apropos of the baby, it is a boy, a fine, thriving healthy one. Mort has not seen it—will not. When Fanny spoke of it as an inducement for him to rally and live—ah! how characteristic of a woman to think *that* argument unanswerable!—he said it had cost him too much. . . . Fanny stooped down and kissed the dead, cold face and I liked her for it. (She has been all that is kind and womanly in the house, ever since the sad event.)[28]

Anna Thomson was only eighteen years old. Mortimer Thomson was so broken up by his wife's death that he did not want the baby, Mark; he gave the child over completely to the care of his wife's mother, who took the child to Minnesota with her. He found Fern's home a welcome solace during the early months of his grief. Gunn reports that he saw him there on January 16, 1859, when he and Haney visited Fern's home. Parton was out of town doing research for his biography of Jackson:

Stayed all day and night, Mort Thomson, Wells and Cahill coming in the evening. Mort looks graver and they say, talks strangely at times, but I was glad to see him behave, comparatively, as usual. We all wrote letters to Jim, at Fanny's suggestion, assuming extreme drunkenness in composition, and I made an imaginary inebriated sketch of the party. The funny character of many of the letters addressed to the Ledger being talked of, Grace fetched a batch, which Mort looked over, culling some for perusal.

On February 24, Gunn reports visiting Oxford Street for Grace's eighteenth birthday:

Haney there, and in the course of the evening, Mort Thomson, Ed Wells and Cahill. Talk, punch, cigars, gambols, boxing!! (I had the gloves on with Cahill and got a "noser" which drew the "claret"!) Kept it up till 1 or so.

In March of 1859 Mortimer Thomson went to Savannah, Georgia, as a reporter for the *Tribune,* and, disguised as a trader, attended the slave auction of Pierce Butler. Sickened by the spectacle of the auction, at which Butler had sold 429 slaves for a total of $303,850, Thomson wrote an article for the *Tribune,* which gained him considerable publicity and was later published in a separate pamphlet as a "sequel" to Fanny Kemble's *Journal of a Residence on a Georgia Plantation.*[29] On March 16, Gunn reported that the previous week he had met Thomson at Fern's, he "having that day returned from Savannah whither he went to report a great slave sale for the Tribune. Marry, the Georgians would have tarred, feathered and ridden him on a rail had they known his mission."

On the same date, Gunn wrote that it was "tavern talk" that Thomson was wooing Grace, and said that he had suspected it. On April 8, 1859, Gunn reported that Jack Edwards, who was at Fern's and Parton's every night copying Parton's manuscript, told him that Thomson was there every night to see Grace. Gunn assumed that Fern wanted the marriage; however, Ethel Parton, Grace's daughter, writes that the marriage was opposed by Grace's family.[30] Gunn reported going to a lecture by Mort Thomson on November 13, 1859. Fern, Parton, and Grace were in the audience, and in the course of the lecture, which was entitled "Pluck," Thomson commended "ceaseless persistence" in suing for a woman's hand in marriage.

In April 1859, however, Gunn had become *persona non grata* at Fern's house, and consequently any further comments that he made about the household were derived secondhand from Haney or other visitors. The reason for the falling out was Gunn's attack upon the *Ledger* in an article he wrote for the *Scalpel* magazine.³¹ Previously Gunn had wanted to write for the *Ledger*, and on April 29, 1858, he wrote that he had gone to see Bonner with ideas for articles, but Bonner had turned him down on every one of them. Gunn, who was always in need of money and would have been glad to receive the money that articles for the *Ledger* would have brought him, noted on February 19, 1859, that Parton told him to submit stories to the *Ledger* and assured him that they would be read. Gunn was doubtful, however, because of his previous criticism of Sylvanus Cobb, Jr., and also because of an article he wrote in *Omnibus*. Gunn's bitterness at Bonner's rejection of his articles probably helped to motivate his attack in the *Scalpel*. It must have seemed to him that everyone he knew wrote for the *Ledger* except him; he knew of course that Fern wrote for the *Ledger*, and on March 16, 1859, he noted with annoyance that Haney had written for the *Ledger*, and that Parton wrote for it regularly every week.

Edward Dixon of the *Scalpel* was eager to obtain an article "trashing" the *Ledger*. On February 10, 1859, Gunn wrote that he was going to do an article on the *Ledger* for the *Scalpel*, and on March 16 he reported that he received fifteen dollars for his *Scalpel* article, "Bonner and the *New-York Ledger*," and that Dixon had told Charles A. Dana of the *Tribune* that he was going to have a "hell of an article" on the *Ledger*, which he called "abominable trash."³²

On April 10, 1859, Gunn learned that there has been a "row" at Fern's house because of his article, the most critical sections of which had been reprinted in the *Century*. Bonner was at the house, and he and Fern were irate about it, Fern vowing that Gunn would no longer be welcome in her home. Bonner was outraged, and in an editorial in the *Ledger* he criticized Gunn, who, he said, was a disappointed author motivated by "sour grapes" (NYL, May 7, 1859). Fern, who felt a tremendous loyalty to Bonner, felt personally attacked, although Gunn had not mentioned her in his article. Gunn in his diary on April 28, 1859, indicated that he believed Fern was angry because he did not mention her work, but her comments indicate that she was angry because of what she considered to be an unfair attack upon Bonner, her trusted friend, by someone she now felt was only pretending to be her friend. On May 7, 1859, Fern wrote an article in her column called "A Social Nuisance," which was aimed at Gunn, whom she perceived as a sycophant:

> If there *is* a nuisance it is your boaster; a fellow whose stock in trade is his chance acquaintance with people of note, male or female; who speaks

of them in the most familiar manner,—as if he were on the most intimate terms of friendship—on all occasions and without occasion;—calling a lady impertinently by her given name, in a saloon or restaurant, that his gaping auditors may infer on what a delightfully free-and-easy footing he stands with her. . . .

The harm such creatures may do, where this species of viper are not understood, may be easily guessed. I say "viper," because such a fellow will not hesitate to sting, even while fawning; he will meanly solicit favors which your good nature grants, to repay them with shrugs and innuendos behind your back, where he thinks he can do so with safety to himself.

Every one who has made a success in the world has been bored and imposed upon by this sort of people. Lucky if the impertinence they return for your kindness has not so disgusted the person sought, as to make him or her suspicious of every new introduction. . . . Nevertheless, if you discover that such fellows have passed your threshold, show them the shortest way over it; they were always ready to sting you even while cringing, they can do no worse than that when you rid yourself of their presence.

Fern apparently felt that Gunn had exaggerated and used his acquaintance with her in order to advance his own fortunes, which assessment she must have based on comments that had been reported to her by others. That she was accurate in her accusation about the "shrugs and innuendos" behind her back and the suggestion that he would "not hesitate to sting, even while fawning" is apparent from Gunn's comments in his diary. Although he crossed out some of the most unkind comments regarding what he assumed were irregularities in Fern's sexual life (assumptions based on gossip and the unconventional aspects of her behavior and of her writing), he apparently discussed them with his friends, even while he was a presumably trusted guest in Fern's home.[33] On March 16, 1859, he wrote, "I have had thoughts in my head, which if guessed at by the indomitable Fanny, would pretty quickly outlaw me from her hospitality."

Before Gunn's *Scalpel* article appeared, he noted on February 19, 1859, that Fern and Parton were househunting. On March 16, 1859, he reported that she had bought a house in New York and that the family planned to move in April. On April 5, he noted that Fern and Parton had moved to the house in New York, but that he had not yet visited them. Fern described her feelings in the *Ledger* in an article entitled "Going to Move":

In those three words how many headaches are breeding. . . . I am to see my bonnet put in the coal-scuttle, and the poker and tongs wrapped up in my dresses, and great slices taken out of my piano, and arms and legs and noses ruthlessly torn from my statues, and my MSS. used for wrapping paper. . . . And in the middle of it all I am to sit down and write, yea, write just as calmly as if I were sitting in a meadow, under a broad green tree. (NYL, April 9, 1859)

Fanny Fern managed to combine her writing and the other aspects of her life—though not without difficulty and not without agitation. She would not have wanted it otherwise, however. In a January 12, 1861, article, she describes and rejects the kind of person whose life is without challenges, the person who is satisfied with eating and sleeping. Such people will miss the "high ecstacies" of life, she says. They "cannot understand why something good to eat cannot cure the heartache." Fern calls them "Happy oysters!" and concludes: "Let them quietly fulfill their destiny to slip down the throat of Time without a hitch in the passage. Stay; would I, then, be a human oyster? No; a thousand times, no!"

14

❧❧

The Civil War and Effie

If ever there was a righteous fight ours is; and that man who needlessly withholds his services, or lazily and dishonorably drawls "peace," because war affects his business, is a traitor, whether he owns it or not.
NYL, September 27, 1862

IN APRIL OF 1859 FERN MOVED INTO A BROWNSTONE IN MANHATTAN that she had purchased at 303 (originally 182) East Eighteenth Street, near Second Avenue. It was in this house that she lived for the next thirteen years, except for trips during the summer, until her death in 1872. During that time she continued to write her weekly column for the *Ledger*, while James Parton pursued his career as a biographer. The houses on the street resembled each other, and soon after she moved into the house Fern found herself one day absentmindedly walking into a strange house. In order to avoid confusion in the future, she purchased a plaster figure of a lamb from the next Italian street vendor who came down the street calling out "Im-a-gees." She chose a lamb for no other reason than that, among the statuettes, lay and religious, it seemed to be the most practical choice. She had the lamb placed above the front door to provide a distinguishing feature to the entrance (EP, 126–127). There it remained until one day it was hit by a snowball and fell, shattered, to the steps.[1]

Inside the house, Fern, who liked "pretty things" (NYL, September 3, 1864), had a number of statues. Her granddaughter remembered that on the marble mantel in the parlor were bronzed plaster busts of Goethe and Schiller. In a window full of flowers and greenery was an alabaster statute of Venus.[2] The reader of *Ruth Hall* recalls Mrs. Hall's shock upon seeing the nude Venus in Ruth's house.

Soon after Fern and Parton moved to East Eighteenth Street, Benjamin Wailes, who had visited Parton to obtain some information about Andrew Jackson, wrote in his diary on July 11, 1859:

Mr. Parton lives in a spacious and elegant house handsomely furnished & parlour containing several pieces of statuary & some paintings on 18

Street near the 2nd Avenue and is now engaged in writing the life of Andrew Jackson in three volumes. . . . Caught a glimpse (as she ascended & decended the stair way before the door at which I sat[)] of "Fanny." She was tidily clad and had a mass of curly or frizzled flaxen locks on her head.[3]

In the 1860s another visitor to the house wrote in the *Boston Chronicle:* "Everything about the house speaks of culture and an artistic woman's dainty care. Pretty pictures on the walls, statuettes around the room, flowers almost always in the vases, and ivy trained carefully over the deep windows."[4] James Parton said of his wife: "She had a particular taste in decorating a house, and knew how to make rooms look exceedingly attractive, and even luxurious, out of very ordinary and inexpensive articles" (JP, 66–67).

During Fern's lifetime her house was a landmark in New York, and was pointed out by the curious and gazed at by Fern's faithful readers. A little girl from the country, who went to see the Fern house in New York, described it thus: "She lives in a big brown house, with the windows all open, and the rest of the people have theirs closed. I knew it was her house before I got there. The bird and the flowers told me so."[5]

In line with Robert Bonner's policy of keeping the *Ledger* a nonpolitical paper, Fern did not become involved with party politics in her column. However, Bonner gave her a pretty free rein, and she was outspoken on whatever issues she wished to address. She wrote in the *Ledger* on November 13, 1858, that she hated having to weigh her words: "If there is anything I hate, it is writing that way; I won't do it for any body except Mr. Bonner, who has too much good sense to ask it—who gives me a wide pasture to prance in because he is sure that I will not jump the fence, though the conservatives sometimes needlessly hold their breath for fear I will."

Sometimes Bonner agreed with her opinions; sometimes he did not. They were in accord on most issues, but two issues on which they did not agree were women's suffrage and doctrinaire religion. On May 29, 1858, Fern unequivocally came out in favor of votes for women:

All my life I have taken the liberty to say what I think, and I am not going to stop now. Though I have not written on this subject, I have done some thinking, and the result will not be satisfactory to the conservative; for I hold up both hands for a woman's ballot box. It implies, in my humble opinion, nothing derogatory to the loveliest feminine traits; no greater exposure than women are every day meeting, in various ways, with the full approbation of husbands, fathers, and brothers, or through their indifference. . . . They may go to the coal-yard, and the wood-yard, and the butcher's and grocer's, without any objection being raised by the men—*not they!* Anywhere but to the ballot-box—that would be unfeminine and indelicate. . . . Men have shown us what they can make it, and certainly by no possibility could it be worse, even if woman had a finger in it. . . . Let [men] bid God-speed to the day when the mothers of their children may be allowed an intelligent and intelligible voice.

How this will be brought about I do not know; that it is only a question of time I am very sure; and I am just as sure that it will in no wise peril connubial puddings, or connubial babies. . . . It is very well for bandboxy men to call Lucy Stone obnoxious names. I have not the pleasure of her personal acquaintance, and I am not sure I should have fought it out with *that* sheriff, but I have read, and I do endorse, her publicly expressed views on Woman voting.

Bonner, however, made clear that he held a different opinion: woman's sphere was in the home. On May 14, 1859, for example, he wrote in an editorial:

What could woman gain of substantial good—what would she lose of innocence, of prestige, of peace, by mingling in the strife and turmoil of the business world. . . . Transplant her from the nursery to the mart, from the boudoir to the bar, from the kitchen and the store-room, if you will to the legislature and the lobby, from the departments of taste and industry which she now appropriately occupies, to the arena of politics and the vortices of speculation—and what would you make of her? What but a compound monster, a *man-woman*. It is a fact patent to all who have read history or taken note of passing events, that she rarely abandons the sphere in which . . . she was *ordained* to move, without leaving her best qualities behind her.

Despite this clear difference in their opinions, Fern continued to assert woman's right to vote—and also woman's right to participate equally in male-dominated professions. And Bonner continued to print her articles.

With respect to doctrinaire religion, Fern was outspoken in her criticism of ministers who insisted upon narrow theology. On January 12, 1867, Fern wrote of her visit to a convent and, condemning the way that she had been brought up to fear and despise Roman Catholicism, she insisted that no one should be criticized because of his or her religion: "What matters it through what door one gets to heaven if he finally gets there, by a pure life and good deeds? What matters it in what dress he kneels to pray, or whether he kneel or stand, or what form of words he uses, or no form at all? And who shall prescribe to all the differing temperaments and natures which God has made, one spiritual shibboleth? *Not I.*"

In a similar article on February 10, 1872, Fern criticized the clergymen who preached abstract doctrine instead of helping people. Such men, she said, put up "doctrinal fences to keep intruders" out. "Creeds!," she said, "I don't know them. . . . I don't ask what my neighbor believes. I want to know *how he lives.*" Bonner regarded Fern's position as dangerous and, although he permitted this article to be printed, he appended a long Editor's Note pointing out Fern's error in not recognizing the importance of doctrine.

Another source of disagreement was Bonner's policy of not printing book reviews or notices in his paper. Fern had written reviews occasionally when she first started writing for the *Ledger* (for example, her review of Whitman's *Leaves of Grass* in 1856). However, Bonner had decided that there was too much "you scratch my back, I'll scratch yours" involved in book reviewing, and, not wanting to be obligated to anyone, he evolved the policy of omitting book reviews entirely. On November 26, 1859, Fern complained that Bonner did not permit literary notices in the *Ledger.* She was aching to review certain books, she said, arguing that women reviewers would be as good or better than men.

In her personal life at this time, Fern's principal concern was the courtship of her daughter by Mortimer Thomson. On July 30, 1859, in an article entitled "All About Lovers," Fern wrote that it was important for young people to have long engagements so that the woman could find out what the man was really like. Her advice is amusing and practical:

Nothing like the old-fashioned long "engagements," say we. Then you have a chance to find out something about a young man before marriage. . . . There are a thousand little things in daily intercourse of any duration, which are constantly resolving themselves into tests of character; slight they may be, but very significant. Some forlorn old lady must have an escort home of a cold evening; she walks slow, and tells the same story many times: see how your lover comports himself under this. He is asked to read aloud to the home circle, some book which he has already perused in private, or some one in which he is not at all interested: watch him then. Notice, also, if he invariably takes the most comfortable chair in the room, "never thinking" to offer it to a person who may enter till he or she is already seated. Invite him to carve for you at table. Give him a letter to drop in the post-office, and find out if it ever leaves that grave—his pocket. Open and read his favorite newspaper before *he* gets a chance to do so. Mislay his cigar-case. Lose his cane. Sit *accidentally* on his new beaver. Praise another man's coat or cravat. Differ from him in a favorite opinion. Put a spoonful of gravy on his meat instead of his potato. Ah, you may laugh! But just try him in these ways, and see how he will wear; for it is not the great things of this life over which we mortals stumble. A rock we walk around; a mountain we cross: *it is the unobserved, unexpected, unlooked-for little sticks and pebbles which cause us to halt on life's journey.*

In a similar vein, on April 14, 1860, Fern told of a woman who tested the aspirants for her daughter's hand by taking them on a journey. It is interesting that in August 1860, Fern and Parton traveled up the Hudson with Grace and Mortimer Thomson.[6]

During the summers of 1859 and 1860 Fern and Parton left New York for a period. In August of 1859 they went to Lake George, and in August of 1860 they took a trip to Lake Superior, where they traveled by steamer across the lake. They were on the *Lady Elgin* steamer on the trip preceding the one on which the ship sank. Grace and Ellen did not accompany them, remaining at the farm of Solon Robinson in Westchester.[7] Fern wrote about this trip in several columns in the *Ledger*. They visited Toronto, which she found too sleepy, although she liked the healthy, smiling faces of the people. From there they traveled by train to Detroit, Fern admiring the "grand old woods" and the country people they saw on the way. Traveling by steamer, Fern criticized the usual way in which ladies made the trip: "striking an attitude in the ladies' saloon" and doing needlework. During the eleven days on the steamer Fern explored the ship, asking questions of the captain and going down below where the steerage passengers were crowded. When the ship docked for freight, she walked briefly around the town they had stopped at. In Chicago, Fern expressed herself "delighted" with the architecture. Traveling by train to Cleveland, they found themselves without a hotel, due to an inauguration of the Perry monument that was to take place the next day. The landlord of a pleasant hotel turned his private parlor into a room for the famous Fanny Fern. Their last stop was Pittsburgh, which Fern pronounced the "dismalest, sootiest, forlornest of cities" (NYL, October 6, October 13, October 20, October 27, November 3, 1860).

Fern was glad to get away from the city for a time during the summer, but during this period she did not like to be too long away. On August 18, 1860, she wrote that although she did not like "reeking city gutters," or "little girls begging pennies" and other city miseries, neither did she like long stretches of "interminable" country days: "The sailor who has all his life buffeted rude and stormy waves, after a week or two in port, goes back to the roar of the winds, and the dash of the sea, with a gusto that no monotony-loving landsman knows."

On August 11, 1860, Fern wrote an article about what she called "Every-Day Follies," which, one suspects, derived from her daughter's preparation for her wedding. The thoughts here expressed reflect the same realistic or cynical attitude toward marriage that one finds at the beginning of *Ruth Hall* where Ruth, on the eve of her marriage, is wondering whether the day might come when she will shrink from her husband (RH, 13). In the article, Fern wrote:

[A]s to marriage—months beforehand the young girl is wholly absorbed in the cut of robes, adaptation of trimmings, and choice of laces, ribbons and ornaments. Not a thought whether the untried future be freighted with happiness or misery. And yet other maidens, as fair and hopeful, have had their matronly hearts wrung by drunkards and libertines, who promised, as solemnly as *her* lover will promise to-morrow, "to love and cherish." Other maidens have tripped smilingly over the paternal threshold to the altar, who have wearily re-crossed it *alone*, to die in the little old room where so many maidenly visions of happiness were conjured up. Other maidens as blithe have accepted a wife's lot, to be humiliatingly questioned, when the feeble mother of many children, as to the expenditure of every pitiable remittance. . . . How many girls would marry if they stopped to think of all these things? After all, then, as the world is bound to go on, and power, whether in the family or on the throne, does not always fall into the hands of magnanimity or justice, one may as well think of ribbons, particularly as that in a man's character which most nearly affects his wife's happiness can never be known, except through the close intimacy of the marriage relation.

At the same time that events in Fern's house were building toward the union of Grace and Mortimer Thomson, events in the country were building toward separation. In keeping with Bonner's policy of maintaining a non-political paper, Fern's columns in the early period of dissension between the states reveal only oblique references to the national situation. On October 22, 1859, for example, in what seems to be a reference to John Brown's seizure of the arsenal at Harper's Ferry the week before, Fern wrote about her preference for people who, though they may be attacked as radicals by their more conservative contemporaries, at least call attention to injustice. These people, she says, are certainly better than "oyster people," who remain "shut up in their own little narrow, inane world, dreading nothing so much as a rap on their shell":

> Do no harm in the world? Did you ever know them [oyster people] do any *good*? Is any mortal better for their having vegetated, and perpetuated their stupid species in it? I trow not. I had rather encounter the rabid ultraist who, though he overshoots the mark, has often a high and noble aim, which his mad but honest zeal may succeed in bringing to the notice of a more judicious philanthropy.

When Lincoln was elected in 1860, there was no discernible comment by Fern, nor was there in the following months as the southern states seceded. However, after the firing on Fort Sumter in mid-April 1861 and Lincoln's call to the militia of the loyal states, Fern described the time as an "electric moment": "It is only in a great crisis, that one becomes fully aware of the importance of popular opinion. When the hearts of thousands beat as one; when the eye of woman flashes . . . ; when men talk in groups, with low, earnest voices . . . ; and at every unusual stir, a thousand pulses leap, it is only at such a time that one can feel it" (NYL, May 18, 1861).

On June 1, 1861, in an article entitled "The Time to Speak Out," Fern praised the man of "bold utterance" who recognized the impossibility of neutrality:

When timidity creeps into its hiding place, or measures its stealthy pace under the transparent mask of neutrality, then—God be thanked for the man of bold utterance! He refreshes us like the quick thunder storm, when the air grows too thick for breath. . . . *There be things worse than death.* When men walk with closed mouths, and averted eyes, nor dare look into the mirror of their own souls, and face the marring of God's image there. . . . When with iron heel they crush out like so many insects, the soul's breath from thousands, and impiously say, "Am I not doing God's service?" Is it a time when the smoke of the pit ascends to the very nostrils, for men to coin pretty phrases?

The following month the Civil War began. Right from the beginning Fern was directly and emphatically Unionist. On June 22, 1861, she criticized young men who were apathetic about national events. Without specifically mentioning the events or Lincoln's call for the militia, she attacked young men who did not take an interest in events and, even more so, men who would not enlist. This was one more time, she said, when she regretted that she was a woman:

We have no words to express our disgust, in a day like this, of the spectacle of a young man thus yawning away existence, so far as any benefit to the great public welfare, through him, is concerned. . . . His well knit limbs should be encased in a petticoat, and a subscription should be immediately raised to present him with a sewing-machine, unless, indeed, the *steel* used in the machinery should be objectionable to his sensitive organization. He should immediately resign his hat to some bonnet, whose owner never so bitterly bewails the fate that assigned her one, as when she sees so sorry a sight as this, when every moment is the hinge of a great event, and the hand-to-hand conflict of life is broken only by the hoarse whisper of brother to brother, "how goes the battle?"

The young men in Fern's family circle were not among the "oyster people" that she criticized. In March 1861 Mortimer Thomson asked to marry Grace. Fern's article in the *Ledger*, "Why Should He?" on March 30, 1861, suggests the difficulty she faced in giving up the daughter that years before she had striven so hard to keep:

How any young fellow can have the face to walk into your family, and deliberately ask for one of your daughters, passes me. That it is done every day, does not lessen my astonishment at the sublime impudence of the thing. There you have been, sixteen, or seventeen, or eighteen years of her life, combing her hair, and washing her face for—*him!* It is lucky the thought never strikes you while you are doing it, that this is to be the end of it all. . . . *He* seems to be of a different opinion; *he* not only insists upon taking her, but upon taking her immediately, if not sooner.

The threat of war and the uncertainty of the times may have accelerated the marriage, or it may have been simply that Grace and Thomson felt they had waited long enough. Whatever the reason, on Sunday, May 12, 1861, they were married.[8] Grace was twenty; Thomson twenty-nine. The article in the *Tribune* was written by Thomson's brother, Clifford, and appeared on May 13:

> Mr. Mortimer Thomson, better known as "Doesticks," was yesterday married by the Rev. Henry Ward Beecher, to Miss Grace Eldredge, eldest daughter of "Fanny Fern." The ceremony took place at the residence of James Parton, esq., the celebrated biographer. The patriotic mother of the bride had an elegant American flag arranged as a canopy, beneath which the happy couple were united.

The diary of Thomas Butler Gunn gives us some details about the wedding. Jesse Haney was present, and Gunn records his account of the wedding:

> The thing was done very quietly, without the delicious theatrical foolery intimated in the "Tribune" paragraph (written by *young* Clif Thomson) though that had been intended. Fan had a flag in the corner of the room, but when Beecher arrived, they forgot the canopy project. No persons were invited, only the persons specially interested, Ned Welles and the Thomsons. The ceremony was of the briefest, not occupying twenty minutes, Grace wearing the $100 dress of lilac silk presented by Stewart to her mother and by her made over to the present Mrs. Thomson. She went through it well, looking like a [sic] honest school girl and appearing perfectly unaffected. They kissed and congratulated her when it was over. . . . Within half an hour of Grace's marriage, she hoped dinner would be ready soon as she was hungry. They rallied her about matrimony developing a good appetite.[9]

The dress that Grace wore was the dress Fern had worn at her marriage to Charles Eldredge, a sample of which is among her papers in the Sophia Smith Collection at Smith College. That Beecher performed the marriage ceremony reflects Fern's regard for him as a "human clergyman." Grace's comment that she was "hungry" after the ceremony indicates the way in which she had been brought up: Fern often wrote with pride of her own healthy appetite and criticized women who seemed to think that it was "un-ladylike" to eat heartily (e.g., NYL, March 21, 1863).

According to the terms of Hezekiah Eldredge's will, Grace was to inherit five thousand dollars at the time of her marriage. In March 1861 Oliver Dyer contacted Joseph Bacon, executor for Eldredge's will, and Bacon replied that, the money having been invested, Grace would receive almost seven thousand dollars, including the interest.[10]

Thomson and Grace set up housekeeping in their own home. Thomson's friend Ned Welles boarded with them.[11] On January 28, 1860, Fern had written a column in the Ledger advising newly married couples to live by themselves—not with relatives—and to live in a house, not a hotel. Also living with them was Thomson's father and his brother Clifford, until Clifford went into the army. Another resident of the house was young Mark Thomson, Thomson's son by Anna Van Cleve. He was two and a half when Grace and Thomson were married.

Like Fanny Fern, Thomson, in his columns, often referred to real people and events. One article by Doesticks that appeared in the Mercury just prior to their marriage gives a humorous account of his going to an auction with the "Curly One," who is Grace Eldredge, in order to furnish the new house.[12]

In July 1861 Thomson was sent to the front as a war correspondent for the Tribune. He also acted as chaplain to the regiment he was associated with. Ethel Parton tells of an incident indicating the regard in which Thomson was held by the men. He did not have a horse, and the government not being able to provide him with one, the men planned a raid on an enemy barn, whence they returned with a "horse for their parson."[13] Thomson also traveled alone on a dangerous mission from Chesapeake Bay to New York in order to obtain assistance for the regiment, which was precariously situated at the time.[14] In July of 1861 James Parton wrote that Thomson had been sent to Arlington Heights and that the family eagerly awaited his letters, which gave lively accounts of events.[15] In the same month Grace wrote to Mrs. Van Cleve that the family was "fearfully excited about war news."[16]

Clifford Thomson was a quartermaster sergeant in the Lincoln Cavalry with the Army of the Potomac. He left New York early in August. In a letter to General Butler, Fern asked Butler to help Clifford Thomson.[17] A letter from Clifford Thomson to Grace from Camp Kearney in 1862 indicates that he was courting her younger sister, Ellen (then seventeen), although the tone of the letter suggests that the relationship may only have been in jest:

From the various camps where we pitched our crowded and leaky tents I addressed letters, loaded with love's fragrant words, to this idol of my heart; in one of those missives I declared my passion and formally offered the corpulent but beautiful young lady my heart, my hand and half of my tent—at the same time I requested this maiden with auburn ringlets to

notify me, in case she did not accept my offer, if she found any other
sweet lipped lady who would. To this elegant and expressive outpouring
of a ruptured heart I received no reply. . . . If you chance to see her will
you casually ask her if she knew me in former years and so lead her to
speak of the soldier that's gone.[18]

Clifford Thomson's letter gives us an indication of the jesting relationship
between him and his new in-laws. Fern's daughters were, apparently, more
outspoken and more likely to engage in repartee with young men than were
other American young ladies of their time. Gunn, for example, commented
when he first met Grace: "A capital, pleasant, frank girl is Grace, possessing
withal a smack of her mother, in her liking for exaggerated remarks on
folks." Nelly, the younger girl, he said, was even more "precociously like
her dam." Gunn, who preferred retiring women, noted that both girls were
"prone to the damnable exaggeration of act and speech of [their] mother,"
which, he lamented, was due to the "heathenish" way in which they had
been brought up. When he heard that Thomson was courting Grace, he
commented: "No such simple-minded worship will be accorded to him as
was offered by" his first wife.[19]

Before she was married, Grace began writing for the New York Ledger.
The first article that can be identified as hers appeared on April 27, 1861,
under the name Mrs. George Washington Wyllys.[20] The style and subject
matter of her articles are very similar to those of her mother. For example,
on December 1, 1861, she wrote:

Sometimes we want to be a man! . . . When the weather is remarkably
muddy, and we've got down-town business to transact, that can't be put
off on any consideration, then we would give any money to be able to put
on something that won't drag and flap round our defenceless ankles every
step we took through the rain—to go whirling off, with our hands in our
pockets, guiltless of gloves, and perfectly indifferent on the subject of
cuffs and undersleeves!
When we see a party of gentlemen go merrily off to play cricket or
baseball, while we, miserable wretch, are doomed to stay behind and
show our crochet-patterns to their wives, and play the agreeable to
women who can't talk of anything but their babies and gowns, through
the burning heat of a summer afternoon, with a tea-party in the perspective, then we would rather be a man! Does anybody blame us?

Although Fanny Fern had raised her daughters to be free of traditional
inhibitions, they were still products of their society. Yet the yearning that
Grace expresses here indicates that although she was bound by the restrictions of her society like any young woman of her day, her upbringing as
Fanny Fern's daughter had taught her not to be ashamed of her unconven-

tional longings. Unlike Alice James, for example, who sat quietly at tea, repressing her desire to run and play, and ashamed of the anger and hostility that made her feel like striking her benign father,[21] Grace was comfortable in her criticism of the restrictions that society placed on women.

Her daughter settled, the events of the war claimed Fern's attention. On August 10, 1861, she noted that the summer reporting of fashions at the resorts was replaced by news of war. She also criticized the men who complained of war "losses" and "prostration of business" due to the war. On August 24 she noted that the country seemed to be thinking "war"; it was common now to see children playing war games: "What has become of those people who objected to seeing a little child play with toy guns or a sword, lest it should develop war-like proclivities?"

On September 7, 1861, Fern published a *Ledger* article entitled "Facing Both Ways," which made clear her unflinching support of the Civil War and her contempt for the uncommitted:

If any body knows a more despicable creature than he who stands perched on the fence of "policy," ready to jump either way, as worldly interest points . . . ;—if any one knows a more despicable creature than this, let him show him up, for I have failed to find him! . . . Out on such time-servers and hypocrites! Their ostrich endeavors to hide their deformed heads, under the mask of "neutrality," will not prevent their detection, and the well-earned contempt of all honest and honorable men.

In a similar article, on November 9, 1861, entitled "On the Fence," Fern criticized the people who would not take a position, but stood ready to support whichever side was in their selfish interest.

One good thing that would come out of the war, Fern believed, was that women would gain more rights. On December 28, 1861, in an article in which she had argued that women should have the vote, Fern indicated that the war would open up opportunities for women:

Well, there's one thing is certain, this war won't leave *women* where it found them, whatever may be said of *men*. The door of the Castle of Folly may be opened by it, and they are gradually coming out into a more bracing atmosphere and one consequence will be, that the great alleged hindrance to female voting, viz., "a want of intelligence," . . . will then be done away with. Meanwhile women who are taxed just the same as if they *were* "intelligent," may work worsted dogs and cats in crochet, awaiting that millennium.

Fern's hard line on the war contrasted sharply with the neutrality of her brother N. P. Willis. Not wanting to offend southern subscribers, Willis did not take a position on the war at all. Fern had satirized him as Hyacinth in

Ruth Hall, and in several articles she specifically criticized Willis's attitude toward the war. On February 22, 1862, using the same satirical name "Hyacinth" and indirectly identifying him by an oblique reference to his book *Pencillings by the Way*, she criticized "Hyppolite Hyacinth's pencillings about the good time he is longing for when his dear polished South 'shall have tearfully forgiven the North!'" Willis was at this time in Washington, and the articles he sent to the *Home Journal* continued to deal with the world of fashion rather than with political issues. On January 11, 1862, Fern wrote: "Suppose I furnish you with some 'War Sketches from the Capitol' after the manner of Hyppolite Hyacinth, giving you non-committal descriptions of tea and dinner parties there, giving you the patterns of tea and dinner service, telling you what the exquisite Mrs. Syllabub immortalized herself by wearing?"

Fern referred to other specific events in her columns during the Civil War. After Lincoln took over the telegraph to protect national security, Fern commented on March 29, 1862, that one could not say that women were the only ones who couldn't keep a secret; the press, she said, could not even keep a national secret. On May 31, 1862, she wrote about "Unrecorded Heroes": the women who fought "the battle of life" at home and the "thousands of brave" privates who would have no monuments erected to them.

In 1862 Fern and Parton spent the summer in New England. Fern wrote about her delightful ride through the countryside and their stay in Northampton, Massachusetts. She also described a visit to the lunatic asylum, commenting on the disproportionate number of women. Fern concluded that if women had the same outlets as men, the proportions would be equal:

I know that in proportion as physical education becomes a religion with the mothers of this country, this will not be so. . . . I know it will not be so, when that millennium comes for women, which is not going to come like a letter through the post, but through mental enlightenment of the masses, and consequent exertion of their own. Then, the number of *female* patients in these institutions will bear some proportion to those, whose active masculine-employments help them to bear the daily frets and vexations, under which the delicate female organization sinks utterly. (NYL, September 20, 1862)

On September 27, 1862, Fern visited the Springfield (Massachusetts) arsenal and commented on the righteousness of the federal cause and the disgust she felt at the men who refused to fight. She also wrote about the soldiers' wives (NYL, November 18, 1862) and the plight of southerners who had remained loyal to the North (NYL, December 27, 1862).

Sometimes Fern found it difficult to remain optimistic that the war would effect changes in the status of women, however. On November 1, 1862, she wrote about the latest fashion she had seen at a public performance: the

ladies in front of her, she said, were wearing "three-foot high hats." Fern
was disgusted with the ridiculousness of the fashion: "Can it be, muttered I
at last, that 'this war' is not going to regenerate our women from such
absurd frivolities after all? One might as well give them up, then, and
heaven have mercy on their future children!"

Fern did not give them up completely, however. The following week she
wrote about her attendance at her first political meeting. The article is a
valuable record of a woman's frustration at the limitations her society
placed on her. More interested in events than were many men, but prevented by her gender from being a participant in those events, Fern gives an
interesting account of the political meeting from the point of view of the
critical observer. Even more valuable for the women among her readers is
the way in which she succeeded in demystifying the all-male event so that
women could perceive it as something that they could participate in some
day. Half the battle for the excluded is the act of becoming familiar with the
event and recognizing that it is something that he or she can, in fact, participate in:

> There was to be a political meeting. Bonfires, speech-making, flag-
> hoisting, and a fine "rumpus" generally. Now I never went to a political
> meeting; and it is a notion of mine, to see every thing there is to be seen
> *once*. . . . And mustn't there be a *beginning* to everything under the sun?
> And wasn't I all ready to begin it? I trust, since I am taxed, I may have the
> use of my *ears* in a free country, provided I hold my tongue, and I'm not
> going to say how long I'll do that. I'd be willing to have them boxed by a
> democrat, if I couldn't have made as good a speech had they given me the
> floor, as *one*, at least, that I heard that night; for I'd have you to know I
> went. There *was* a crowd. What of that? I've been jostled quite as much
> getting in and out of the opera, and such places. And there was a racket. A
> hall full of gossiping women couldn't have made a greater, and I hope
> that is doing it full justice. And then there was preliminary hemming and
> hawing, and flattering one another, before one another's faces, and I
> didn't perceive that the recipients blushed, or were more averse to swal-
> lowing a big dose of it, than a pack of the sisters would have done under
> similar circumstances. And there were big truths, wrapped up in as many
> unnecessary swathings of words, as if "rambling women" had been the
> speakers; and the audience were as "fidgetty" as a woman-audience; all
> the difference was that they kept looking at their watches, instead of set-
> tling bracelets and finger-rings.

It was soon after this article was written that Fern's granddaughter was
born. On December 1, 1862, Grace gave birth to a daughter, Grace Ethel.
Thomson was not home for the birth of his child, but he returned from the
front three weeks later when Grace, having contracted scarlet fever from her

little stepson, Mark, died at the age of twenty-one. Mark, who was staying
with Grace at the time, and who, unknown to her, was coming down with
scarlet fever, apparently infected her when she brought him up into her bed
to look at the baby.[22] She died on December 23, 1862, a day after the fourth
anniversary of the death of Thomson's first wife.

Thomson was devastated by the deaths of his two wives, each leaving him
with a newborn baby. He never recovered. In fact, his career, which had
been so promising, ended at that point. Did he blame himself? Or did he
simply give up? One does not know. But after the death of his second wife,
his personal life, and as a consequence, his professional life also, quickly
deteriorated. After Grace died, little Ethel came to live with her grandmother, James Parton, and her aunt, Ellen, who was eighteen when her
sister died. Thomson signed over the child for three years, and although he
indicated that he did not want to give her up permanently, he never re-
claimed her.[23] He stayed in New York for a while, and his daughter had
vague memories of her handsome father throwing her up in the air when she
was very young, or running into a burning church nearby to rescue the
historic Peter Stuyvesant Chair.[24] Soon, however, Thomson went to Minnesota, and over the years he wrote sporadically for the newspapers. He apparently lived a rather irregular life. In 1873 James Parton reported seeing
him in New York. He was destitute and looked very ill. He asked Parton for
money, which Parton gave him.[25] Parton wrote that there was talk that he
might be put in an institution, and both he and Ellen insisted that Effie must
never know how her father lived.[26] When Thomson died in 1875 at the age
of forty-three, he was said to have developed a dependency on opium.[27]

For Fanny Fern also the loss of her daughter Grace was a devastating
blow. Having struggled up from the desolation of her first daughter's death
and the deaths of her young sister, her mother, and her first husband, Fern
must have felt that she had left tragic times behind her. On January 10,
1863, she published in the *Ledger* an article entitled "Death," which derived
from Grace's death:

> *You* know what it is, and *you*, and *you*, to stand, with straining eye-
> balls, and watch the dear form grow more and more shadowy, as it re-
> cedes through the dark valley. To stretch forth your warm, eager hands to
> help and succor it, and feel them thrust back with an iron grasp. To pour
> out words of agonized love only to have them inexorably intercepted. To
> sob, to moan, only to that appalling silence and those freezing limbs. To
> call back the love that, in days gone by, had answered in brimming meas-
> ure to the faintest smile of yours. . . . [T]o have cruel memory stand up
> and draw aside the curtain from the bright past, and force you, shudder-
> ing, to look on this picture and then on *that!*

After her long struggle to keep her daughter when she was threatened
with the loss of her child by her father-in-law's will, and after the trium-

phant reclaiming of Grace from an unkind grandmother, which is portrayed in *Ruth Hall*, Fern must have felt the bitter irony of Grace's death at such a young age. She had witnessed the childbirth-related deaths of so many young women: her sister Ellen; N. P. Willis's wife, Mary Stace; her brother Richard's wife, Jessie Cairns; Mortimer Thomson's first wife, Anna Van Cleve. And now her daughter Grace. She found it difficult not to torture herself with recriminations and thoughts of "possible omissions" and of the "terrible 'if'" which might have prevented her daughter's death. She indicates in this article that she feels that one could go insane if one was not able to believe in some kind of eternity. Only this, she says, can "deaden the dull earth sound on the coffin-lid" (NYL, January 10, 1863). The following week in her column she expressed gratitude to the "human" clergyman who was able to speak "convincing words to the ear of despair" (NYL, January 17, 1863).

After Grace's death, Fern continued to write her column as she had always done, intermixing comments on issues and events with comments deriving from her personal life. On January 24, 1863, in an article entitled "Washing the Baby," she introduced little Effie to the public:

> You may think it a very simple thing to wash a baby. You may imagine that one feels quite calm and composed, while this operation is being faithfully and conscientiously performed. That shows how little you know. When I tell you that there are four, distinct, delicate chins to be dodgingly manipulated, between frantic little crying spells, and as many little rolls of fat on the back of the neck that have to be searched out and bathed, with all the endearing baby-talk you can command, the while, as a blind to your merciless intentions; when I tell you, that of all things, baby won't have her ears or nose meddled with, and that she resents any infringement on her toes with shrill outbreaks, and that it takes two people to open her chubby little fists, when water seeks to penetrate her palms. . . . When I inform you that every now and then you must stop in the process to see that she is not choking, or strangling, or that you have not dislocated any of her funny little legs, or arms, or injured her bobbing little head, you can form some idea of the relief when the last string is tied, and baby emerges from this her daily misery, into a state of rosy, diamond-eyed, scarlet-lipped, content, looking as sweet and fresh as a rosebud, and drowsing off in your arms. . . . Ah me! how shall one keep from spoiling a baby? Ah me! how can one ever give brimming enough love-measure—to this—*the motherless.*

The loss of Grace was hard for Fern to accept, but the advent of Effie into their home brought a new joy to Fern and Parton, who were mother and father to the child. If Fern had indeed lost a child early in the marriage as her article seems to suggest (NYL, August 22, 1857), Effie took the place of the child they did not have. As Fern later told Grace Greenwood of Effie, "*She* is my poem."[28] One year after Grace's death, Fern wrote that although "heart-wrenchings" are legion, we still reach out our hands for the gilded bubble of hope. . . . When our dearly-beloved children are taken from us, our torn heart-strings hasten to twine about *their* children" (NYL, December 12, 1863). James Parton grew to love the child so much that, years later, when Fern died, he could not bear to give up the little girl that he had raised as his own. He said that he could never repay her for the joy she had brought into his life. When Ethel Thomson came of age she legally changed her name to Ethel Parton.[29]

Several articles that Fern wrote in February of 1863 suggest that there were those who questioned Fern's motive in taking over the care of little Effie. On February 7, 1863, Fern published an article in the *Ledger* entitled "Self-Constituted Judges." One suspects that the reference is to Parton's relatives, who did not seem ever to approve of what Fern did:

> There are few things in this world more painful than a persistent and wilful misappreciation of one's opinions, motives, and actions by others. To be accused of meannesses, from which the soul shrinks with horror; to do a generous action, and have it laid to the account of self-seeking, or self-interest; to have every nerve and fibre alive with anxiety on some subject, of which one is accused of criminal and heartless indifference; to have one's tears and smiles analyzed to discover, if possible, some ingredient of falsity; to have critical, loveless, pharasaical eyes scanning all your honest strivings to do right; *always* to have one's point of view condemned because it *is* one's point of view; in your parching thirst for *justice*, to have an empty cup held mockingly to your lips, all this might well paralyze soul and action, in those who thus suffer, were there no self-reliance, or no other tribunal than the warped judgment of humanity.

In the face of criticism, Fern's "self-reliance" once again was able to sustain her, coupled with the belief in a higher justice. In this article Fern makes clear how throughout her life she was able to defy family and custom in her struggle to maintain her independence. In her youthful defiance of her father and the clergymen and teachers who attempted to instill in her the fear of a Calvinist God; in her defiance of her family and her in-laws who attempted to force her to remain with her abusive second husband; in her defiance of critics and convention which condemned her for her satirical treatment of male authority in *Ruth Hall;* and in her defiance of her more conventional peers who criticized her search for a "freer range" for women: in all of these struggles Fern had to rely first of all upon herself. But, as is often the case with the powerless in society, she found strength in the belief that there was a higher authority for the essential rightness of her position.

After Grace died, Fern found it difficult to bear the comments of outsiders, who thought to philosophize away her grief. In a February 21, 1863, article she points out how much easier troubles are to bear when they are "Other People's Troubles." Then one can be philosophical about death. But, says Fern, what a difference it makes if the hearse stands at one's own door.

Also in February, Fern wrote an article that suggests that she had found out something about Mortimer Thomson that indicated he had betrayed her daughter's trust. In an article entitled "Retribution" published on February 21, 1863, she wrote:

> What worse punishment could be the portion of any human being than to bear about with him the hourly consciousness of having repaid trust with treachery; child-like confidence with betrayal; and with having worn to the eyes of innocence a life-mask, even though they be closed in death before the dreadful secret be discovered, which would have extinguished happiness, and poisoned peace forever.

One wonders if Thomson's dissipations preceded his wife's death. Gunn comments in his diary that after Grace died, it was discovered that Thomson had spent almost her whole inheritance in the year and a half they had been married. Of the seven thousand dollars that she inherited from her grandparents, only fifteen hundred was left when Grace died. Gunn reports that Fern asked Thomson to put that amount into a trust for Ethel, but he refused.[30] There is an unfortunate irony inherent in Thomson's apparent misuse of his wife's money. Hezekiah Eldredge had drawn up his will in the way that he did so that Fanny Fern would not be able to get her hands on his money: his granddaughters were not to get a penny until they married, when he assumed that their husbands would have control of the money. That Grace's husband thus was enabled to spend Grace's money meant that Grace's daughter did not get any of her mother's inheritance. This must have been one more example to Fern of the inequities for women inherent in a system of patriarchal control of money.

In February 1863 Fern and Parton went to Washington, D.C., where Parton was beginning research for his next book, a study of General Benjamin Butler.[31] Fern wrote three articles from Washington, describing her visit to such places as the Senate, the Patent Office, the Smithsonian Institute, and the White House. At the Senate, she said, she felt so patriotic that she almost forgot her "bonnet" and was ready to make a speech (NYL, March 21, 1863). She arrived in Washington during a period of heavy rain and sleet: "The streets were a quaking jelly of mud, filled with a motley procession of dirt-encrusted army-wagons, drawn by wretched-looking horses, the original color of whose hide was known only to their owners. Military men swarmed on the sidewalks, gossipped on the steps of public buildings, filled hotel entries, parlors and dining-rooms, and splashed through mud-puddles with a recklessness born of camp-initiation" (NYL, March 21, 1863). On

March 3, 1863, Congress passed a conscription act. Two weeks later there were draft riots in New York City that lasted four days. Fern and Parton, however, were probably not in New York at this time. They had gone to Lowell, Massachusetts, to stay with General Butler and his wife while Parton interviewed the general.[32]

In August of 1863 Fern and Parton traveled to Saratoga, and on September 5, 1863, she described the ladies' fashionable dress. On September 12, she described a visit to Vermont, and reported the sadness of being at a country train depot and watching the crowd gather to meet the train that was carrying a dead soldier's body (NYL, September 19, 1863). Later in September she was back in New York and commenting on the troops stationed there in a "city camp." The article "Our City Camps" is particularly interesting as a summation of Fern's quarrel with the restrictions of her society and as a statement of her reaction to them. She wrote of how she wanted to go straight up to the soldiers and talk to them about the war, but, as a woman, she could only use her eyes and "do the pretties," as if life were "no more earnest" to her than to any "female butterfly":

Well—one thing I know. If I have to gnaw this file much longer, some Lunatic Asylum will have the pleasure of inscribing my name on its books; for there is not a day that I don't feel it in my feet to jump over some five-barred gate, that custom and "propriety" have set up, to limit female range within the scented clover-fields of lethargic inanity. Now that I have cleared my throat, I tell you—I want a freer range. In plain Saxon, I want to "loaf" about, and see something besides ribbons and laces. I want to be able to go out evenings alone, if the whim suits me, without being spoken to, on any legitimate and proper errand I may see fit. I would like to go to see ship-yards, and wharves, and iron works, and station-houses, and hospitals, and jails, and penitentiaries; and if there must be riots, I want to see *them*, as well as political meetings, where people are pulled out by the head and shoulders for bad sentiments and bad manners. I know this is neither "refined" nor "lady-like," according to the present perverted sense of these words; and I know you are ready to ask, "Wouldn't I like to be drafted?" Yes sir; and if I were, I hope I would not buy "a substitute." . . . I would agree to subscribe to almost anything, so that I need not lace, pin, and button on so many things every morning, only to take them off every night, and hold them up every time it rained or is damp, and be frightened to death for fear some human hoof will tear them or some human lips spit upon them. I would agree to anything a self-respecting woman might, could I only have an escape-valve for the superfluous electricity, that refuses the usual conductors of needles and thread, and new bonnets, and flies from my head to my heels, till I long to be a locomotive or a comet. Between you and me, I think the amount of it is, that I want to be taken care of and petted as a woman and yet to have the independence of a man. (September 26, 1863)

With an interest in events, Fern found herself confined by her gender to the sidelines along with women whose only interests were fashion or domestic chores. Unable and unwilling to find an outlet for her energies in the usual inane feminine pursuits of embroidery and dress, there were times, she said, when she felt as if she were being driven insane by society's having closed up all active outlets to her. In an 1866 article she commented that it was no wonder women gave so much attention to dress. There was nothing else for them to do that would occupy their minds sufficiently, and if they did not have something to occupy their minds, they would go insane thinking of the oppressiveness of their situation: "You see, my dear, a woman mustn't think, if she wouldn't land in a Lunatic Asylum" (NYL, March 24, 1866).

In "Our City Camps" Fern also made clear her opinion on the draft. The draft law of March 1863 enabled a man to purchase a substitute or to pay the government a fee to avoid being drafted. This meant that the well-to-do could be exempted, and the law was called discriminatory. The four-day draft riots in New York City that month developed after the posting of a list of draftees, all of whom were laborers. The rioters' principal anger was directed at the government conscription offices, but they also struck out at all those whom they blamed for the war: they hanged blacks, robbed Unionists and looted their homes, attacked the mayor's house, and burned the *Tribune* office. Although Fern did not approve of the violence and the misdirected anger, she did agree with the criticism of the discriminatory conscription law. On March 5, 1864, she wrote sarcastically about men who, when drafted, find a substitute because they suddenly realize that they are not as well as they used to be, or they suddenly discover they are the sole support of a widowed mother, whom they had previously ignored. She was to return to this theme in later articles. For example, on May 27, 1865, just after the war ended, she was sarcastic about the "six-foot cowards" who no longer have to grumble about the draft "that is to tear them from families for which they never half provided."

Fern was particularly contemptuous of men who opposed the war on a monetary basis. On September 17, 1864, she wrote:

I have little patience with your *"men of today,"* who, with no thought or care for the future of their children or their country, seeing only the increased cost of living and increased taxation, ignobly shirking self-denial and effort, clamor like grown-up babies for *"peace;"* . . . as if a country that was worth living in was not worth fighting for; as if more than three years of battling, two hundred and fifty thousand lives, and four thousand

million of dollars, were to have their finale in inglorious subjection to
rebeldom. The men who hold these views, whether in Wall Street or
behind drygoods-counters, in pulpits or in colleges, had better go home
and tend the babies while the women finish the fighting.

At the same time that Fern was writing these bold words, of course, she
also was "tending the baby." From time to time she shared with her readers
some of the joys and difficulties of doing so. Her pictures of mothering,
which derive from her own experience, are as relevant today as they were
when they were written. On May 16, 1863, she described the anxieties of
trying not to "wake the baby":

How many tunes have sometimes to be hummed, how many walkings up
and down the floor, how many trottings, how many rockings, how many
feedings, before this desirable event comes off. At last the little lids give
promise of drooping, the little waxen paws fall helpless, the little kicking
toes are quiescent, mamma draws a breath of relief, as she pushes her hair
off her heated face, and baby looks as if nothing on earth could ever
disturb its serenity. Won't there? Tramp, tramp, tramp, comes the baby's
papa up stairs with a pair of creaking boots. Mamma rushes to the nursery door, with warning forefinger on her lip and an imploring "John,
dear, the baby! it is the nurse's day out—pray don't wake her up." "John
dear," true to his sex, creaks on, and argues this wise, "My dear, I've
often noticed that it isn't *that* kind of noise that ever wakes baby." Of
course, mamma is too much of a woman not to know that a *man is never
mistaken* even with regard to a subject he knows nothing about; but it
strikes her that sometimes strategy is a good thing; so the next day she
places his slippers below stairs in a very conspicuous and tempting position, trusting that his tired feet may naturally seek that relief. I say *naturally*, because she knows that he would as soon thrust his feet into two
pots of boiling water as put them in those slippers, if he thought the idea
emanated from a *female* mind, so naturally does the male creature hedge
about his godlike dignity. Well, baby is quieted and patted down again. . . .
Just then "dear John" appears again, and wants something; a bit of
string, or a bottle, maybe, but whatever it is he is sure it is on the top shelf
in the closet of that room; and though he is not going to use it immediately, he wants it *found* immediately because—he *wants* it! and because
"though impatient woman can never wait an instant for anything," man
is very like her in that respect, though he don't see it. So the search is
instituted, and down tumbles one thing and then another off the shelves,
rattling and rustling and bumping, and finally it is discovered that "the
pesky thing" isn't there, but is down in the kitchen cupboard; this piece of
information dear John conveys to his wife in a shrill "sissing" whisper,
"because a whisper," he says, how loud soever, "never yet woke up
baby!"

Just then the large violet eyes unclose and the little mouth dimples into a pretty smile of recognition, and "dear John," whose attention is called to it, explains, peeping into the crib, "Well now, who'd have thought it," and creaks off down stairs after his bottle or ball of string, as calm as a philosopher; and then asks his wife at dinner "if she has mended that lining in his coat-sleeve that he spoke about at breakfast time."

Fern's nickname for Parton, who sometimes was abstracted, was "the philosopher" or "the biographer." On July 11, 1863, she wrote in a column entitled "The Married Philosopher":

Mr. Jones is what is usually termed a philosopher—i.e., a being who is always up in the clouds, intently contemplating some ideal self-inflated air-balloon. Any unhappy individual addressing him a question, must be content to wait a week for an answer, or receive one as far distant from the subject in hand as is the political North from the political South.

The following week, in order to give equal time to their eccentricities, Fern wrote about "The Married Philosopher's Wife":

It has occurred to me, since writing a description of "The Married Philosopher," that his wife, Mrs. Jones, may also be said to have *her* little peculiarities. Not that she would ever admit that she was different from anybody else, which is the more particularly absurd, because her everyday goings-on never had, or will have, a parallel. . . . Mr. Jones often remarks that there is so much variety in Mrs. Jones' composition that it is quite equal to being in the society of several women.

As the Civil War continued, Fern urged retrenchment among civilians and praised the U.S. Sanitary Commission, which had been approved by the government to provide food and clothing as well as medical care for the soldiers (NYL, August 1, 1863, June 18, 1864, July 30, 1864).

In August of 1864 Parton and Fern took Effie to the mountains for a week. Parton reported in a letter that he had returned from a trip to the Isle of Shoals to find his wife "completely exhausted from the heat and the baby" and planned to take her to the Catskill Mountain House.[33] After their return from the Catskills, Parton and Fern spent ten days at Fortress Monroe in Virginia as guests of General Butler.[34] Butler, who had come to know Fern and Parton when the latter was writing his biography, enjoyed Fern's company and valued her opinions. In 1866, for example, he sent a copy of a report to Parton requesting that he let Fern read it: "I should like the fine instincts of an intelligent woman upon it."[35]

Fern was seasick on the trip to Virginia, but, Butler reported in a letter to his wife, she and Parton were unusually interested in everything they saw.[36] They went out into the field and stayed at the army camp. Fern wrote about the trip in her columns. On October 8 she wrote about a visit to the army hospital, commenting that those who whined for an "inglorious peace" should see the "many-sided phases of agony" in the hospitals instead of seeing only the "holiday-aspect of war." On October 15 she described her conversations with some of the three hundred Union soldiers who had been prisoners of war and whose exchange had just been effected. They told her about the horrors of the Confederate Libby Prison, which only increased her reason for opposing an easy peace.

On October 22 Fern told about the adventures of a "Woman at Headquarters," where she particularly enjoyed the evening campfires, "round which you can sit and talk with intelligent men till the small hours about other things than 'bonnets.'" On October 29 and November 5 she described some of the things she had seen: the desolation and the beauty of the South; the "fine soldierly appearance of our colored troops"; a photographer's shed in the woods where she had her picture taken; and the meticulous housekeeping of some of the men, which surprised her. She rode on horseback to the front lines with General Birney and, as she said later, ruined her dress "touching off a thirty-two pounder Parrot gun commissioned to throw shells into Petersburg" (NYL, November 19, 1864, May 27, 1865). Looking at the James River in Virginia, she realized that she too "would have loved this beautiful country" if she had been born there; but "having ever been to the North and seen what Southern eyes must see there," she could never again have been "contented and happy with [her] Southern birth-right and its accompanying curse" (NYL, October 29, 1864). The curse, of course, was slavery.

When President Lincoln was assassinated on April 15, 1865, six days after Lee's surrender, Fern wrote from New York that the city was in mourning. Thousands mourned him as they would mourn one of their own, she said, and if they did not mourn him, they should, for it was to him that they were "more indebted than any other for permission to draw breath" in this country (NYL, May 13, 1865). On May 27, 1865, she celebrated the end of the war in her column "The Last Four Years": "I thank God that the dear lost lives, from our President down, have not been in vain; that the blood the monster slavery would have lapped up triumphantly has only gone to strengthen the roots of the tree of Liberty."

15

"At My Post"

What if you are so constituted that injustice and wrong to others rouses you as if it were done to yourself? What if the miseries of your fellow beings, particularly those you are powerless to relieve, haunt you day and night? . . . What if you feel like rolling up your sleeves and engaging in deadly combat with every disgusting sham and humbug that comes in your way? . . . What if you cannot carry out the creed of so many [men] of the present day. . . . who with a man's chances fold their supine hands over all these abuses, turn a deaf ear to all these cries of distress. . . . What to them is the future of others, if their selfish present be undisturbed? . . . Well, rather than be that torpid thing, and it a man, I would rather be a woman tied hand and foot, bankrupt in chances, and worry over what I am powerless to help. At least I can stand at my post, like a good soldier, because it is my post; meantime—I had rather be taken off that by a chance shot, than rust in a corner with ossification of the heart.

NYL, February 2, 1867

THE CIVIL WAR OVER, FANNY FERN CONTINUED TO WRITE, as she had before, on issues and events, child rearing and education, women's follies, men's tyrannies, and—that all-pervading question—women's rights. Ethel Parton, Fern's granddaughter, describes the relationship between Fanny Fern and the public:

With every passing year, her hold on her public strengthened, rather than waned. They felt they knew her better and better, as indeed she grew to know them. They sensed, rightly, her complete sincerity. She said many things that needed saying, and she said them effectively. . . . Above all, she was an intensely vital creature. . . . She became to thousands as real a person as their next door neighbor. Her weekly visit, by way of the *New York Ledger*, was an event eagerly looked forward to. When the *Ledger* arrived in a family of good size, with father and mother and grown sons and daughters, many were the quarrels as to who should have the first reading of Fanny Fern's column. (EP, 161–162)

Fern received an extraordinary amount of mail from her readers, some asking advice, some thanking her for the comfort or encouragement that her words had given them, others taking issue with something she had written about, some seeking help, and many simply writing to pour out their troubles as they might to a warm friend. Some letters were sent in care of the *Ledger;* others were sent directly to her home. Her granddaughter tells us that there was never a day when the letter box at 303 East Eighteenth Street did not contain letters from *Ledger* readers; usually, it was overflowing (EP, 162). To some of these letters Fern wrote a personal reply. Occasionally she answered a letter in her column if it seemed of general interest. But although she could not possibly answer all of the letters, she read all of them, and she took very seriously her role as public mentor (EP, 164). An article published in the *Ledger* on February 18, 1860, gives us an idea of some of the letters she received. Although it was impossible to answer so many letters, she indicated that she sympathized with their contents and told the writers they were welcome to write if it would "ease their bosoms":

Don't you suppose I feel grateful to the man who sent me a box of nice, warm soles to slip in my boots this cold weather? Don't you suppose that the mother who sent me a daguerreotype of her dead boy, made my heart glow with that sweet and touching proof of confidence toward a stranger? Don't you suppose that the little girls off in the prairies who sent me some flower-seeds in a nice little letter, made me very happy? Don't you suppose I would have written a love letter for that entranced young man, to the girl he adored yet was afraid of, had I time? Do you suppose I didn't cry over that poor wife's letter, the shadow on whose hearthstone, cast by an intemperate but dearly loved husband, was growing darker and darker every day? Do you suppose I was not grateful for the offer of that "young carpen*tier* only nineteen years old," who kindly offered to construct for me a handy writing desk, to be made evenings, when his day's toil was over? . . . Do you suppose I wouldn't read several MSS. a month, give my opinion, and find a publisher, were the days longer, and my head stronger?

The character of some of these letters is suggested also by the selections quoted in *Ruth Hall,* which gives a further idea of Fern's reaction to them. Although she was amused at the outrageousness of some of the letters, she was intensely sympathetic to the letters that told of personal tragedies, suffering, and loneliness. She was also gratified by the letters which indicated that her column had been of help to people. "This will repay many a weary hour," Ruth says as she reads a letter from a man who says he is "a better son, a better brother, a better husband, and a better father" than he had been before he began reading her articles (RH, 183). On February 23, 1861, after commenting on the unfairness of "those jackels," the literary critics who are motivated by personal pique or petty animosities, Fern notes that it is the letters more than anything else that tell an author what her work means to her readers:

A letter comes to you; then another, and another, till, mayhap if you are lucky, you have done counting them; full of love and appreciation, of what you know, better than anybody can tell you, is very faulty. . . . It may be a man, or woman, or child, whose spiritual eyes gaze into yours, . . . over miles and seas far away, and [who] claims you for a dear though unseen friend; blessing you for some word of yours that came like a cordial, when heart and soul grew faint, to make life's paths easy to the tired feet. Ah! then your tears fall as you say, *this repays me for all my toil, this is better than a diploma from any college.*

As Fern's granddaughter noted, a large minority of these letters were from men, but the majority were from women. Fern received letters from women of all ages and economic backgrounds. Despite the ill-treatment she had received from women in her personal life, her sympathies were with women generally. After she had been writing her *Ledger* column for fourteen years, she wrote: "I wish I could ease all the burdens of the persons who write to me for sympathy and advice; more especially those of my own sex" (NYL, August 6, 1870). On October 28, 1871, in reply to a letter she had received from a woman whose baby had died, Fern wrote that she knew that she could not say anything that would lessen the woman's pain. "I shall not *reason* with you, now," she said, "for that were worse than useless. I only reach out my woman's hand, and clasp yours in sympathy, although we never have and never may meet in this world."

The clasp of this "woman's hand," reached out in sympathy, was understood by Fern's readers. Receiving hundreds of letters a week, many from women who wrote to Fanny Fern about the tragedies and sometimes horrors of their personal life that they could not tell to anyone else, Fern was probably closer to the "pulse" of American womanhood than anyone else of her generation. It was from these letters that Fern gained her wide knowledge of "women's wrongs." In an article published in the *Ledger* on August 10, 1867, she said to those who did not understand her insistence upon the desperation of so many women: "You should have read the letters I have received; you should have talked with the women I have talked with; in short, you should have walked this earth with your eyes open, instead of shut, as far as its women are concerned."

Clearly, Fern was psychologically astute and sensitive to the problems women wrote to her about; she probably was also very good at reading between the lines. When Fern wrote about women in her columns, she wrote both from her own experience as a woman and from her knowledge of what was in the private hearts and minds of women all over the country.

It is this, perhaps, that helps to explain her continuing popularity. Initially, she had become popular because of her candid and satirical columns, which, based as they were on her own experience and observation, rang true for her readers. That they continued to ring true long after Fern herself was no longer the victim she portrayed in her early work was owing to her close relationship with female suffering through her correspondence.

It is important to recognize this aspect of Fern's work in order to understand the full significance of Fern's columns for today's readers. On January 30, 1869, Fern wrote:

I know scores of bright, intelligent women, alive to their fingertips to everything progressive, good and noble, whose lives, hedged in by custom and conservatism, remind me of that suggestive picture in all our Broadway artist-windows, of the woman with dripping hair and raiment, clinging to the fragment of rock overhead, while the dark waters are surging round her feet.

This is not an affectedly melodramatic picture of women's lives during the period that Fern wrote; it derived from Fern's own experience and also from the accumulation of years of letters from women whose lives were a constant struggle against mental, emotional, and physical annihilation. It is the depth and breadth of her knowledge gained from women themselves—in that pre-Freudian age of reticence and suppression—that make Fern's columns such a valuable source of information about the situation of American women in the nineteenth century. When she wrote metaphorically of women suspended over an abyss, clinging only to a "fragment of rock," or when she wrote of women's "legal murders" (NYL, March 12, 1870), she was describing a situation that was based on the confidences of thousands of women.

Fern and Parton spent the summers of 1865 and 1866 in Brattleboro, Vermont, taking with them Fern's daughter, Ellen, and her granddaughter, Ethel. They did not like the artificialities of resort life, and chose instead to board in a farmhouse. Leaving the city at the end of June, they remained in the country until October. Previously Fern had indicated that she did not enjoy staying in the country for too long a period, but now she was glad to go. One of the reasons for her change of mind was her desire to give little Effie a summer in the country. "Sometimes," she wrote on July 8, 1865, "I get so depressed and heart-sick at all this misery in New York, and no help for it, or none that is at *all* adequate and no prospect of anything different." "Childhood in New York is terrible," she said, "whether in silk or with unwashed feet. It is old in fashion and old in crime before it is out of short frocks."

But Fern herself also was happy to leave the city for a spell. In 1866 she wrote: "Peace—blessed peace! here again among the mountains[.] Now, if one can resist the old habit of reading the city newspapers, there is a Paradisaical chance for happiness for some weeks to come" (NYL, August 11, 1866). She was also glad to get away from the care of keeping a house. "I hate care, I hate a kitchen," she wrote on July 21, 1866.

Sometimes, though, it was difficult to write while in the country: "I'd just like to have you, Mr. Bonner, try to write in view of those splendid trees and that great, cool, lazy, comfortable-looking mountain" (NYL, August 26, 1865). Her columns continued throughout the summer, however, and they give an idea of her life while she was in the country: going for walks or drives, exploring the countryside, going to the country fair, or just sitting in the shade of a tree and playing with her granddaughter (NYL, August 12, 1865, August 18, 1865, October 6, 1866). Fern makes clear her distaste for city ladies who do not know how to enjoy the country:

> *I* do not find the day long in the country. I could sit lazily under that tree, all day, in a trance of cat-like purring enjoyment. But I'll tell you what rouses me out of it. That group of city ladies, who come sailing past, inside those enormous hoops, freighted with round trimming, and square trimming, and pointed trimming, and tripping daintily lest an atom of dust should invade those precious dry-goods. . . . And now, a little two-and-a-half year older toddles up to me on the grass and says, "Tell me, what are the trees whispering about?" *She's* the girl for me. Do you suppose those dressed-up ladies ever have such a thought as that? (NYL, August 12, 1865)

When the summer was over, Fern was reluctant to return to the city: "To lose October! the golden month of all the year in the country, that one may come to town, to see that a dusty house is put in shining order; that's what I call a trial." With characteristic determination, however, she tackled the job, and when she was finished, she took "a cake of glycerine soap to remove the working traces from her hands" and put her "fingers in writing order." "After all," she said, "this had to be done; and one's life can't be all play, and I must be woman enough to take my share of the disagreeables, instead of shirking them like a great coward; for all that, I like a tree better than a broomstick; a fine sunset better than a gridiron" (NYL, October 21, 1865, October 13, 1866).

Fern's reluctance to return to the city did not only derive from her love of nature. She took very seriously the social problems that were only too apparent in the city. In the country she could put them out of her mind—for a time, at least—but in the city they pressed upon her:

> It seems dreadful to take all this wretchedness, and waste of life, as a matter of course, and that with which we have nothing to do. We can't get used to the worn faces, the hurried footsteps, the jostling indifference,

the dust, and grime, and shabbiness through which we plunge at every turn. Visions of moss-dripping rocks, huge and grand; sweet, grassy roads, full of birds, and darting squirrels; plentiful orchards and barns. . . . Oh, we had much rather think of these, and close our eyes on all this maelstrom-misery, and tinselled grandeur. We feel stifled. We throw up the window, and wonder what can ail us? for unrest, unquiet, and strife, seem to be in the very atmosphere that we breathe. (NYL, October 27, 1866)

In spite of—or perhaps because of—the pain expressed here, Fern's sense of injustice was so strong that throughout her career on the Ledger she made it her business to visit places in New York that were not only unpleasant but were considered off limits for women of her class. On February 10, 1866, she complained that conservative custom prevented her from doing— or writing about—much that she would like to:

People who visit a great city, and explore it with a curious eye, generally overlook the most remarkable things in it. They "do it up" in Guide-Book fashion, going the stereotyped rounds of custom-ridden predecessors. If my chains were a little longer, I would write you a book of travels that would at least have the merit of ignoring the usual fingerposts that challenge travellers. I promise you I would cross conservative lots, and climb over conservative fences, and leave the rags and tatters of custom fluttering on them, behind me, as I strode on to some unfrequented hunting ground.

Although her "chains" were not long enough to take her everywhere she would have liked to go, Fern visited places and areas in New York City that most women of her class did not see. She used her columns to call attention to injustice and to bring to her readers, particularly her women readers, pictures of the unpleasant realities of life from which so many of them were sheltered—and with which Fern believed they should be familiar. Early in her career she had taken her readers into the Five Points area of New York, which was at the time the most notoriously impoverished and most crime-ridden area of the city. She wrote with disgust of the pious who went into these areas of the city offering only pious cant and Bible tracts. What was needed, Fern asserted, was practical help, and she praised the efforts of the man who had established the Five Points House of Industry, which provided jobs and job training as well as an educational day-care center—all of which he had to do on his own because he could obtain no funds from any religious or municipal organization (MWT, October, 15, 1853, October 22, 1853).

In 1853 Fern wrote about her visit to the Tombs prison (MWT, November 12, 1853), and in 1858 she wrote three columns about her visits to the prison on Blackwell's Island (now known as Welfare Island) in the East River. Fern was very modern in her analysis of criminal or antisocial behavior, looking at the environmental causes rather than judging from a pompous holier-than-thou standard:

Shall I pity these poor wrecks of humanity less, because they are so recklessly self-wrecked? because they turn away from my pity? Before I come to this, I must know, as their Maker knows, what evil influences have encircled their cradles. How many times when their stomachs have been empty, some full-fed, whining disciple, has presented them with a Bible or a Tract. . . . I must go a great way back of those hard, defiant faces, where hate of their kind seems indelibly burnt in; back—back—to the soft blue sky of infancy, overclouded before the little one had strength to contend with the flashing lightning and pealing thunder of misfortune and poverty which stunned and blinded his moral perceptions. (NYL, August 14, 1858)

On May 4, 1867, Fern wrote that she thought "it would be cheaper to pick children out of the streets," and give them a decent life where they could learn to be good, than to "build jails and penitentiaries and gibbets to punish them when they grow up."

Fern was also critical of the penal system. Some of her criticism is evident in the novella "Fanny Ford," where she portrays the harsh and contemptuous treatment of the prisoners (FF, 133–136, 169–170). In her Blackwell's Island columns she calls for a more enlightened attitude toward prisoners, including some kind of work provided for them when they are released. "Anything but shutting a man up with hell in his heart to make him good," she concluded (NYL, August 14, 1858).

In May 1871 Fern visited a reformatory for women and was appalled at the gloomy surroundings and the rigid, inhuman attitude of the administration. She left feeling utterly crushed. Unlike many women of her class, Fern was able to put herself in the place of these female criminals. Having done so, she evolved her critique of a penal system which did not reform:

If *I* had by circumstances drifted in there, I should have scaled the walls the first chance, or else gone mad in such dismal surroundings, and with such dreadful memories to keep me silent company. This is *not* the way to reform such persons, I am sure of it. Anybody who has studied human nature or the subject, must know that. But alas! too often *they* are placed in control, who, with the best intentions perhaps, have done neither. (NYL, May 27, 1871)

Poverty and crime were not the only subjects that Fern brought to the attention of her comfortable middle-class readers, particularly her female readers. In February 1866, in an article entitled "Where the Money Is Made," Fern wrote about her visit to the Fulton Street Market and contrasted the ignorant frivolity of a fashionable woman's life with life in the business district. Such women had no idea how the money was made that they and their husbands both squandered; but, Fern concluded, even if she showed them, they would not be interested, and they would have only contempt for the woman who was:

I had just come from a different part of the city, where *the money is made to buy* those pretty boots, and silk stockings, and rich dresses; and it struck me how little those women even dreamed, how it looked down there. . . . I would have taken her little gaiter boots past the huge quarters of beef and mutton, and the stacks of pie, and the piles of peanuts, and the tubs of butter, and the great round cheeses; past the ruddy old women sitting at their stalls, with one layer of woolen shawl over another, till their natural proportions were a matter of mystery, sipping their hot cups of coffee, and chatting with everybody, and here I would have asked my lady if she herself, after all, were any happier? and then I would have taken her across the street to the dock wharfs, through carts laden with the skins of animals just taken from a huge vessel. . . . Perhaps she would have applied her handkerchief to her nose, and cried "enough," but I would have made her go on; up the big swarming street on the bank of the river, past all those dingy warehouses, labelled all over with "hides" and "oil" and "cordage," and "flour," and "beans," and "pork," and "tallow," and "pig-iron," and all such little luxuries, in whose dingy counting-rooms the fathers, and husbands, and brothers of these delicate ladies garnered up the dollars for the drygoods on their sweet backs. I would have shown her the old loafers just fit to put upon the stage of a theatre with their brimless hats, and patched jackets, and rainbow trousers, and blear eyes, and blue noses, and indescribable boots, with both hands in their own pockets, until they could find one of their neighbor's that was worth transferring them to. I would have pointed out the little beggars, running off with bruised oranges, and bananas, and lemons, and pocketing isolated cocoa-nuts and apples, and looking longingly at the great bales of cotton. . . . Then, if her pretty head was not crazed, dodging dirty carts and dirtier drivers, and her boots too tired to proceed, she should look at her favorite and elegant Adolphus, as he emerged from the dingy counting room, and buttoned up his disgusted and wearied nose for an omnibus ride to a very different and much sweeter smelling locality.

I think *that* could be a new experience for my lady—don't you? . . . But, bless me! what's the use of throwing any "pearls" but a jeweler's before such *fine* ladies. They would only think you were some horrid creature who wore your own hair and wanted women to vote. (NYL, February 24, 1866)

On March 10, 1866, Fern wrote about a visit to the Newsboys' Lodging House. Calling her readers' attention to the boys of seven to ten years old who, orphans generally, sold newspapers on the streets of New York, she urged that something be done for these children. She herself did not have a solution, or the power to effect one if she had, but she admired the very human proprietor of the lodging house, who had at least provided the children with a clean place to live and a caring environment. "Few people who stop these little fellows in the street to purchase a paper, ever glance at their faces, much less give a thought to their belongings, associations or condition," Fern said, pointing out that people *should* know and see how they lived. She contrasted these poor boys to the indulged darlings of some of her readers. Her method in this and in other portrayals of injustice was to force people to acknowledge, and, if possible, to identify with or at least to recognize the humanity of people less fortunate than they. Although she did not have an agenda for reform, she believed that the greatest motivation for reform was the ability to identify with the unfortunate or the exploited. As long as one could think of them as "the other" or "they," one could perhaps rest content with their suffering.[1]

On August 4, 1866, Fern described her visit to the morgue at Bellevue Hospital. On November 3 she described seeing a woman who was drunk. She said it was the first time she had seen a *lady* in this condition, but she went on to discuss the increased use of what she called "stimulants" by women, often on the prescription of a physician. Here Fern was referring not only to alcohol, but also to laudanum, or opium, which was routinely prescribed for women who complained of "nervousness" or other vague symptoms of unhappiness. "These are dangerous remedies," Fern said, "and the more so, because many of our women would be very glad of anything to deaden the pain, and disappointment, and ennui of their lives." One cannot help but see the connection between the women who were thus prescribed for in the mid-nineteenth century, and the twentieth-century women for whom doctors have prescribed tranquilizers or other drugs to "deaden the pain" of living.

On January 5, 1867, Fern reiterated her call for women's suffrage. The well-to-do woman who selfishly opposed it, Fern said, "may never see or think of those other women, who may be lifted out of their wretched condition, of low wages and starvation, by this very lever of power." Moreover, such misery was not confined to the poor: if one could "draw aside the veil" from many homes in the affluent areas of New York, one would see women who suffered "defilement and brutality" from the tyranny of husbands and fathers. All women would benefit from the vote, Fern said, asserting that there was not one reason against it that was even worth considering.

Also in January, Fern wrote a long article entitled "The Working-Girls of New York." James Parton, who was writing for the *Atlantic Monthly* at the time, had told the editors about his wife's article, and they were interested in publishing it. Fern had thought she could publish it in the *Atlantic Monthly* under her real name, rather than as Fanny Fern, which is how she was able to publish "A Literary Couple" in *Galaxy* also in 1867. However, Robert Bonner wanted the article, and he exercised his right as the exclusive publisher of Fern's work.[2] The article was published in the *Ledger* under the name Sara P. Parton rather than the name Fanny Fern. It appeared in the column usually reserved for Bonner's editorials. Fern began:

Nowhere more than in New York does the contrast between squalor and splendor so sharply present itself. . . . Jostling on the same pavement with the dainty-fashionist is the care-worn working-girl. Looking at both these women, the question arises, which lives the more miserable life—she whom the world styles "fortunate," whose husband belongs to three clubs, and whose only meal with his family is an occasional breakfast? . . . Or she—this other woman—with a heart quite as hungry and unappeased, who also faces day by day the same appalling question: *Is this all life has for me?* (NYL, January 26, 1867)

Having established this connection between the working woman and the fashionable woman, Fern went on to discuss the low salary, poor working conditions, and "dark, cheerless tenement houses" of the seamstresses, shop-girls, and female factory operatives. Her vivid pictures of the homes and workplaces of these women indicate that she had visited them and had talked with the women she writes about. Her picture of the women working in a hoop factory is suggestive of Melville's "Tartarus of Maids." The main difference is that the young women in Melville's story could look forward to marriage as a salvation from their daily grind. Fern notes that although working women might look forward to marrying in order to escape from the terrible conditions under which they worked, that route was often an illusion: the desperate young women would simply find themselves back at the tenement but "with this difference, that their toil does *not* end at six o'clock, and that from this bargain there is no release but death" (NYL, January 26, 1867).

Fern's solution to this problem is very modern—and one that even today has not yet been wholly effected: that women should receive equal pay for equal work, and that they should have access to all jobs for which they are qualified—without regard to gender. Meanwhile, she was glad to see new job opportunities open to women. Printers, waiters, clerks, minters, as well as physicians, artists, and lecturers: these are only some of the jobs that Fern commented on as they opened up to women—despite heavy criticism from her conservative contemporaries. Fern wrote on April 7, 1866: "I always make it a rule to stand by my own sex in any and every attempt to earn their own livelihood innocently and honestly." She also applauded any measures that would improve their lives. On December 5, 1868, Fern wrote about the work that benevolent ladies' groups had been doing in setting up respectable boardinghouses for working women. She congratulated these "excellent ladies who do something besides talk."

In "The Old Problem," on March 30, 1867, Fern portrayed an all-too-common scene, illustrating her belief that one must consider environmental causes for antisocial behavior:

> When the weary Barney McGuire, with his tin dinner pail, crosses at night the threshold of his miserable tenement-house home, and sees the same stereotyped dismal picture, of a frouzy wife at the wash-tub, and a dozen fractious children, quarrelling at her draggled skirts, I cannot but feel a strong sympathy for Barney; and when I read in the morning paper that he was on trial "for a drunken brawl" the evening before, I well understand that he might be drawn into it because he was too utterly disheartened to sit down amid the filthy, uncomfortable surroundings of the dirty little room he called "home."
>
> But what of *Mrs.* Barney McGuire? that human fixture, with her per-petual baby, and its snarling brothers and sisters, whose disputes she has only time to settle with a hasty slap or a rough pitch out of her way? Though it is very hard for Barney, I think it is much harder for her, and I can't think that Barney betters matters much, by giving her only enough of his sympathy and presence as to run for the doctor at the birth of their thirteenth child.

It is significant that Fern looked at the effects of poverty on women as well as on men. In this essay she sympathizes with the poor laborer and *also* with his wife. Fern was impatient with those who would piously judge or blame the victims of poverty; she looked for other solutions. This is partic-ularly evident in her writing on prostitution. When she visited Blackwell's Island, Fern wrote of the prostitutes she saw there, refusing to abide by the taboos of her time which insisted that such women should not even be named. Arguing against the double standard of those who would cross the street to avoid one of these women, while at the same time inviting to their homes the men who patronized them, Fern denied the arguments of legisla-tors and public officials that such women were "mere animals, naturally coarse and grovelling" (NYL, August 28, 1858). Once again, she was able to put herself into the place of "the other"—in this case a most shocking identification for her readers. Having worked as a seamstress, Fern knew how impossible it was to live on such a meager income; she also knew from experience how few job opportunities were open to women. This made her sympathetic to the plight of working women who gave up in their attempts to earn their living by conventionally respectable means. "Where's the mar-vel?" she asked, when commenting on the numbers of poor women who turned to prostitution (TF, January 29, 1853).

While Fern was writing about these issues, her life at 303 East Eighteenth Street went on as usual. Occasional references to family issues appear in her column. On March 3, 1866, for example, she wrote about having a furnace installed. This was an innovation, and Fern's column, which was written humorously, tells of the way in which she handled two potentially dangerous situations. In both instances, Fern reveals herself as a quick-thinking, take-charge person in emergencies. In one instance the maid was overcome by fumes escaping from the furnace. Fern ran to her assistance, quickly throwing open the windows and working with the woman until she came to. The other instance occurred one evening when no one was at home but Fern, her daughter, and little Effie. They smelled smoke, and going into the basement, found that the ceiling was ablaze. Fern sent Ellen with the baby to a neighbor's and commandeered a man from the street. A neighbor joined them, and together they set up a water chain from the pump and tore up the floorboards, saturating the area with water until the fire was out.

On April 14, 1866, Fern wrote about "Mr. Fern on the Jury." "Who's to console *me* for my solitary dinners," she asked, and what about Mr. Fern's writing deadlines and his weak stomach? "Suppose *I* go in your place?" she said to him. "Now there's an idea! Shouldn't I like to twist up those lawyers? I have a great mind to try it." Fern's granddaughter occasionally appeared in her column also. On June 30, 1866, Fern wrote "A Grandmother's Dilemma," describing her recognition of Effie's buoyant spirits, which she would not destroy in order to make the child into a well-behaved automaton: "I have given it up; with shame and confusion of face, I own that child *governs me*. I know her *heart* is all right; I know there's not a grain of *badness* in her; I know she would die to-day, if she hadn't those few flaws to keep her alive. In short, she's *my grandchild*. Isn't that enough?"

Fern also wrote about going to concerts, lectures, and the opera. On December 1, 1866, she reiterated her dislike of what she called artificial music:

When I go to a fashionable concert, and the lady *"artiste,"* I believe that is the regulation-word, comes out in her best bib and tucker, with a gilt battle-axe in her back hair, and a sun-flower in her bosom, led by the tips of her white gloves, by the light of a gleaming bracelet, and stands there twiddling a sheet of music, preparatory to the initiatory screech, I feel like screeching myself. . . . Then if you only knew the agony of perspiration I'm in, when drawing near the end of one of her musical gymnastics, she essays to wind up with one of those swift, deafening *don't-stop-to-breathe finales*, you *would* pity me. I get hysterical. I wish she would split her throat at once, or stop.

Fern and Parton spent the summer of 1867 once again in the mountains. Fern was glad to get away from the city. On May 18, however, she wrote about her annoyance at all of the preparations that had to be made before she could go: "How disgusting is the road women must travel to assure all this happiness. Woolens and furs to be put safely out of reach of moths. House cleaning and carpet shaking to be done. Dresses to be bought, and horror! worse than all, to be fitted. Trunks to be packed—writing to be done, weeks ahead. My brain spins to think what a purgatory one must travel through, to reach that serene heaven, the bird-peeping morning of the country."

In July 1867 Fern and Parton sailed up Lake Champlain to St. Albans and spent the summer in Highgate Springs, Vermont. They settled in a farmhouse, which they regarded as the healthiest environment for Effie. Fern wrote on July 6: "I consider it a crime to defraud childhood of its happy country experience. At no *fashionable* place of resort can this be attained." At such resorts, she said, a child must change its clothes a half dozen times for "show parade in a public parlor." In the country no one cared about clothes, she said, and the happy child could "dig in the dirt, and roll in the grass, and tumble in the barn, unchecked by care of the sacred dry-goods." Adults, too, could dress casually. A woman could wear her "morning calico" all day and a pair of stout boots; she could go over fences and across fields, climb hills, and lounge on the grass (NYL, September 14, 1867).

One complaint that Fern had about summer resorts was that other residents pointed out the famous Fanny Fern, commenting on her appearance, her children, her husband, her manners:

"Is that hair her own?" What can she be saying to that man, who is *not* her husband? What an affectation in her always to wear black. For pity's sake, when does *she*, who is forever flying about, find time to write? Don't you suppose that her husband does it for her? *Her* children are no brighter than other people's, as far as I can see. I wonder how her house looks? . . . [A]s to her looks, did you ever see one of these scribbling women who wasn't a fright? Where there are brains, my dear, never do you look for grace, or beauty, or taste in dress; put *that* in your notebook. Hark! there's the dinner-bell; now we'll see whether she eats with her knife, like the rest of the strong-minded. (NYL, September 28, 1867)

In 1867–1868 Charles Dickens was visiting the United States, and in January 1868 Fern and Parton went to hear him speak at Henry Ward Beecher's church. Parton was quite taken with the writer, but Fern was not impressed. She wrote in a letter to General Butler:

I have been to hear the great Dickens. I hate him. No old girl could be vainer. He travels about with a lot of men—millinery in the shape of becoming lights—a crimson screen behind to tone down the rubicund John Bulliam of his face. . . . Mr. Parton clapped his hands till they were blistered, when he heard him—and turning around to me with glowing

face, said, "Fanny, what do you think of that?" "I hate him," I said, with
my eyes on his two vests and the obnoxious rosebud. I wanted to see a
man.[3]

The New York Press Club invited Dickens to a dinner that was to take
place on April 18. Only men were members of the Press Club; only men
were invited to the dinner. Some of the members objected, saying that there
were eminent women journalists who should be invited to the dinner. James
Parton wrote to James T. Fields on February 29, 1868: "There ought to be
ladies at the Press dinner to Dickens."[4] Three women applied for member-
ship in the Press Club, among them Fanny Fern, but their applications were
laughed at. The more conservative members of the club refused to permit
women to be present at the dinner, unless they were seated in the gallery
simply to watch the proceedings. The women refused to attend under such
conditions, and the dinner went on without them. On May 16 Fern published a column describing the situation:

There was lately a dinner given in New York to a literary gentleman of
distinction. One of the gentlemen invited to attend it, said to his wife: "It
is a shame that ladies should not attend this dinner. *You* ought to be
there, and many other ladies who are authors." Acting upon this impulse,
he suggested to the committee that ladies should be invited. The answer
was . . . "It would be so awkward for the ladies." . . . [A]s to the question
of "awkwardness," the boot, I think, was on the other foot. . . . In short,
these men would be obliged to conduct themselves as gentlemen were
ladies present; and they wanted a margin left for the reverse. They preferred a bar-room atmosphere to the refining presence of "lovely woman,"
about whom they wished to hiccup at a safe distance.
    Perhaps, in justice, I should add, that it was suggested, that they might
perhaps see the animals feed from "the musicians' balcony," or listen to
the speeches "through the crack of a door," with the servants, or in some
such surreptitious and becoming and complimentary manner, which a
woman of spirit and intelligence would, of course, be very likely to do.
(NYL, May 16, 1868)

After this incident, the women newspaper writers decided to form their
own club, which they named Sorosis,[5] and the following year the members
of Sorosis were invited to the New York Press Club Dinner at Delmonico's.
Fanny Fern and James Parton were at the head table, and the first toast was:
"Woman's kingdom: if it is not kingdom come, it is kingdom coming."[6]
Although this occasion represented a victory for literary women, there was
still a long way for them to go, as indicated by the *Atlantic Monthly's* refusal to invite its women contributors to its twentieth-anniversary dinner in
1877.[7]

Fanny Fern was asked to be the first president of Sorosis, but she declined, accepting a post as one of the vice presidents, and Alice Cary was elected president. Cary resigned because of illness, and Jane Croly (Jennie June) became president.[8] This was the first women's club in the United States. The women received a great deal of criticism for their action, but the idea of women's clubs soon caught on and Sorosis became a model for women's clubs all over the country. Fern defended the formation of the club in her June 6, 1868, column:

Yes; they have "done it." Ladies—fie, for shame on them!—have "organized a club!" They meet at a perfectly respectable and fashionable restaurant; they lunch there; they eat there; they talk there; but their offence seems to consist in the fact that the matter and manner of their talk, on those occasions, is as yet an undivulged secret. . . . One editor so far forgot good breeding—if he had any—as to caricature in an engraving ladies of irreproachable standing in the community—one of them being represented as unable to sit up, and in a reclining posture, with a book falling from her hands.

Comment on this is needless, to those acquainted with the members of the Ladies' Club. Such impertinent coarseness only recoils on the perpetrators. . . . Now, I fail to see why it is not just as right, when the wives of these men are left to take care of themselves . . . , that they should not have equal privileges. I fail to see why it should be assumed that, because they do so, they are disgracing themselves, any more than that their husbands, and fathers, and brothers are doing the same. Nay more, I say that, where a man has need of such relaxation and amusement, his wife has five times the necessity for it, owing to . . . the endless, wearing, petty details of her life, and the lack of out-of-door relief from the same.

16

Last Years

Ah! leave us a few more blessed days and nights like these, for who knows whether September will ever come again to some of us?
NYL, October 15, 1870

WHEN FANNY FERN DECLINED TO ACCEPT THE PRESIDENCY OF SOROSIS or to participate actively in the club—although she lent her name to it—it may have been simply because, although she sympathized with the idea of the club, she did not want to take the time that active involvement would have entailed. But there is another reason why she did not become involved in the club, a reason that was a secret from all but her immediate family. The year before the Dickens dinner, Fern had discovered that she had a terminal cancer. She continued to write her column as though nothing was wrong, and, as long as she continued to look well, no one suspected that she was ill. After her death her husband described Fern's attitude toward her illness:

She suddenly became aware that she was afflicted with mortal disease. I well remember the moment when the certainty of this fact became manifest to her mind. A flush spread over her face, but she said nothing except that she should go at once to the doctor for his final opinion. Her life during the next six years was a contest with death; and what made it the more remarkable was, that the conflict went on in secrecy. From the moment when she discovered her condition, she determined that, if she could not avoid being sick, she would at least avoid appearing so. Her most intimate friends and nearest neighbors saw her for years come and go, visited her, and received her visits, without suspecting her condition; supposing, all the while, that she, if no other woman in the world, was in perfect health. Her appearance was even improved at times by the flush which pain brought to her cheeks; and, until within the last year of her life, her appetite was keener, her spirits higher, and her capacity for enjoying life greater than before. (JP, 71–72)

Fern's columns continued as they had before, and her readers would not have guessed from her columns that anything was wrong. In retrospect, however, one can find occasional references which suggest her knowledge of the imminent fatality with which she was living. Given James Parton's dating of the onset of her illness as occurring after her fifty-fifth year, a close analysis of her columns suggests that she first learned of her illness early in 1867. On March 23 of that year she published in the *Ledger* an article entitled "A Child's Mission," which described the joy that a young child can bring into the life of one who is in the depths of despair. Effie was four years old. The article, which is also interesting as a portrayal of Fern's relationship with her little granddaughter, is significant as a record of her state of mind upon the realization of the imminence of her own death:

> I think there is nothing on earth so lovely as the first waking of a little child in the morning. The gleeful, chirping voice. The bright eye. . . . The perfect happiness—the perfect faith in all future to-morrows!
>
> We who have lain our heads on our pillows so often, with great sorrows for company; . . . We who have awoke in the morning, with a sharp shuddering cry at the awful reality, and closed our eyes again wearily upon the sweet morning's light . . . ; we who have risen, and with a dead, dull weight at the heart, moved about mechanically like one walking in sleep, through the gray, colorless treadmill routine of to-day, a wonder to ourselves—ah! with what infinite love and pity do such look upon the blithe waking of the little child! As it leaps trustfully into our arms, with its morning caress and its soft cheek to our face, how hard it is sometimes to keep the eyes from overflowing with the pent-up pain of the slow years. Oh, the sweet beguilement of that caress! . . . The saucy little challenge "to play!"
>
> *We* play? We swallow a great sob and get obediently down on the carpet to "build block-houses"; and when the little one laughs, as the tall structure reels, and topples, and finally falls over, and merrily stands showing the little white teeth and clapping hands, and peeping into our face, and says reproachfully, What are you thinking about? Why don't *you* laugh?—we thank God she has so long a time before she finds out that grieving "why." . . . And in spite of ourselves, we laugh.

This column brings a new note to Fern's columns: although she had been sharp and cynical in the past, and although she had certainly written of loss and suffering and the burdens that come with living, previous columns had always reflected a snap-to mentality, that is, a realization that it is profitless to bemoan one's fate and a determination to swing into action. In this article she indicates that she is ready to throw in the towel, that it is only the child Effie who gives her the strength to rise above despair. This column is, however, an isolated instance of such an attitude, and it is its difference and its singularity that suggest that it marked the period during which Fern first became aware that she was dying.

Reading this column with a knowledge of the secret of which Fern had just become aware gives a powerful poignancy to Fern's portrayal of the contrast between the confident joy of the young child and the despair of the adult who feels "a dull, dead weight at the heart." Moreover, any reader who has experienced difficulty responding to a child's challenge to play in the midst of distractions of less import than one's impending death can recognize the effort required by Fern in the incident described in this column. The column also provides an indication of the almost superhuman effort that was to characterize Fern's last years. Despite her initial response of an incredulous "We play?" she swallows a great sob and joins in the happy game. Fern's response to the child's challenge foreshadows her response to the challenge of death during the remaining years of her life: she refused to succumb to despair and joined in the game of life with her usual gusto. This is all the more remarkable since all of the conventions of her culture would have encouraged her to do otherwise. At a time when women were encouraged by their society to appear sick when they were well, when female hypochondria was regarded as fashionable and ladylike behavior, Fern was doubly unusual in that she not only condemned what she called "fashionable invalidism" among women who were well (NYL, July 27, 1867), she also refused to become an invalid when she was in fact ill.

James Parton indicates that after the realization of her illness, Fern continued her life as before. Her columns, which continued to appear every week, were as caustic and as outspoken as they had always been. In July 1868 she published a new collection of her essays, *Folly As It Flies,* her first adult collection in eleven years. Two years later she published *Ginger-Snaps,* and 1872 marked the appearance of *Caper-Sauce.* Knowing that her years were limited, she apparently wished to get together her articles as quickly as possible. One suspects also that, knowing she was dying, she wanted to publish these collections of her articles in order to assure an income for her daughter and granddaughter. James Parton, when he was writing *Fanny Fern, A Memorial Volume,* which was published in 1873, the year after her death, said that part of his motivation in preparing the book was to provide an income for Effie.[1]

From June to late September of 1868 Fern and Parton, along with Ellen and Effie, spent the summer at a hotel in Stockbridge, Massachusetts.[2] In an article on July 18, 1868, she reasserted her vigorous good health and stated her impatience with the celebrity hunters who still pursued her:

[I]f you see me coming in to dinner, and think it worth while to announce the fact, in a place where there is a dearth of news, just do it quietly, so that I sha'n't feel like throwing a biscuit at your head, and don't think because I am a literary woman, and a member of the "Sorosis" that I live on violets and dew—I don't. I wear awful thick shoes, and go out in the mud, and like to get stuck there; and I am horrid old—fifty-six—and ugly besides; and I shall speak when I feel like it, and when I don't, I sha'n't, because it is too much to be on my good behavior all the year round, and this is my vacation.

In Stockbridge Fern relived the memories of visiting her sister Louisa in Stockbridge when she, Fern, was a schoolgirl (NYL, August 1, 1868). For years Fern and Parton had been contemplating buying a house in the country, although they were never to do so:

> [W]e cross the meadow—to the tell-tale willows, behind which the river hides, and listen to its peaceful flow; and say for the thousandth time, that we *will* own "a place" in the country; but, nevertheless, it is ten to one, that next summer will find us staring at the "place" of somebody else, and allowing him the privilege of keeping it in order for us, and settling the bills for the same. Alas! that the tools with which scribblers work can be sharpened and kept from rusting only on that grindstone—*the city.* (NYL, August 15, October, 24, 1868)

The summer was flawed by sickness, however. Both Parton and Fern were ill.[3] Fern was confined to bed for over a week with a sore throat and total loss of speech, and even after she got out of bed she was uncharacteristically tired all the time (NYL, September 19, 1868).

In 1868 Parton edited *Eminent Women of the Age,* a collection of biographical sketches of prominent women. Grace Greenwood (Sara Lippincott) wrote the article on Fern, and Fern wrote one on Gail Hamilton (Mary Abigail Dodge).[4] The following year Gail Hamilton wrote several letters to Parton and Fern, complaining of her ill-treatment by Ticknor and Fields, who paid her less than they did their male contributors.[5]

Early in 1868 Harriet Beecher Stowe wrote to James Parton thanking him for his kind words about her in his article on the need for an International Copyright Law, published in the *Atlantic Monthly* in October 1867. In her letter she included mention of Sarah Willis, whom she had known as a "bright laughing witch of a half saint, half sinner" in her sister's school in Hartford.[6] Fern replied to Stowe on February 14, 1868, in a letter accompanying Parton's:

> My dear "Miss Harriet"—
> That's the title you had in the old school days. So I shall stick to it. I say Amen to all Mr. Parton has written. I also say, that he is no more fit to make a bargain than your dear Mr. Stowe is. I say that I have to put him up to all the impudence he has, & that I daren't leave his side a moment when a bargain is imminent, lest he should "put his foot in it." He will dig & delve forever & be forever fleeced by those publishing wolves I am afraid. I think you and I will understand "speaking up in meetin'" for

them, and will act for ourselves. I wish they were all like Bonner of the Ledger, who sent me the other day a check for five hundred (over & above the liberal pay I get every week) as an expression of his "good will," & it is not the first time he has remembered me in this way. But make what we may, New York is a horrid vortex & swallows it all up.[7]

Fern's letter provides an interesting look at the relationship between her and James Parton. Whitman had blamed Fern for Parton's insistence that he return the money he owed Parton, and Fern's portrayal of Parton's lack of forcefulness in business relationships suggests that Whitman was right—that it was Fern who took the strong stand. The letter is also interesting as a comment on society's expectations for men and women. Stowe's husband had done the negotiating for her before *Uncle Tom's Cabin* was published, and his failure to take a strong stand had lost her thousands of dollars.[8] Fern did her own negotiating, or had a lawyer do it for her. As she makes clear in this letter to Stowe, husbands are not necessarily better at business negotiations just because they are men.

This letter opened up a correspondence between Stowe and Fern in which they discussed, among other things, women's suffrage and women's rights. Stowe declared on July 25, 1868: "Yes, I do believe in Female Suffrage— The more I think of it the more absurd this whole government of man over woman looks. . . . I hold to woman's rights to the extent that a woman's own native name never ought to die out and be merged in the name of any man whatever."[9] Stowe also wrote to congratulate Parton through Fanny Fern on his antismoking article, which, according to his biographer, ironically gained more attention than anything else he wrote.[10] Although Fern had been writing against smoking for years, Parton was a heavy smoker who had recently given up the habit. In 1869 Stowe wrote to Parton and Fern about the controversial article she was writing on Byron's incestuous relationship with his half-sister. They encouraged her to write the truth, and when the article was published in the *Atlantic Monthly* in September 1869 it created a scandal.[11]

In the spring of 1869 Fern and Parton traveled to Washington, where Parton apparently sought assistance in developing an International Copyright Law.[12] In her column in the *Ledger* on April 10, 1869, Fern described sitting in the lobbyists' room in the White House, and expressed her approval of the fact that a woman, Vinnie Ream, had been commissioned to make the statue of Lincoln.

The days at home were brightened by the presence of Fern's granddaughter, whose reminiscences provide us with a vivid picture of life in Fern's household from the child's perspective. In an article entitled "A Little Girl and Two Authors," published in 1941, Ethel Parton describes how as a very young child she could go to her grandmother, "Nanny," with any question and expect to have the question answered and/or discussed reasonably and without impatience or ridicule. Once, for example, she was bewildered by the fact that several days' rain had prevented a planned outing to Central Park, and she went to ask her grandmother why the rainy days did not alternate with sunny days, which, to her child's mind, seemed a fairer arrangement. Her grandmother "did not laugh"; she explained that "weather happens just anyhow," and the child and her grandmother "gravely" discussed the problem.[13]

Ethel Parton tells of a rare instance when she had been punished by her grandmother by being confined to her room. As she lay in her bed she pondered what she regarded as the injustice of the punishment, and, her resentment growing, she climbed out of bed, and, still wearing her long white nightgown, descended the stairs into the parlor, where Fern and Parton were entertaining guests. The small child marched up to her amazed grandmother, stamped her foot, and declared: "You are a bad, Bad, BAD woman!" Fern was so amused at the child's audacity that little Effie (who was probably around three or four at the time) was passed around the equally amused guests: "I remember among them Horace Greeley's round, beaming face, set in its sunflower fringe of white whiskers—and then [I was] carried upstairs in the arms of James Parton and put back in bed, where, having relieved my mind, I curled down willingly enough, with a cracker and my doll for company."[14]

Fern believed that schooling should not begin until a child was seven. At that time it was decided that, instead of sending Effie to school, she would be instructed at home by James Parton. Ethel Parton remembered with joy their daily sessions in his study at the top of the house. Her education was not confined to those hours, however; he taught spontaneously in their daily companionship as well. Every day Fern would make out a list of necessary errands, and Parton, accompanied by Effie, would go out for a walk after breakfast. Ethel Parton remembers particularly their visits to grocer and butcher, when Parton would explain any new and unusual foods, and she would beg him to purchase them. One day they found the "great black furry carcass of a bear" at the butcher's, and Parton ordered bear steak. That night the little girl was excited to have bear for dinner, although it was pretty tough and it gave Parton a "frightful attack of indigestion."[15]

As Fern occasionally mentioned in her columns, she had a very sensitive nose. This caused her, late in life, to prohibit the cooking of pungent vegetables like turnips and cabbage. Only when Fern and Parton were away did the household staff cook the forbidden vegetables. One of little Effie's first attempts at letter writing was five words written in all capitals, which her Aunt Ellen mailed to Fern: "DEAR NANNY WE HAVE TERNIBS."[16]

In June 1869 Fern and Parton and their family left the city for Cape Ann. After taking the train and steamboat to Boston, Fern walked on the Boston Common with Effie, recalling her days there both as a child and later as a mother of her own little girls, one of them Effie's mother. They visited

Mount Auburn Cemetery, where were buried Fern's first husband and her two daughters. Fern noted that she, too, would be buried there some day, and her comments reveal the anguish that she felt at the realization that she would never see Effie grow up: "The hardest pang I shall know, between now and then, will be letting go the little hand that clasped mine to-day, as I walked about there" (NYL, August 7, 1869). Although Fern's readers would not have known of Fern's fatal illness, today's readers who know of it can see the heartache that underlay these words; the thought of leaving little Effie again motherless must have been hard to bear. In fact, that she was able to live as long as she did seems to have been due almost to a sustained act of will motivated by her determination to remain with Effie as long as she possibly could.

At Cape Ann Fern went for walks along the beach and admired the wild beauty of the ocean. She had a number of complaints about the place, however: the washing was poorly done, and she did not enjoy the bread or the minister's sermons, both of which she said were indigestible (NYL, August 14, August 21, August 28, September 18, September 25, October 2, 1869). Before going back to New York the family stopped at Plymouth, where Fern visited a women's prison and wrote about the poor conditions, particularly the lack of any facilities for the women's babies (NYL, October 9, 1869). She also visited Daniel Webster's house, remembering how she had admired him before his failure to oppose slavery (NYL, October 16, 1869).

Back in New York Fern continued to confront the "woman question" in her column. The women of 1869, she said, were "howling for their rights," and she urged them on. On October 23, 1869, she wrote about a woman in an earlier period whose rights were so circumscribed that she was reprimanded by the church fathers for advising her husband to buy land. On November 6, 1869, she wrote of specific American women who had "helped themselves to their rights." And on November 13, 1869, she attacked the New York daily press for its mean-spirited and flippant treatment of women's issues. On December 18 she wrote on women's salaries, advising women to earn their own money when they could rather than becoming simply the "serf" of a tyrannical husband.

On February 19, 1870, Fern wrote a humorous article about her illness. Her readers would not have understood the seriousness of the illness that confined her to her bed. Knowing the seriousness of her illness, however, and knowing that, although she would rally temporarily, she would not recover, one can see the bitter anguish in her distress at being ill:

I know nothing more distressing to a self-helpful person than to be laid on the shelf—sick! To lie like a baby and be fed; to have your face and hands washed, and your hair combed for you; to be read *to*, instead of reading yourself; for, after all, how is anyone to guess that which you like best in your morning paper to hear? To have somebody else, over-water your pretty plants, or forget to water them altogether. . . . Now I *hate* to be waited on. It hurts my independence. I hate to lie in bed. . . . I like sunlight and tornadoes of fresh air. I hate gruel and messes and drugs, and hot pillows. I like ale, and a long walk, and light, easy clothing.

In 1868 and 1870 there was a series of interchanges in the *Ledger* between Fern and Henry Ward Beecher. On May 2, 1868, Fern had written an article criticizing Beecher for advocating candy for children, which elicited a reply from Beecher. Fern, whose concern with nutrition and tooth decay was surprisingly modern, maintained that candy as a regular diet for children was unhealthy. Then, on February 5, 1870, Beecher wrote in the *Ledger* about a box of candy that had been sent to him. Fern replied on February 26 that she was a faithful adherent of his, "leaving out the candy."

In 1936 Fern's granddaughter published "A New York Childhood: The Seventies in Stuyvesant Square," an article in *The New Yorker* describing her life in New York at this time. She recounts walks and omnibus rides with Parton and Fern, both of whom made the walks entertaining as well as educational. She walked on Fifth Avenue, in Gramercy Park, to which they had a key, and in Stuyvesant Square, as well as taking less conventional trips to the business district and the waterfront. On one occasion Parton took her for a walk around sordid neighborhoods near the East River. During these walks she sometimes met other literary personalities. Among those she remembered were Bret Harte, who forced an unwanted kiss on the indignant child, and William Cullen Bryant, "bearded, grave, and looking as if he came out of an illustrated Bible." Horace Greeley visited the house, sometimes bringing his little girl, Gabrielle, to play with Effie. Similarly, Thomas Nast, who had married Parton's cousin Sarah Edwards, visited with his daughter Julia, who was also Effie's playmate. During this time Fern and Ethel sometimes amused themselves on their walks by trying to guess what type of people lived in the houses they passed and inventing stories about those they did not know. One day they passed a very lavishly decorated house, and when Ethel wondered about who lived there, her grandmother answered sharply, "A thief." Ethel, who till then had thought of thieves as "homeless wretches," was surprised, but Fern explained that the resident of the house was Peter Sweeny, a member of the Tweed Ring which at that time was looting the city through Tammany Hall, the corrupt political machine.[17]

Ethel Parton describes entertainment at 303 East Eighteenth Street as "simple and informal." On New Year's Day Fern had for years followed the tradition of conducting an open house. The custom required a gentleman to visit a number of different homes on New Year's Day; by the time the man had drunk punch at several homes, he was often in a state of intoxication before he finished his calls. However, in the 1870s, like other hostesses in New York who had become tired of holding an open house for inebriated gentlemen, Fern adopted the custom of simply leaving a beribboned basket tied to the front door on New Year's Day in which callers could leave their cards. Ethel remembers that the basket was always full to overflowing and describes how one morning-after she found a number of cards which had fallen to the ground, their owners having been too unsteady to aim accurately into the basket. Some of these cards had collected in the sodden cavity of a top hat that one of the callers had lost.[18]

In March 1870 Fern and Parton traveled to Philadelphia, Baltimore, and Washington en route to Virginia. Fern's columns describe the deterioration of the hotels as they proceeded south (NYL, April 2, 1870). Always the prey of celebrity hunters, Fern was amused by a visit to the opera in April of that year after she had returned to New York. During the performance she overheard people talking about her with pretended familiarity:

In two orchestra chairs, directly in front of me, sat a lady and gentleman, both utter strangers to me. Said the *gentleman* to his companion, "Do you see the lady who has just entered yonder box?" pointing, as he did so, to the gallery; "well, that is Fanny Fern."—"You know her, then?" asked the lady.—"intimately," replied this strange gentleman—"*intimately.* Observe how expensively she is dressed. See those diamonds, and that lace! Well, I assure you, that every cent she has ever earned by her writings goes straightway upon her back." Naturally desiring to know how I did look, I used my opera-glass. The lady was tall, handsome, graceful, and beautifully dressed. The gentleman who accompanied me began to grow red in the face, at the statement of my "intimate" acquaintance, and insisted on a word with him; but the fun was too good to be spoiled. (NYL, April 9, 1870)

During the summer of 1870 Fern and Parton took Ellen and Effie to Orchard Beach in Maine for the summer. Fern, her health failing, would have been content to remain in the city rather than undertake the effort required to move to the country for the summer, but she felt it would be a crime to keep Effie in the city all summer: "Were it not for Bright Eyes, my heart would fail me at thought of leaving" (NYL, June 11, 1870). That summer they also visited Litchfield and saw the Beechers' home (NYL, July 23, 1870). Henry Ward Beecher replied to this article in the *Ledger* on August 6, expressing pleasure that she had gone to Litchfield. At Orchard Beach Fern and her family stayed in a hotel, having decided that boarding at a farmhouse was not for them. On September 10, 1870, she wrote in the *Ledger* describing their activities. Her illness was not incapacitating until her last year, and she enjoyed the rest and beauty of the site:

What do we do all day at the sea-shore? Why we "lay off." . . . What with bathing and getting dry—what with riding and walking, both on the beach and in the woods— . . . what with receiving letters, and answering them—what with discussing the war news—what with watching the young people pair off in a state of bread-and-butter felicity, and hoping that the wool may continue to be pulled over their bright eyes— . . . what with seeing new phases of human nature at every step, and being astonished to see how soon some people are sounded and how fathomless are others—what with eating and drinking, and hating to go to bed and hating to get up, I hope you understand that we have enough to do.

On October 15, 1870, Fern wrote of her reluctant good-bye to the beach, indicating that she tended to linger to "make much of the present gladness." Her comments indicate her awareness of the fact that such enjoyment might not come again.

At the end of 1870 James Parton went on the lecture circuit. Fern traveled with him to Boston, where she wrote home to Ellen that she had "grown fat!"[19] On December 9 she wrote to Effie, telling her of a visit to the house she grew up in:

My little dear Pet:

I should write a word to "Aunt" [her daughter Ellen] or Julia [Fern's sister]. I am going to write to you. I think of you all the time. . . . I look into all the shop windows and wonder what you would like. I have bought something for Nelly & Susan, but that is a *secret.* The Common looks very green & nice and when I walk there, I wish so much that you were running down the paths before me. . . . I went Sunday with Jim [James Parton] to see the house where I used to play when I was a little girl. *Such* a time as I had to find the old street I used to live in. . . . [T]hey have had time since then to pull all the houses and gardens to pieces and build great stores instead. And worse than all they had taken away the name of the street and given it a new one. They called *my* street Congress Street instead of Atkinson. But I found a big policeman & he told me about it, & then Jim & I poked round to find the pretty garden I used to play in & the house with the honeysuckle over the door—but oh dear! Instead of honeysuckle over the door—a lot of old frowsy Irish heads peeped out of the windows! ten or eleven at each window, & said "See the lady!" & the garden had gone, & a house stood on it—& I said to Jim—"Oh dear I feel like Rip Van Winkle." Wasn't it too bad? . . . & then I came home to the hotel—and felt as if I ought to be an old lady if I ain't! but instead I ate turkey & mince pie & drank some wine & saved the ice-cream for you! I wasn't going to freeze that turkey up in my stomach! and in the evening I drank tea with Mrs. Dana & Hartley & Henrietta kept saying "tell us some more things about that dear little Effie." Tomorrow I am going to Newton to see cousin Imogen's [N. P. Willis's daughter] little baby—with Mary Jenkins [Fern's sister]. Jim goes

away to lecture every night & comes home in the morning, & I put a few
of his old boots outside the door—to make them think a man inside!
Goodbye darling. I shall soon be home & bring you something finally.

Fanny[20]

  Fern's column during her last two years was as varied as ever. On January
7, 1871, she described her visit to Boston where Parton was lecturing. On
February 11 of the same year she wrote about a fashionable reception she
had been to, lamenting the formality and the crowding, and on March 3 and
11 she wrote about the discomfort and frivolousness of women's fashions.
On June 10 she noted that offers were pouring in from country boarding
places offering free board if she would agree to stay there. However, she
said she knew such offers were not really "free"; she wanted to be able to
say what she really thought of any place that she went.
  The last two summers of her life Fern went with her family to Newport,
where they rented a cottage. In 1871 she was able to join in the social activities of the place, her illness still not being known to those outside her family. She and Parton were members of the Town and Country Club of
Newport, an organization of literary people that grew out of their activities
that summer. Among its other members were Julia Ward Howe, who was
president at this time, Colonel Thomas Wentworth Higginson, and Helen
Hunt Jackson. A Mock Commencement organized by the club was the high-
light of the summer of 1871. Julia Ward Howe wrote in her *Reminiscences*
of the "brilliant conjunction of stars" and "the delicious fooling" of that
evening. The evening began with the "faculty," including Fern and Parton,
marching up the aisle with mock solemnity, wearing academic caps and
gowns. Howe acted as college president, and the various members of the
faculty gave mock orations. The program for the occasion, printed in Latin,
is among Fern's papers in the Sophia Smith Collection at Smith College. It
lists a lecture entitled "Thesis Rhinosophica: Our Noses and What to Do
with Them," by "Francisca Felix Parton, Jacobi Uxor," and another lecture
entitled "Oratio Historioni: The Ideal New York Alderman," by "Jacobus
Parton." Fern gave her talk, which Howe illustrated on the blackboard by
the equation:

$$\text{"Nose} + \text{nose} + \text{nose} = \text{proboscis}$$
$$\text{Nose} - \text{nose} - \text{nose} = \text{snub."}[21]$$

Fern became very fond of Newport, and in an article on July 22, 1871,
described Newport as "Our Emerald Isle": "Newport remains the gem of
seaside resorts, combining as it does, society or seclusion at your pleasure."
  Particularly during these last years, Fern was resentful of enforced society; she wrote in the *Ledger* on July 29, 1871, of her annoyance at strangers

or acquaintances that she met at summer resorts who acted as though she should be "on call" to entertain them:

[I]t is a mistaken idea that overworked literary people go into society to amuse and entertain the crowd. . . . There must be *some time* for rest, even for these servants of the public. Said a person, one evening, to me, at a place of summer resort, "Fanny, they say you can do this, and that, and the other thing; and yet you have *done nothing to amuse us* since you came here." "Very good," replied I, "we will talk about that when you do something for *my* amusement. You are an idler, I am a worker, and I came here to do just what you complain of—*to rest."* . . .
Now nothing can be more delightful than to make agreeable acquaintances. . . . But this prying open leaves, even humble Fern leaves, with curious, not loving fingers, merely to pass an idle hour, . . . is quite another *branch* of the business.

Fern also wrote with annoyance about the way in which people seemed to demand the mother's personality and talent from the daughters of literary women. Fearing gossip, and also unsure of herself, her daughter Ellen was quiet in company. Fern said that she herself was used to gossip and knew how to handle it, but it would take a young person a long time to reach that point. Others might criticize such a daughter for not "shining," but Fern knew that the worst error of parents was to try to mold or mend a child's nature (NYL, September 2, 1871). Ellen had been precocious and outspoken as a child and young girl, which is apparent in Gunn's diary: he criticized Ellen, whom he knew from age eleven to fourteen, saying that she was unfortunately too much like her mother.[22] Moreover, the "incorrigible Nettie" in *Ruth Hall*, who was based on Ellen, is portrayed as similarly precocious (RH, 192). It is surprising, then, to see Ellen at twenty-seven criticized for being too quiet. If as Fern says in this article, within the family circle Ellen was "witty and sparkling," but in company was quiet, one can only conclude that the restrictions of her society—the fear of criticism and ridicule—had made her cautious. It is, perhaps, a bitter comment on the repressive effects of conventional society (which conventions Fern criticized all her life) to see this change in Fanny Fern's daughter from the lively, outspoken child and young girl to the young woman who was *so* quiet that her reticence was widely commented upon.[23]
At the end of the summer Fern wrote an "Adieu to Newport" which revealed her uncertainty about the future. She was sorry to leave "the happy hours and friendly faces" she had known in Newport. "Brick pavements," she said, would soon "clip her wings": "I shall not soar again till I see another bright June. Shall I see it? Neither you nor I know" (NYL, October 21, 1871).
Back in New York Fern soon felt the effect of the "brick pavements."

That winter her house was broken into by burglars for the fifth time. In exasperation, Fern wrote about the experience in the *Ledger* on December 16, 1871:

Being an author, and the wife of an author, I can never cease wondering at this distinguishing mark of their preference. Now if they want plunder, why not go to head-quarters—to Robert Bonner, for instance. . . . I have neither cashmere shawls nor diamonds. All the silver I ever owned, they relieved me of two years since. . . . There's nothing to pay them for a sixth visit save our respective manuscripts, which I defy them either to sell or decipher. . . . What did they take? I'll tell you what they *didn't* take, for which I get on my knees to them, whether they are in jail or out. The life of my little grandchild, who unsuspectingly ran up stairs alone, to get some little plaything, and tripped down, singing, to say "she couldn't get the closet door open." The wretch was in there. That, taking other gold, he left the gold that was shining on *her* flossy head, is matter of praise enough for me. I wouldn't lift a finger to point him out if I could; when that soft little breathing was so near him, and he didn't stop it, for fear of possible detection.

Previously burglars had taken whatever valuable jewelry there was in the house; another time, after living in the house for a week while Fern and her family were in the country, they had stolen all of the silver (which Fern and Parton had vainly hidden behind some books).[24] Fern's casual reference to Robert Bonner's house as being more worth robbing than her own was apparently taken seriously by at least one reader of the *Ledger*. A few days after Fern's column appeared thieves broke into Bonner's house and carried off all of his silver (JP, 68). With James Parton lecturing successfully, Fern was often asked why she did not lecture. She replied in her column that she had no desire to lecture (NYL, December 23, 1871), sarcastically commenting that her sphere was home, "especially when I'm asked to do anything outside of it that I don't want to do!"

Early in 1872 Fern attended a meeting for the relief of needy women. She heard a number of speeches, each speaker tearing down the methods and ideas of the other speakers. Fern wrote that she had noticed this divisiveness in almost all attempts to benefit women. Recognizing what is a common failing of philanthropic enterprises, Fern wrote on February 24, 1872: "There *are* great 'wrongs' to be righted for women. And if the time spent in calling names were spent in redressing them by each, according to their peculiar gift and light, neither underrating the other, there would be much more accomplished."

On March 25 Fern wrote about unfortunate scenes that she had witnessed in the streets: a drunken man punching his wife, a drunken woman slapping her little girl, and a five-year-old boy pleading with the policeman not to arrest his father. On May 11 she wrote about the "life of the company," the man who shines in company but is surly and silent when alone with his family.

It was a long winter for Fern, but with the spring she felt as if she had gained new life. On June 1 she wrote about the "glory and beauty of each new spring." On June 15 she wrote about the pleasures of being a grandmother, "to have one's children's children at our knee; to tell them wonderful tales of their parents' childhoods; to come between them and the harm of "*too* much *governing.*"

Except for the temporary rally when the warm weather came, Fern's health had declined considerably since the previous year. Some time during this year, or earlier, she underwent radical surgery in an attempt to arrest the cancer.[25] She lost the use of her right arm and began writing her columns laboriously with her left hand. Then when she lost the use of her left arm, she dictated her columns to her husband or her daughter. James Parton tells of how they tried to persuade her to give up writing her columns, but she insisted: "No! I must do it; for as long as people see my pieces in the *Ledger* every week, they cannot say that I am sick" (JP, 75).

She suffered from intense pain, but in June she was able to go by steamboat to Newport for the summer. It was an agonizing trip, yet after she arrived in Newport she wrote about the experience, making it the subject of a jest, and sent it to the *Ledger* (JP, 75; NYL, August 3, 1872). Her friends and her readers were unaware of the seriousness of her illness, but it was clear that she was ill. By the end of the summer, her condition had deteriorated so that she could no longer walk outside. When she felt well enough, she went for rides in the carriage, but it required two hours of agony to get her dressed, and she had to carry stimulants and opiates with her in case the pain became unbearable (JP, 80). Her readers could not read the pain and suffering in her columns, which were written with the same vitality and wit that they always had been. She referred to her illness casually in one of her columns, but in such a way that no one would have suspected it was to be fatal. On July 27 she wrote about taking a nap, indicating that she could never be bothered to do so: "I never could see the sense of turning day into night in that fashion, when there is never half daylight enough, as it is, to do what one wishes—when one day's work has overlapped another ever since I could count." On one of her drives Fern saw a woman of advanced years, who lived in a pretty cottage that she had bought herself after many years of "arduous toil in a profession the most difficult, perhaps, of all for a woman." It was a gratifying sight, Fern said, to see her thus rewarded (NYL, August 24, 1872).

At the end of the summer Fern returned to New York. This trip was even more difficult than the trip to Newport. She had to be carried on to the steamer. Colonel Higginson helped her family get her onto the ship, and Parton wrote from New York to thank him on September 23: "We had a terrible time all the way, and Mrs. Parton, I fear, has written her last piece and taken her last ride. She has had a bad day, and declines fast. Still, her strength is amazing, and she may rally when the weather is cooler."[26]

Fern did not rally, however. She was in great pain, and she could not lay her head back without assistance. Yet she retained her sense of humor until the last, making jocular comments about the ludicrousness of her condition. The night that she died she helped dress her granddaughter for a birthday party, and when she knew that she would not last the night, she told her husband and daughter not to tell Effie if she should die during the night. "Tell her after breakfast," she said. She died at six o'clock on the evening of October 10, 1872 (JP, 84). Two days later her last article was published in the *Ledger*. It was entitled "End of the Summer Season," but it seemed to signify also the end of her life. The incredible strength and courage which led her to defy death as she had defied so many other crushing blows in her life enabled her almost to find victory in her defeat. After this long "contest with death," she was asserting her will even as she closed her eyes to the "sparkle and sunrise":

As for me, whether I go early or late, whether my eyes are open or shut, memory will always make pictures for me of dear blessed Newport, full of sparkle and sunrise . . . which makes me say with Festus, "Oh, God, I thank thee that I live."

On November 2, 1872, the editorial page of the *New York Ledger* was deeply edged in black, and Bonner announced the death of Fanny Fern to his readers. Some of the daily papers had already printed the story, but, as a weekly, the *Ledger* required two weeks to go to press. Most readers throughout the country, however, first learned of her death from the *Ledger's* announcement. The following week Bonner wrote at length about Fern's life and work: "Her success was assured, because she had something to say, and knew how to say it. . . . , giving the world a piece of [her] mind, and the world was glad to get it. . . . With all her intellect and genius, had there not been added to these her courage, her honesty of purpose, and her faithfulness of heart, she would not have been Fanny Fern" (NYL, November 9, 1872). Similar obituaries appeared in all the leading newspapers. The following week the *Ledger* published a letter from a freight conductor who, in noting the Pullman car that had been named after Fanny Fern, commented: "As I looked at it, the many helpful words she has written came to my mind and I said to myself—'Fanny Fern is a name that will be remembered as long as memory lasts.'"

Fern was buried in Mount Auburn Cemetery in Cambridge, Massachusetts, with her first husband, Charles Eldredge, and her daughters Mary Stace Eldredge and Grace Eldredge Thomson. Robert Bonner erected a marble monument, the design of which was planned by Fern's daughter Ellen Eldredge.[27] Like the freight conductor, Fern's generation was convinced that her name would live forever. The monument, which is in the shape of a large cross, is embellished with fern leaves and bears only the name "Fanny Fern."

"Paper Pellets":
The Spectrum of Ideas

I believe that when one woman is pushed to the wall, all her sex are injured by it, and though she may box my ears for seeing it, it only shows what moral and mental rasping the poor thing has experienced that she cannot see a friend in Fanny Fern.

NYL, September 12, 1868

THROUGHOUT HER TWENTY-ONE-YEAR CAREER as a newspaper columnist, Fanny Fern wrote on many subjects: literature, prison reform, prostitution, venereal disease, family planning, divorce, education, child rearing, and rights for women. In this chapter I will look at Fern's position on these issues—many of which have been introduced in the previous chapters—and then turn to the two issues that have emerged as the most important ideas in Fern's work: her critique of the domestic scene in America and her call for economic independence for women.

Fern also wrote occasionally on what were regarded as traditional "women's topics." At the outset of her career, when she herself was reeling from the loss of so many loved ones (mother, sister, child, and husband within a two-year period), she wrote a number of articles on death and dying, particularly the deaths of young children. She also wrote from the perspective of someone who believed in a divine power, but her religious belief was never dogmatic. When religion is mentioned in Fern's work it is often in conjunction with death. Fern's attitude is summarized in the column she wrote after the death of her daughter Grace: the accumulation of these losses, she said, would have been impossible to bear without the solace of a belief in immortality (NYL, January 10, 1863). The subjects of death and dying, which in the twentieth century have been labeled "sentimental," were never romanticized in Fern's work; her treatment of these subjects was not affected or contrived. She was writing candidly about her own experience.

Literature and Writing

Fern criticized authors who were imitative and praised writers who could strike out bravely on their own, without regard to criticism by conservative critics who could not tolerate deviations from the genteel style and subject matter of most popular writing. It is from this perspective that Fern praised Whitman's *Leaves of Grass.* Other writers she specifically praised in her columns include Charlotte Brontë and Harriet Beecher Stowe, Stowe for taking a strong stand on a controversial issue and Brontë for writing frankly and without regard for the inhibiting "feminine proprieties" of the period (OB, May 28, 1853; NYL, June 6, June 13, July 4, 1857, November 17, 1860).

Among the specific faults that Fern criticized in literature were artificial language and unnecessary esoteric "dictionary words," for example, such phrases as "amethystine light of iridescent eyes" (NYL, January 19, 1861). She was also sarcastic about the use of clichéd or tired metaphors. In her ridicule of one such example, the "fair young creature of seventeen summers," Fern asked ironically, "What becomes of her winters?": "I entreat the humanitarian to make some inquiry into the circumstances of this abridged young creature, so long defrauded by unprincipled story and novel writers, of her inalienable woman's rights to *winter* in our midst" (NYL, April 28, 1860). Fern was also impatient with books that relied for interest on thrilling or sensational events, and she was critical of novelists who killed off a character, usually a woman, because they did not know what to do with her (NYL, April 20, 1861). Particularly significant was her criticism of the heroines of male writers:

> What was the heroine of the book like? I'll tell you. She was one of those soft, senseless, silky, creamy, yielding, "clinging" creatures. . . . A thing so profoundly impressed with man's superiority, that she would no more think of venturing on a sentiment, that was not an echo of his opinions, than she would think of altering the Litany. A being, always trembling with suspense, till her lord has pronounced his mutton chop and coffee good. Who laughs, or is serious, according to his direction. In fine, who pleases him best, the nearer she approaches idiocy. . . .
> The most unnatural and improbable thing on earth is generally a male-writer's heroine. . . . [She has] no more symmetry, or human semblance, than a child's crude drawing. (NYL, October 10, 1863)

Fern was also outspoken on editorial and publishing practices. As we saw in an earlier chapter, she was critical of editors whose reviews of books were not based on the quality of the books themselves—editors who reviewed books favorably because they wanted a return favor from the publisher or author, or, conversely, editors who reviewed books unfavorably because of envy or personal pique against the author or publisher (OB, September 25,

1852; NYL, September 26, 1859, February 18, 1871). She was particularly critical of editors who reviewed books by women unfairly, either criticizing the book because of jealousy or reviewing the woman and not the book (e.g., NYL, November 15, 1856, May 23, 1857, May 30, 1868).

In an 1871 essay, Fern, who wrote often on the subject of writing, answered one of the many letters she received from students asking her to write their compositions for them. She was critical of the artificial way students were made to write compositions and sympathized with the beleaguered students (NYL, December 16, 1865). Once, she said, she was sent a prize essay that she recognized as one of her articles that a student had copied and submitted as his/her own. However, she did not wholly blame the students, given the conditions under which they were required to write (NYL, June 9, 1860). To a New York school committee that had sent her a composition the committee believed to be plagiarized from her work, she wrote that its members should take a look at one of her articles, "A Word to Parents and Teachers," in *Fresh Leaves,* and she advised the committee to rethink its teaching of composition:

> Do you not agree with me that obliging children to *write at a mark,* is offering a premium for plagiarism? I could wish a thorough reform in the department of Composition, as taught at present in our schools. If (and this has happened more than once) an Editor, short of topics, does not hesitate to copy an entire article of mine & pass it off for an Editorial, how can you expect a poor cornered child, with the fear of punishment before its eyes if it cannot perform impossibilities, to be more scrupulously honest?[1]

Fern's advice to the writer was that one should write about something one knows, in one's own natural language, without padding or artificial embellishment (NYL, March 14, 1857, July 15, 1871).

To would-be professional writers Fern had two principal pieces of advice. First, she advised hard work: "Work early and work late, if you would excel. Never rely on *natural* genius; none but a *natural* fool ever does that" (MWT, November 19, 1853). Second, she advised the writer to be original: "Don't filch whole sentences from other writers, without honest quotation marks. Don't treat us to Dickens and water. . . . Be yourself, or be nothing. . . . If you have nothing to say, don't say it; if you have, for patience' sake, use your own words to do it in, though they may be rough as a nutmeg-grater" (NYL, August 22, 1857, July 27, 1861).

Social Criticism

In addition to speaking out on literary matters, Fern addressed a number of controversial social problems. Her positions on prison reform and on prostitution have been discussed in the earlier chapters with respect to specific articles: she criticized a justice system that emphasized punishment rather than rehabilitation, and she denounced a legal and economic system that made it impossible for a woman to earn a living wage and then condemned her (in effect, wrote her off as subhuman) when she was driven to prostitution as a means of support. Fern was also outspoken on the issue of venereal disease. At a time when "respectable" women were not supposed to know that prostitution or venereal disease existed, Fern brought the facts out into the open: forty years before the publication of Ibsen's *Ghosts*, Fern wrote about venereal disease, calling attention to the way in which the sexual double standard affected the lives of women. Like the white wives of southern slaveholders who pretended not to know of their husband's illegitimate black children, women were expected to pretend not to know of their husbands' philandering before or after marriage—even when they themselves were infected by the disease and they saw their children die at an early age from congenital syphilis (e.g., NYL, October 24, 1857, August 28, 1858).

Another controversial subject that Fern addressed was the need for family planning; the unrestricted births of too many children were responsible for the ill health of many women, she said. Although Fern did not name any specific method of birth control, she stressed the need for family planning and made clear her belief that men as well as women were responsible for controlling the number of their children (e.g., NYL, March 12, 1870).

Fern also wrote boldly on the question of divorce. Noting that no work is more demeaning than a demeaning marriage, Fern wrote in 1857 that it would be better for a woman to leave her husband than remain in a brutalizing marriage—even if it meant leaving her children (which at that time would have been the case):

Better let her leave them, than remain to bring into the world their puny brothers and sisters. Does she shrink from the toil of self-support? What toil, let me ask, could be more hopeless, more endless, *more degrading* than that from which she turns away? . . . Let a woman who *has the self-sustaining power* quietly take her fate in her own hands, and right herself. Of course she will be misjudged and abused. *It is for her to choose.* (NYL, October 24, 1857).

Children's Literature, Education, and Child Rearing

In addition to her eight books for adults, Fern published three books for children: *Little Ferns for Fanny's Little Friends* (1853), *The Play-Day Book* (1857), and *A New Story Book for Children* (1864). These books contain articles that had been previously published in the newspaper as well as original pieces that Fern wrote for the books. Many of the stories derive from her own childhood; others are based on events and people that she had observed. As children's books, they differ in two important ways from many children's books published today. First of all, like most children's stories of the time (and unlike much of the "hygienic" children's literature of today), Fern's stories often tell of children's deaths and other sad events.[2] Second, Fern's children's books make available for children the same subjects of social criticism that she developed in her columns for adults. The books are serious, nonsatirical attempts to speak to children in a friendly, confidential manner about values and social concerns, but through the medium of short stories about children. Fern, who used her pen to create and form public opinion, also used her pen to educate and mold young minds and hearts; she sought to create the kind of adults who eventually would overturn the injustices that she criticized in her columns.

All of Fern's stories have to do with human relationships, and Fern's method is to portray the positive or negative behavior of the people in the story in such a way that her meaning will be clear. Unlike the moralistic Sunday School tales, which focus on children's behavior, Fern's stories often portray adults whose behavior is criticized. In one story, which is written from the point of view of a child, the child says that she and her sister will not go to the circus if their black nanny is not permitted in. In "The Wild Rose," a mother's kind and charitable attitude toward the Native Americans is contrasted favorably with her husband's hatred of them. In many stories the child reader is led to identify with the less fortunate child: the poor, the disabled, the immigrant. Society is criticized for not giving women the pay they deserve for their work. Also criticized are parents—fathers as well as mothers—who do not spend time with their children (See also NYL, May 30, 1863, December 28, 1867). Young girls are told: "Don't mind being called 'a tom-boy'—run, jump, shout, fly kites, climb boards, tangle your hair, soil your hands and tear your aprons, and Nature will reward you with strong straight backs, full chests, bright eyes, rosy cheeks, and a long life." Boys are told not to inflict injury on anyone: "It is not 'fun' to give pain to the weak, the timid, the helpless; it is not 'fun' to play the tyrant."[3]

Fern's interest in the formative value of children's literature is indicative of another significant theme in her work: the question of child development. Writing much in advance of her time, Fern discussed what she regarded as the common errors of child rearing and children's education. Many of her ideas on education have become accepted practice. She deplored the conditions in the schools: dark, crowded, unventilated schoolrooms where young children sat on backless benches for long periods at a time bent over work or reciting endlessly. One point that she stressed often was that young children who had spent a good part of the day in school should not be burdened with homework after school hours. Praising the new concept of the kindergarten, which had come from Germany, Fern asserted that small children should have small tables and chairs proportioned to their size where they could sit in small groups. The school day should not be too long, she said, and there should be a long lunch hour with plenty of time for the children to play actively outside.[4]

Fern's ideas on child rearing were also progressive. First of all, she recognized children's individuality. She warned parents not to try to make them all the same (NYL, January 23, 1858; Folly, 296–298); she also cautioned parents not to try to make their children replicas of themselves (NYL, July 12, 1862, September 2, 1871). Because she looked at children as individuals, Fern was particularly concerned about what she called "children's rights." She urged adults to make an effort to put themselves in the child's place (NYL, April 5, 1862, December 15, 1860, May 7, 1870). Fern also emphasized that a parent should not favor one child over another (NYL, February 28, 1857). She was particularly concerned about the common practice of favoring the boys in a family over the girls. Boys, as well as girls, she said, should be taught reciprocity. Sisters should not be made to do everything for their brothers in the belief that one is training the girl to be a good wife someday; parents should also ask themselves if they are training their boy to be a good husband. Under the present system, Fern said, where the girl is taught self-sacrifice and the boy is indulged at the expense of his sisters, "a monstrous little tyrant is produced" (NYL, August 29, 1863, September 29, 1866).

Fern's ideas on discipline were advanced for her period. She urged an end to severe and cruel punishments—physical and verbal. Parents, she said, would do well to think about their own infractions before they punished a child (NYL, May 4, 1861, April 24, 1858). On the other hand, Fern did not approve of indulgence. Parents, she said, should "be firm, but kind" (NYL, September 3, 1859, July 27, 1861, August 8, 1863, June 17, 1865). At the same time, she said, parents should not be afraid to love their children: "Too much indulgence has ruined thousands of children. *Love* not one" (NYL, September 2, 1871).

Fern's insights into child psychology were unusually perceptive. She noted that sometimes what is identified as "naughtiness" could be more accurately described as "ennui": an intelligent and active child needs something interesting to do (NYL, May 14, 1864, October 19, 1867). She also pointed out that parents can crush the truth in a child by punishing for confessions, and warned that disproportionately severe punishment or unreasonable rules will only make a child sneaky, evasive, and dishonest. "Do anything," she said, "but offer a premium for slyness and deceit to your children" (OB, May 15, 1852; NYL, May 18, 1872). Fern also advocated honesty and openness with children, with respect to sex as well as other matters (NYL, February 19, 1859).

Domesticity
and the Economics of Independence

Fern gives considerable attention to all of the preceding ideas. However, if one were to ask what ideas emerge as the most important in her work—the

most important to her and also the most important for the readers of today—one would point to Fern's critique of the domestic scene in America
and her call for women's independence.

In Mary E. Wilkins Freeman's 1891 short story, "The Revolt of
'Mother,'" Sarah Penn says to her daughter:

You ain't found out yet we're women-folks, Nanny Penn. . . . One of
these days you'll find it out, an' then you'll know that we know only what
men-folks think we do, so far as any use of its goes, an' how we'd ought
to reckon men-folks in with Providence, an' not complain of what they do
any more than we do of the weather.[5]

Despite individual differences among nineteenth-century women writers regarding the ideology of domesticity, this advice, handed down from mother
to daughter, can be said to represent the one tenet of a woman's domestic
life—and since her life at the time was primarily domestic, of her life in
general—that remained a given in the lives of nineteenth-century American
women of all classes and backgrounds.[6]

One woman who did question male authority, without qualification and
without apology, both in her private life and in her public voice, was Fanny
Fern. Her main theme was that women should be treated as individuals, not
as voiceless, unthinking adjuncts to their husbands, fathers, or brothers.
Fern's attitude can be gleaned from two short articles that she wrote early in
her career.

"The Tear of a Wife" was published in 1852. Fern began this article with
a quotation from a contemporary newspaper: "The tear of a loving girl is
like a dew-drop on a rose; but on the cheek of a wife, is a drop of poison to
her husband." In response to this comment, Fern wrote sarcastically:

It is "an ill wind that blows *nobody* any good." Papas will be happy to
hear that twenty-five dollar pocket-handkerchiefs can be dispensed with
now, in the bridal *trousseau.* Their "occupation's gone"! Matrimonial
tears "are poison." There is no knowing what you will do, girls, with that
escape-valve shut off; but that is no more to the point, than—whether
you have anything to smile at or not; one thing is settled—*you mustn't
cry!* Never mind back aches, and side aches, and head aches, and dropsi-
cal complaints, and smoky chimneys, and old coats, and young babies!
Smile! It flatters your husband. He wants to be *considered* the source of
your happiness, whether he was baptized *Nero* or *Moses!* Your mind
never being supposed to be occupied with any other subject than himself,
of course a tear is a tacit reproach. Besides, you miserable whimperer,
what have you to cry for? A-i-n-t y-o-u m-a-r-r-i-e-d? Isn't that the *sum-
mum bonum*—the height of feminine ambition? You *can't* get beyond

that! It's the *jumping-off* place! You've arriv!—got to the end of your journey! Stage puts up *there!* You've nothing to do but retire on your laurels, and spend the rest of your life endeavoring to be thankful that you are Mrs. John Smith! *"Smile!" you simpleton!* (OB, August 28, 1852)

The second article, "Awe-ful Thoughts," was published in 1856 in response to a quotation which stated: *"[A]we . . .* is the most delicious feeling a wife can have toward her husband." Fern wrote:

"AWE!"—awe of a man whose whiskers you have trimmed, whose hair you have cut, whose cravats you have tied, whose shirts you have "put into the wash," whose boots and shoes you have kicked into the closet, whose dressing-gown you have worn while combing your hair; . . . who has hooked your dresses, unlaced your boots, fastened your bracelets, and tied on your bonnet; who has stood before your looking-glass, with thumb and finger on his proboscis, scraping his chin; whom you have buttered, and sugared, and toasted, and tea-ed; whom you have seen asleep with his mouth wide open! Ri—diculous! (NYL, November 1, 1856)

These two articles give us an idea of Fern's perspective. Laughing at and consequently undercutting the hallowed image of husbands and marriage, Fern wrote from the perspective that marriage is *not* the romantic institution it was believed to be and that husbands are *not* gods.

In her critique of the domestic scene Fern developed her argument around certain major assertions. Her first assertion was that the current concept of marriage was not just; it gave men all of the advantages. Fern said that she would like to make a bonfire of all the books of advice to women (OB, February 14, 1852). "There is not one sensible or *just* book of advice for women," she said; they are all "selfish" and one-sided" and would make a woman "reflect *his* thoughts, *his* opinions, narrow as they often are, as if God had endowed her with no individuality, no brain to think, or heart to feel" (NYL, March 17, 1860). Women are told by pulpit and press to hide their own irritations and put on an angelic smile for their husbands, Fern said; at the same time they are told that they must expect harsh words from their husbands. "Away with such one-sided moralizing," she wrote in 1857; and she added in 1861, "We believe in laying down no rule of conduct for the wife which will not apply equally to the husband" (NYL, October 24, 1857, June 18, 1861).

Fern's second assertion was that marriage has been falsely romanticized. In "A Whisper to Romantic Young Ladies," published in 1852, Fern pulled the rug out from under the romantic notion of marriage. Responding to a quotation idealizing marriage, she wrote:

Girls! *that's a humbug!* The very *thought* of it makes me groan. It's all moonshine. In fact, men and moonshine in my dictionary are synonymous. . . . When . . . your wedding dress is put away in a trunk for the benefit of posterity, if you can get your husband to *smile* on anything short of a "sirloin" or a roast turkey, you are a lucky woman. . . . Lovers have a trick of getting disenchanted, too, when they see their Aramintas with dresses pinned up around the waist, hair powdered with sweeping, faces scowled up over the wash-tub, and soap-suds dripping from red elbows.

We know these little accidents never happen in novels—where the heroine is always "dressed in white, with a rose-bud in her hair," and lives on blossoms and May dew! There are no wash-tubs or gridirons in *her* cottage; *her* children are born cherubim, with a seraphic contempt for dirt pies and molasses. *She* remains "a beauty" to the end of the chapter, and "steps out" just in time to anticipate her first gray hair, her husband drawing his last breath at the same time, as a dutiful husband *should;* and not falling into the unromantic error of outliving his grief, and marrying a second time!

But this humdrum life, girls, is another affair, with its washing and ironing and cleaning days, when children expect boxed ears, and visitors picked-up dinners. All the "romance" there is in it, you can put under a three-cent piece! (TF, June 12, 1852)

Not only did Fern insist that marriage was not idyllic, she also pointed out that it was often destructive to women. One of her most moving articles is the short piece "Owls Kill Humming-birds," published in 1852, which depicts the tragedy for a woman of marriage to a Casaubon:

If you have the bump of mirthfulness developed, don't marry a tombstone. . . . You go plodding through life with him to the dead-march of his own leaden thoughts. *You* revel in the sunbeams; *he* likes the shadows. You are on the hill-tops; he is in the plains. Had the world been made to his order, earth, sea, and sky would have been one universal pall. . . .

No—no—make no such shipwreck of yourself. Marry a man who is not too ascetic to enjoy a good, merry laugh. *Owls kill humming-birds!* (TF, December 11, 1852)

In this article Fern's use of the word *kill* can be interpreted figuratively to mean the wearing down of a woman's spirit. However, in other articles she makes clear that she also believed that marriage could literally kill. Women, she said, were worn down by neglect and cruelty, and worked to death by too much housework and too many children. As Fern wrote in 1861, "Life for most women is a horrid grind. They are placed in a treadmill and then taunted for being narrowed down to its peck-measure limit" (NYL, March

23, 1861). Men would hang themselves, she said, if they had to do the repetitive, grinding work that women do three hundred and sixty-five days a year (NYL, June 8, 1861). For most women "the only day of rest is the day of their death" (NYL, March 11, 1865). Fern also used strong words about the women and children who were destroyed by the venereal disease that their husbands brought home. It was all of these abuses of male authority that caused Fern to conclude that some marriages were "legal murders." She wrote in 1870:

What do I mean by "legal murders"? Well, if a woman is knocked on the head with a flat-iron by her husband and killed, or if arsenic is mixed with her food, or if a bullet is sent through her brain, the law takes cognizance of it. But what of the cruel words that just as surely kill, by constant repetition? What of the neglect? What of the diseased children of a pure, healthy mother? What of the ten or twelve, even healthy children, "who come," one after another, into the weary arms of a really good woman, who yet never knows the meaning of the word *rest* till the coffin-lid shuts her in from all earthly care and pain? . . . I could write flaming words about "the inscrutable Providence which has seen fit to remove our dear sister in her youth from the bosom of her young family," as the funeral prayer phrases it.

Providence did nothing of the sort. Poor Providence! It is astonishing how busy people are making up bundles to lay on *His* shoulders! I imagine Providence meant that women, as well as men, should have a right to their own lives. (NYL, March 12, 1870)

In this article and elsewhere, Fern made clear that it was not *Providence* that caused the premature deaths of women; the deaths of many women were caused by the selfish attitude of husbands who had absolute authority over their wives, and were permitted by culture and the law to mistreat, use, or neglect their wives with impunity.

As Fern realized, the problem was that not only was the concept of male authority protected and countenanced by society, but, for the most part, women themselves did not question it. Consequently, the third aspect of Fern's argument was that women needed to assert themselves and put a stop to their enslavement and victimization. Although they might love their families, she said, they should not sacrifice themselves for anyone. She wrote in 1869:

Nobody will thank you for turning yourself into a machine. When you drop in your tracks, they will just shovel the earth over you, and get Jerusha Ann Sombody to step into your shoes. . . . So you just take a little comfort yourself as you go along, and look after "No. 1." (NYL, September 4, 1869)

In a society that believed the ideal woman to be totally selfless and acquiescent, Fern's assertion that a woman must look out for "No. 1" was startling. But, she said, the insane asylums and cemeteries were full of women who had been denied their individuality by husbands who treated them like machines. Broken in body and/or spirit, they went insane or died of overwork (NYL, September 20, 1862).

Given this assessment of marriage, the fourth aspect of Fern's argument was to urge women to develop themselves intellectually and financially so that they could be independent of marriage as a means of fulfillment and/or support. Women, she said, need to take time to cultivate themselves by reading and writing, either to find employment outside the home or simply to save themselves from "dying," literally or figuratively. "Be clean but not too clean," she wrote in 1872. "Stop and take a breath and while you stop . . . to rest, read. So shall the cobwebs be brushed from your neglected brain, and you shall learn that something else besides cleanliness is necessary to make home *really* home" (NYL, April 6, 1872). She also advised women to write—for publication, if they had the talent—but also just for themselves. Surprisingly modern in her realization of the therapeutic value of writing, Fern insisted that a woman who was unhappy and depressed could find comfort in expressing her thoughts on paper (NYL, August 10, 1867). Fern also believed that married women could be financially independent. If a hardworking wife "has any gift besides motherhood," she said, "she will want to use it to support herself" (NYL, July 9, 1870).

Finally, Fern's solution to the dilemma in which women found themselves was not only for women to assert their independence, either by independent action within the home or by pursuing financially rewarding occupations outside the home; she also urged men to take an active part in the domestic scene. Men need to become partners in the domestic scene, helping with child care and housework, she said, and in general making the home a pleasant place to be; they should not be simply the selfish recipients of female service. Writing of the "*mutual* obligations" of the married couple (NYL, June 18, 1861), Fern urged men and women to "pull evenly in the matrimonial harness" (NYL, October 4, 1856). This meant that a man should do his best to make his home bright and cheerful, not expect his wife to do all the soothing while he remained surly and irritable (NYL, October 4, 1856, June 18, 1861, July 9, 1870). In addition, she urged the husband to help with the housework if necessary. And, most important, she said, a father should help with the children: "Don't be too dignified or manly (?) to tend your own flesh-and-blood baby, when your wife has little or no assistance" (NYL, March 6, 1858, November 18, 1865). A husband should recognize when his wife has too much to do, Fern said, and help her (NYL, May 26, 1866).

Fanny Fern believed in the family state, but as she wrote early in her career, "If you are romantic, dig clams, but don't get married" (OB, August 14, 1852). Moreover, although she was fond of children, she did not idealize motherhood. She insisted that mothers *and* fathers should share in child rearing. Fern was not a theorist; she dealt with life as it was lived. Her articles portray real-life situations with which she had become familiar through experience and/or observation. She satirized the pretensions and abuses of male authority and criticized injustice wherever she found it. If she did not portray marriage and domestic life as all sunshine and flowers, it was because she did not see them that way. As she said in 1852, "I have seen too much of life to be merry at a wedding" (OB, May 1, 1852)

The most revolutionary aspect of Fern's assessment of the domestic scene was her conclusion that women would never be free of male domination until they were financially independent. In her drive for independence, she realized that even when a woman was wealthy because of her husband's or father's status, as long as she was dependent upon men—husband, father, brother—for financial security, she could have no autonomy as a human being. The woman's opinions were not listened to; her conversation was regarded as trivial. She had no more autonomy in society than a child. Fern herself said that she resented the "fence that was put up around women to keep them from seeing anything but feathers and bracelets." When women are interested in other matters, she said, they are "patronizingly soothed like some amiable lunatic or else majestically snubbed" (NYL, December 28, 1861). Having the vote would help, Fern said, and other rights were important. But if women were to be taken seriously, she concluded, they would have to be able to earn and possess money independently of the men in their life.

In expressing these sentiments Fern was far in advance of her time. Her contemporaries—male and female—were highly critical of a woman who was assertive enough to compete with men and defy the restrictions placed on women's activities by the "cult of the lady."[7] In an 1857 article, Fern advised women to follow her example, despite criticism and accusations of being unfeminine. Women should not be intimidated by the criticism of "conservative old ladies of both sexes," she asserted. As she said of Harriet Hosmer, the sculptor, she was glad that she "had the courage to assert herself—to be what nature intended her to be—a genius—even at the risk of being called unfeminine, eccentric, and unwomanly" (NYL, December 19, 1857).

Moreover, Fern commented, once a woman becomes successful, she need not worry about her critics:

Take your rights, my sisters; don't beg for them! Never mind what objectors say or think. Success will soon stop their mouths. Nothing like that to conquer prejudice and narrowness and ill-will. (NYL, July 16, 1870)

And, as she said in an 1866 article supporting women lecturers against the criticism they received: "They can stand the spiteful criticism with a good house over their independent heads, secured and paid for by their own

honest industry, . . . with greenbacks and Treasury notes stowed away
against a rainy day" (NYL, December 8, 1866).

Not only would success silence the critics or soften their sting, but women
would receive better treatment once they were independent. They would not
be vulnerable to insult or "rough usage"; even naturally rude people would
be self-seeking enough to modify their behavior around an independent—
and consequently powerful—woman.

> She won't *have* rough usage. She will be in a position to receive good
> treatment from *motives of policy,* from those natures which are incapable
> of better, and higher. She will, in short, stand on her own blessed inde-
> pendent feet as far as "getting a living" is concerned, as I do to-day.
> (NYL, September 16, 1869)

Fern's main argument in favor of economic independence for women derived from her own experience in being coerced into marriage as a means of
support. Marriage, she insisted over and over, should not be viewed as a
way of "getting a living." No way of getting a living, she said, was harder.
Moreover, the independent woman would not need to be driven to marry
someone she did not love and respect just to keep the wolf from the door. In
response to a newspaper writer who had criticized female physicians, Fern
wrote in the *Ledger* on July 16, 1870:

> Why shouldn't women work *for pay?* Does anybody object when women
> *marry for pay?*—without love, without respect, nay with even aversion?
> . . . How much more to be honored is she who, hewing out her own path,
> through prejudice and narrowness and even insult, earns honorably and
> honestly her own independence.

Fern advocated that all avenues of employment be open to women as they
were to men and that women receive equal pay for equal work. In 1857 she
commented after seeing women working in the Philadelphia mint: "I was
glad, as I always am, in a fitting establishment, to see *women* employed in
various offices . . . and more glad still, to learn that they had respectable
wages" (NYL, July 18, 1857). Fern's position on this matter grew out of her
own experience of poverty. When she was living in poverty and trying to
support herself and her children by working as a seamstress, she was never
able to earn more than fifty to seventy-five cents a week.

Fern also urged economic independence for women because she believed
that too many women lived purposeless lives and that economic endeavors
would give them purpose. The average middle-class woman's life was trivi-
alized, a round of fashions and social calls. The woman who is constantly
going to the doctor, Fern said, may not even be sick: "Half the time nothing
in the world ails [her] but the want of some absorbing occupation or inter-

est" (NYL, October 10, 1868). In an article about women's art, Fern commented that she was always glad to see women do a meritorious thing: "Every such step helps lift them from that torpid aimlessness which is the bane of so many women's lives" (NYL, June 3, 1865). In 1868 she commended the "self-supporting women" who put "to shame the useless lives of the idle ladies who remorselessly wear out the souls of men in vain struggle for fashionable supremacy" (NYL, December 5, 1868).

Finally, Fern wanted to see women active outside the home because, as she wrote about women lecturers, every woman has a right to use her "God-given talents": "If the lady had a gift for something else than 'darning stockings' all her life, she had a right, and did well to exercise it" (NYL, May 23, 1863).

What had happened to bring Fanny Fern to a position so different from that of most of her contemporaries? During the time she was living in poverty, and as she portrays so graphically in *Ruth Hall*, Fern found that her friends and relatives wanted to have nothing to do with her. Friends she had entertained at her home when she was in comfortable circumstances were embarrassed to know her in her poverty. Once she became famous, however, people who had cut her on the street were anxious to know her; her relatives and friends all sought to be remembered by the famous writer. This experience caused Fern to recognize with bitterness the gap between society's ostensible values and the reality of the effect of poverty. Although it was an accepted fact in American capitalistic society that in a man "money talks," nineteenth-century Americans regarded the fluid social structure as a male phenomenon. Women were outside the money economy; they were simply expected to reflect the status of their male protectors. Nineteenth-century American middle- and upper-class white women were conditioned to believe that their value as women was intrinsic, that they needed only to be good wives and mothers and devoutly religious and they would be respected and esteemed for their "womanly" qualities.[8]

Fern's descent into poverty showed her the hypocrisy behind the facade of society's values; she concluded that in American society "worth"—with respect to women as well as men—was in actuality measured in dollars. In effect, Fanny Fern was radicalized by her widowhood and the ensuing circumstances. As long as she was dependent upon her male relatives, she was powerless to determine her own fate or the fate of her children.

Two factors in Fern's private life are particularly significant in assessing her independent stance: her second marriage, which was a marriage of convenience that she had entered into under pressure from her father; and the terms of her father-in-law's will, which withheld money from her children unless she agreed to give them up. These two experiences helped drive Fern into her position on the financial independence of women. Forced into a brutalizing marriage, and threatened with the loss of her children by her father-in-law's will, she recognized the vulnerability of the woman who was economically dependent. It was only after she acquired money of her own that she gained the power of self-determination. And even after she married a third time, she refused to give up the independence she had struggled so hard to win.

In order to come to this position of independence Fern not only defied tradition, she also diverged from the religious teachings of her society. Although she was criticized for her defiance, Fern refused to accept the religious view that woman was dependent by nature and divine law. Responding directly to theologians such as Horace Bushnell and John Todd, who, writing against women's rights, warned of the dangers of women "unsexing" themselves by pursuing "masculine" activities, Fern cited examples of specific women working in the eighteenth and early nineteenth centuries. Such women, Fern said sarcastically, "did not ask leave of Doctors Bushnell or Todd to step out of [their] 'God-appointed woman's sphere'" (NYL, November 6, 1869). Moreover, unlike many of the women writers of her period who portrayed religion as an aid in women's "practice of submission," Fern saw religion as a spur to female achievement.[9] In Susan Warner's *The Wide, Wide World* (1851) and Maria Cummins's *The Lamplighter* (1854), for example, religion helps the heroine gain a victory over self and assists her in her struggle to put down her feelings of rebellion. Fern's Ruth Hall, however, finds in religion the encouragement she needs to continue her struggle for independence in defiance of society and of her male relatives (RH, 123).

In this respect Fern's *Ruth Hall* is closer to the slave narrative of Harriet Jacobs, *Incidents in the Life of a Slave Girl* (1861), than to the novels written by middle-class white women of the period. Both Jacobs and Fern were critical of the church as an institution when it diverged from the Christian principles of love and charity.[10] And both rejected the attempts of others to use religion to force submission: Fern rejected the patriarchal preaching that would make a woman passive in the name of "femininity"; Jacobs rejected the teachings of slavery, the "patriarchal institution" which claimed that slavery was the ordinance of God.[11] Jacobs, who had hidden for seven years in a tiny space in her grandmother's house rather than surrender to her white master, gained encouragement from religion to defy her master and the society that would enslave her.[12] Both Fern and Jacobs maintained a strong religious belief, but they rejected the patriarchal religion that would crush them; instead their spiritual beliefs helped provide them with the strength to rebel.

Susan Warner's heroine in *The Wide, Wide World* is taught submissiveness by her mother, who counsels passive acceptance in the face of her father's tyranny.[13] Fern and Jacobs, however, differentiate between acts of Providence and man-made cruelty. As Jacobs writes in *Incidents in the Life of a Slave Girl,* "When separations come by the hand of death, the pious soul can bow in resignation, and say, 'Not my will, but thine be done, O Lord!' But when the ruthless hand of man strikes the blow, regardless of the misery he causes, it is hard to be submissive."[14]

This similarity between Fern and Jacobs cannot be ascribed simply to coincidence—they knew each other quite well—and there are other important parallels in their work.[15] Jacobs was driven to her desperate action by the same two motives that drove Fanny Fern. First, they shared a desire to preserve their sexual integrity. In Fern's *Rose Clark,* Gertrude Dean, whose story was based on the second marriage of Fern herself, shudders at the footsteps of the husband whom she does not love, whose financial power gives him the right to use her sexually even while she despises him; she can see her "bill of sale" on all of his possessions (RC, 235–238). In desperation, Fanny Fern left her husband, just as Harriet Jacobs fled rather than submit sexually to the master whom she despised. The situation of the slave woman is not wholly comparable to that of the free woman, who has rights and privileges and the respect of society, all of which are denied the slave. There are similarities, however, in the lack of power and the sexual vulnerability of both women.

The other parallel between Fern and Jacobs is the motivating factor of their children. Fern, as we have seen, was driven to seek her independence by the terms of her father-in-law's will, which would have taken her children away from her. Similarly, Jacobs was driven to run away in order to save her children. Her grandmother urged her to stay, but she saw her masters' plan to put her children "into their power in order to give them a stronger hold" on her. She realized that the only way she could save her children was to leave: "Nothing less than the freedom of my children would have induced me" to run away.[16] Jacobs, of course, sought more than independence; she sought freedom also. But a comparison of the two writers provides a significant comment on the position of women in nineteenth-century America: slave or free, women were dependent upon and answerable to men; without autonomy in society or in the home, their bodies and their children were not their own.

What was most unusual about Fern's concept of the independent woman was that not only did most people of the time not believe that women should be financially independent, but those who did think women should have the right to earn a living generally were speaking of the single woman. Fern, however, did not view career and marriage as an either-or situation. Nor did she view a woman's professional career as only a stopgap measure to fill in the period between childhood and marriage. She viewed the independent woman as remaining independent after and during marriage. She recognized the difficulties, but she did not see the two as mutually incompatible. She wrote in the *Ledger* on September 18, 1869:

Woman, be she married or single, being able to earn her own living independent of marriage—that often harder and most non-paying and most thankless road to it—will no longer have to face the alternative of serfdom or starvation, but will marry, when she does marry, for love and companionship, and for cooperation in all high and noble aims and purposes, not for bread and meat and clothes.

And in a July 9, 1870, article called "Self-Supporting Wives," in response to a newspaper writer who had worked himself "into a foam" at the idea of such wives, Fern wrote that women need not spend their lives suppressing their own worries to soothe irritable husbands; if they have the will and the ability to do so, they can go out into the world and support themselves.

Combining marriage and a career was not easy, Fern admitted. And in some cases, the right kind of man not being available, it might not be possible. She found it difficult to conceive of a woman doctor simultaneously carrying on the vocation of wife and mother, for example, and she noted that few men of her day would be unselfish enough to be a good husband to an artist wife (NYL, October 17, December 19, 1857, December 31, 1859). However, she believed that independence in marriage, such as she herself had attained, was possible and preferable (NYL, July 8, 1871).

Ruth Hall was unlike most other American novels of the period in that most nineteenth-century American writers portrayed the female protagonist as submissive to male authority and ultimately content with the domestic sphere, while Fern portrayed a protagonist who was bold, defiant, and a formidable economic competitor. It was this final point, Fern believed, that made the concept of financial independence for women so unpalatable to nineteenth-century American men. On September 21, 1872, a month before she died, Fern wrote of a conversation she had heard regarding a widow who had taken over her husband's construction business and managed it brilliantly. Fern was appalled to hear not one word of praise for this admirable woman. Even men from whom she would have expected sympathy could only ask, "Where was the baby?" or other sniping questions. Fern found no fault in the woman's character; yet she was universally criticized. Why? Fern asked herself: "At last I hit upon it. . . . She was *not* 'the clinging vine'!" This was what men objected to: she was able to function independently of and in a position superior to men, not only keeping the books but also superintending work on the building site and paying the men's salaries. It was this image of the woman having power over men that was so threatening. As Fern had concluded about men's opposition to women's voting: "This would place in our hands a weapon of power which they are very unwilling we should wield" (NYL, May 29, 1858).

A financial competitor wields a certain amount of power—power that Fern did not believe men were ready to see in women. Fern was not humble—that is, not "feminine"—in her recognition of her own power.

When she was criticized by another woman writer for being "egotistical" because she referred to herself as famous, she replied that she did not believe in false modesty (NYL, December 10, 1864). Fanny Fern proudly asserted that she had attained her success on her own; she did not, like many women writers of the period, humbly ascribe her success to a husband or father or brother, or even to God.[17] On July 19, 1856, after she had bought a house with her own money, she wrote an apostrophe to her inkstand, "My Old Ink-Stand and I," in which she gloried in how "they," she and her inkstand, had done it all by themselves: bought a brand new house (with title deed and insurance to prove it), fine furniture for the house, and food, clothes, and toys for her children.

This kind of self-assertion in a woman was shocking and somewhat unnerving to men. When Fern was criticized by an editor for not doing her own washing, she replied: "As long as Mr. Bonner pays me enough to buy out the editor's office, I will do just what the editor would do—turn from the washtub to the inkstand" (NYL, September 18, 1869). The suggestion that she had the power to buy and sell the editor who had criticized her was discomfitting to the editor—as she obviously intended it to be. Fanny Fern's challenge to men was loud and clear:

I believe in the woman *that is to be*. . . . She has as yet had to struggle with both hands tied, and then had her ears boxed for not doing more execution. . . . Cut the string gentlemen. . . . Pooh! You are afraid. (NYL, June 18, 1870).

In 1852, one year after Fanny Fern began her career, she wrote on the Fourth of July that it was ironic to see *women* celebrating their independence, "dragging around with their fetters at their heels." "They'll know better when I get up that Fern Insurrection!" she said (OB, July 10, 1852). The revolution that Fern referred to here might have been interpreted as a political one, or her words could simply have been interpreted as a joke. In retrospect, however, and after examining her writings over the twenty-one years of her career, one can see that she did indeed preach revolution. It was not a political revolution, however; it was a gender-related economic revolution. "I want all women to render themselves independent of marriage as a mere means of support," she wrote in the *New York Ledger* on June 26, 1869. This was the "Fern Insurrection."

EPILOGUE

In Her Own Voice

I thank the gods that [she] has had the courage to assert herself—to be what nature intended her to be—a genius—even at the risk of being called unfeminine, eccentric, and unwomanly. "Unwomanly?" because crotchet-stitching and worsted foolery could not satisfy her soul! . . . Well let her be unwomanly, then, I say; I wish there were more women bitten with the same complaint; let her be "eccentric," if nature made her so, so long as she outrages only the feelings of those conservative old ladies of both sexes, who would destroy individuality by running all our sex in the same mold of artificial nonentity—who are shocked if a woman calls things by their right names. I am glad that a new order of women is arising . . . , who are evidently sufficient unto themselves, both as it regards love and bread and butter; in the meantime, there are plenty of monosyllabic dolls left for those men who, being of small mental stature themselves, are desirous of finding a wife who will "look up to them"

NYL, December 19, 1857

FANNY FERN EMERGES AS AN IMPORTANT FIGURE in nineteenth-century American literature and American cultural history primarily because of the singularly individualistic perspective from which she wrote. At a time when a strident individualism was the identifying characteristic of [white] male Americans, and women were praised for their dependency and selfless passivity, Fanny Fern advocated and practiced—both in her life and in her writing—individualism for women.[1] Criticized as "unfeminine" and "unwomanly," Fern did not capitulate to the censorious pressures of her convention-bound contemporaries—neither the literary critics nor her personal acquaintances and family connections. In her writings she spoke her mind on issues and events, regardless of the reception she knew her words would receive. The individualistic character of Fern's voice is apparent in all aspects of her writing: her subject matter, her writing style, and the positions she took.

Many of the topics she chose to write on were regarded by her contemporaries as taboo, especially for women, and many others were controversial because of Fern's stance. Although she also wrote on acceptable "women's" topics, Fern's columns, for the most part, were polemical and satirical, stripping the conventional facade from sacrosanct institutions and traditions that she regarded as inhibiting and unjust, particularly for women.

Her style was original and satirical. Criticized as "vulgar" by conventional critics because of her frank style and subject matter, Fern wrote on subjects that ladies were not supposed to mention and in language that was clear and abruptly concise. She did not mince words or beat around the bush; in fact, she criticized genteel women writers who, she said, "circumlocute about the alphabet in such a way, every time they open their mincing lips" (NYL, December 30, 1865).

Even more important, Fern's individualistic stance is reflected in the courageous and sometimes unpopular positions she took on controversial issues. She spoke in her own woman's voice—at a time when women, like children, were expected to "be seen and not heard."

A consideration of Fern's position on the issues here discussed provides us with a significant clue regarding the question of canon formation in the United States, that is, the way that books have attained canonical status. In analyzing the issue of canon formation, we are faced with the question of why Fanny Fern, a writer whose work was so compelling during her lifetime and is still timely today, has not only not been canonized, but has been completely invisible. As I suggested earlier, the principal reason why the name of Fanny Fern was allowed to fall into oblivion was because her work was wholly at odds with the traditions of American culture that the influential formers of canons have sought to preserve.[2] One can point to other reasons—her name, her early sentimental writings—but these are not sufficient to have caused the total suppression of her work. Other now-famous writers have what might be regarded as odd names (Mark Twain, for example) or wrote potboilers early in their career (see, for example, Whitman's early sentimental fiction and temperance novel). The irony implicit in the fact that Fern was criticized by her contemporaries for her "unfeminine" writing, while twentieth-century critics disparaged her work because they regarded it as too "feminine," suggests that it was the content of her work that made it unpalatable to critics of both centuries, who were either unable or unwilling to confront the issues that she raised. In the twentieth century Fanny Fern was damned as a sentimentalist and stereotyped as one of the "mob of scribbling women," and the revolutionary content of her work was comfortably ignored. Her work remained out of print for over a hundred years and has been absent from anthologies and college syllabi as well.

The female individualism in Fern's writing is the principal reason why her work has been obscured for so long. All societies are logophobic; that is, they are fearful of discourse that threatens the structure of society.[3] In her insistence on individualism for women, Fern was making a claim that threatened the principal assumptions of American society. Condemned as a sentimentalist, however, she was effectively removed from discussion.

In a male-structured society, where the power structure depends upon phallocentric assumptions, an aggressively female perspective is a threat to the structure of society and all of its institutions: cultural, educational, economic, political. American history provides us with a long history of the suppression of women who have attempted to speak out. That more women did not speak out during the formative years of our nation, when all of the national rhetoric focused increasingly on individualism and freedom, is not surprising when one considers what happened to women who made themselves conspicuous. The case against Anne Hutchinson in 1637 was a case not only against religious dissent but also against a woman who presumed to interpret Scripture for herself and for other women. In his history, Edward Johnson deprecates the effrontery of the "weaker sex" in trying to set up a "Priest of their own," and calls Anne Hutchinson a "Master-piece of Women[']s wit."[4] The 1640 trial of Ann Hibbens revealed the same fear of the threat to the civic order posed by an assertive woman. Couching their argument in religious rhetoric, her judges concluded that her greatest sin was that of "transgressing the rule of the apostle [Paul] in usurping the authority over him whom God hath made her head and husband."[5] Fifteen years later Hibbens was executed as a witch; as a sympathetic clergyman observed at the time, she "was hanged as a witch only for having more wit than her neighbors."[6] The threat of witchcraft accusations became a means of enforcing the apostolic injunction; any woman who presumed to be different was in danger of being accused of witchcraft. The first witch executed in Massachusetts was Margaret Jones, whose success as a physician made her suspect.[7]

These were, of course, extreme measures; for the most part they were not necessary. Societal pressure and conditioning were effective means of preventing women from posing a threat to the status quo by going outside the place that society had assigned them. The emphasis on woman's "place" is indicative of society's need to maintain the existing structure. In 1855, the year that Ruth Hall was published, Ralph Waldo Emerson was invited to speak at a women's rights convention in Boston. Emerson told the audience of women that he did not object to women voting, because their vote would counteract the ignorant immigrant vote. But, he said, "the best women do not wish these things": equality of education and employment, property rights, suffrage. People who ask for these "rights," Emerson asserted, "do not have the support or sympathy of the truest women." True women, he said, would not want to leave their "place" in the home because they know that "out of place they lose half their weight." A "masculine woman is not strong," he insisted, "but a lady is." Women, Emerson averred, are "the civilizers of mankind"; their function is to "embellish trifles."[8] It was this kind of appeal to the elevated status of women, ostensibly sympathizing with while in reality diminishing women, that was an effective silencer. After all, if no "true woman" would want such things, the woman who spoke up was denying her womanhood.

Even worse was the explanation for the woman who went outside her household sphere. Particularly revealing is the statement of John Winthrop regarding the reason Governor Edward Hopkins's wife had become insane. Winthrop wrote in 1645 that she had "lost her understanding . . . by occasion of giving herself wholly to reading and writing and had written many books. . . . If she had attended her household affairs, and such things as belong to Women, and not gone out of her way to meddle with such things as are proper for men whose minds are stronger, etc., she had kept her wits, and might have improved them usefully and honorably in the place God had set for her."[9] In the history of American culture, female individualism has been regarded as suspect because it constitutes a threat to the social order. The woman who attempted to go out of her place was a dangerous aberration. Like the protagonist in Charlotte Perkins Gilman's "The Yellow Wallpaper," Governor Hopkins's wife sought to write, but in a society that denied her that function—a society that forced her to remain voiceless—she could only go insane. This, Fern insisted, was often the result for the woman who had no other outlets but those prescribed by the restrictions of her "place": "Over the needle, a woman may think herself into an Insane Asylum, while the active, out-door turmoil of business life is at least a *sometime* reprieve to *him*" (NYL, October 1, 1859, March 24, 1866).

The uniqueness of Fern's position can be understood in terms that have been applied to film criticism. As Laura Mulvey concludes in her pioneering article identifying the masculine gaze in film, women have been portrayed in films as the object of the male gaze, passive beings to be fetishized and appropriated by the masculine perspective.[10] Women in nineteenth-century American society were similarly objectified. Herman Melville, for example, wrote in *White-Jacket* (1850): the best of "chamber furniture . . . is the sight of a lovely wife."[11] A female person was seen primarily as an object of the male perspective, the effect of which was to diminish and depersonalize the individual woman. Fern, however, reversed the concept of the controlling gaze. She did not drop her eyes to the floor demurely and modestly as a woman of her generation was expected to do. In her fiction and in her newspaper articles the gaze is aggressively feminine: a woman looking *at men*, appraising, sometimes admiring—Fern was even unusually frank in her appreciative comments about the male body—in a way that was thought to be the prerogative of the male gaze.

Even more important, Fern's gaze was not only aggressively feminine, replacing and refusing to be appropriated by the male gaze; in looking at men, she was often critical of what she saw. Fern satirized and ridiculed the

pontifications and injustices of men and masculine society in graphic language and recognizable detail. Moreover, when men looked back—returned the gaze—they found that Fern was laughing at them. Recognizing
the power of laughter, Fern commented in a review of her husband's book
on humorous poetry that there were no women poets in the book: it is
"lucky for the male sex," she said, that women have not written humorous
poetry (NYL, August 2, 1856).

Post-Freudian analysis has identified male resistance to this kind of female
assertion as the male fear of castration. Feminist critic Hélène Cixous, who
ridicules this fear, as well as the Freudian concept of penis envy, has insisted
that men must overcome their fear and meet the woman as a person with
her own wholly female drives and desires instead of seeing her as a wounded
male intent on mutilation: "You only have to look at the Medusa straight
on to see her. And she's not deadly. She's beautiful and she's laughing."[12]

Like Cixous, Fern insisted upon the femaleness of her perspective. Early
in her career she replied to a reader who had taken her for a man that she
was, in fact, a "female woman" (OB, January 31, April 17, 1852). The use
of the word *female* here might seem redundant, but in the context of Fern's
writing it is not. She insisted that a strong woman was not a masculine
woman, or a man in female dress, or a woman who was usurping the role of
men; a strong woman was a strong *woman*. Impatient with critics who
could not understand an assertive woman except in masculine terms, Fern
commented, "Isn't it the funniest thing in life, that a woman can't be vital
and energetic, without being thought masculine?" (NYL, November 19,
1870).

Fern acknowledged and asserted her femaleness, and part of her assertion
involved the mandate to women to speak up, to use their female voices to
critique injustice from their own point of view. Fern insisted that a woman's
point of view counted as much as a man's. In "An Explosive Burst," she
wrote:

> I like a person who sticks to an opinion, or a friend, though he should
> be blown out of the mouth of a cannon every ten minutes for doing it. Of
> course, this is "horrid unfeminine,"—I know that too; but why a woman
> has not a right to love and hate persons and things as well and as strongly
> as a man; and why she has not a right, like him, to resent a manifest
> injustice, and why her individualism in matters of opinion and everything
> else should not be respected equally with his, I have yet to learn. (NYL,
> June 18, 1864)

In an article on women lecturers, Fern pointed out the need to hear the
woman's point of view. Responding to critics who claimed that a woman
had "nothing new" to bring forward, Fern asserted that even if she did not,

her woman's perspective was itself valuable because it gave "the presentation of a familiar theme, from a *feminine* point of view" (NYL, March 12, 1864).

One way in which women could let their voices be heard was by writing. This was the route that Fern chose, and in 1867 she wrote an article advising other silenced women to write: "I look around and see innumerable women, to whose barren, loveless life this would be improvement and solace, and I say to them, write! Write, if it will make that life brighter, or happier, or less monotonous. Write! it will be a safe outlet for thoughts and feelings. . . . [L]ift yourselves out of the dead-level of your lives. . . . Fight it! oppose it, for your own sakes and your children's! Do not be *mentally* annihilated by it" (NYL, August 8, 1867). Over a hundred years later Hélène Cixous wrote a similar article, whose language is uncannily reminiscent of Fern's: "Woman must write her self: must write about women and bring women to writing. . . . Write, let no one hold you back, let nothing stop you. . . . For when the Phallic period comes to an end, women will have been either annihilated or borne up to the highest and most violent incandescence. Muffled throughout their history, they have lived in dreams, in bodies (though muted), in silences."[13]

That Cixous and other feminist critics still feel the necessity to urge women to use their woman's voice is indicative of the extent to which resistance to the individualism of women has continued through the twentieth century, in American society and in other cultures as well. Looking now at American culture, the question we must ask ourselves centers around the question of societal structure: Has it changed? Is it more receptive today to the female individualism contained in Fern's writing? The evidence suggests that the logocentric—or phallogocentric—nature of American society continues to be resistant to the aggressive assertions of the woman's voice.[14] We have only to look at the escalating violence against women that is evidenced in popular culture today as well as in the gory statistics of police calendars to recognize that, as women have begun to speak out, they have also been increasingly silenced.[15] Analyses of films, television shows, popular music, and MTV videos, not to mention "snuff" pornography, show an alarming increase in the portrayal of women as victims: objectified, degraded, and— that ultimate silencer—killed. Similarly, police statistics show rapidly rising figures of crimes against women.[16] We remember that Fern's contemporary—and presumed friend—who was impatient with her independent behavior recommended that her husband "horsewhip her until she prayed for mercy."[17]

It is an irony that is not wholly accidental that Fanny Fern, who had been dismissed by twentieth-century (male) critics as a sentimentalist, too silly and too "feminine" to be worthy even of consideration, is in fact the most threatening and the most aggressively feminine writer of the period. Turning her gaze on men, usurping the power of the gaze and meeting men's assertions with laughter and ridicule, Fern constitutes a potent threat to the masculine power structure. Her life and work provide us with a penetrating look at nineteenth-century society from the perspective of a frank and outspoken woman; they also provide us with a compelling example of a woman who refused to be silenced.

NOTES

Prologue. Who Is Fanny Fern?

1. Nathaniel Hawthorne, *Letters to William Ticknor, 1851–1869*, ed. C. E. Frazer-Clark, Jr., 2 vols. (Newark, N.J.: Carteret Book Club, Inc., 1972), 1:78.

2. Fred Lewis Pattee, *The Feminine Fifties* (New York: D. Appleton-Century, 1940), 110–118. Fern's work was very popular in the nineteenth century. Until recently, however, it was ignored in the twentieth century, and Fern was disparaged as "a sentimental nonentity," "the grandmother of all sob sisters." See, e.g., Pattee, *The Feminine Fifties*, 110–118; and James D. Hart, *The Popular Book* (New York: Oxford University Press, 1950), 97. Robert P. Eckert, Jr., in "Friendly, Fragrant Fanny Ferns," *The Colophon* 18 (September 1934), unpaged, accepts the portrayal of Fern in the hostile *Life and Beauties*, and although he corresponded with Ethel Parton and obtained some valuable information, his is not an objective evaluation. Serious twentieth-century scholarship on Fanny Fern (which, sigificantly, between 1950 and 1991 has been published primarily by women scholars) began in 1954 with two articles by Elizabeth Bancroft Schlesinger, "Proper Bostonians as Seen by Fanny Fern," *New England Quarterly* 27 (March 1954):97–102; and Schlesinger, "Fanny Fern: Our Grandmother's Mentor," *New York Historical Society Quarterly* 38 (October 1954):501–519. Helen Papashvily devotes several pages to a discussion of Fern's career in *All the Happy Endings* (New York: Harper, 1956), 123–125. Papashvily, however, shows little understanding of Fern's work, commenting, for example, that "it was only her brother, not the whole male sex, she wanted to discipline" (125). A pioneering effort was the privately printed pamphlet, Florence Bannard Adams, *Fanny Fern, or a Pair of Flaming Shoes* (Trenton, N.J.: Hermitage, 1966). This was followed by Patricia McGinnis, "Fanny Fern, American Novelist," *Biblion* 2 (Spring 1969):2–37. An important article was Ann Douglas [Wood], "The 'Scribbling Women' and Fanny Fern: Why Women Wrote," *American Quarterly* 23 (Spring 1971): 3–24. Although Douglas's article is important for its careful research and interpretive assessment of Fern's work in relation to other women writers, and although she astutely recognizes the importance to Fern of the need for "*self*-expression" for women, Douglas is not free from the bias against women writers as sentimental and irrational that was promulgated by Pattee. For example, at the end of her article she says that Fern went on writing "hysterically" for the rest of her career (24), when, in fact, Fern's work, which was never hysterical, was even more measured or less angry later in her career than it was early in her career.

It was twelve years before anything else on Fern was published. In 1983 and 1984 Fern appeared as part of two separate works on women writers: Linda Huf, "*Ruth Hall* (1855): The Devil and Fanny Fern," in *A Portrait of the Artist as a Young Woman: The Writer as Heroine in American Literature* (New York: Ungar, 1983), 16–35; and Mary Kelley, *Private Woman, Public Stage: Literary Domesticity in Nineteenth-Century America* (New York: Oxford University Press, 1984), passim. I began working on Fern in 1981, and discussed her work briefly in the notes to my book, *The American Narcissus: Individualism and Women in Nineteenth-Century*

American Fiction (New Brunswick, N.J.: Rutgers University Press, 1984), 260–261. My works on Fern include Joyce W. Warren, "Profile of Fanny Fern," *Legacy* 2 (Fall 1985): 54–60; Warren, Introduction to *Ruth Hall and Other Writings* (New Brunswick, N.J.: Rutgers University Press, 1986), ix–xlii; Warren, "Subversion versus Celebration: The Aborted Friendship of Fanny Fern and Walt Whitman," in *Patrons and Protégées: Gender, Friendship, and Writing in Nineteenth-Century America,* ed. Shirley Marchalonis (New Brunswick, N.J.: Rutgers University Press, 1988), 59–93; "The Gender of American Individualism: Fanny Fern, the Novel, and the American Dream," in *Politics, Gender, and the Arts,* ed. Ronald Dotterer and Susan Bowers (Selinsgrove, Pa.: Susquehanna University Press, 1991); and "Text and Context in Fanny Fern's *Ruth Hall:* From Widowhood to Independence," in *Joinings and Disjoinings: The Significance of Marital Status in Literature,* ed. JoAnna S. Mink and Janet D. Ward (Bowling Green, Ohio: The Popular Press, 1991), 67–76; and "Fanny Fern's *Rose Clark*," *Legacy* 8 (Fall 1991). Recent scholarship includes David Reynolds, *Beneath the American Renaissance* (New York: Knopf, 1988), 402–407; and Susan K. Harris, "Inscribing and Defining: The Many Voices of Fanny Fern's *Ruth Hall,*" in *Nineteenth-Century American Women Writers: Interpretive Strategies* (New York: Oxford University Press, 1990), 111–127. (This chapter appeared earlier under the same title in *Style* 22 [Winter 1988]: 612–627).

One measure of how completely Fanny Fern has been ignored by the literary and academic community is the dearth of M.A. and Ph.D. theses that have been written on her work. In the 120 years since her death, only two master's theses and one doctoral dissertation have been written solely on Fanny Fern, and she has appeared prominently in few others. The first was Mae Weintraub Zlotnik, "Fanny Fern: A Biography" (Master's thesis, Columbia University, 1939). This was followed by Elaine Gellis Breslaw, "Popular Pundit: Fanny Fern and the Emergence of the American Newspaper Columnist" (Master's thesis, Smith College, 1956). Twenty years later Fern was an important part of Susan Geary's Ph.D. dissertation at Brown University, "Scribbling Women: Essays on Literary History and Popular Literature in the 1850's" (1976). Although a number of graduate students are currently involved in work on Fern, the first doctoral dissertation to appear that was written wholly on Fern was Stewart Desmond, "The Widow's Trials: The Life of Fanny Fern" (New York University, 1989).

In the twentieth century Fern's work has also been excluded from anthologies, even anthologies of women's writings published in the 1980s. The first twentieth-century anthology to include Fern's work was Judith Fetterley's 1985 collection, *Provisions: A Reader from 19th-Century American Women* (Bloomington: Indiana University Press, 1985), 241–260. The first major anthology to include a representation of Fern's work was *The Heath Anthology of American Literature,* ed. Paul Lauter et al. (Lexington, Mass.: D. C. Heath and Company, 1990), 1:1899–1907.

3. *Harper's New Monthly Magazine* 9 (July 1854): 277.
4. Reprinted in *The Living Age* (November 19, 1853), 485.

1. Deacon's Daughter

1. See birth records from the City Clerk's office in Portland, Maine.
2. Except in references to her birth, where I have used the birth certificate

first appears in letters to her from her first husband before their marriage in 1837. After that time she rarely used the form *Sarah,* although it was used by those who knew her as a young girl. *Sara* is the spelling used on all but one of her business contracts, her prenuptial agreement, her will, and the only article published in the *Ledger* under her real name. Information about Fanny Fern's early life is taken primarily from documents in the Sophia Smith Collection, Smith College, Northampton, Mass.; the Maine Historical Society, Portland, Maine; Ethel Parton, "Fanny Fern, An Informal Biography" (unpublished manuscript in the Sophia Smith Collection); James Parton, *Fanny Fern, A Memorial Volume* (New York: G. W. Carleton, 1873); and Fern's newspaper articles.

3. See Abner Morse, *Genealogical Register of the Descendants of Several Ancient Puritans* (Boston: H. W. Dutton & Son, 1859), 2:205–223; Ethel Parton, "Fanny Fern," and the Willis Family section of the pamphlet vertical file in the Genealogy Room of the New York Public Library. See also *New England Historical and Genealogical Register* (Boston: Samuel Drake, 1847–1865) 1:184, 10:289, 16:388, 27:316, 31:344, 21:187. Also extant is the manuscript "Biography of My Grandfather, Nathaniel Willis," by Richard S. Willis, dated February 27, 1890, in the Detroit Public Library.

4. Morse, *Genealogical,* 210, 213.

5. For information about the career of Nathaniel Willis, Jr., Fern's father, see, in addition to the previously listed genealogical works, William Willis, *History of Portland from 1632–1864* (Portland: Bailey & Noyes, 1865), 600; and Nathaniel Willis, "Autobiography of a Journalist," in Frederic Hudson, *Journalism in the United States from 1690 to 1872* (New York: Harper & Brothers, 1873), 289–293. Willis's claim that he was the founder of the *Recorder* was disputed; however, Willis's name is the only one on the first edition of January 3, 1816.

6. Although the town records in Portland were destroyed by the same fire that destroyed the Willis's house, I was able to determine the location of the Willis house from information derived from interviews with contemporaries of the family. See, e.g., "N. P. Willis and Early Portland," anon., n.d., Joint Free Public Library of Morristown and Morris Township, New Jersey. See also Federal Writers' Project Staff, *Maine: A Guide to Down East* (Boston: Houghton Mifflin, 1937), 176.

7. See the *Boston City Directory,* 1810–1820. See also the records in the *Registry of Deeds,* vol. 262, Court House, Boston, Massachusetts.

8. Morse, *Genealogical,* 214.

9. Records of the Park Street Church, Congregational Library, Boston, Massachusetts.

10. Nathaniel Willis, letter to James Parton, June 20, 1868, Houghton Library.

11. James Parton, letter to James T. Fields, February 13, 1867, Huntington Library, San Marino, California.

12. Undated newspaper clipping in the Saugus Public Library, Saugus, Massachusetts.

13. Circular advertising the Emerson Ladies' Seminary dated October 26, 1824, Lynn Historical Society.

14. Material in Saugus Public Library prepared by Richard Provenzano for the Saugus Historical Society, 1981.

15. D. Hamilton Hurd, *History of Essex County, Massachusetts* (Philadelphia: J. W. Lewis & Co., 1888), 1:419.

16. Horace H. Atherton, *History of Saugus, Massachusetts* (Saugus: Citizens Committee of the Saugus Board of Trade, 1916), 74.

17. Linda Guilford, *The Use of a Life: Memorials of Mrs. Z. P. Grant Banister* (New York: American Tract Society, 1885), 45–46. See also Robert Haney, "The Story of Joseph Emerson and His Female Seminary at Saugus," a talk given in Saugus on November 15, 1987, manuscript at the Saugus Public Library; and Harriet Webster Marr, "Joseph Emerson, Educator," in *Essex Institute Historical Collections* 3 (July 1953):205.

18. Marian Lansing, ed., *Mary Lyon Through Her Letters* (Boston: Books, Inc., 1937), 34–35.

19. Guilford, *Use of a Life*, 50–51.

20. Ibid., 41.

21. Ibid., 49.

22. Circular advertising the Emerson Ladies' Seminary, October 26, 1824.

23. Guilford, *Use of a Life*, 36.

24. Ibid., 39.

25. Ibid., 43.

26. Their birth dates were as follows: Nathaniel Parker, 1806; Louisa, 1807; Julia, 1809; Sarah, 1811.

27. The letters from Nathaniel P. Willis to Louisa Willis are in the Princeton University Library. In them Willis sends his love to Sarah and to Julia, indicating that both sisters were at Saugus. Although all of the letters are undated, in this letter N. P. Willis refers to the wedding of Mary Woods that he had just attended. The records in *The Vital Records of Andover to 1850* in the Andover Historical Society, Andover, Massachusetts, indicate that the wedding took place on September 27, 1822, which enables us to establish the approximate date of this and other letters. We know, for example, that the letter in which Willis tells about visiting the school preceded that of September 27 because in it Willis refers to the bride by her maiden name.

28. Undated newspaper clipping in the Saugus Public Library. See also E. P. Robinson, *Sketches of Saugus*, newspaper clipping book in the Boston Public Library, sketch no. 6.

29. Mary Willis, letter to Nathaniel P. Willis, December 19, 1823, in the Sophia Smith Collection. In this letter, Mary mentions all of the children except Sara and Louisa, which might indicate that they were not at home. However, we know that Louisa was at home the previous month because her brother wrote to her in Boston on November 9, 1823 (letter in Princeton University Library). This suggests that Sara was also at home, and that Mary simply neglected to include her and Louisa in her letter. That they were no longer at Saugus is suggested by the fact that they are not listed in the catalog for the Emerson Ladies' Seminary for 1823, in the Lynn Historical Society, although, according to Joseph Emerson's brother, Ralph Emerson, "The pupils in the preparatory school were probably not included in the catalogue" (Ralph Emerson, *Life of Rev. Joseph Emerson* [Boston: Crocker & Brewster, 1834], 262). That Fern and her sisters left the seminary in the fall of 1823, however, is apparent from her family's mention that she left the seminary when there was a severe epidemic (e.g., Ethel Parton, "Fanny Fern," 36); most sources indicate that there was a severe typhoid epidemic at the school in the fall of 1823 when many parents withdrew their children. See, Atherton, *History of Saugus*, 72;

Hurd, *History of Essex County,* 1:419; and newspaper clippings in the Saugus Public Library.

30. Guilford, *Use of a Life,* 54.

31. Ibid., 57.

32. Catalog of Adams Female Academy, 1853, p. 8, in the trustees' records in Derry, New Hampshire.

33. Guilford, *Use of a Life,* 57–62.

34. Mary Lyon, letter to Hannah White, July 2, 1824, in Lansing, *Mary Lyon,* 47.

35. Mary Lyon, letter to Amanda White, September 26, 1824, ibid., 49.

36. Guilford, *Use of a Life,* 73–75. See also reminiscences of a student at the academy in the New Hampshire Historical Society.

37. Guilford, *Use of a Life,* 56; Mary Lyon, letter to Hannah White, in Lansing, *Mary Lyon,* 47.

38. See copy of the Adams Female Academy 1827 diploma in Foster McCrum Palmer's unpublished essay, "The Adams Female Academy Diploma of Maria Chickering," in the Taylor Library in East Derry, New Hampshire.

39. Guilford, *Use of a Life,* 67.

40. Mary Lyon, letter to Amanda White, September 24, 1824, Lansing, *Mary Lyon,* 48.

41. Guilford, *Use of a Life,* 73.

42. Ellen Eldredge, letter to Robert Bonner, May 23, 1874, New York Public Library.

43. Guilford, *Use of a Life,* 55–56, 65, 76.

44. Ibid., 60–61, 68.

45. Ibid., 85.

46. Ibid., 64.

47. Ibid., 76–77.

48. See, e.g., Richard B. Sewall, *The Life of Emily Dickinson* (New York: Farrar, Straus and Giroux, 1974), 2:358–361.

49. Guilford, *Use of a Life,* 80–81.

50. Ibid., 85–87.

51. See the Park Street Church historical records at the Congregational Library, Boston, Massachusetts.

52. Notice in the *Connecticut Courant,* November 5, 1827, cited in Mae E. Harveson, *C. Esther Beecher, Pioneer Educator* (Philadelphia: Science Press, 1932), 44.

53. Catharine Beecher, *Educational Reminiscences and Suggestions* (New York: S. B. Ford & Co., 1874), 47–48.

2. Hartford Female Seminary

1. Fanny Fern, "Suggestions on Arithmetic," July 1829, school composition written at the Hartford Female Seminary, in the Sophia Smith Collection, Smith

College, and in James Parton, *Fanny Fern, a Memorial Volume* (New York: G. W. Carleton, 1873), 38–42.

2. Although I have not been able to locate a catalog for 1827 or 1830, Sarah Willis is listed as a student at the Hartford Female Seminary in the school catalog for 1828 and 1829. Copies of the 1828 catalog for the Hartford Female Seminary are in the Stowe-Day Foundation and the Connecticut Historical Society, both in Hartford. A copy of the 1829 catalog is in the Connecticut State Library in Hartford. The new seminary building opened in November 1827, but since the first entry in Sara Willis's school album (a gift from her brother N. P. Willis, currently in the Sophia Smith Collection, Smith College) is September 16, 1828, she probably did not begin at the seminary until the term after it opened, in May 1828. This date is supported by her statement in a school composition in 1829 that she first arrived at the seminary in the month of May (Sophia Smith Collection), and by her comment in the *New York Ledger* on February 26, 1870, that she went to the Hartford Female Seminary when she was sixteen (she turned seventeen in July 1828).

It is more difficult to determine when she left the seminary. A letter from Harriet Beecher Stowe to Mary Dutton on May 25, 1830, which is in the Beinecke Library at Yale University, indicates that Sara Willis was at the seminary for the summer term that year, and the last entry in her school album is dated September 1830. Ethel Parton says that she remained at home for six years before she was married in May of 1837 ("Fanny Fern, An Informal Biography [unpublished manuscript in the Sophia Smith Collection, Smith College], 76), which suggests that she completed her studies in Hartford at the end of the winter term in April 1831. This would be supported by Catherine Beecher's insistence that her students remain for the full three-year course.

3. Letter in *Reunion, Hartford Female Seminary* (Hartford: Case, Lockwood & Brainard Co., 1892), 67.

4. John C. Parsons, "Dr. Hawes and the Seminary," in *Reunion, Hartford Female Seminary,* 57–58.

5. Mary Kingsbury Talcott, "Description of the Hartford Female Seminary," 1830 (unpublished manuscript, Stowe-Day Foundation, Hartford).

6. Catharine Beecher, *Educational Reminiscences and Suggestions* (New York: S. B. Ford & Co., 1874), 47–48.

7. Catharine Beecher, letter to Mr. and Mrs. Willis, May 27, 1829, Sophia Smith Collection, Smith College.

8. Catharine Beecher, "Educational Reminiscences," *American Journal of Education,* ed. Henry Barnard (Hartford: American Journal of Education), 1878), 77.

9. Kathryn Kish Sklar, *Catharine Beecher: A Study in American Domesticity* (New Haven: Yale University Press, 1973), 79.

10. Mae E. Harveson, *C. Esther Beecher, Pioneer Educator* (Philadelphia: Science Press, 1932), 40–41.

11. Lyman Beecher Stowe, *Saints, Sinners and Beechers* (Indianapolis: Bobbs-Merrill, 1934), 115.

12. Sklar, *Catharine Beecher,* 93.

13. Ibid., 98.

14. Ibid.

15. Thomas Woody, *A History of Women's Education in the United States* (New York: Science Press, 1929), 1:355.

16.   Catharine Beecher, *Suggestions on Education, Presented to the Trustees of the Hartford Female Seminary* (Hartford: Packard & Butler, 1829), 12–25, 74–77. This is variously titled *Suggestions Respecting Improvements in Education, Presented to the Trustees of the Hartford Female Seminary.* Also Harveson, C. *Esther Beecher*, 41; *Hartford Courant*, October 21, 1823.

17.   1831 Catalog for the Hartford Female Seminary, 12–13, in the Connecticut State Library in Hartford.

18.   1831 Catalog for the Hartford Female Seminary, 7–8; 1828 Catalog for the Hartford Female Seminary, 14, Stowe-Day Foundation, Hartford.

19.   Harriet Beecher Stowe, letter to Mary Dutton, May 25, 1830, Beinecke Library, Yale University.

20.   Harriet Beecher Stowe, letter to James Parton, n.d. [1868], Sophia Smith Collection, Smith College.

21.   Harriet Beecher Stowe, letter to James Parton, February 6, 1868, Sophia Smith Collection, Smith College.

22.   Harriet Beecher Stowe, letter to Sarah Willis Parton, n.d., [1868], Sophia Smith Collection, Smith College.

23.   James C. Derby, *Fifty Years among Authors, Books and Publishers* (New York: G. W. Carleton, 1884).

24.   Sarah Willis's school album is in the Sophia Smith Collection, Smith College.

25.   Harriet Beecher Stowe, letter to Sarah Willis Parton, February 12, [1868], Sophia Smith Collection, Smith College.

26.   Ethel Parton, "Fanny Fern at the Hartford Female Seminary," *New England Magazine* 24 (March 1901):98.

27.   Catharine Beecher, letter to Mr. and Mrs. Willis, May 27, 1829.

28.   Ibid.

29.   Harriet Beecher Stowe, letter to Sarah Willis Parton, February 12 [1868], Sophia Smith Collection, Smith College.

30.   Mary E. Dewey, ed., *The Life and Letters of Catharine Sedgwick* (New York: Harper & Brothers, 1871), 225–226. That Fern visited her sister Louisa at Stockbridge is clear from an article in the *Ledger* on August 1, 1868. In this article, however, she says that she was a "romping school-girl" in nearby Pittsfield. In an interview in *The Life and Beauties of Fanny Fern* (New York: H. Long and Brother, 1855), 219, Fern's father also refers to her having attended a school in Pittsfield. Her sister married on May 31, 1824. Sarah Willis had left the Emerson Female Seminary in the fall of 1823. It is known that she and her sister Mary later attended the Adams Female Academy in Derry, New Hampshire, which was founded in 1824. However, Sarah and Mary are not listed in the 1824 or 1825 catalogs; they are listed in the 1826 catalog. Sarah might have attended a school in Pittsfield in 1824–1825, but the records of the Pittsfield Female Academy do not show her name. However, the available records only cover the years 1822–1826. Since the school began as a boarding school in 1827, it is possible that Fern was a student there in 1827 before she went to the Hartford Female Seminary. See records at the Berkshire Athenaeum, Pittsfield, Massachusetts.

31.   The significance of Catharine Sedgwick in these two areas is apparent from the comments of her contemporaries. Emily Dickinson's father, for example, admired Sedgwick because she gave him "a conscious pride" that American women could compete with writers of other countries, both male and female. See letter from

Edward Dickinson in Richard B. Sewall, *Life of Emily Dickinson* (New York: Farrar, Straus and Giroux, 1974), 49. In *Woman in the Nineteenth Century*, Margaret Fuller praised Sedgwick's position on women's rights. See *The Writings of Margaret Fuller*, ed. Mason Wade (New York: Viking, 1941), 207–208.

32. Sklar, *Catharine Beecher*, 147.

33. For information about N. P. Willis, see Henry A. Beers, *Nathaniel Parker Willis* (Boston: Houghton, Mifflin, 1885); and Cortland P. Auser, *Nathaniel P. Willis* (New York: Twayne, 1969).

34. Beers, *Willis*, 46–47.

35. Catharine Beecher, *Arithmetic, Explained and Illustrated, for the Use of the Hartford Female Seminary* (Hartford: P. Canfield, 1828), Preface.

36. Harriet Beecher Stowe, letter to Sarah Willis Parton, n.d., Sophia Smith Collection, Smith College.

37. Although Catharine Beecher did not believe that women were powerless, she felt that their influence should be rooted safely within the family. For Beecher's views on women's role and her conception of the domestic value of education for women, see, e.g., Catharine Beecher, *Suggestions on Education; The Elements of Mental and Moral Philosophy, Founded upon Experience, Reason, and the Bible* (Hartford: Peter B. Gleason & Co., 1831); *An Essay on Slavery and Abolitionism, with Reference to the Duty of American Females* (Philadelphia: Henry Perkins, 1837); and *A Treatise on Domestic Economy, for the Use of Young Ladies at Home, and at School* (Boston: Marsh, Capen, Lyon, and Webb, 1841). For a good analysis of Catharine Beecher's views on women's role, see Jeanne Boydston, Mary Kelley, and Anne Margolis, *The Limits of Sisterhood: The Beecher Sisters on Women's Rights and Women's Sphere* (Chapel Hill: University of North Carolina Press, 1988), spec. 114–124.

3. *"Bread-Making and Button-Hole Stitching"*

1. Henry A. Beers, *Nathaniel Parker Willis* (Boston: Hougton Mifflin, 1885), 17–18.

2. For a detailed discussion of the concept of women's role in nineteenth-century America, see Barbara Welter, "The Cult of True Womanhood," *American Quarterly* 18 (Summer 1966):151–162, 173–174. Welter writes: "The attributes of True Womanhood, by which a woman judged herself and was judged by her husband, her neighbors, and society could be divided into four cardinal virtues—piety, purity, submissiveness and domesticity. Put them all together and they spelled mother, daughter, sister, wife—woman. Without them, no matter whether there was fame, achievement or wealth, all was ashes." Although, as Mary Beth Norton points out in "The Paradox of 'Women's Sphere,'" one should not equate prescriptive behavior with actual behavior, Welter's analysis gives us an idea of the behavior that was expected of women of Fanny Fern's generation. See Norton, "The Paradox of 'Women's Sphere,'" in *Women of America*, ed. Carol Ruth Berkin and Mary Beth Norton (Boston: Houghton Mifflin, 1979), 139–149.

3. Nathaliel P. Willis's poem written for his sister Sarah Willis, "To My Wild Sis," is in the Sophia Smith Collection, Smith College.

4. Nathaniel P. Willis, letters to John B. Van Schaick, are in the Historical Society of Pennsylvania, Philadelphia, and the Pennsylvania State University Library, University Park. See also Willis's letters to his friend George Pumpelly, e.g., January [1830], June 30 [1829], in the Butler Library, Columbia University. In January [1830], Willis wrote:

"*Vive l'amour*" is still my slogan. I was landed in the street last Thursday night in my stocking feet from a ten foot window—a descent made in the hurry of an escape from a man who keeps a pretty woman, *who* keeps me. So I button'd my suspenders (thermometer at zero) and sans cravat or cloak, hurried home. The "impertinent intruder" was said to have gone to Salem—blast his genitals—and nobody expected him at midnight, to interrupt honest men in their amusement.

5. Nathaniel P. Willis, letters to J. B. Van Schaick, September 1 [1828]; February 3 [1829]; February 18 [1829], Historical Society of Pennsylvania.

6. N. P. Willis, letters to J. B. Van Schaick, November 27 [1828]; February 18 [1829], Historical Society of Pennsylvania.

7. Records of the Park Street Church, in the Congregational Library, Boston, Massachusetts.

8. Beers, *Willis*, 90, 92–93.

9. Ibid., 89.

10. N. P. Willis, letter to J. B. Van Schaick, February 14, n.d. [circa 1827–1831], Pennsylvania State University Library.

11. N. P. Willis, letter to J. B. Van Schaick, January 11 [1829], Historical Society of Pennsylvania.

12. N. P. Willis, letters to J. B. Van Schaick, April 12 [1829]; April 20 [1829], Historical Society of Pennsylvania.

13. N. P. Willis, letter to J. B. Van Schaick, February 26 [1831], Historical Society of Pennsylvania.

14. Horace Mann, letter to Mary Peabody, December 22, 1836, Massachusetts Historical Society.

15. Nathaniel P. Willis, letter to Hannah Willis, September 12, 1835, in Beers, *Willis*, 99.

16. N. P. Willis, letter to J. B. Van Schaick, November 23, [1828], Historical Society of Pennsylvania.

17. N. P. Willis wrote to his fiancée two weeks before the wedding: "I should never have wished to marry you if you had not been religious, for I have confidence in no woman who is not so." See Beers, *Willis*, 176.

18. Correspondence between Sarah Payson Willis and Charles Harrington Eldredge [1836–1837], Sophia Smith Collection, Smith College.

19. J.C.A., letter to Sarah Willis, undated, Sophia Smith Collection, Smith College. Also among Fern's papers in the Sophia Smith Collection is a letter from John James Flournoy to N. P. Willis, dated April 7, 1830, declaring his passionate love for Willis's sister Sarah and asking permission to marry her. The letter is accompanied by a note from Paul M. Trevant, dated April 10, 1830, stating that Flournoy had given him other such letters to mail, but he had not sent them. Flournoy had apparently suffered a nervous breakdown and, according to Trevant, his doctor had advised that if he could become settled on this subject, he might get better. Also included are passionate verses by Flourney written to Sarah Willis.

20. Boston City Directory (Boston: Charles Stimson, 1836).

21. Charles Eldredge, letter to Sarah Willis, n.d., Sophia Smith Collection, Smith College.

22. Mary Eldredge's will is in the Sophia Smith Collection, Smith College.

4. Marriage, Motherhood, and Money

1. I have not been able to determine the exact date of Fern's daughter Mary's birth. Most sources indicate that she was born in 1838, but nowhere are the month and date given, and the Boston City Registry has no record of her birth. According to the inscription on her tombstone at Mount Auburn Cemetery in Cambridge, she was seven years old when she died. If she was a full-term baby conceived after her parents' marriage in May 1837, she would have to have been born in February or early March of 1838 in order to have been seven when she died on March 17, 1845.

N. P. Willis's hope that his family would love his English bride is suggested by the poem he composed when he sailed for the United States with her in May 1836. "Lines on Leaving Europe" concludes with this plea:

> Room in thy heart! The hearth she left
> Is darkened to lend light to ours.
> There are bright flowers of care bereft,
> And hearts—that languish more than flowers.
> She was their light—their very air;
> Room, mother, in thy heart! place for her in thy prayer!

In Henry A. Beers, *Nathaniel Parker Willis* (Boston: Houghton Mifflin, 1895), 179. Fern's attitude toward Mary Stace Willis is apparent in her 1852 reference to the "sweet English Mary" whom her brother had brought home with him (*Olive Branch*, August 15, 1852).

2. Cambridge, Massachusetts, Middlesex County *Register of Deeds*, 376:578–579.

3. See *Boston City Directory*, 1839. For records of Hezekiah Eldredge's purchases in Brighton, see especially, Cambridge, Mass., Middlesex County *Register of Deeds*, 323:367; 330:22; 337:602–603; 353:552–553; 368:198–199; and particularly the map of his lands in Brighton at the end of volume 469.

4. In Elizabeth Stuart Phelps's 1877 novel, *The Story of Avis* (New Brunswick, N.J.: Rutgers University Press, 1985), for example, when Avis Dobell receives the check in payment for her portrait of Ostrander, the check is made out to her father (75).

5. There are many examples of nineteenth-century women writers whose husbands or fathers lost their earnings through mismanagement of the funds. Among writers, the father of Susan and Anna Warner used his daughters' money as fast as they could earn it, and the husband of Rose Terry Cooke made it necessary for his wife to continue to write for a living because, after their marriage, he used up all of her savings in ill-advised investments.

6. See Cambridge, Massachusetts, Middlesex County *Register of Deeds,* 383:291; 385:9.

7. See Cambridge, Massachusetts, Middlesex County *Register of Deeds,* 398:1; 399:158–159, 533; 400:7; 404:274–275; 405:73, 367; 408:77–78, 80–81; 407:195; 417:572.

8. See *The Case of Joseph Jenkins versus Charles H. Eldredge, et al.,* in Equity, in the Circuit Court of the United States, for the First Circuit—District of Massachusetts (Boston: Freeman and Bolles, 1843). A copy of this publication is in Fanny Fern's papers in the Sophia Smith Collection at Smith College. A duplicate copy is in the Massachusetts Historical Society in Boston. I want to thank Alfred R. Williams, Massachusetts real estate consultant, for taking the time to explore the complexities of this case.

9. I have put together the story of this complicated case from the following records: *The Case of Joseph Jenkins versus Charles H. Eldredge,* ibid; *Federal Cases,* 13: 462–519, New York University Law Library; the private papers of Joseph Jenkins in the Massachusetts Historical Society; the private papers of Fanny Fern in the Sophia Smith Collection at Smith College; and the records at the National Archives and Records Administration, Boston.

10. See specifically, Eldredge's petition, the Master's Report, and the Final Decree in the "Final Record Book," vol. 31, in the Records of the U.S. Circuit Court for the District of Massachusetts, National Archives, Boston, Massachusetts.

11. Petition of Charles H. Eldredge, "Final Record Book," 31:338–340.

12. Ibid., esp. pp. 331, 346–349, 386, 388–389, 405–406.

13. Ethel Parton, letter to Robert P. Eckert, Jr., June 23, 1934, private collection: "Whatever she accepted from him she accepted with bitter reluctance, because of his open resentment of Charles Eldredge's inconvenient selection of a time to die. He had liked and admired him while living, as a rising young financier, but when things went smash, he held him wholly to blame." See also Ethel Parton, "Fanny Fern, An Informal Biography" (unpublised manuscript in the Sophia Smith Collection, Smith College), 100–101.

14. See, e.g., N. P. Willis, letters to J. B. Van Schaick, September 1 [1828], February 3 [1829], and February 18 [1829], Historical Society of Pennsylvania, Philadelphia.

15. Master's Report, "Final Record Book," 31:276–278.

16. Petition of Charles H. Eldredge, "Final Record Book," 31:351.

17. Sarah P. Eldredge, letter to Richard Willis, February 20, 1844, Sophia Smith Collection, Smith College. Richard Storrs Willis's response to the family tragedies reported to him while he was in Germany is suggested in a letter from him to Bayard Taylor in July 1845. N. P. Willis had arrived in England, and Richard expected his brother to come to Germany: "I hope he will come, but I should almost fear to see him, after our frightful family calamities, and the *reality* of them which one so near & dear to me as he, would certainly bring with him" (Olin Library, Cornell University, Ithaca, New York).

18. See Harriet Beecher Stowe, *Uncle Tom's Cabin* (New York: Harper & Row, 1965), e.g. 82–91.

19. Other deaths from childbirth in Fanny Fern's family include the death of Richard Willis's wife, Jessie Cairns Willis, in 1858 and the death of Fern's daughter, Grace Willis Thomson, in 1862.

5. "Dark Days"

1. See Ethel Parton, letter to Robert P. Eckert, Jr., June 23, 1934, private collection. Also see Ethel Parton, "Fanny Fern, An Informal Biography" (unpublished manuscript in Sophia Smith Collection, Smith College), 100, and James Parton, *Fanny Fern, A Memorial Volume* (New York: G. W. Carleton, 1873), 49.
2. See, e.g., Ethel Parton, letter to Robert P. Eckert, Jr., June 9, 1934, private collection.
3. Susan (Capen) Douglas Willis's will and account books are in the Massachusetts Historical Society. A copy of the prenuptial agreement is in the Boston Court House, Suffolk County *Register of Deeds,* 500:225–226.
4. That Fern's mother, if living, would have helped her daughter's situation somewhat is suggested several times in Fern's articles. See, e.g., "I Want My Mother," *New York Ledger,* April 29, 1871.
5. See also Fanny Fern's articles, specifically, *New York Ledger,* February 26, 1859; *Olive Branch* September 4, 1852, and January 8, 1853. Also see Fanny Fern, *Ruth Hall and Other Writings,* ed. Joyce W. Warren (New Brunswick, N.J.: Rutgers University Press, 1986), 66–67, 70–72, 87–88. Fern's comments about her father's stinginess are recorded in the Diary of Thomas Butler Gunn, October 24, 1856, Missouri Historical Society, Saint Louis, Missouri.
6. Fanny Fern, *Fresh Leaves* (New York: Mason Brothers, 1857), 9–43.
7. William Endicott, *Reminiscences of Seventy-Five Years* (Boston: Massachusetts Historical Society, 1913), 9–10. See also William Endicott letter to Dr. Horace Bumstead, January 14, 1913, cited in Mae Weintraub Zlotnik, "Fanny Fern: A Biography (Master's thesis, Columbia University, 1939), 11 notes.
8. See, for example, Ralph Waldo Emerson, *Journals and Miscellaneous Notebooks,* ed. William H. Gilman et al., 16 vols. (Cambridge: Harvard University Press, 1960–1982), 9:273. Despite an occasional cry of pain in his journals, Emerson's public writings and even his private writings maintain the persona that he strove to present to the world: individualistic to the extent that he could remain untouched by the loss of other human beings. When his son Waldo died, Emerson wrote a letter, "I chiefly grieve that I cannot grieve; that this fact takes no more deep hold than other facts" *(Letters of Ralph.Waldo Emerson,* ed. Ralph L. Rusk, 6 vols. [New York: Columbia University Press, 1939], 3:9. For a detailed analysis of this aspect of Emerson's and Thoreau's individualism, see Joyce W. Warren, *The American Narcissus: Individualism and Women in Nineteenth-Century American Fiction* (New Brunswick, N.J.: Rutgers University Press, 1984), 35–43, 60–69.
9. The extent to which Henry David Thoreau sought to maintian a persona of total self-reliance is apparent in his response to his brother John's death from lockjaw. When John died, Thoreau did not write in his Journal for many months, and when he resumed writing, he did not mention his brother's death. When he did refer to John's death in letters, he wrote emotionlessly. That he was in fact very strongly affected by his brother's death is apparent in the psychosomatic lockjaw and ill health he suffered from for many months after John's death *(The Writings of Henry David Thoreau,* Walden Edition, 20 vols. [New York: AMS Press, 1968], 6:41–42; 8:106).
10. See Ethel Parton, letter to Robert P. Eckert, Jr., June 23, 1934, in which she specifically answers his question about her grandmother's poverty:

Most of my information on such points I had, of course, from my Aunt Ellen. Her memory of those years of struggle and poverty was all too vivid, though she was still a young child. But I have heard of them also from my great-aunt Julia Willis, who spent a year with us here in Newburyport after I was a young woman grown. My Aunt Ellen, who was devoted to her mother, might have been considered biased, and her mother's partisan, perhaps. But Aunt Julia was an exceptionally cool and clear-brained old lady, never involved in family feuds, nor likely to have her recollection of fact distorted by her emotions. So while my knowledge of detail is slight, I feel that on the essential situation I have a right to speak with assurance.

Regarding Julia Willis's honesty, see letter from Sarah Willis Eldredge to Richard Willis, February 20, 1844, where she tells of how her mother asks Julia if it is true that Ellen is dead. When Julia responds that she is dead, her mother says that it must be true because Julia "never told a lie" (Sophia Smith Collection, Smith College). In *The Life and Beauties of Fanny Fern* (New York: H. Long and Brother, 1855), 219–222, Nathaniel Willis is quoted as saying that he contributed eight hundred dollars to Fern and her children after Charles Eldredge died, before and after her marriage to Farrington, but that he stopped helping her because she wrote him "unwomanly and unfilial" notes asking him for money. He said that he believed the Eldredges contributed an equal sum. It is difficult to know how much credence to give this statement, first, because it is printed in a hostile book whose author's purpose was to discredit Fern, and, second, because Willis was being interviewed after the publication of *Ruth Hall* and was attempting to defend himself against the criticism contained in the book.

11. Mary Andrews Denison's protest novel, *Edna Etheril, The Boston Seamstress* (New York: Burgess, Stringer & Co., 1847), which describes conditions in Boston at the time that Sarah Eldredge was working as a seamstress, indicates that seamstresses were paid six cents a shirt (40). Other sources indicate that a seamstress, working twelve to fifteen hours a day, could not make more than ten shirts a week. See David Reynolds, *Beneath the American Renaissance* (New York: Knopf, 1988), 352.

12. I have not been able to locate the date of the teacher's examination in the records in Boston. It is mentioned by Ethel Parton "Fanny Fern," 103–105, and James Parton, *Fanny Fern,* 50.

13. Ethel Parton tells us that her grandmother said that although the portrayal of the exam in *Ruth Hall* was humorous, it was "much nearer truth than any one would be likely to suppose" ("Fanny Fern," 104).

14. See *Boston City Directory* (Boston: Charles Stimson, 1846–1853); Abner Morse, *Genealogical Register of the Descendants of Several Ancient Puritans* (Boston: H. W. Dutton & Son, 1859), 2:213–223; and the papers of Josiah F. Bumstead in the Massachusetts Historical Society.

15. Ethel Parton, letter to Robert P. Eckert, Jr., June 6, 1934, private collection.

16. The date of the Farrington marriage is given as January 15, 1849, in the *New England Historical and Genealogical Register* (Boston: Samuel G. Drake, 1849), 3:195. However, the records at the Park Street Church, where the ceremony was performed, list the date as January 17, 1849. The difference in dates may simply be an error, or the two different dates may indicate that the marriage happened the

way that Gertrude Dean's second marriage did in *Rose Clark:* Stahle tricked Gertrude into marrying him by having the wedding announced in the newspaper as though it had already taken place (Fanny Fern, *Rose Clark* [New York: Mason Brothers, 1856], 233). If the Farrington marriage occurred in the same way, the date of the actual marriage would be January 17; the premature announcement would be the January 15 date that is recorded in the *Register.*

    17. See *Boston City Directory* for 1849.

    18. Ellen E. Parton, letter to J.P.C. Winship, February 28, 1899, Sophia Smith Collection, Smith College.

    19. Ethel Parton, letter to Robert P. Eckert, Jr., June 9, 1934, private collection.

    20. This theme appears in a number of nineteenth-century novels. See, e.g., E.D.E.N. Southworth's *The Hidden Hand* (1859); Wilkie Collins, *The Woman in White* (1859–1860); and Louisa May Alcott, "A Whisper in the Dark" (1863).

    21. Fanny Fern portrays this situation in "The Step-Mother," Boston *Olive Branch,* February 7, 1852.

    22. Ellen E. Parton, letter to J.P.C. Winship, February 28, 1899, Sophia Smith Collection, Smith College.

    23. *Boston City Directory,* 1850.

    24. See letter from William H. Dennett, variously spelled Dennet, to Fern's daughter, Ellen Eldredge Parton, March 2, 1876, Houghton Library, Harvard University.

    25. Sarah P. Farrington, letter to Thomas Farrington, January 28, 1851, Sophia Smith Collection, Smith College.

    26. See also Fern, *Rose Clark,* 246.

    27. Ethel Parton, letter to Robert P. Eckert, Jr., June 23, 1934. See also statement by Ethel Parton in the Farrington Papers, Sophia Smith Collection, Smith College.

    28. Letter from Thomas Farrington "To Whom it May Concern or For Mrs. S. P. Farrington," January 28, 1851, Sophia Smith Collection, Smith College.

    29. Clipping from the *Boston Daily Bee,* February 25, 1851, Sophia Smith Collection, Smith College.

    30. The last year that Samuel P. Farrington is listed in the *Boston City Directory* is 1850. That he wrote letters to his wife pretending affection and falsely asking her to join him, as Stahle did in *Rose Clark* (252–253) in order to give Gertrude no legal weapon against him, is suggested by Fern's note on the envelope containing the Farrington Papers in her papers at Smith College. "My daughter Grace will understand the *duplicity* of S. F.'s letters," she wrote, but there are no letters from Samuel Farrington among the papers. One suspects that the letters were destroyed by her family after her death. Or Fern herself may have destroyed them after Grace's death, since after Grace died, there would be no one living who would understand the letters; her daughter Ellen was too young at the time of her marriage to Farrington to understand the situation.

    31. In February 1850, Edwin Forrest filed a divorce suit against his wife accusing her of adultery. N. P. Willis defended her to his friends and in April wrote a defense in the *Home Journal.* Forrest named Willis and his brother Richard Willis as correspondents in the case, and in June 1850 Forrest attacked Willis in the street. There was a countersuit by Mrs. Forrest beginning in December 1851. Mrs. Willis sat in the courtroom with her husband, and Mrs. Forrest was ultimately cleared of

all charges. The trial proceedings were recorded in *The New York Times* from December 18, 1851, to February 2, 1852. See also Henry A. Beers, *Nathaniel Parker Willis* (Boston: Houghton Mifflin, 1885), 307–326. On July 16, 1851, at around the time that his sister was beginning to write, the Boston *Daily Evening Transcript* announced: "Mr. Forrest has commenced proceedings in the U.S. Court against N.P. Willis in action for libel setting damages at $20,000."

32. When Willis was in England in 1835 he was insulted in a magazine article by Captain Marryat, who wrote in the *Metropolitan:* "Although we are acquainted with the birth, parentage, and history of Mr. Willis, . . . we will pass them over in silence; and we think that Mr. Willis will acknowledge that we are generous in so doing." Willis replied in the *Times,* and Marryat challenged him to a duel. The two were ready to fight the duel, but at the last minute their seconds were able to settle the dispute (Beers, *Willis,* 197–205).

33. Of Fanny Fern's eight siblings, only Lucy Bumstead and N. P. Willis would have been in a position to help her monetarily, and they are the only two that Fern seems to have been bitter about: except for her father and in-laws, they are the only relatives she satirized in her story in *Ruth Hall.* Lucy was married to the well-to-do Josiah Bumstead, and Willis was a successful journalist, whose wife had brought him a comfortable income. Two of her sisters were dead (Ellen in 1844 and Louisa in 1849). Mary was herself a widow, her husband, Joseph Jenkins, having died in 1843 during the suit that his father had brought against Charles Eldredge. Julia was unmarried and dependent upon her male relatives. Fern's younger brother, Richard, had just returned from Germany at the end of 1848 and was a struggling musician. His fortunes changed for the better at the same time Fern's did: he married the wealthy Jessie Cairns on September 30, 1852. His memorial tribute to her written for their three little daughters when their mother died in 1858 describes how he was an impoverished musician and she his music pupil when they met. (See the papers of Richard and Jessie Willis in the Ward Family Papers in the Bryant Library, Roslyn, New York.) I have been able to find very little information about Fern's other younger brother, Edward. He is seldom mentioned by the other members of the family. There are two letters from N. P. Willis in the Fales Library at New York University regarding some kind of trouble that his brother was in. Both of the letters are to correspondents in Ohio, and if the brother referred to is Edward, they suggest that Edward Willis was living in Ohio at the time of his sister's difficulties. One has been dated 1852 in another hand. In the first letter to Edmunds Pierrepont in Columbus, Ohio, dated October 25, N. P. Willis writes:

> Your letter touching my unhappy brother puts me under great obligation to you, everything with regard to him being of course of the deepest interest to us. Mr. Cartwright a merchant from that part of the country now in Boston puts the merits of the case in a totally different light, however, acquitting my brother of everything but rudeness & indiscretion. I trust in God it is so.

In the second letter, postmarked November 28, Willis writes to an unknown correspondent in Akron, Ohio:

> I received yours of November 16 & am exceedingly obliged to you for such welcome intelligence. My brother is at present in France, I believe, tho' I hear he designs returning. He has not written to me in many months.

Richard Willis stated in January of 1852 that he had no idea where his brother Edward was living. (See Richard Willis's testimony in the Forrest trial recorded in *The New York Times* on January 13, 1852). Edward Willis was apparently unsettled in 1851–1852, and would not have been in a position to help his sister. He died prematurely in 1853 at the age of thirty-six.

34. Louisa May Alcott, *Behind a Mask* (New York: Quill, 1984), 59. Although Jean Muir fabricated this particular story, Alcott's reference to the threat would have been thoroughly understood by her readers, and Jean's choice of this story was clearly one that would gain her sympathy.

35. E.D.E.N. Southworth, *The Hidden Hand* (New York: Dillingham, 1888), 442.

36. Ethel Parton, letter to Robert P. Eckert, Jr., June 23, 1934.

37. Ibid.

6. The Birth of Fanny Fern

1. See especially, Ethel Parton, letter to Robert P. Eckert, Jr., June 9, 1934, private collection.

2. Fern's movements at this time can be established from a combination of sources. In her 1856 article "My Old Ink-Stand and I," Fern indicates that early in her career she occupied an attic room in a boardinghouse run by Mr. and Mrs. Griffin. The *Boston City Directory* for 1850–1853 lists a boardinghouse run by George Griffin at 31 Brattle Street in Cambridge. That Fern was living in Cambridge early in 1853 is clear from her contract with Derby and Miller dated May 2, 1853, which lists her residence as Cambridge. At some point, she apparently lived in a boardinghouse on Mount Vernon Street. (See Ethel Parton's manuscript biography, "Fanny Fern," 118, in the Sophia Smith Collection, Smith College, Northampton, Massacusetts.) Since there is a Mount Vernon Street just up the hill from the Boston Common, Fern may have been in this boardinghouse when Ellen wandered away from the Common to look for dandelions. Or, since there is a Mount Vernon Street in Cambridge, this could have been her 1853 Cambridge address.

3. "The Model Husband" (Boston *Olive Branch*, June 28, 1851) is the first of seven articles that can be positively identified as Fern's appearing in the *Olive Branch* before Fern began using the Fanny Fern signature. It was later said that her first article was "The Model Minister." However, this latter article did not appear in the *Olive Branch* until April 24, 1852, when she had been writing under the Fern signature for seven months. What was erroneously remembered as "The Model Minister" was probably "The Model Husband." The editor wrote an introductory note to "The Model Husband," which he seldom did, suggesting that he was introducing a new contributor. Fern remembered *The Mother's Assistant* as having been the periodical that bought her first article; however, the only article by her that I have been able to find in this journal was published in December 1851. See letter to the *Nation*, undated clipping from the 1860s in the Horace Greeley Papers, New York Public Library. Fern writes that her first article was in a "one-horse religious

magazine in Boston, called *The Mother's Assistant* or some such name." She said the remuneration was fifty cents and that she had to climb "four pair of stairs five times to the office of the editor to get it, besides being put through this catechism: "Widow eh? But you have on black! Children? How many? Girls or Boys?"

Fern's obituary notice in *The Nation* 15 (October 17, 1872): 251 states that her first article appeared in *The Carpet-Bag*, a comic weekly. However, I have not been able to find an article that could be by Fern published in *The Carpet-Bag* before June 28, 1851, when "The Model Husband" appeared in the *Olive Branch*. Nor have I found any other source that mentions *The Carpet-Bag*.

4. In order to determine the facts of Fern's early attempt to publish her articles, I have used the following sources: James Parton, *Fanny Fern, A Memorial Volume* (New York: G. W. Carleton, 1873), 50–52; Ethel Parton, "Fanny Fern, An Informal Biography" (unpublished manuscript in Sophia Smith Collection, Smith College), 110–112; and Fern's own newspaper articles. In addition, I have consulted the files of the newspapers in which her early articles were published. Also relevant is Fanny Fern, *Ruth Hall and Other Writings*, ed. Joyce W. Warren (New Brunswick, N.J.: Rutgers University Press, 1986), 120–122, 125. I have not been able to locate the newspaper in which her first article was reprinted, although I have located other early reprints.

5. Nathaniel Parker Willis, letter to Sarah Eldredge Farrington, n.d., Sophia Smith Collection, Smith College.

6. Nathaniel Parker Willis, "To My Wild Sis"; envelope containing poem and letter, Sophia Smith Collection, Smith College.

7. For example, after printing Fanny Forrester's and Grace Greenwood's work, Willis printed comments praising their work. In the *Home Journal* he calls Fanny Forrester a "woman of genius" (July 25, 1846) and writes a tribute to the "genius" of Grace Greenwood (June 19, 1847). He prints and reprints their work and comments favorably in short notes or in articles specifically on the writer. See also, e.g., *Home Journal*, February 14, 1846, February 21, 1846, April 18, 1846, July 25, 1846, April 3, 1847. That Willis did not generally pay his contributors is apparent from James Parton's comments in *Triumphs of Enterprise, Ingenuity, and Public Spirit* (New York: Virtue & Yorston, 1874), 16–17.

8. See e.g. George Templeton Strong, *Diary*, ed. Allen Nevins and Milton Halsey Thomas (New York: Octagon Books, 1974), 2:122. Strong writes after going to a small party at Richard Willis's: "Great respect for Richard Willis, his only drawback his brother, N. P. Willis, author of the Blidgims story & (according to common report), of other things only not quite so flagitious. Wish *he* would go to Australia." See also the review of *Ruth Hall* in the *Hartford Courant*, December 19, 1854: "The style is Fanny Fern's, and resembles that of no other writer. Like Willis's it is brilliant and sketchy, but has more pathos and humor inwrought into its very texture."

9. See Nathaniel Parker Willis, letter to Richard Storrs Willis, June 2 [1853], Princeton University Library.

10. James C. Derby, *Fifty Years Among Authors, Books and Publishers* (New York: G. W. Carleton, 1884), 220.

11. See Ellen Tucker Emerson, *The Life of Lidian Jackson Emerson*, ed. Delores Bird Carpenter (Boston: Twayne, 1980), 82–83.

12. Ralph Waldo Emerson, *Complete Works*, Centenary Edition, ed. Edward W. Emerson, 12 vols. (Boston: Houghton Mifflin, 1903–1904), 2:272.

13. Harriet Martineau, *Autobiography*, ed. Maria Weston Chapman (Boston: James R. Osgood, 1877), 1:384–385.

14. Henry A. Beers, *Nathaniel Parker Willis* (Boston: Houghton Mifflin, 1885), 306–307.

15. This article appears to be by Fanny Fern: it is signed "Aunt Emma," and Fern often called herself "Aunt" when writing for children; it appears in the "Youth's Department," which is where other articles by Fanny Fern appeared at this time; the style sounds like Fern's; and the facts that the article refers to about the author's life coincide with the facts of Fern's life.

16. The editor of the *True Flag* describes Fern's first appearance at his office in his anonymously published *The Life and Beauties of Fanny Fern* (New York: H. Long and Brother, 1855), 39–42. This was a hostile work, in which the editor, William Moulton, sought to defame Fanny Fern in order to avenge himself upon her for leaving his employ and then for satirizing him in *Ruth Hall*. Although one therefore must question the accuracy of his description, it is interesting to see the scene from the editor's perspective.

17. *Life and Beauties*, 43.

18. *The Mother's Assistant, Young Lady's Friend*, 22 (December 1851):187–188.

19. The files of the *Olive Branch* are in the American Antiquarian Society, Worcester, Massachusetts.

20. The files of the *True Flag* are in the American Antiquarian Society, Worcester, Massachusetts.

21. Fanny Fern's earnings can be determined from Derby, *Fifty Years*, 199–200, her own comments, and the comments of the editors for whom she wrote (Boston *Olive Branch*, January 6, 1855; Boston *True Flag*, January 13, 1855).

22. For example, the New York *Musical World and Times*, on January 22, 1853, several months after Fanny Fern began writing for it, printed a reply to the often asked question, "Who is Fanny Fern?":

Various paragraphs purporting to be correct answers to this question, are going the rounds of the press. One says Fanny Fern is N. P. Willis; another, that Eppes Sargent is the "critter"; a third, that Park Benjamin is the veritable Fanny; a fourth, that she is a maiden sister of Richard Storrs Willis of the *New York Musical World*; a fifth announces, with a great flourish, that the mystery is at last solved, and that Mrs. Harriet Beecher Stowe, the authoress of *Uncle Tom's Cabin*, is the real Fanny Fern; Mrs. Ellett suffers herself to be announced by a Cincinnati publisher as Fanny Fern . . . ; sundry papers insist that Fanny is a sister of Oliver Dyer . . . ; others, that she is a Southern lady, and the wife of a distinguished politician; and the last and most popular rumor is that Fanny Fern is the Rev. Thomas F. Norris.

23. Ellen E. Parton, letter to J.P.C. Winship, February 28, 1899, Sophia Smith Collection, Smith College.

24. In addition to Fanny Forrester and Grace Greenwood, other alliterative writers included Minnie Myrtle, Essie Evergreen, and Lottie Laurel. An example of the "pretty" writing that was associated with these alliterative names is this piece from Lottie Laurel:

Wandering through a lovely garden, where the most delightful perfumes were wafted on every passing breeze from a thousand bright-eyed flowers, and where tinkling fountains, and warbling birds, made heavenly melody, I saw among a bed of lilies a beautiful little being whose dress seemed sunbeams and dew-drops woven together, while a radiant star glittered on its fair and tiny forehead. (*New York Ledger*, April 28, 1855)

25. Ann Douglas [Wood] discusses the dualistic quality of the name Fanny Fern, "Fanny" representing the "satanic," and "Fern" representing the sentimental ("The Scribbling Women and Fanny Fern: Why Women Wrote," *American Quarterly*, 23 [Spring 1971]: 17–18). It is important to recognize, however, that such dualism is only the effect of the name for twentieth-century readers. From the perspective of the author herself, there was no dualism in the name at all. The ferns she had in mind were *not* delicate and ethereal, and their association with her mother was not with sentimentality but with strength. Moreover, one cannot assume, on the other hand, that her association of the name Fanny with mischief, which Douglas cites in Fern's article "Tom Versus Fan" (Boston *True Flag*, July 10, 1852), predated her own use of the name. For a very different association, see the story "Woman's Rights" by Haddie Lane in *Godey's Lady's Book* 40 (April 1850):269–273. The Fanny in the story is a submissive and dutiful young woman who meekly accepts her father's abuse.

26. In July 1856 Fanny Fern and her husband, James Parton, went to court in Philadelphia and successfully prevented William Fleming from publishing a book under the name Fanny Fern. On August 2, 1856, Fanny Fern printed an article in the *New York Ledger* describing her triumph, "A Premonitory Squib Before Independence."

7. Columnist and Author

1. For Fern's earnings at this time, see Boston *Olive Branch,* January 6, 1855, and Boston *True Flag,* January 13, 1855.

2. James Parton, *Triumphs of Enterprise, Ingenuity, and Public Spirit* (New York: Virtue & Yorston, 1874), 16–17.

3. Henry A. Beers, *Nathaniel Parker Willis* (Boston: Houghton Mifflin, 1885), 321. Also see Willis's letters to the *Home Journal,* in 1852. His letters were written from the south until October 2, 1852, when he returned and was living on the Hudson.

4. Fanny Fern's articles are printed, quoted from, or referred to in the *Home Journal* between August 21, 1852, and October 6, 1853, during which time N. P. Willis was not in the office. On June 4, 1853, *Fern Leaves* was given a long and very favorable review in the *Home Journal,* apparently written by James Parton, and the second series of *Fern Leaves* was announced on August 13, 1853.

5. See also, Milton Flower, *James Parton, the Father of Modern Biography* (Durham, N.C.: Duke University Press, 1951), 23–24. Willis sold his house in Manhattan in the spring of 1853, but he had continued to live in the country the previous winter while his new house was being built because the doctors had told him that the

city would be bad for his health. He moved into his house in July 1853 (Beers, *Willis*, 327–328). Parton's break with Willis must have come in September or October of 1853. He apparently was still at the *Home Journal* at the end of the summer: the *Musical World and Times*, on August 27, 1853, referred to him as the music critic of the *Home Journal*. The last article on Fanny Fern (except for a review of her children's book on December 16, 1853) appeared on October 6, 1853. This suggests that Willis did not return to the *Home Journal* office until the fall of 1853. Parton's biography of Horace Greeley was published in December 1854, and he said that he began work on it a few months after he left the *Home Journal* and that he worked on it for eleven months, which would mean that he left the *Home Journal* in September or October of 1853 (*Triumphs of Enterprise*, 19–20).

6.   Hezekiah Eldredge's death certificate is in the records of the Secretary of State, State House, Boston, Massachusetts. His will is in the Register of Probate Court, Boston, Massachusetts.

7.   A copy of Mary Eldredge's will, dated March 17, 1855, is in the Sophia Smith Collection, Smith College. In a codicil dated January 27, 1857, Mary Eldredge directed her lawyer to "procure two gold rings with daguerrotype miniatures" of Charles Eldredge to be presented to Fern's daughters "as tokens of remembrance from me." Since all of the money, the portrait of Charles Eldredge, the family silver and china, and the household furnishings were given to persons outside the family (with the exception of one hundred dollars given to Nancy Watson, "a member of my family"), these "tokens" seem a deliberate insult to Fern and to the Eldredges' only grandchildren.

8.   Hezekiah Eldredge's will.

9.   James C. Derby, *Fifty Years among Authors, Books and Publishers* (New York: G. W. Carleton, 1884).

10.   Ibid., 208–209.

11.   Fanny Fern, letter to Derby and Miller, February 8, 1853, Chicago Historical Society.

12.   The original contract with Derby and Miller for *Fern Leaves* is not among Fern's papers at Smith College. However, a supplemental agreement dated May 2, 1853, which is among her papers, refers to the original contract, which it says was signed on February 10, 1853, Sophia Smith Collection, Smith College. A letter from Oliver Dyer to Derby and Miller, dated April 28, 1853, in the Chicago Historical Society, contains a statement from Fern asking to transfer negotiations for her royalties to Dyer and her brother, Richard Willis.

13.   See, e.g., *Musical World and Times*, October 15, 1853.

14.   James D. Hart, *The Popular Book* (New York: Oxford University Press, 1950), 93.

15.   See, e. g., *Putnam's Monthly* 2 (November 1853): 103.

16.   *New York Mirror*, cited in *Musical World and Times*, October 15, 1853.

17.   *New Haven Palladium*, cited in *Musical World and Times*, October 15, 1853.

18.   *Home Journal*, June 4, 1853.

19.   The opera "La Sonnambula" with Madame Sontag was performed at Castle Garden on Monday evening, July 25, 1853. It is cited in the *Musical World and Times* and in the *Home Journal* on July 30, 1853.

20.   Fanny Fern, letter to J. C. Derby, n.d., Chicago Historical Society. Also printed, with modifications, in Derby, *Fifty Years*, 210–211.

21. Richard Storrs Willis is first listed in the *New York City Directory* in 1852. Another Richard Willis, a music teacher, is listed earlier. R. S. Willis began using his middle name, Storrs, after he moved to New York in order to differentiate himself from the other Richard Willis. Richard Willis had been in Germany from 1842 to 1848. He returned to the United States in October 1848. For several weeks he lived with his brother N. P. Willis in New York and then moved to New Haven. He returned to New York to edit the *New York Musical World and Times* and was married in September 1852. For a record of his movements see his testimony in the Forrest trial recorded in *The New York Times* on January 13, 1852.

22. N. P. Willis, letter to Richard Willis, June 2 [1853], Princeton University Library. Although the year is not given on the letter, it can be dated positively as 1853 because of the reference to Richard Willis's review of *Fern Leaves*, which appeared in the *Musical World and Times* on May 28, 1853. The date on this letter is not clear, but I believe the letter is dated "June 2nd." It might be read as "June 29"; however, Willis's numeral nine at this time was usually rounded, and this figure is clearly a long straight diagonal line. There is a curlicue at the top of the line, which could be the circle of the nine, but it is probably the symbol for the ordinal number, which Willis usually used in dating his letters, and the diagonal line is the slash line that Willis often placed after the date of the month and before the year. That Willis does not refer to the "Apollo Hyacinth" article of June 18 or to the satiric portrayal of their father in Fern's article in the *Musical World* on June 11 indicates that the letter was written before rather than after these articles appeared. He only mentions Richard's review and its portrayal of Fern's poverty.

23. E.g., *The Life and Beauties of Fanny Fern* (New York: H. Long, and Brother, 1855), 27–36.

24. On March 19, 1853, the *Musical World* commented, "Many articles of an inferior character are now going the rounds of the press accredited to Fanny Fern which were never written by her; while scores of her best productions . . . are copied from paper to paper . . . without any credit being given her for them." On June 11, 1853, the *Musical World and Times* printed a notice that it was taking legal action against any newspaper editors who printed Fanny Fern's articles without giving credit to the *Musical World*.

25. Since Fanny Fern died in 1872, she was not living when Henry Ward Beecher was accused of adultery with one of his parishioners. There is no way of knowing which side Fern, who had always liked Beecher, would have taken in this scandal, which divided the Beecher family.

26. In 1851 the London Crystal Palace Exhibition Building, a spectacular cast-iron-and-glass structure designed by Joseph Paxton, was built in London. Two years later a similar structure was built in New York on the site that is now Bryant Park. The style was later used in building the dome of the U.S. Capitol. The Crystal Palace Exhibition in New York was designed to display artworks and manufactured goods from all over the world from 1853 to 1854. It was the first World's Fair in the United States. It burned down on October 5, 1858. One aspect of this article may have inspired the Emily Dickinson poem describing the "menagerie" character of other people.

27. *Home Journal*, October 6, 1853.

28. Derby, *Fifty Years*, 211–213. This letter, although it is undated, can be dated in late June of 1853 because of the reference to an article that had appeared in the *Olive Branch* on June 18, 1853.

29. Mary Eldredge's death certificate is in the office of the Secretary of State, State House, Boston, Massachusetts.

30. Contract with Mason Brothers is in the Sophia Smith Collection, Smith College.

31. James Hart, *The Popular Book*, 94. See also John S. Hart, *Female Prose Writers of America* (Philadelphia: E. H. Butler, 1857), 471–472.

32. Fern's trip to Niagara Falls is described in the children's story "The Journey," in *The Play-Day Book* (New York: Mason Brothers, 1857), 35–56, published in 1857. This story contains other material that Fern uses in *Rose Clark:* the descriptions of the train wreck, the hotel, the falls, and the people she encountered.

33. Letter from Samuel Blatchford to J. C. Derby, September 17, 1853; James H. Collins, letter to Samuel Blatchford, September 8, 1853; copy of the divorce decree, September 7, 1853, Sophia Smith Collection, Smith College. It is not clear whether the date on the decree is the date of the divorce or simply of the copy. The original record is not available, having been destroyed in the Chicago fire in 1871. However, the divorce must have been obtained between May and September 1853 because in the supplemental contract with Derby and Miller, which is dated May 23, 1853, Fern is identified as Sarah P. Farrington, while in the later contracts on September 6 and 8, 1853, she is identified as Sara P. Eldredge. Farrington may have reappeared in Fern's life as Stahle attempted to do in the life of Gertrude Dean in *Rose Clark* (New York: Mason Brothers, 1856). Stahle attempted to obtain money after Gertrude had become famous (345–346). However, Fern had been advised by Derby's lawyer that her former husband was not entitled to any of her money. There is no evidence that Farrington appeared years later after Fern's death as Mary Kelley suggests in *Private Woman, Public Stage: Literary Domesticity in Nineteenth Century America* (New York: Oxford University Press, 1984), 266. The 1873–1874 letters between Parton and Ellen Eldredge that Kelley cites refer to Ethel's father, Mortimer Thomson, who they feared would attempt to claim his daughter. Parton and Ellen did not want Effie to know about the irregular life that her father led. James Parton, letters to Ellen Eldredge, May 14, 1873, October 6, 1873, n.d. [1873], and February 4, 1875, Houghton Library, Harvard University.

34. *Life and Beauties*, 55–59. That Dyer was in Boston in October is apparent from his letter to the *Musical World and Times* from Boston, dated October 24, 1853 (New York *Musical World and Times*, October 29, 1853). There was no article from Fanny Fern this week in the *Musical World*, which suggests that she was also away.

8. Ruth Hall

1. Contract between Mason Brothers and Sara P. Eldredge, February 16, 1854, in Sophia Smith Collection, Smith College.

2. For example, a British review printed in *The Living Age* on November 19, 1853, wrote: "If Fanny Fern, with her insight into motives, her laughing contempt for cant and conventionalism, her knowledge of life and power of pathos, has constructive ability, she will write a connected tale fit to take a high place among works of fiction." The reviewer for the *Hartford Courant*, reviewing *Fern Leaves*, Second

Series, in June 1854, wrote that he hoped Fanny Fern would write a continuous story, and predicted great popularity for such a book.

3. Ethel Parton, letter to Robert P. Eckert, Jr., June 6, 1934, private collection.

4. James C. Derby, *Fifty Years among Authors, Books and Publishers* (New York: G. W. Carleton, 1884), 219.

5. Derby, *Fifty Years*, 208–209, says that he paid her ten cents per copy for her first book, and the contract for *Fern Leaves*, Second Series, dated September 6, 1853, indicates that she was also paid ten cents per copy for *Fern Leaves*, Second Series, although she was only paid six cents per book for her children's book, *Little Ferns for Fanny's Little Friends* (Auburn, N.Y.: Derby and Miller, 1853). See contract in Sophia Smith Collection, Smith College.

6. Review of *Fern Leaves*, *The Living Age* 3 (November 19, 1853):485.

7. Nathaniel Hawthorne, *The Letters of Hawthorne to William Ticknor, 1851–1869*. 1910. Ed. C. E. Frazer Clark, Jr. (Newark, N.J.: Carteret Book Club, 1972), 1:78.

8. Fred Lewis Pattee (*The Feminine Fifties* (New York: D. Appleton-Century, 1940), 111, 115, 120, for example, struggles to explain what he calls Hawthorne's "infatuation" with Fanny Fern and concludes that Hawthorne did not know about Fern's anger at her family and thus could not judge the novel accurately—which is no explanation at all, especially since the autobiographical aspects of the book had nothing to do with Hawthorne's assessment of it, as is apparent from Hawthorne's later comment (Ethel Parton, "Fanny Fern, An Informal Biography" [unpublished manuscript in Sophia Smith Collection, Smith College], 128).

9. For a discussion of *Ruth Hall* as a female *kunstlerroman* see Linda Huf, *A Portrait of the Artist as a Young Woman: The Writer as Heroine in American Literature* (New York: Ungar, 1983), 16–35. The only other detailed discussions of *Ruth Hall* are my Introduction to *Ruth Hall and Other Writings* (New Brunswick, N.J. Rutgers University Press, 1986) and Susan K. Harris, "Inscribing and Defining: The Many Voices of Fanny Fern's *Ruth Hall*," in *Nineteenth-Century American Women Writers: Interpretive Strategies* (New York: Oxford University Press, 1990), 111–127. This chapter appeared earlier under the same title in *Style* 22 (Winter 1988): 612–627.

10. Grace Greenwood, "Fanny Fern,—Mrs. Parton," in *Eminent Women of the Age*, ed. James Parton et al. (Hartford: S. M. Betts, 1868), 74.

11. For a detailed discussion of Mason Brothers' advertising campaign, see Susan Geary, "Scribbling Women: Essays on Literary History and Popular Literature in the 1850's" (Ph.D. dissertation, Brown University, 1976), 47–56; see also the section of this dissertation published in "The Domestic Novel as a Commercial Commodity: Making a Best Seller in the 1850s," *Papers of the Bibliographical Society* 60 (1976): 365–394. Also see Patricia McGinnis, "Fanny Fern, American Novelist," *Biblion* 2 (Spring 1969):13–19.

12. See, e.g., *New York Tribune*, November 15, 1854, p. 1.

13. See, e.g., *New York Tribune*, December 14, 15, 16, 18, 19, 1854.

14. See, e.g., *New York Tribune*, December 18, 1854.

15. See, e.g., *New York Tribune*, December 13, 1854.

16. See, e.g., *New York Tribune*, December 25, 1854.

17. See, e.g., *New York Tribune*, February 17, 1855.

18. See, e.g., *New York Tribune*, April 11, 1855.

19. The German translation, *Fanny Ford und Ruth Hall*, was published in Pesth and Leipzig in 1856. On May 3, 1856, the *New York Ledger* reported that *Ruth Hall* had been translated into French and was being serialized in *L'Assemblée Nationale*; however, a search through the issues of this periodical between 1855 and 1857 in the Bibliothèque Nationale and the Bibliothèque de L'Institut de France in Paris failed to locate the serialization.

20. *London Atlas*, printed in the *True Flag*, March 17, 1855.

21. *Putnam's Monthly* 5 (February 1855): 216.

22. *Protestant Episcopal Quarterly Review* 2 (April 1855): 301.

23. *Albion*, in *The Life and Beauties of Fanny Fern* (New York: H. Long, and Brother, 1855), 224.

24. See, e.g., *Southern Quarterly* 27 (April 1855):449; *National Era* 9 (April 5, 1855):55; *True Flag*, January 13, 1855; *Olive Branch* 19 (December 30, 1854):2; *Knickerbocker* 45 (January 1855):84–86.

25. See e.g., *Protestant Episcopal Quarterly Review* 2 (April 1855):300; *Putnam's Monthly* 5 (February 1855):216;*Olive Branch* 19 (December 30, 1854):2; *Dansville* (N.Y.) *Republican*, December 27, 1854, cited in the *Olive Branch*, January 13, 1855.

26. *True Flag*, January 13, 1855.

27. New Orleans *Crescent City*, in the *Olive Branch*, January 13, 1855.

28. Although *The Life and Beauties of Fanny Fern* was published anonymously, it was probably the work of William U. Moulton, the *True Flag* editor who had revealed Fern's identity, and whose series of articles is reprinted in the book. In the novel *Ruth Hall*, Mr. Tibbetts, who was based on the *True Flag* editor, threatens Ruth when she tells him she will no longer write for his paper (157), and as Florence Bannard Adams notes, in the argument between the *True Flag* and the *Olive Branch* in January 1855, Moulton is identified by name in the *Olive Branch* on January 13, 1855. See *Fanny Fern, A Pair of Flaming Shoes* (West Trenton, N.J.: Hermitage Press, 1966), 11.

29. *Olive Branch* 19 (December 30, 1854):2. The review is unsigned, but it may have been by "S," a woman who had been contributing to the *Olive Branch* before and during the time that Fern gained her popularity as a contributor. One suspects that she was jealous of Fern's popularity, for her own writing was quickly eclipsed by Fern's. On April 17, 1852, "S" wrote an article in the *Olive Branch* criticizing Fern. She comments that she would like to see Fern get married, to take some of the nonsense out of her—though she says no sensible man would marry a woman like Fern.

30. Caroline Healey Dall, Review of *Ruth Hall*, *The Una* (March 1855), 42–43.

31. Sarah Josepha Hale, *Godey's Lady's Book* 50 (February 1855): 176; and 45 (November 1852):490.

32. Haddie Lane, "Woman's Rights," *Godey's Lady's Book* 40 (April 1850):269–273.

33. Ellen Louise Chandler Moulton, letters to Phillips, Sampson, & Co., June 17, 1854, and October 3, 1854, Boston Public Library, Boston, Massachusetts.

34. *New York Atlas*, March 17, 1855.

35. Mary Eldredge's will is dated March 17, 1855, Sophia Smith Collection.

36. Interview with Richard Storrs Willis, *Detroit Free Press* [1872], undated clipping, Sophia Smith Collection, Smith College. Fern also visited Richard Willis in

his home. See letter from James Parton to Ellen Eldredge and Ethel Thomson, May 5, 1874, Houghton Library, Harvard University. Parton mentions that he had met a man who "had met all of us at your uncle Richard's."

37. See Hope Willis Rathbun, letter to Florence Snow, July 23, 1966, in Sophia Smith Collection, Smith College, which indicates that Fanny Fern remained a persona non grata for years in N. P. Willis's family. The wife of N. P. Willis's son, Grinnell Willis, however, reported that "he always laughingly said that 'Aunt Sarah put my father in his place.'" See Katherine Willis, letter to Ethel Parton, November 13, 1931, Sophia Smith Collection, Smith College.

38. Lucy Bumstead, letters to James Parton and Ellen Eldredge Parton, 1872 and 1876, Houghton Library, Harvard University. Lucy's son, Freeman Bumstead, and his wife Mary were witnesses to Fanny Fern's will, dated January 7, 1871, Sophia Smith Collection, Smith College.

39. That Fern remained on amicable terms with her sisters Julia and Mary is clear from letters referring to visits to and by them. See, e.g., Fanny Fern, letter to Ethel Parton, December 9, 1871, Sophia Smith Collection, Smith College. See also James Parton, letters to Ellen Eldredge Parton, which mention letters and visits to and from them, March 21, 1875, and November 9, 1874, Houghton Library, Harvard University.

40. *New York Times,* December 20, 1854.

41. *New York Tribune,* December 16, 1854.

42. *Hartford Courant,* December 19, 1854, p. 2.

43. See, e.g., *Hartford Courant,* December 19, 1854, p. 2; *Peterson's Magazine* (Philadelphia), February 1855; *New York Times,* December 20, 1854; *Troy Daily Budget,* in *New York Tribune,* December 19, 1854; *Boston Post,* in *New York Tribune,* December 19, 1854.

44. *Graham's Magazine* 60 (August 1857).

45. *American Publisher's Circular & Literary Gazette* 2 (October 4, 1856): 603.

46. Michel Foucault, *The Archaeology of Knowledge and the Discourse on Language,* tr. A. M. Sheridan Smith (New York: Harper, 1972), e.g., 203, 216, 224, 227.

47. See, e.g., Jacques Derrida, *Writing and Difference,* tr. Alan Bass (Chicago: University of Chicago Press, 1978); *Of Grammatology,* tr. Gayatri Chakravorty Spivak (Baltimore: Johns Hopkins University Press, 1976); and *Positions,* tr. Alan Bass (Chicago: University of Chicago Press, 1981). In *Positions* Derrida summarizes his position: "I have attempted to systematize a deconstructive critique precisely against the authority of meaning, as the *transcendental signified* or as *telos,* in other words history determined in the last analysis as the history of meaning, history in its logocentric, metaphysical, idealist . . . representation" (49–50). Regarding the dismantling technique, he writes: "Dissemination would be not only the possibility for a mark to 'disembed' itself. . . . It is also the possibility of deconstructing . . . , or, if you prefer, of unsewing . . . the symbolic order in its general structure *and* in its modificaitons, in the general *and* determined forms of sociability, the 'family' or culture" (*Positions* 85).

48. Marx and Engels published *The Communist Manifesto* in 1847. In 1867 Marx published *Das Kapital,* explaining that all of history is determined by economic conditions. Between 1852 and 1862 he wrote for the *New York Herald.* Fern, as an avid reader of newspapers, must have been familiar with his work during these years while he was evolving his ideas for *Das Kapital.*

49. Adams, *Flaming Shoes*, 23.

50. Augusta Jane Evans, *St. Elmo* (1866; reprinted N.Y.: Cooperative Publication Society, 1896), 562.

51. An interesting exception to this pattern is Hagar in *The Deserted Wife* by E.D.E.N. Southworth (1855), who is deserted by her husband and pursues a profitable career as a singer. At the end of the novel, however, she is reunited with her husband, and, although she no longer "worships" him, the author tells us, she does not continue with her career.

52. Nina Baym, *Woman's Fiction: A Guide to Novels By and About Women in America, 1820–1870* (Ithaca: Cornell University Press, 1978), 35.

53. Ibid., 48–49.

54. Jane Tompkins, *Sensational Designs: The Cultural Work of American Fiction, 1790–1860* (New York: Oxford University Press, 1985), 125.

55. See Jacques Lacan, *Ecrits, A Selection*, tr. Alan Sheridan (London: Tavistock, 1977). In his analysis of the way in which a person formulates his/her identity, Lacan discusses "certain critical moments that mark the history of men's mental genesis, each representing a stage in objectifying identification" (17). Although Lacan's masculinist orientation would not allow him to see the gender bias of this symbolic order, his description of the way in which the individual develops his/her identity through a series of contacts with the "Other" is useful in understanding the process by which Ruth Hall defines herself.

56. *New York Ledger*, February 16, 1856. The only exceptions to this ecumenical spirit that I have found in Fern's work have to do with money. In *Ruth Hall* there are two references to the term "Jew" as a synonym for greed (90, 145). I have found no similar references in all of her newspaper articles except for an 1853 article which uses the term "Scot" as a synonym for someone who is tightfisted. Although modern readers are aware of the prejudice inherent in such stereotypes, unfortunately they were common in Fern's day. Harriet Beecher Stowe, for example, uses the same stereotype in a letter to Fanny Fern in 1868, where she describes a publisher with whom she "had a long haggling battle the other night in which he cheapened literary wares in the style of a Jew peddler" (Sophia Smith Collection, Smith College).

57. For a discussion of the figure of the "b'hoy" in nineteenth-century popular literature and his derivation from the concept of the lower-class firemen as a representative of American republicanism, see Sean Wilentz, *Chants Democratic: New York City and the Rise of the American Working-Class 1788–1850* (New York: Oxford University Press, 1984), 263; and David Reynolds, *Beneath the American Renaissance* (New York: Knopf, 1988), 463–464.

58. Charlotte Brontë, letter to Elizabeth Gaskell, 1852, quoted in Winifred Gerin, *Elizabeth Gaskell: A Biography* (New York: Oxford University Press, 1976), 132. Gaskell was apparently familiar with the poem *Ruth* by George Crabbe, which appeared in Crabbe's *Tales of the Hall* in 1819. I am indebted to Victoria Warren for first calling my attention to Gaskell's novel in relation to *Ruth Hall* and also for the insightful suggestion that, since the word "ruth" means "compassion," both Fern and Gaskell might have intended the name Ruth as an ironic comment on the lack of compassion shown toward the title character. Although there are many sources that might have provided Fern with the suggestion of the name for her heroine (e.g., the biblical Ruth, Wordsworth's poem), the combination of the two names, Ruth and

Hall, in Crabbe's work in conjunction with the appearance of Gaskell's novel in 1853 is particularly significant.

59. Horatio Alger, *Ragged Dick* (New York: Macmillan, 1962), 43–44. Of the 106 books that Alger wrote, only one had a female protagonist, *Helen Ford* (1866). Although the heroine is self-reliant like Alger's male heroes, and at the beginning of the novel she works hard and earns her own living to support her indigent and impractical father, Alger apparently did not know what to do with her. He resolved the problem in a traditional manner: her father inherits a fortune, and Helen gives up her career.

60. Elizabeth Cady Stanton, Review of *Ruth Hall, The Una* (February 1855): 29–30. The negative review of *Ruth Hall* by Caroline Healey Dall in the March issue of *The Una* (discussed earlier in the chapter) was in part a response to this favorable review by Elizabeth Cady Stanton. Dall began her review by saying that Stanton was "one of the most able and earnest advocates of our cause," but insisted that Stanton did not understand the "whole field covered by the book," by which she meant Fern's satire of her relatives and Fern herself. Dall, who was from the Boston area, knew people who knew Fern and the Willises. It is clear from her review that she did not like what she had heard about Fern; whereas Stanton could recognize the significance of the novel, Dall's opinion was colored by society's prejudices.

61. *Harper's New Monthly Magazine* (March 1855): 551.

62. *Southern Quarterly* 27 (April 1855):443, 449–450.

63. *Putnam's Monthly* 5 (February 1855): 216.

9. Robert Bonner and James Parton

1. Helen Gurley Brown, *Having It All: Love, Success, Sex, Money: Even If You're Starting With Nothing* (New York: Simon & Schuster, Linden Press, 1982).

2. Mary Noel, *Villains Galore* (New York: Macmillan, 1954), 93.

3. For a discussion of the prevalence of prurient sexuality and gore in nineteenth-century American popular literature, see David Reynolds, *Beneath the American Renaissance* (New York: Knopf, 1988), 211–224.

4. For information about Robert Bonner and the *New York Ledger*, see Matthew Hale Smith, *Twenty Years among the Bulls and Bears of Wall Street* (Hartford: J. B. Burr & Co., 1870), 214–230; Frederic Hudson, *Journalism in the United States* (New York: Harper and Brothers, 1873), 646–655; James C. Derby, *Fifty Years among Authors, Books and Publishers* (New York: G. W. Carleton, 1884), 200–207; Ralph Adimari, "Bonner and the *Ledger*," *American Book Collector* 6 (May-June, 1935): 176–193; James Playstead Wood *Magazines in the United States* (New York: The Ronald Press, 1949), 86–89; Elaine Breslaw, "Popular Pundit: Fanny Fern and the Emergence of the American Newspaper Columnist" (Master's thesis, Smith College, 1956), 15–24; Frank Luther Mott, *A History of American Magazines*, 5 vols. (Cambridge: Harvard University Press, 1957), 2:23–24, 356–363.

5. Smith, *Twenty Years*, 216–217, 221. Bonner signed the name of Dr. Thomas Chalmers, a famous Scottish theologian (1780–1847). Chalmers, a

preacher and professor of Moral Philosophy at the University of St. Andrews, had published *Commercial Discourses* (1820), which was designed to instill the life of commercial men with the spirit of the gospel. He wrote articles and preached in London, and in 1843 he led a withdrawal of 470 ministers from the General Assembly to establish the New Church of Scotland.

6. See Derby, *Fifty Years,* 202–203; Smith, *Twenty Years,* 217; Noel, *Villains,* 64.

7. Ibid. James Parton, *Fanny Fern, A Memorial Volume* (New York: G. W. Carleton, 1873), 57, says that Bonner had to borrow the money to pay her.

8. See Robert Bonner, letter to James Parton, August 4, 1866: "I will pay you for any further articles you may write $25 each, so that you and Fanny can have the same pay" (Houghton Library, Harvard University).

9. See the letters of E.D.E.N. Southworth to Robert Bonner at Duke University, particularly: n.d. from Prospect Cottage; February 18, 1861; and Bonner to Southworth, September 20, 1857; see also a contract agreement dated January 27, 1863.

10. Fred Lewis Pattee, *The Feminine Fifties* (New York: D. Appleton-Century, 1940), 186.

11. Walt Whitman, *New York Dissected,* ed. Emory Halloway and Ralph Adimari (New York: Rufus Cockwell Wilson, Inc., 1936), 230.

12. Smith, *Twenty Years,* 221-222; Derby, *Fifty Years,* 203.

13. The loyalty of Bonner's writers is reflected in E.D.E.N. Southworth's refusal in 1867 to write a story for *The Saturday Night,* which had offered her ten thousand dollars.

14. Derby, *Fifty Years,* 204.

15. Smith, *Twenty Years,* 214.

16. Noel, *Villains,* 86.

17. See the letters of E.D.E.N. Southworth to Robert Bonner at Duke University, e.g., 1862 [n.d.]: "It is a striking fact that although duty and circumstances oblige me to do a great deal for other people—some of whom have no claim upon me—no one in this world but yourself ever does anything for me. And often when I feel over-burdened by the mass of helpless—I had nearly said—good-for-nothing people—that lean on me, there comes some unexpected and unearned kindness from you to reconcile me. May Heaven reward and bless you;—the only benefactor I ever had in this world." Similarly, on March 29, 1887, she wrote: "You have been 'a tower of strength' to me for thirty years. . . . I think every one of your writers, printers, proof readers and all, must feel as the great Henry Ward Beecher and my small self do—that to please Robert Bonner is a sufficient motive for doing our very best."

18. For a discussion of Bonner's advertising method, see Derby, *Fifty Years,* 204; Smith, *Twenty Years,* 218–219; Noel, *Villains,* 67–73.

19. James Parton, "*Jane Eyre* and *Shirley,*" *Home Journal* (January 5, 1850).

20. James Parton, *Triumphs of Enterprise, Ingenuity, and Public Spirit* (New York: Virtue & Yorston, 1874), 13–21. See also Milton Flower, *James Parton, The Father of Modern Biography* (Durham, N.C.: Duke University Press, 1951), 25–26. The contract between James Parton and Mason Brothers is in the James Parton Papers, Houghton Library, Harvard University. Parton was paid a royalty of ten cents per book, as opposed to Fern's fifteen cents per book.

21. The Diary of Thomas Butler Gunn, Missouri Historical Society, Saint Louis.

22. Gunn diary, e.g., June 5, 1859, June 26, 1859.

23. James Parton, letter to J. T. Fields, February 13, 1867, Huntington Library, San Marino, California.

24. *The Home Journal*, January 13, 1855.

25. The Pre-nuptial Agreement between Sara Payson Eldredge and James Parton, dated January 5, 1856, is in the James Parton Papers, Houghton Library, Harvard University. Attached to it is an additional agreement dated June 16, 1856, naming Lowell Mason, Jr., as cotrustee with Oliver Dyer.

26. The Married Woman's Property Act was passed in New York State in 1860. One of its provisions was that, upon marriage, a woman could retain possession of property that she possessed before her marriage.

27. The wedding certificate of Sarah Payson Eldredge and James Parton, dated January 5, 1856, is in the James Parton Papers, Houghton Library, Harvard University.

28. See, e.g., *New York Herald* (January 7, 1856): 1.

29. See, e.g., Julius Ward, "James Parton," *New England Magazine* (January 1893): 630, 636–638.

30. Gunn diary, January 11, 1858. See also, e.g., August 1, 1856, August 17, 1856, October 3, 1856, December 7 and 22, 1856, December 30, 1857, February 21, 1858, February 24, 1858, April 23, 1858, January 16, 1859, February 23, 1859.

10. Walt Whitman

1. The similarity between these two books was first suggested by Clifton Furness and Alfred Goldsmith and has been noted by successive Whitman scholars. See Clifton J. Furness, introduction to Walt Whitman, *Leaves of Grass* (New York: Columbia University Press, Facsimile Text Society, 1939), ix–x. See also Walt Whitman, *I Sit and Look Out: Editorials from the "Brooklyn Daily Times,"* ed. Emory Holloway and Vernolian Schwartz (1932; reprint, New York: AMS Press, 1966), 211; and Clara Barrus, *Whitman and Burroughs: Comrades* (New York: Houghton Mifflin, 1931), 178. More recently, it has been noted by Justin Kaplan, *Walt Whitman: A Life* (New York: Simon and Schuster, 1980), 216; and Paul Zweig, *Walt Whitman: The Making of the Poet* (New York: Basic Books, 1984), 42. Zweig comments that Whitman "almost surely" got the idea for the cover and title from *Fern Leaves*. There had been other "Leaves" books prior to Fern's (e.g., Grace Greenwood's *Greenwood Leaves* in 1850), but *Fern Leaves* was so well known and so unusual in its satiric content that it seems most likely that it was the principal source for Whitman's cover and title, if only because Whitman, who was an eager promoter of his own book, would not have been unaware of the benefits of such an association.

2. See, e.g., Zweig, *Walt Whitman*, 231.

3. For sales figures for *Fern Leaves*, see John S. Hart, *The Female Prose Writers of America* (Philadelphia: E. H. Butler, 1857), 472. As of June 1, 1854,

there were 70,000 copies of *Fern Leaves* sold in the United States and 29,000 sold in Great Britain. *Fern Leaves, Second Series*, published May 1854, had sold 30,000. Whitman's own comments regarding the sales of *Leaves of Grass* appear in Horace Traubel, *With Walt Whitman in Camden*, 6 vols. (Boston: Small, Maynard, 1906–1982), 2:471–472; 3:115–116.

4. Fern's novel *Ruth Hall* (1855) was reprinted in 1986 by Rutgers University Press. The edition contains approximately a hundred of her newspaper articles. See *Ruth Hall and Other Writings*, ed. Joyce W. Warren.

5. The receipt and Whitman's explanation are printed in Traubel, *Whitman in Camden*, 3:235–239. For an analysis of the Whitman-Parton debt, see Oral S. Coad, "Whitman vs. Parton," *Journal of the Rutgers University Library* 4 (December 1940):1–8; and Milton Flower, *James Parton, The Father of Modern Biography* (Durham, N.C.: Duke University Press, 1951), 48–49, 240–241. See also the letters of Ethel Parton and William Sloane Kennedy, and others, in the Rutgers University Library, New Brunswick, New Jersey.

6. Traubel, *Whitman in Camden*, 3:235–236.

7. See, e.g., the editorial comment in Whitman, *I Sit and Look Out*, 211; and Walt Whitman, *New York Dissected*, ed. Emory Holloway and Ralph Adimari (New York: Rufus Rockwell Wilson, Inc., 1936), 153.

8. Fred Lewis Pattee, *The Feminine Fifties* (New York: D. Appleton-Century, 1940), 110–118. Gay Wilson Allen, *The Solitary Singer* (New York: Grove Press, 1955), 177, calls Fern a "purveyor of sentimental pap." Other Whitman scholars who have accepted this opinion of Fern's work apparently without reading it include Henry Canby, *Walt Whitman: An American* (Westport, Conn.: Greenwood Press, 1943), 122, 301; Frances Winwar, *American Giant: Walt Whitman and His Times* (New York: Harper and Brothers, 1941), 183–184; and Kaplan, *Walt Whitman*, 216.

9. This has been the assumption of almost every Whitman scholar. See, e.g., Barrus, *Whitman and Burroughs*, 178; Whitman, *I Sit and Look Out*, 211; Whitman, *New York Dissected*, 153; Winwar, *American Giant*, 183–184, 202; Canby, *Walt Whitman*, 122; Kaplan, *Walt Whitman*, 216; Zweig, *Walt Whitman*, 279–280.

10. Kaplan, *Walt Whitman*, 216.

11. MS biography of Walt Whitman by Clifton Joseph Furness (cited in Flower, *James Parton*, 48).

12. Whitman, for example, wrote his own anonymnous reviews of *Leaves of Grass* and flattering articles about himself. Kaplan, *Walt Whitman*, 207–209, comments that Whitman had learned his lessons from P. T. Barnum. Quentin Anderson, in his introduction to Walt Whitman, *Walt Whitman's Autograph Revision of the Analysis of "Leaves of Grass"* (New York: New York University Press, 1974), 11, comments that "Whitman threw himself into the effort to make himself known with a single-mindedness unexampled among great writers."

13. See Samuel Wells, letter to Walt Whitman, June 7, 1856, Feinberg Collection, Library of Congress. The passage from this letter is quoted incorrectly by Kaplan, *Walt Whitman* (216), and Edwin Haviland Miller, *Walt Whitman: The Correspondence* (New York: New York University Press, 1961), 2:44, both of whom say that Wells had called Fern and Parton "rich and enterprizing," whereas it is clearly their publishers that Wells refers to.

14. Whitman, *New York Dissected,* 130–131.

15. Undated clipping in Sophia Smith Collection; also Horace Greeley, letter to Fanny Fern, August 16, 1870, Houghton Library, Harvard University.

16. Zweig, *Walt Whitman,* 271.

17. Thomas Butler Gunn, Diary, May 15, 1856, Missouri Historical Society, Saint Louis.

18. Gunn diary, June 1856. A section of the diary is published by John Francis McDermott, "Glimpses from the Diary of Thomas Butler Gunn, 1856–1860," *American Literature* 29 (November 1957):316–319.

19. McDermott also comes to this conclusion; see ibid., 316.

20. MS of letter reproduced in William White, "Fanny Fern to Walt Whitman: An Unpublished Letter," *American Book Collector* 11 (May 1961):8–9.

21. Norton had written a quasi-favorable review of *Leaves of Grass* for *Putnam's Monthly* in September 1856, but he made this comment to his friend, James Russell Lowell, confessing that he himself had trouble with the book's "disgusting" coarseness; see Charles Eliot Norton, *Letters,* 2 vols. (Boston: Houghton, 1913), 1:135.

22. Ralph Waldo Emerson, *Complete Works* Centenary Edition, ed. Edward W. Emerson, 12 vols. (Boston: Houghton Mifflin, 1903–1904), 3:231–233.

23. Walt Whitman, *Leaves of Grass,* Norton Critical Edition, ed. Sculley Bradley and Harold W. Blodgett (New York: Norton, 1973).

24. Walt Whitman, *Collected Writings: Prose Works, 1892,* ed. Floyd Stovall, 2 vols. (New York: New York University Press, 1963–1964), 2:389.

25. Ibid., 1:225–226.

26. Among the critics who have recognized Whitman's limited view of women are D. H. Lawrence, *Studies in Classic American Literature* (1932; reprint, New York: Viking, 1971), 167; Leadie Mae Clark, *Walt Whitman's Concept of the American Common Man* (New York: Philadelphia Library, 1955), 95–107; Nina Baym, "Portrayal of Women in American Literature, 1790–1870," in *What Manner of Woman: Essays on English and American Life and Literature,* ed. Marlene Springer (New York: New York University Press, 1977), 220–221; and Arthur Wrobel, "'Noble American Motherhood': Whitman, Women, and the Ideal Democracy," *American Studies* 21 (Fall 1980):7–25.

27. Whitman, *Leaves of Grass,* 96–99.

28. Ibid., 48.

29. Whitman, *Collected Writings,* 2:389.

30. Ibid., 2:389, 372. Whitman, *Leaves of Grass,* 401; Whitman, *Collected Writings,* 2:364, 397.

31. Whitman *Leaves of Grass,* 101–103. I have not discussed the question of Whitman's ambivalence about his own sexual identity here because it does not seem to have had a significant effect on his attitude toward woman's role. Although one might argue that it was his ambivalence about his own sexual identity that enabled Whitman to recognize in women the same physical nature that he felt in himself, there is no evidence that it enabled him to transcend the conventions of his time with respect to his conception of the role of women in society.

32. See the *Brooklyn Daily Eagle,* August 19, 1846, September 11, 1846, November 20, 1846, and January 29, 1847. Some of these articles are reprinted in *The Uncollected Poetry and Prose of Walt Whitman,* ed. Emory Holloway, 2 vols.

(Gloucester, Mass.: Peter Smith, 1972), 1:137; and *The Gathering of the Forces of Walt Whitman*, ed. Cleveland Rodgers and John Black, 2 vols. (New York: Putnam's, 1920), 1:148–151. For a discussion of Whitman's work on the *Eagle*, see Thomas Brasher, *Whitman as Editor of the "Brooklyn Daily Eagle"* (Detroit: Wayne State University Press, 1970).

33. *Brooklyn Daily Times*, July 19, 1857, reprinted in Whitman, *I Sit and Look Out*, 53–54.

34. *Brooklyn Daily Eagle*, February 11, 1847, reprinted in Florence B. Freedman, *Walt Whitman Looks at the Schools* (New York: King's Crown Press, 1950), 165–166.

35. *Brooklyn Daily Eagle*, November 9, 1846; see *Uncollected Poetry and Prose*, 132.

36. *Brooklyn Daily Times*, September 2, 1857, reprinted in Whitman, *I Sit and Look Out*, 113–114.

37. *Brooklyn Daily Eagle*, February 18, 1847, reprinted in Rodgers and Black, *Gathering of the Forces*, 1:73–74.

38. *Brooklyn Daily Eagle*, September 8, 1846.

39. See *Brooklyn Daily Times*, March 13, 1859; and *Brooklyn Daily Eagle*, April 13, 1846, March 12, 1847, and May 29, 1847. See also, Whitman, *I Sit and Look Out*, 117–118.

40. Charles W. Eldridge, "Walt Whitman as a Conservative," *New York Times*, June 7, 1902.

41. Justin Kaplan, for example, claims that the "I" of *Leaves of Grass* "is almost as often a woman as a man" (*Walt Whitman*, 63). Other critics have attempted to make a case for Whitman as a proponent of women, even a feminist. See Judy Womack, "The American Woman in 'Song of Myself,'" *Walt Whitman Review* 19 (June 1973):67–72; Kay F. Reinartz, "Walt Whitman and Feminism," *Walt Whitman Review* 19 (December 1973):127–137; Lottie L. Guttry, "Walt Whitman and the Woman Reader," *Walt Whitman Review* 22 (September 1976):102–110; Muriel Kolinsky, "'Me Tarzan, You Jane': Whitman's Attitudes toward Women from a Women's Liberation Point of View," *Walt Whitman Review* 23 (December 1977):155–165; and Harold Aspiz, *Walt Whitman and the Body Beautiful* (Urbana: University of Illinois Press, 1980), chapter 7.

42. Ethel Parton, letter to William Sloane Kennedy, February 10, 1897, Rutgers University Library.

43. Whitman met Dyer frequently at Fern's and Parton's, but he had first known him ten years earlier when they both worked on the *Brooklyn Daily Eagle*.

44. Whitman's letter and the receipt are printed in Traubel, *Whitman in Camden*, 3:237–239.

45. Ethel Parton, letter to William Sloane Kennedy, February 10, 1897, Rutgers University Library.

46. Ethel Parton, letter to William Sloane Kennedy, February 15, 1897, Rutgers University Library.

47. William Sloane Kennedy, "Did Walt Whitman Leave a Debt Unpaid?" (unpublished manuscript, n.d., Rutgers University Library).

48. Kaplan, *Walt Whitman*, 33–38, describes how Whitman accepted the role of guru, or head of an apostolic church whom his disciples exalted to Christlike proportions.

49. Most Whitman scholars who have made the assumption that Fanny Fern was in love with Whitman have either cited no source or have cited an anonymous "intimate friend" of Whitman as the source. See, e.g., Whitman, *I Sit and Look Out*, 211. That this intimate friend was Ellen O'Connor is clear from the letters of William Sloane Kennedy in the Rutgers University Library. See also Barrus, *Whitman and Burroughs*, 178; and Kaplan, *Walt Whitman*, 224–225.

50. That Ellen (Nelly) O'Connor was in love with Whitman is apparent from her letters in the Feinberg Collection at the Library of Congress, 1864 to 1870, culminating in the letter of November 20, 1870, printed in full in Florence B. Freedman, *William Douglas O'Connor: Walt Whitman's Chosen Knight* (Athens: Ohio University Press, 1985), 246–248:

> I always know that you know that I love you all the time, even though we should never meet again, my feelings could never change, and I am *sure* that you know it as well as I do. I do flatter myself too, that *you* care for *me*,—not as I love you, because you are great and strong, and more sufficient unto yourself than any woman can be..

Whitman was critical of the way O'Connor treated his wife; he lived for ten years as part of the O'Connor family, helping Nelly O'Connor with household chores, exploring Washington with her, and she darning his socks and stitching the little notebooks he kept notes in. When he was seriously ill in 1873, she was his constant visitor and nurse. In 1872 Whitman's friendship with O'Connor ended in a violent quarrel. Although the reason for the quarrel has been given out as having to do with black civil rights or the Franco Prussian War, it is clear that there was more involved than an abstract argument. That O'Connor urged his friend John Burroughs to maintain secrecy about the quarrel suggests that the reason was personal, and the fact that O'Connor left his wife on the night of the quarrel suggests that the reason for the quarrel somehow involved Nelly. One clue is found in O'Connor's short story "The Carpenter," published in *Putnam's* in January 1868. The story protrays a man who is "tortured by the deep suspicion that his beloved wife is drifting from him into love with his bosom-friend." See Freedman, *William Douglas O'Connor*, 149–150, 210, 246–260, 340; Freedman, "New Light on an Old Quarrel: Walt Whitman and William Douglas O'Connor, 1872," *Walt Whitman Review* 11 (June 1965):27–52; Jerome Loving, *Walt Whitman's Champion, William Douglas O'Connor* (College Station: Texas A&M University Press, 1978), 99–102; Traubel, *Whitman in Camden*, 3:509; Miller, *The Correspondence*, 2:193–198, 204–207.

51. Ethel Parton, letters to William Sloane Kennedy, February 10 and 15, 1897.

52. This was told to me by James Parton II, the great-grandson of Fanny Fern. He learned it from Ethel Parton, Fern's granddaughter, who was present at the time.

53. Ethel Parton, letter to William Sloane Kennedy, February 10, 1897.

54. Walt Whitman, "Free Academies at Public cost," *Brooklyn Daily Times*, July 9, 1857, reprinted in Whitman, *I Sit and Look Out*, 53–54.

55. For example, Holloway and Adimari (in Whitman, *New York Dissected*, 152) say that the disparaging reference to Fanny Fern "may have been only

Whitman's opinion of her as a writer"; and Allen (in *Solitary Singer*, 210) explains it by saying that Whitman was "probably contemptuous of her sentimental journalism."

56. *Memoirs of Margaret Fuller Ossoli*, ed. Ralph Waldo Emerson, William Henry Channing, and James Freeman Clarke, 2 vols. (1852; reprint, New York: Burt Franklin, 1972), 2:67.

57. For comments regarding Fanny Fern's original style, see *Harper's Monthly* 9 (July 1854):277.

58. James Fenimore Cooper, *The Ways of the Hour*, in *Complete Works*, 32 vols. (New York: Putnam, 1893), 24:312.

11. Famous and Infamous

1. Fern is referring to herself in the opening quotation. "A Story About Myself," published in *A New Story Book for Children* (New York: Mason Brothers, 1864), 7, begins: "Nobody could be more astonished than I, to find myself famous. I never dreamed of it, when I sat in a small room, at the top of the house where I lodged, scribbling over a sheet of coarse foolscap with *noms de plume*, out of which I was to choose one for my first article."

2. The statement by Lord Byron, "I awoke one morning and found myself famous," is quoted in Sir Thomas Moore, *The Life and Letters of Lord Byron* (London: John Murray, 1860), 159.

3. Manuscript dated December 1868, from the private collection of James Parton III. Fern's acerbic sense of humor is also evident in a letter she wrote the following year to a correspondent whom she had apparently criticized:

My dear "Slack."

The biographer [James Parton] says, you will be mad with me, for what I wrote you. No you won't. Nobody can be mad with me, without I choose to let them. I don't choose to let you. You haven't the slightest idea how you'd admire me, did you know me!

Fanny Fern, letter to "Slack," October 1869, Lloyd W. Smith Collection, Doc. No. 2509, Morriston National Historical Park, Morristown, New Jersey.

4. James Parton, letter to Childs and Peterson, who were collecting information for Allibone's *Dictionary of Authors*, April 29, 1858, Historical Society of Pennsylvania, Philadelphia.

5. Fanny Fern, letter to the New Bedford *Mercury*, January 31, 1855, Alderman Library, University of Virginia.

6. See, for example, Boston *Olive Branch*, January 22, 1853; *New York Ledger*, March 12, 1859.

7. Thomas Butler Gunn, Diary, April 10, 1859, Missouri Historical Society, Saint Louis.

8. Gunn diary, April 8, 1859, June 5, 1859.

9. Gunn diary, e.g., September 16, 1856, October 31, 1856, May 8, 1859, June 1, 1859, June 5, 1859, July 21, 1859, August 21, 1859.

10. Gunn diary, December 27, 1856.
11. Gunn diary, March 16, 1859.
12. Gunn diary, see, e.g., March 27, 1856, March 12, 1859, March 16, 1859, April 10, 1859, May 1, 1859, June 5, 1859. On May 1, 1859, he wrote:

> She dresses immodestly, exposing her bosom, more than women generally do in ball costume. She makes smutty jokes. She compliments (!) male visitors by supposing them to have begotten illegitimate children. . . . She will call attention to her feet, to other portions and the least intellectual ones, of her body. She hung up one of her shoes, near the gas, in the room I occupied, one night, I suppose to set me regaling my mind with speculations about it. (I grinned, got a book and never looked at the shoe.) . . . She showed me a letter Jim sent to her down south, a letter written for her eye alone and for her prurient, nasty taste. . . . She openly hints at her sexual desires.—All of which is less harmless than her writings.

It is obvious from this passage that the sober Gunn did not understand Fern. She apparently enjoyed shocking him (putting her shoe in his room, for example), and, as her newspaper columns make clear, she was clearly being sarcastic when she "complimented" a man on his illegitimate children.

13. Harriet Prescott Spofford, "James Parton," *The Writer* 5 (November 1891):231.
14. Caroline Chesebro', *Isa, A Pilgrimage* (Clinton Park, N.Y.: Redfield, 1852), 296–299: "Two ways of escape at this time unexpectedly, certainly providentially, opened for Isa: through the marriage covenant, which she had set at naught, mocked, defied—and with it defied the world's opinion and that confidence, without which human life were, to women, nothing worth. . . . [But Isa couldn't see] the hand of God stretched out to her through these men."
15. Gunn diary, March 6, 1858.
16. Gunn diary, March 16, 1859.
17. Gunn diary, e.g., December 27, 1856, April 8, 1859, August 6, 1859, August 11, 1859, December 12, 1859.
18. Gunn diary, December 25, 1858; Christmas program in Gunn diary, December 27, 1858.
19. Gunn diary, July 12, 1861.
20. Gunn diary, September 18, 1861.
21. Julius H. Ward, "James Parton," *New England Magazine* (January 1893): 629.
22. Gunn diary, e.g., June 5, 1859. In 1891 Harriet Prescott Spofford wrote somewhat tactlessly and without full knowledge of the situation that Parton had been unhappy during his marriage to Fern. Spofford, who knew Parton in Newburyport during the later years of his life, and who ends by comparing Parton to Christ, clearly was not an objective analyst. She lays all the blame on Fern for any difficulties the couple had during the early years of their marriage, and apparently was unable to admit even that the marriage was consummated. "James Parton," 231–234.
23. Gunn diary, September 18, 1861.
24. Gunn diary, November 2, 1860, November 7, 1860, July 12, 1861.

25. Gunn diary, July 12, 1861, September 18, 1861.
26. Gunn diary, January 1–4, 1861
27. Ibid.
28, Gunn diary, December 31, 1860
29. Gunn diary, e.g., December 19, 1858, December 25, 1858, March 16, 1859, April 25, 1859, January 28, 1859, May 1, 1859.
30. Ellen Eldredge, letter to Robert Bonner, August 28, 1873, Robert Bonner Papers, New York Public Library.
31. James Parton, letter to Charles Eliot Norton, August 19, 1864, Houghton Library.
32. Review of *Fern Leaves, Home Journal*, June 4, 1853.

12. *"Fanny Ford" and* Rose Clark

1. See, e.g., Jacques Derrida, "Differance," *Speech and Phenomena*, tr. David B. Allison (Evanston: Northwestern University Press, 1973), 140, 150. Derrida writes, for example: "Every concept is necessarily and essentially inscribed in a chain or a system, within which it refers to another and to other concepts, by the systematic play of differences. Such a play, then—differance—is no longer simply a concept, but the possibility of conceptuality, of the conceptual system and process in general" (140).
2. Margaret Fuller, *Woman in the Nineteenth Century*, in Bell Gale Chevigny, *The Woman and the Myth: Margaret Fuller's Life and Writings* (Old Westbury, N.Y.: The Feminist Press, 1976), 248.
3. Samuel Blatchford, letter to J. C. Derby, September 17, 1853, Sophia Smith Collection, Smith College. Oliver Dyer's defense of Fanny Fern in Boston is reflected in *The Life and Beauties* (New York: H. Long, and Brother, 1855), 55–59. The author sarcastically calls him (as John Walter) "Fanny's man-at-arms" and describes how "Walter" confronted him and other editors who had criticized Fern.
4. Review of *Rose Clark, Harper's New Monthly Magazine* 12 (December 1855): 260.
5. See, e.g., Derrida, *Of Grammatology*, tr. Gayatri Chakravorty Spivak (Baltimore: Johns Hopkins University Press, 1976), 49.
6. Review of *Rose Clark, New York Daily Tribune* (December 6, 1855): 6.
7. Review of *Rose Clark, New York Times* (November 30, 1855): 3.
8. Review of *Rose Clark, Boston Daily Bee* (December 8, 1855), printed in the *New York Times* (December 12, 1855): 5.
9. Review of *Rose Clark*, New York *Mirror*, quoted in *New York Times* (November 30, 1855): 5.
10. Review of *Rose Clark, Boston Daily Bee*.   ——
11. Review of *Rose Clark, Harper's*.
12. Review of *Rose Clark* in *Maysville Eagle, New York Entre'Acte, Boston Saturday Evening Gazette*, quoted in the *New York Times* (December 12, 1855): 5. Also, New York *Mirror*, quoted in the *New York Times* (November 30, 1855): 5.

13. Herman Melville, letter to Nathaniel Hawthorne, quoted in Lewis Mumford, *Herman Melville* (New York: Harcourt, Brace & Co., 1929), 155.

14. Fern took the quotation from Mrs. Gaskell's *Life of Charlotte Brontë*, published in 1857. Some women writers accepted the conventional view of women and joined in the criticism of Fern. In a letter telling of her own difficulty in earning money by her writing (which suggests that she may also have been jealous of Fern), one woman writer criticized Fern's writing as "vulgar": "Because Mr. Bonner of the Ledger, thinks enough of Fanny Fern to give her $6000 a year to write for him exclusively, that does not prevent me from thinking her writings vulgar trash." See C. B. Cheeseborough, letter to Paul Hamilton Hayne, September 16, 1872, Perkins Library, Duke University.

For a good discussion of the restrictions on women writers, see Nina Baym, *Novels, Readers and Reviewers: Responses to Fiction in Antebellum America* (Ithaca: Cornell University Press, 1984), 257. Baym writes of the restrictions on nineteenth-century women writers: "Women may write as much as they please providing they define themselves as women writing when they do so, whether by tricks of style—diffuseness, gracefulness, delicacy; by choices of subject matter— the domestic, the social, the private; or by tone—pure, lofty, moral didactic."

15. Review of *Isa*, by Caroline Chesebro', *Southern Literary Messenger* (May 1852): 319.

16. Review of *The Curse of Clifton*, by E.D.E.N. Southworth, *Graham's Magazine* (April 1853): 508–509.

17. Review of *Hagar the Martyr*, by E. Marion Stephens, *National Era* (June 14, 1855): 95.

18. "Literary Women," *The Living Age* (June 25, 1864): 609–610.

19. Advertisement for *Rose Clark*, *New York Times* (December 6, 1855): 5.

20. S. Austin Allibone, *A Critical Dictionary of English Literature and English American Authors* (Philadelphia: Lippincott, 1872), 2:1520.

21. Review of *Rose Clark*, *New York Times*.

13. *"A Practical Bluestocking"*

1. Grace Greenwood, "Fanny Fern—Mrs. Parton" *Eminent Women of the Age*, ed. James Parton et al. (Hartford: S. M. Betts, 1868), 80.

2. Horace Greeley, quoted in the *Home Journal*, March 6, 1852.

3. Fanny Fern, "Mrs. Adolphus Smith Sporting the 'Blue Stocking,'" *Fern Leaves, Second Series* (New York: Derby & Miller, 1854), 101–102. The name "Adolphus Smith" was the name of a man whose property Fern's father-in-law held a mortgage on. See Middlesex County *Register of Deeds*, 1822 and 1823, 247:79, Cambridge, Massachusetts. It was also the name of a woman who burned to death in Northfield, Massachusetts, as reported in the *Olive Branch*, August 23, 1851, which was around the time that Fern's first articles were being published in the *Olive Branch*.

Other women writers reported the same difficulty. See, e.g., C. B. Cheeseborough, letter to Paul Hamilton Hayne, September 16, 1872, Perkins Library,

Duke University. Cheeseborough writes: "I have written when sick in bed, written when I have been nursing the sick of my family, written when I have been bowed down by grief caused by death in my family, written when I have been moving, written when I have been cooking and sweeping and dusting. Can you wonder that sometimes I have written so badly?"

Fern's sympathy for struggling women writers is suggested by her 1858 letter to an unknown woman who had written to ask her for help in publishing her manuscript:

My dear Madam.

I received you letter, & sympathize with you in your misfortunes. I also have mentioned your case to Mr. B[onner], as detailed in your letter. This of course cannot secure the acceptance of the mss. unless Mr. B[onner] should find it adapted to his uses & have occasion for it; though I should be most glad for your sake should this prove to be the case. I have a friend in your city—an editor, Col. Fitzgerald of *The City Item.* Perhaps he might accept your articles— you could but ask; you will of course take a specimen with you when you go.

With kindest wishes for your future

I am Yours truly
Fanny Fern

Fanny Fern, letter to "Dear Madam" January 28, 1858, Lloyd W. Smith Collection, Doc. No. 4830, Morristown National Historical Park, Morristown, New Jersey.

4. The Pre-nuptial Agreement between Sara P. Eldredge and James Parton is in the Houghton Library, Harvard University.

5. Mrs. James Parton, "A Literary Couple," *Galaxy* (1867): 606–610.

6. Emily Dickinson, "I'm Wife," *The Complete Poems of Emily Dickinson* (Boston: Little, Brown, 1960), 94. That Emily Dickinson was familiar with and liked Fern's work is suggested by a letter from her sister in which she says that she was reading aloud "spicey passages from Fern leaves" to entertain their father. See Millicent Todd Bingham, ed., *Emily Dickinson's Home: The Early Years as Revealed in Family Correspondence and Reminiscences* (New York: Dover Publications, 1967), 312.

7. "Fanny Fern at Home," *Boston Chronicle,* undated clipping [mid-1860s] in Sophia Smith Collection, Smith College.

8. "A Trio of Famous Women," undated clipping [1867], in the Horace Greeley papers, New York Public Library.

9. Thomas Butler Gunn, Diary, March 16, 1859, Missouri Historical Society, Saint Louis.

10. Gunn diary, August 9, 1857.

11. See, e.g., David Reynolds, *Beneath the American Renaissance* (New York: Knopf, 1988), 405.

12. Gunn diary, December 27, 1856, June 5, 1859.

13. Gunn diary, e.g., June 26, 1859.

14. Gunn diary, February 19, 1858.

15. Perkins was the son of Mary Beecher Perkins, sister of Catharine Beecher and Harriet Beecher Stowe, and the father of Charlotte Perkins Gilman (1860–

1935). For references to Perkins in the life of Fern and Parton, see, e.g., Gunn diary, August 21, 1856, and the letter from Fern to Mortimer Thomson in 1859 asking him to pick up three tickets for the opera, including one for Perkins. The letter is undated, but Fern mentions that the tickets are to hear Matilda Heron at Niblos; Heron was performing "Camille" at Niblos from November 28 to December 1, 1859 (letter in Kenneth Spencer Research Library, University of Kansas). See also Frederick B. Perkins, letter to James Parton [n.d.], Houghton Library, Harvard University.

    16. Jacobs's reticence about revealing this part of her background is apparent from a letter from her to Amy Post, April 4, [1853], in Harriet Jacobs, *Incidents in the Life of a Slave Girl*, ed. Jean Fagan Yellin (Cambridge: Harvard University Press, 1987), 234–235.

    17. See, e.g., Fanny Fern, *New York Ledger*, January 11, 1862, February 22, 1862. See also Harriet Jacobs, letter to Amy Post, [1852], *Incidents*, 232.

    18. For the dating of Jacobs's movements at this time, see Jacobs, *Incidents*, 180, 183, 185, 188, 194, 199, 288. She arrived in Philadelphia in the third week of June 1842 and, after a short stay in New York, went to Boston. She soon returned to New York, where she obtained a position as nursemaid in the family of Nathaniel P. Willis at the Astor House. In the summer or fall of 1843 she fled to Boston, returning to New York in the winter. Again threatened by her previous owner, she fled to Boston with her daughter in October 1844, and remained in Boston throughout the winter. After Mary Willis died in March 1845, Jacobs accompanied Willis and his child to England, returning in the winter of 1846. For two years she and her daughter Louisa lived in Boston, where she supported herself as a dressmaker. Fern's husband died in October 1846, and it was probably during the years 1847 to 1848, when Fern also attempted to support herself and her children by sewing, that Fern was grateful for Jacobs's friendship and came to know her daughter. In January 1849 Fern married Farrington. At this time, Louisa was sent to school in Clinton, New York, and, Jacobs, missing her daughter, went to sew in the home of a lady she knew (was this the newly married Fern?). In March 1849 Jacobs went to Rochester. In the fall of 1850 she again became a nursemaid in the home of N. P. Willis, who had remarried. In the spring of 1851, threatened by the husband of her young owner and the provisions of the Fugitive Slave Law of the previous year, Jacobs was sent by Mrs. Willis with the Willis's baby to Mrs. Willis's parents in New England, who sent her to stay in the country. She may again have seen Fern, who had left her husband in January and was at this time under intense criticism from relatives and friends. It may be this period that Fern was referring to when she said that Jacobs was one of the few people who had stuck by her.

    19. Ibid., 241.

    20. On March 16, 1859, Gunn says he thinks that Louisa Jacobs left Fern's home because Fern did not want her as a competitor to Grace. However, this assertion is not consistent with the fact that Fern apparently treated Louisa as a marriage candidate; nor is it consistent with Gunn's reporting that the male visitors, through attracted to her, will not marry her because of her origins. Then, on July 12, 1861, he says that the Rogerses have told him that the reason Jacobs left was because Fern was jealous of her with James Parton. Given their animosity toward Fern, the Rogerses are hardly a reliable source of information. There is no

other source of information to confirm their allegations. Louisa Jacobs's departure probably had to do with her mother's plans; in 1858 Harrient Jacobs traveled to England in an attempt to get her book published there.

21. For information about the life of Mortimer Neal Thomson, see Fletcher D. Slater, "The Life and Letters of Mortimer Thomson" (Dissertation, Northwestern University, 1931); copy also in the Houghton Library, Harvard University.

22. Fanny Fern, in letters from James Parton to Mrs. Van Cleve, April 20, and May 23, 1858, Houghton Library, Harvard University.

23. Greenwood, "Fanny Fern—Mrs. Parton," 79. Fern wrote back that she had said to Parton that she had "'a good mind to send the rest of the set flying out of the window!' His less impetuous hand stayed me. I assure you it was no virtue of mine. My blood is quick and warm."

24. All her life Margaret Fuller suffered from incapacitating headaches. See Fuller's 1838 journal cited in Bell Gale Chevigny, *The Woman and the Myth: Margaret Fuller's Life and Writings* (Old Westbury, N.Y.: The Feminist Press, 1976), 37.

25. For other comments by Gunn, see his diary, March 16, 1859. See James Parton, letters to James Freeman Clark, July 5, 1870; to James T. Fields, June 16, 1870; to Warland Clapp, November 30, 1869, Houghton Library, Harvard University. In the latter, for example, he says "my physical stamina is not great." See also the letter from Fanny Fern to Horace Greeley, which was written for James Parton, who appended a postscript from "her headachy husband," February 28 [n.d.], Horace Greeley papers, New York Public Library.

26. Manuscript dated May 22, 1857, in the Alderman Library, University of Virginia.

27. Of course, it is possible that Fern had an abortion. Gunn writes about the availability of abortions, and on March 16, 1859, he comments, "As Parton once said, When an American woman becomes pregnant, her first thought is, shall I take a pill and get rid of the trouble?" However, it is doubtful that Fern would have written about the baby in her column and discussed names with her daughters if she was going to have an abortion. It is more likely that she had a miscarriage, or that she had begun to reach menopause and mistakenly believed she was pregnant.

28. Gunn diary, December 24, 1858.

29. Mortimer Thomson, "A Great Slave Auction," *New York Tribune*, March 9, 1859; *Auction Sale of Slaves at Savannah, Georgia, March 2d and 3d, 1859* (New York: American Anti-Slavery Society, 1859).

30. Ethel Parton, notes in the Sophia Smith Collection, Smith College.

31. Thomas Butler Gunn, "Bonner and the *New-York Ledger*," *The Scalpel* 11 (April 1859): 54–62.

32. Charles Dana was probably glad to hear that the *Scalpel* was to print a critical article on the *Ledger*. He had had his own problems with the *Ledger*. On June 13, 1856, when Horace Greeley was in Washington and Dana was in charge of the *Tribune* it had printed an advertisement for the *Ledger* accompanied by an editorial denouncing the paper. The advertisement was a full page of Cobb's next novel, published as an advertisement in the *Tribune* and other papers. Bonner had paid $1,500 for it. The other papers had printed the advertisement without comment. Bonner was outraged at Dana's editorial, and the *Tribune* printed an apology.

33. Gunn's negative comments about Fern focused on her presumed sexual irregularities and what he regarded as vulgarities in her behavior and in her writing. That he shared these opinions with his friends is apparent from his comments in his diary about conversations he has had with others. See, e.g., March 16, 1859.

14. The Civil War and Effie

1. Ethel Parton, "A New York Childhood: The Seventies in Stuyvesant Square," *New Yorker* (June 13, 1936): 32.
2. Ibid.
3. Benjamin L. C. Wailes, Diary, July 11, 1859, Perkins Library, Duke University.
4. *Boston Chronicle*, undated clipping in Sara Parton papers, Sophia Smith Collection, Smith College. Because of the reference to Fern's granddaughter, who was born in 1862, the article can be dated from the mid-1860s.
5. *New York Evening Sun*, June 18, 1892, clipping in the Sara Parton papers, Sophia Smith Collection, Smith College.
6. Thomas Butler Gunn, Diary, August 3, 1860, Missouri Historical Society, Saint Louis.
7. Gunn diary, August 11, 1859, August 22, 1860, September 14, 1860. See also the letter from Fanny Fern and James Parton to General George Morris on October 1, 1860. Fern writes that they have just returned from Lake Superior, "where we had a most delightful trip and *didn't* get wrecked in the 'Lady Elgin' though we were in her only a few hours previous" (Alderman Library, University of Virginia).
8. Abner Morse, from information in his *Genealogical Register* (Boston: H. W. Cutton & Son, 1859), 2:184–223, in a privately printed "Willis Genealogy" in 1863 (New York Public Library) gives the date of the wedding as May 2, 1861, but it is clear from the *Tribune* article and Gunn's diary that the date was May 12, 1861.
9. Gunn diary, May 14, 1861.
10. Joseph N. Bacon, letter to Oliver Dyer, March 1, 1861, James Parton papers, Houghton Library, Harvard University.
11. . Gunn diary, March 3, 1861. Gunn describes Welles as having a crush on Thomson and says at one point that he was jealous of Anna and Grace. Gunn says that Welles's friendship with Thomson was one-sided, with Welles attempting to please Thomson by doing small favors, while Thomson jestingly called him "Jane." Gunn reports that after Thomson's marriage to Grace, Welles boarded with them. Gunn does not suggest that Welles was homosexual, only that he admired and wanted to be liked by Thomson. Ethel Parton confirms that after Thomson's marriage Welles lived with him and Grace. See letter from Ethel Parton, in Fletcher D. Slater, "The Life and Letters of Mortimer Thomson" (Dissertation, Northwestern University, 1931), 197–198.

That Thomson's father, his brother Clifford, and his son, Mark, were also living with them is clear from Grace Thomson's letter to Mrs. Van Cleve, July 29, 1861,

Houghton Library, Harvard University. I quote the letter at length for the information it provides:

First I will tell you what you seem most anxious to know—Mort is not in any way connected with the Army although he would have been—he says—had it not been for our marriage. When the news of that dreadful defeat, came to us last Monday Mort was sent on to the Army at Arlington Heights for the *Tribune*. He went at fifteen minutes notice and could not even bid little Mark good bye as he was out with the nurse walking. . . . I felt so badly about his going away that he wanted to stay but I would not have him give up so fine a chance; and one which I know he had been wishing for, for any foolishness of mine. That my love for him should stand in the way of his success is something that would never permit.

Cliff is regimented in the Lincoln Cavalry and starts next week for the war and then I shall feel quite deserted. He has been a great comfort to me since Mort went away. I love him dearly and he has often told me that except for his Mother I was dearer to him than any woman in the world. I shall miss him dreadfully but he is a brave boy and I am glad he is going to aid in the good cause. . . .

Mr. Thomson is boarding with us since his wife went away, and Ned Welles has been with us ever since the first week of our marriage. Cliff is with us too.

The baby is perfectly well and often speaks of you. I was singing him some little nursery rhymes the other day and he said "Grandma Keve told Mark that." I send you a little bit of his hair that I snipped off for you.

The folks in [E]ighteenth St. are all well but fearfully excited about the war news. Nelly is going to stay with me while Mort is gone. He made her promise to. She is a dear girl and Mark is very fond of her.

12. Mortimer Thomson, *Mercury* [1861], undated clipping in Gunn diary, 1861.

13. Slater, "Thomson," 198.

14. Ibid., 199.

15. James Parton, letter to Mrs. Van Cleve, July 20, 1861, Houghton Library, Harvard University.

16. Grace Thomson, letter to Mrs. Van Cleve, July 29, 1861, Houghton Library, Harvard University.

17. Fanny Fern, letter to General Benjamin F. Butler, n.d., Sophia Smith Collection, Smith College.

18. Clifford Thomson, letter to [Grace Eldredge Thomson], January 11, 1862, New-York Historical Society, New York, New York.

19. Gunn diary. September 7, 1856, April 10, 1859, May 1, 1859, May 15, 1859, May 31, 1859, January 8, 1860, March 16, 1860.

20. Grace's articles under the name Mrs. George Washington Wyllys appeared in the *Ledger* between April 27, 1861, and April 12, 1862, which suggests that she had signed a one-year contract.

21. Alice James's comment is quoted in Jean Strouse, *Alice James: A Biography* (Boston: Houghton Mifflin, 1980), 120.

22. Gunn diary, December [31] 1862; Slater, "Thomson," 199.

23. See Gunn diary, December 1862. See also James Parton, letters to Ellen Eldredge, n.d. [1873], and May 14, 1873, Houghton Library.

24. Slater, "Thomson," 201.

25. James Parton, letters to Ellen Eldredge, n.d. [1873], May 14, 1873, October 6, 1873, and February 4, 1875, Houghton Library.

26. James Parton, letter to Ellen Eldredge, n.d. [1873]:

I have heard nothing additional from him—not even an acknowledgement of the money I have sent to him. Don't worry. He is utterly powerless—in body, in mind, in purse. He cannot maintain himself for a week—much less another. You need fear nothing. If he should apply to you for money, it would be madness in you to send it. Refer the whole thing to me, and I will see if he cannot be got back to Minnesota, or into some institution. . . . [Effie] must *never* know of these things.

That Thomson was as hard up as Parton represented him to be is apparent from a letter dated August 25, 1873, from Thomson to Thurlow Weed, whom he did not know, asking Weed for a loan of fifty dollars. He told Weed that he had been sick and that his nurse had pawned his clothing (leaving him the pawn tickets) and that he was in desperate need of money. He said that he was asking Weed because he had already made "heavy drafts on my nearer friends" (University of Rochester Library, Rochester, New York).

27. *Graphic* (June 26, 1875): 895, cited in Slater, "Thomson," 202.

28. Grace Greenwood, "Fanny Fern,—Mrs. Parton," *Eminent Women of the Age*, ed. James Parton et al. (Hartford, Conn.: S. M. Betts, 1868), 84.

29. Milton Flower, *James Parton, the Father of Modern Biography* (Durham, N.C.: Duke University Press, 1951), 105-106. See also letters from James Parton to Ethel Thomson [later Parton], 1873-1876, in the Houghton Library. Papers regarding Ethel Parton's change of name are in the Sophia Smith Collection, Smith College.

30. Gunn recorded in his diary the information about Thomson which he received in a letter from Jesse Haney: "It having become necessary for him to take out letters of administration upon her estate, it was discovered that he had spent all but $1500 of the money; in other words, that he had managed to knock down about $5500 in a year and a half! . . . This last $1500 he refuses to settle upon the child, but intends to use it while studying medecine! Here's a precious fellow! . . . There never could have been any good in this man. No human being's character could slough away like this unless it had been rotten in the beginning" (Gunn diary, December [31] 1862).

31. In a letter to General Benjamin F. Butler, dated February 23, 1863, James Parton tells him that he arrived in Washington "last week" (Benjamin F. Butler papers, Library of Congress).

32. Flower, *Parton*, 65-66. James Parton, letter to Benjamin F. Butler, January 19, 1863, and March 12, 1863, Benjamin F. Butler papers. Parton's comments regarding Fern indicate that she accompanied him.

33. James Parton, letter to Benjamin Franklin Butler, August 19, 1864, in Benjamin Franklin Butler, *Private and Official Correspondence*, 5 vols. (Privately issued, 1917), 5:79.

34. Sarah Butler, letter to James Parton, May 21, 1864, Houghton Library.
35. Benjamin F. Butler, letter to James Parton, January 15, 1866, *Correspondence*, 5:696–697.
36. Benjamin F. Butler, letters to Sarah Butler, September 7 and 8, 1864, *Correspondence*, 5:126–127.

15. "At My Post"

1. The ability to make the reader identify with the "other" is similar to the technique used by Harriet Beecher Stowe in *Uncle Tom's Cabin*, when she forced her white Northern readers to identify with the slaves she portrayed, particularly the mothers.
2. In a letter to James T. Fields, dated December 18, 1866, at the Huntington Memorial Library, San Marino, California, James Parton wrote: "Mr. Bonner has gobbled up the article which Mrs. Parton earlier proposed to send to you." The article was published in the *Ledger* on January 26, 1867.
3. Fanny Fern, letter to General Benjamin F. Butler, in Benjamin Franklin Butler, *Private and Official Correspondence*, 5 vols. (Privately issued, 1917), 5:718–719.
4. James Parton, letter to James T. Fields, February 29, 1868, Huntington Memorial Library.
5. The name Sorosis meant "an aggregation." The stated object of the club was "the promotion of agreeable and useful relations among women of literary, artistic, and scientific tastes; the discussion and dissemination of principles and facts which promise to exert a salutary influence on women and on society, and the establishment of an order which shall render the female sex helpful to each other, and actively benevolent in the world." See Jane C. Croly, *The History of the Women's Club Movement in America* (New York: Henry G. Allen & Co., 1898), 15–19, 24–25. See also *Report of the Twenty-first Anniversary of Sorosis* (New York, 1890), 25.
6. *New York World* 10 (November 28, 1869):1.
7. For a discussion of this event and the response, see Susan Coultrap-McQuinn, *Doing Literary Business: American Women Writers in the Nineteenth Century* (Chapel Hill: University of North Carolina Press, 1990), 2–7. On December 17, 1877, H. O. Houghton & Co., publishers of the *Atlantic Monthly*, gave a dinner party to celebrate the twentieth anniversary of the magazine and the seventieth birthday of John Greenleaf Whittier. Although a number of women were contributors to the magazine, no women were invited to the dinner. Fern's comment that one reason why men preferred not to have ladies present at the Press Club dinner for Dickens was because the men wanted to have tobacco and wine is confirmed by the *Atlantic Monthly's* actions after the response to its exclusion of women from the anniversary dinner: in future celebrations where women were to be present, the publishers' celebrations in 1880 (for Oliver Wendell Holmes) and in 1882 (for Harriet Beecher Stowe) were *breakfasts* where wine would not be a factor. It is also interesting that the *New York World* article regarding the New

York Press Club dinner at Delmonico's in 1869 to which women were invited for the first time concluded with the words: "scarcely any wine was drunk" (*New York World* 10 [November 28, 1869]:1). It would seem that if women were to be wholly accepted as equals professionally, they would have to overcome their image as inhibitors of male camaraderie.

    8. Croly, *History*, 15–17.

16. Last Years

    1. James Parton, letter to Robert Bonner, May 23, 1873, Robert Bonner papers, New York Public Library. See also James Parton, *Fanny Fern, A Memorial Volume* (New York: G. W. Carleton, 1873), 5–6.

    2. In a letter to James Freeman Clark, dated September 17, 1868, James Parton wrote that he and Fern planned to leave Stockbridge "one week from tomorrow" (Houghton Library, Harvard University).

    3. Fern's illness is recorded in the *New York Ledger*, September 19, 1868. Parton's illness as well as Fern's are mentioned in James Parton's letter to James C. Derby, August 22, 1868, University Research Library, University of California, Los Angeles. Parton says that he has been sick for five weeks. Fern, he says, is also sick: "You may judge how low she was reduced when I tell you that she was perfectly submissive and reasonable."

    4. In a letter to James Parton, dated March 23, 1868, Grace Greenwood said that the article was difficult for her to write because she was not personally acquainted with Fern (Houghton Library, Harvard University). She was, however, familiar with Fern's works. She apparently did not share the opinion of some of her contemporaries that Fern's writings were harmful for children. As noted earlier, Caroline Healey Dall, for example, asserted that she kept Fern's books away from her children. See Dall's review of *Ruth Hall*, *The Una* (March 1855): 42–43. Greenwood wrote to Fern in August 1870, sending Fern a picture of her daughter, who she said would like to meet Fern: "The first novel she ever read was your 'Ruth Hall.' She was then about eight years old" (Sophia Smith Collection, Smith College).

    5. Mary Abigail Dodge [Gail Hamilton], letters to James Parton and Fanny Fern, September 15, 1869, September 27, 1869, October 11, 1869, December 7, 1869, Sophia Smith Collection, Smith College. She also asked Fern how she could call her husband "Jim." Fern wrote back offering to help her with her publishers, and incidentally telling her that Parton called her "Fan." Hamilton thanked her for her offer of help, adding a P.S.: "Fan is not half so bad as *Jim!*" Parton later wrote to James Freeman Clark at the *Atlantic Monthly* asking why the editors "behave like princes to me" and have been so niggardly to Hamilton. James Parton, letter to James Freeman Clark, March 29, 1870, Boston Public Library. For a discussion of the circumstances, see Susan Coultrap-McQuin, *Doing Literary Business: American Women Writers in the Nineteenth Century* (Chapel Hill: University of North Carolina Press, 1990), 120–128.

    6. Harriet Beecher Stowe, letter to James Parton, February 2, 1868, Sophia Smith Collection, Smith College.

7. Fanny Fern, letter to Harriet Beecher Stowe, February 14, 1868, Schlesinger Library, Radcliffe College.

8. Stowe's publisher, John P. Jewett, offered her fifty percent of the royalties if she would put up five hundred dollars. Calvin Stowe rejected this offer, accepting a ten percent royalty instead (Charles Edward Stowe, *Life of Harriet Beecher Stowe* [Boston: Houghton, Mifflin, 1890], 158; Forrest Wilson, *Crusader in Crinoline: The Life of Harriet Beecher Stowe* [Philadelphia: J. B. Lippincott, 1941], 277; E. Bruce Kirkham, *The Building of Uncle Tom's Cabin* [Knoxville: University of Tennessee, 1977], 140–149).

9. Harriet Beecher Stowe, letters to Fanny Fern, July 25, 1868, and February 12 [1868], Sophia Smith Collection.

10. Milton Flower, *James Parton, the Father of Modern Biography* (Durham, N.C.: Duke University Press, 1951), 95. Harriet Beecher Stowe, letter to Fanny Fern, February 15, 1868, Sophia Smith Collection, Smith College.

11. Harriet Beecher Stowe, letters to Fanny Fern and James Parton, June 1, 1869, and July 25, 1869, Sophia Smith Collection, Smith College.

12. Flower, *Parton*, 110–111.

13. Ethel Parton, "A Little Girl and Two Authors," *The Horn Book Magazine* 17 (March-April 1941):81–82.

14. Ibid., 82.

15. Ibid., 82–84.

16. Ibid., 85.

17. Ethel Parton, "A New York Childhood," *New Yorker* (June 13, 1936), 37–46.

18. Ibid., 46.

19. Fanny Fern, letter to Ellen Eldredge, November 15 [1870], Sophia Smith Collection.

20. Fanny Fern, letter to Ethel Thomson [later Parton], December 9 [1870], Sophia Smith Collection, Smith College.

21. Julia Ward Howe, *Reminiscences, 1819–1899* (Boston: Houghton Mifflin, 1899), 402–405. See also undated newspaper clipping, "Town and Country Club of Newport," and the Latin program for the Mock Commencement prepared by Professor Lane of Harvard University; both in the Sophia Smith Collection, Smith College.

22. For example, Gunn refers to Ellen as Fern's "youngest brat, who promises to be dreadfully like her." He says that she is an "obnoxious girl" who is "horribly, precociously like her dam" and predicts that any man who marries her will have a hard time with her. See Thomas Butler Gunn, Diary, April 10, 1859, May 1, 1859, December 26, 1859, February 8, 1860, March 16, 1860, Missouri Historical Society, Saint Louis.

23. After Fern's death, James Parton helped Fern's daughter, Ellen, and granddaughter, Ethel, to settle in Newburyport, Massachusetts. It was difficult for Parton to separate himself from Effie, who was not quite ten at the time of her grandmother's death. Although he had raised the child as his own since she was an infant, he had no legal claim to her. Parton remained in New York, where he completed *Fanny Fern: A Memorial Volume* the year after Fern's death. The book was printed by the Women's Printing House. (See letter from the press, July 18,

1873, in the Houghton Library, Harvard University.) Parton wrote to Ellen and Effie and visited them often. Eventually he bought a house in Newburyport, which he shared with them. See letters from James Parton to Ellen Eldredge and Ethel Thomson, 1873–1876, Houghton Library. Brought together by the child, "Effie," James Parton and Ellen Eldredge found themselves drawn to each other. They were married on February 4, 1876. The marriage was found to be invalid under Massachusetts law, which prohibited marriage between stepfather and stepdaughter, but they were able to marry in New York, and Ellen received her inheritance from Hezekiah Eldredge's will. (See the letters from Ellen Eldredge and James Parton to Robert Bonner in the Robert Bonner Papers, 1873–1874, New York Public Library. See also the letters from Joseph Bacon to Ellen Eldredge and James Parton, August 14, 1876, and April 30, 1878; also Amos Noyes, letter to James Parton, February 26, 1878 Houghton Library, Harvard University.) It is interesting that Parton's marriage to Fern's daughter was in a sense foreshadowed by the ending to Fern's 1855 story, "Fanny Ford." Also, as her daughter said in a letter to Robert Bonner on February 7, 1876, her mother had "with her dying breath," wished them to "always live together" (Robert Bonner papers, New York Public Library). It is also interesting that Thomas Butler Gunn described Ellen as being so much like her mother. As a private woman, she may have been a good deal like her mother, but as a public woman she was not: as we have seen, she was quiet in company (which Fern never was) and, despite the urgings of publishers and editors, she was proud of the fact that, as she said in a letter to Robert Bonner, unlike her mother (and her sister) she never wrote for the public (Ellen Eldredge, letter to Robert Bonner, n.d. [1873], Robert Bonner Papers).

24. Ethel Parton, "A New York Childhood," 32–35.

25. Harriet Prescott Spofford refers to Fern's "severe surgery" in "James Parton," *The Writer* 5 (November 1891): 232. Although no sources mention the nature of the surgery or the type of cancer, the symptoms are consistent with breast cancer, and one suspects that the surgery involved a mastectomy.

26. James Parton, letter to Thomas Higginson, September 23, 1872, Houghton Library, Harvard University.

27. It is not clear whether Ellen Eldredge designed the monument or modified an existing design. On May 14, 1873, James Parton wrote to her enclosing four designs for the monument from which she was to choose one, but on May 19, 1873, he wrote telling her that Robert Bonner said to send her design even though it would cost a thousand dollars and approving her wish that the "true fern" be used and that the base be made smaller (letters in the Houghton Library, Harvard University).

17. "Paper Pellets": The Spectrum of Ideas

1. Fanny Fern, letter to William B. Eager, n.d., John Hay Library, Brown University.

2. I am referring, for example, to children's textbooks, for which many publishers have developed stringent guidelines which prohibit all references to

death, religion, or fantasy, as well as the portrayal of "bad" characters or the criticism of adult authority.

3.   See, for example, Fanny Fern, *Little Ferns for Fanny's Little Friends* (Auburn: Derby and Miller, 1854), 16–19, 35–36, 45–47, 47–51, 59–60, 61–66, 66–69, 89–94, 94–99, 100–103, 104–108; *The Play-Day Book: New Stories for Little Folks* (New York: Mason Brothers, 1857), 64–69, 102–106, 107–119, 155–159, 194–203, 72–75, 76–88, 91–95, 96–101, 102–106, 120–123, 133–139, 153–159, 184–190, 194–203, 242–247.

4.   See, e.g., Boston *Olive Branch,* June 18, 1853; New York *Musical World and Times,* August 20, 1853; and *New York Ledger,* March 7, 1857, April 17, 1858, October 29, 1859, November 24, 1860, February 22, 1862, November 29, 1863, February 11, 1865, May 5, 1866; November 4, 1871.

5.   Mary E. Wilkins Freeman, "The Revolt of Mother," in *A New England Nun and Other Stories* (New York: Harper & Brothers, 1891), 451–452.

6.   For a discussion of the definition of womanhood in nineteenth-century America see Barbara Welter, "The Cult of True Womanhood: 1820–1860," *American Quarterly* 18 (Summer 1966): 151–162, 173–174. Welter writes: "The Attributes of True Womanhood, by which a woman judged herself and was judged by her husband, her neighbors, and society could be divided into four cardinal virtues—piety, purity, submissiveness and domesticity. . . . Without them, no matter whether there was fame, achievement or wealth, all was ashes." One cannot assume that all men and women shared these beliefs. Feminist-abolitionists in the mid-nineteenth century, for example, although they accepted the virtues of piety, purity, and domesticity, urged women's right to pursue other activities than the domestic, and they rejected the concept of submissiveness. See, e.g., Blanche Glassman Hersh, *The Slavery of Sex: Feminist-Abolitionists in America* (Urbana: University of Illinois Press, 1978), 189–190, 208–209. Recent studies of male-female relationships in the mid-nineteenth century indicate that although "the mid-nineteenth-century exalted the idea of a loving, companionate, egalitarian marriage, . . . in reality, the wife remained subordinate." See Ellen K. Rothman, *Hands and Hearts: A History of Courtship in America* (New York: Basic Books, 1984), 145. See also William Leach, *True Love and Perfect Union: The Feminist Reform of Sex and Society* (New York: Basic Books, 1980); and Karen Lystra, *Searching the Heart: and Romantic Love in Nineteenth-Century America* (New York: Oxford University Press, 1989). Lystra writes that although patriarchal control in a household had come into question in the nineteenth century, "hierarchical gender distinctions nonetheless remained powerful" (230, 236).

7.   For an analysis of the problems faced by twelve women in mid-nineteenth century America who attempted to combine a successful writing career with the period's limiting definition of womanhood, see Mary Kelley, *Private Woman, Public Stage: Literary Domesticity in Nineteenth-Century America* (New York: Oxford University Press, 1984). The problems faced by Charlotte Perkins Gilman (1860–1935) indicate that the situation was not much changed a generation later. Gilman's struggle to maintain her identity under the pressures of domestication (and the ideas of the most advanced medical opinion of the time) is chronicled in her story "The Yellow Wallpaper" (1892). Rather than go mad like the woman in the story, Gilman left her suffocating marriage to pursue a successful writing career. In important respects Gilman's ideas parallel those of Fern. Like Fern earlier,

Gilman advocated autonomy for women, which they both believed could only come through economic independence. Like Fern also, Gilman criticized the foolishness of women's fashions and urged more sensible dress for women; she decried the tyranny and selfishness of men; and also like Fern, Gilman wrote frankly about venereal disease, attacking the wall of silence that society had erected to prevent women from knowing about it (this at a time when there was no cure for the disease, antibiotics had not been invented, and marriage to an infected man would infect his wife and cause birth defects or the death of his children). See Charlotte Perkins Gilman, "The Yellow Wallpaper" (1892) and other short fiction, particularly "If I Were a Man" (1914), "Making a Change" (1911), "An Honest Woman" (1911), "The Widow's Might" (1911); her novels *The Crux* (1911) and *What Diantha Did* (1912); her utopian novels *Moving the Mountain* (1911) and *Herland* (1915); and her nonfiction works, particularly *Women and Economics: A Study of the Economic Relation between Men and Women as a Factor in Social Evolution* (1898).

8. In an article entitled "The True Woman" in the *Ladies' Repository* in August 1853, the Reverend Jesse T. Peck expressed the general opinion of his age. "The true woman," he said, was "timid, shrinking, and retiring"; whereas man is suited to the "rude antagonisms and fierce collisions" of a public and professional life, woman is "meant for kindlier labor, where delicate sentiment, deep felt sympathy, devout affection, and subduing tenderness, can soften the asperities of life" (337).

9. Jane Tompkins in *Sensational Designs: The Cultural Work of American Fiction, 1790–1860* (New York: Oxford University Press, 1985) points out that the use of religion in most nineteenth-century women's fiction is to aid the heroine in submission not to man, but to God (162–163). However, the result in this world was the same: the woman could not rebel against the injustice of men. Tompkins points out the powerlessness of nineteenth-century American women but notes that rebellion was impossible because "they lacked the material means of escape or opposition" (161). The domestic novelists, Tompkins asserts, portrayed the way in which women forced themselves to submit to what appeared to be a necessity, and made it a source of power. Fanny Fern sought another way out: she advised women to gain "the material means" that would make rebellion possible.

10. See, for example, Harriet Jacobs, *Incidents in the Life of a Slave Girl*, ed. Jean Fagan Yellin (Cambridge: Harvard University Press, 1987), 70–72, 74; Fanny Fern, *New York Ledger*, February 10, 1872.

11. See, e.g., Jacobs, *Incidents*, 18, 70–71, 74.

12. Ibid., 91, 155.

13. Susan Warner, *The Wide, Wide World*, ed. Jane Tompkins (New York: The Feminist Press, 1987), 12.

14. Jacobs, *Incidents*, 37.

15. For several years I had used *Ruth Hall* and *Incidents in the Life of a Slave Girl* as pivotal texts in a course on nineteenth-century American women writers, noting the similarities between them. Jean Fagan Yellin also notes the relationship between the two works in the notes to her edition of *Incidents* (254). However, it was not until my discovery of the diaries of Thomas Butler Gunn in the Missouri Historical Society in March of 1987 that I knew for a certainty that Jacobs and Fern knew each other, and that they knew each other well.

16. See Jacobs, *Incidents*, 95–96.

17. Women writers often modestly ascribed their success to others. Harriet Beecher Stowe claimed that she did not write *Uncle Tom's Cabin;* God did, she said. See, e.g., Charles Edward Stowe, *Life of Harriet Beecher Stowe* (Boston: Houghton, Mifflin, 1890), 156; and *Life and Letters of Harriet Beecher Stowe,* ed. Annie Fields (Boston: Houghton, Mifflin, 1897), 163–165. Sarah Josepha Hale took pleasure in the fact that her husband's name bore the celebrity for any praise she might receive. See Hale, *Woman's Record, or Sketches of All Distinguished Women from 'The Beginning' till A.D. 1850 (1853, 1869, 1876)* (New York: Harper & Brothers, 1853), 686–687.

Epilogue. In Her Own Voice

1. For a comprehensive analysis of the masculine character of nineteenth-century American individualism, see Joyce W. Warren, *The American Narcissus: Individualism and Women in Nineteenth-Century American Fiction* (New Brunswick, N.J.: Rutgers University Press, 1984).

2. With respect to canon formation, Jane Tompkins in *Sensational Designs: The Cultural Work of American Fiction, 1790–1860* (New York: Oxford University Press, 1985) describes classic texts "as the bearers of a set of national, social, economic, institutional, and professional interests" (xii); "the literary works that now make up the canon," she writes, "do so because the groups that have an investment in them are culturally the most influential" (5).

3. See Michel Foucault, *The Archaeology of Knowledge and the Discourse on Language,* tr. A. M. Sheridan (New York: Pantheon Books, 1972), 219, 234.

4. Edward Johnson, "Wonder-Working Providence of Sion's Saviour," *The Puritans,* ed. Perry Miller and Thomas H. Johnson, 2 vols. (New York: Harper, 1963), 1:156.

5. Nancy Cott, ed., *Root of Bitterness: Documents of the Social History of American Women* (New York: Dutton, 1972), 47–58.

6. Justin Winsor, *Memorial History of Boston,* ed. William F. Poole, 4 vols. (Boston: Osgood and Co., 1880–1881). 2: 141.

7. Ibid., 133.

8. Ralph Waldo Emerson, *Complete Works,* Centenary Edition, ed. Edward W. Emerson, 12 vols. (Boston: Houghton Mifflin, 1903–1904), 11:403–426.

9. John Winthrop, *Winthrop's Journal,* ed. James K. Hosmer, 2 vols. (New York: Scribner's, 1908), 2:225.

10. Laura Mulvey, "Visual Pleasure and Narrative Cinema," *Screen* 16 (Autumn 1975):6–18.

11. Herman Melville, *White Jacket, The Writings of Herman Melville,* 12 vols. (Evanston and Chicago: Northwestern University Press and Newberry Library, 1968–1991), 5:46.

12. Hélène Cixous, "The Laugh of the Medusa," tr. Keith Cohen and Paula Cohen, *Signs* 1 (Summer 1976):885.

13. Cixous, "Laugh," 875–877. See also Julia Kristeva, *Desire in Language: A Semiotic Approach to Literature and Art,* tr. Thomas Gora, Alice Jardine, Leon

S. Roudiez (New York: Columbia University Press, 1980). Although Fern cannot be said to share these critics' identification of a special, nonlinear quality of feminine writing, she foreshadowed their insistence on the need for the woman's perspective or voice.

14. The term "phallogocentric," a conflation of "logocentric" and "phallocentric," is used to suggest the male-dominated ideology of the central culture.

15. Although specific figures are not available on a year-by-year basis, experts agree that there has been a substantial rise in the number of violent crimes against women since the 1960s. The rapid escalation in the past fifty years is documented by Diana Russell's San Francisco study. See Jane Caputi and Diana E. H. Russell, "'Femicide': Speaking the Unspeakable," *MS.: The World of Women* 1 (November 1990):34–37.

16. I do not mean to say that women's increased autonomy is the only reason for the increasing violence against women. Other factors are, of course, important, for example, the increase in violence in general in our society and the increase in number and in the graphic portrayal of acts of violence in the popular entertainment media.

17. Thomas Butler Gunn, Diary, September 18, 1861, Missouri Historical Society, Saint Louis.

INDEX

Adams Female Academy, 20–24, 319n30
"Adieu to Newport" (Fern), 283
advertising, 149, 335n11, 340n18; of *Ruth Hall*, 121, 122–124
Albion (London), criticism of Fern, 125
Alcott, Louisa May, 88; at *New York Ledger*, 148
Alger, Horatio, 139, 339n59
"All About Lovers" (Fern), 238
American Monthly Magazine, 39, 50; failure, 52
The American Narcissus: Individualism and Women in Nineteenth-Century American Fiction (Warren), 1, 313n2, 362n1
Americans, Native, 28, 292
Andover Theological Seminary, 43
"Angel Comforters" (Fern), 81
"The Angel over the Right Shoulder" (Phelps), 212
"Apollo Hyacinth" (Fern), 95–96
Arthur, Timothy S., at *New York Ledger*, 148
Atlantic Monthly, 151, 265–266, 275, 276; discrimination, 270
authority, male, 2, 154, 200, 304; abuses by, 297, 299; questioning, 294; threatened, 130
"Awe-ful Thoughts" (Fern), 295

Banister, Zilpah. *See* Grant, Zilpah Polly
Barnum, P. T., 162
Baym, Nina, 133, 349n14
Beecher, Catharine, *Fig. 8*, 12, 24–25, 44, 183, 318n2, 320n37; at Hartford Female Seminary, 27–38; social causes, 28
Beecher, Rev. Edward, 24, 25
Beecher, Rev. Henry Ward, 32–33, 113, 157, 162; adultery accusation, 333n25; criticism by Fern, 279; marriage of Eldredge, G., 242; relations with Bonner, 147
Beecher, Rev. Lyman, 24, 28, 37–38
Beers, Henry, 97
behavior: antisocial, 267; environmental causes, 267; proper, 30, 31, 34, 124–125, 208, 233; sexual, 50
"Behind a Mask" (Alcott), 88

bigotry, 157
Blackwell's Island (prison), 263, 267
"Boarding-House Experience" (Fern), 119
"Bogus Intellect" (Fern), 214
Bonner, Robert, *Fig. 12*, 284; advertising campaign, 149, 340n18; on death of Fern, 286; at *New York Ledger*, 143–149; relations with Fern, 146–149, 181; on suffrage, 237; treatment of staff, 148, 276, 340n17
"Borrowed Light" (Fern), 113, 167
Boston Chronicle, 236
Boston Recorder, 9, 10, 46
Brimstone Corner, 6
Brontë, Charlotte, 1, 138, 208
Browning, Elizabeth Barrett, 1
Brooklyn Daily Times, 173
Bryant, William Cullen, 279; at *New York Ledger*, 148
Bumstead, Freeman (nephew), 83, 337n38
Bumstead, Josiah F. (brother-in-law), 20, 327n33; support, lack of, 83
Bumstead, Laura (niece), 83
Bushnell, Horace, 302
"A Business Man's Home" (Fern), 77
Butler, Gen. Benjamin F., 243, 251, 252, 255, 269
Byron, George Gordon (Lord), 179; incest, 276

Calvinism, 6, 12, 17, 24, 28, 29, 43, 157, 250
canon, formation, 177–178, 307, 362n2
Caper-Sauce (Fern), 274
Cary, Alice, 148; in Sorosis, 271
Cary, Phoebe, 148
castration, fear of, 310
Chandler, Ellen Louise, 127
"A Chapter on Literary Women" (Fern), 215
Chesebro', Caroline, 183, 208
Child, Lydia Maria, 104
child rearing, 56; attitudes of Fern, 187, 244–245, 257, 291–293; improvements, 199; religion in, 12–13; rigidity in, 89; writings on, 2, 89, 288
"Children of Adam" (Whitman), 168
"A Child's Mission" (Fern), 273